The Ethics of Captivity

The Ethics of Captivity

EDITED BY LORI GRUEN

OXFORD
UNIVERSITY PRESS

OXFORD
UNIVERSITY PRESS

Oxford University Press is a department of the University of Oxford.
It furthers the University's objective of excellence in research, scholarship,
and education by publishing worldwide.

Oxford   New York
Auckland   Cape Town   Dar es Salaam   Hong Kong   Karachi
Kuala Lumpur   Madrid   Melbourne   Mexico City   Nairobi
New Delhi   Shanghai   Taipei   Toronto

With offices in
Argentina   Austria   Brazil   Chile   Czech Republic   France   Greece
Guatemala   Hungary   Italy   Japan   Poland   Portugal   Singapore
South Korea   Switzerland   Thailand   Turkey   Ukraine   Vietnam

Oxford is a registered trademark of Oxford University Press
in the UK and certain other countries.

Published in the United States of America by
Oxford University Press
198 Madison Avenue, New York, NY 10016

© Oxford University Press 2014

CIP data is on file at the Library of Congress

ISBN 978-0-19-997799-4 (hbk.); 978-0-19-997800-7 (pbk.)

9 8 7 6 5 4 3 2
Printed in the United States of America
on acid-free paper

CONTENTS

ACKNOWLEDGMENTS

I am grateful to all the contributors to this volume for their thoughtful engagement with the complexities of captivity. I am especially appreciative of the candor, passion, and expertise that authors in Part One shared. I would also like to thank the photographers who agreed to allow their photographs to be included here, particularly Jo-Anne McArthur, award-winning photojournalist whose work documenting human relations with other animals across the globe is featured in the film *The Ghosts in Our Machine* and her book *We Animals*; Frank Noelker, whose photographs of captive animals in zoos, published in *Captive Beauty*, and chimpanzees in sanctuaries have been widely exhibited and deeply inspirational; Isa Leshko, who will be publishing her important work *Elderly Animals*; Susan Weingartner, an animal advocate who found her gift in photographing animals; and Amy Fultz, who in addition to being a marvelous photographer is Director of Behavior, Research and Education at Chimp Haven. Special thanks to the incarcerated students I have worked with over the years and to a very dear group of chimpanzees who started me thinking about the ethics of captivity almost a decade ago: Sarah, Sheba, Emma, Harper, Keeli, Ivy, and the late Darrell. Alexis Sturdy, Maddie Neufeld, Kristen Olson, and pattrice jones provided inspiration and/or assistance along the way. I am delighted that Peter Ohlin has enthusiastically supported this volume and thank him and Emily Sacharin for seeing it into print.

CONTRIBUTORS

Irus Braverman is Professor of Law and Adjunct Professor of Geography at SUNY Buffalo. Her current interests lie in the interdisciplinary study of law, anthropology, and animality. Braverman has written about zoos, animals in the city, and the in situ–ex situ divide in nature conservation. She is the author of *House Demolitions in East Jerusalem: "Illegality" and Resistance* (2004), *Planted Flags: Trees, Land, and Law in Israel/Palestine* (2009), and *Zooland: The Institution of Captivity* (2012). Braverman is currently coediting *The Expanding Spaces of Law: A Timely Legal Geography* and completing a manuscript entitled *Managing Wildlife*.

John Bryant, James Davis, David Haywood, Clyde Meikle, and Andre Pierce are currently enrolled in college courses while they are collectively serving 225 years in a maximum security men's prison. Haywood, Meikle, and Pierce have been university students since 2009, Bryant and Davis since 2011.

Alasdair Cochrane is Lecturer in Political Theory at the University of Sheffield. A prominent theme of his research has been the value of liberty to animals. This is most directly discussed in *Animal Rights without Liberation* (2012), and "Do Animals Have an Interest in Liberty?" *Political Studies* 57 (2009). He is also the author of *An Introduction to Animals and Political Theory* (2010).

Margo DeMello is a cultural anthropologist and currently lectures at Central New Mexico Community College. She is the Human-Animal Studies Program Director for the Animals and Society Institute, and President of House Rabbit Society, an international rabbit advocacy organization. Her books include *Stories Rabbits Tell: A Natural and Cultural History of a Misunderstood Creature* (2003), *Why Animals Matter: The Case for Animal Protection* (2007), *Teaching the Animal: Human Animal Studies Across the Disciplines* (2010), *Speaking for Animals: Animal Autobiographical Writing* (2012), and *Animals and Society: An Introduction to Human-Animal Studies* (2012).

Catherine Doyle is the Director of Science, Research and Advocacy for the Performing Animal Welfare Society (PAWS) in California, which operates three sanctuaries and cares for more than 100 rescued and retired wild animals, including eight elephants. She received her master of science in anthrozoology from Canisius College, where her research focused on elephants' perceptions of keeper-elephant interactions. She has studied captive conditions for elephants since 2003 and has been actively involved in issues affecting the welfare and conservation of elephants, including work as elephant campaign director for In Defense of Animals.

Karen S. Emmerman wrote a dissertation in ecofeminist animal ethics, "Beyond the Basic/Non-basic Interests Distinction: A Feminist Approach to Inter-species Moral Conflict and Moral Repair." She is a co-organizer of the University of Washington Critical Animal Studies Working Group, board member of the UW Center for Philosophy for Children, and Adjunct Lecturer in the UW Philosophy and Comparative History of Ideas departments. She also teaches philosophy to K-12 students in public schools; in 2013–2014 she is Philosopher-in-Residence at John Muir Elementary in Seattle, Washington.

Lauren Gazzola is a longtime animal rights and social justice activist. She is a member of the SHAC 7, six individuals and a nonprofit organization prosecuted under the controversial Animal Enterprise Protection (now Terrorism) Act for their participation in the Stop Huntingdon Animal Cruelty campaign to close Huntingdon Life Sciences. She has volunteered at the California Anti-SLAPP Project, as a literacy tutor at New York City's Grand Street Settlement, and with a youth HIV/AIDS awareness and community outreach group. She served 40 months incarcerated in a federal prison in Connecticut.

Lori Gruen is Professor of Philosophy, Feminist, Gender, and Sexuality Studies, and Environmental Studies at Wesleyan University where she also coordinates Wesleyan Animal Studies and directs the Ethics in Society Project. She is the author, most recently, of *Ethics and Animals* (2011) and coeditor with Carol Adams of *Ecofeminism: Feminist Intersections with Other Animals and the Earth* (2014). She is currently working on two projects: one develops an account of resistance self-respect inspired by her work teaching incarcerated men; the other explores human relations to captive chimpanzees, drawing lessons from the lives of some of the chimpanzees she has come to know, respect, and love.

Alexandra Horowitz teaches psychology at Barnard College, Columbia University. Her dissertation was one of the first to address the cognition and metacognition of domestic dogs. The Horowitz Dog Cognition Lab at Barnard conducts research on a wide range of questions, including dog olfaction, interspecies play behavior, and attributions of secondary emotions to dogs.

In addition to many scholarly articles relating to dog behavior and cognition, Horowitz is the author of *Inside of a Dog: What Dogs See, Smell, and Know* (2009) and *On Looking: Eleven Walks with Expert Eyes* (2013).

Miriam Jones logged a couple of decades doing everything from teaching high school English to GLBTQ activism before she found her way to the animal liberation movement 15 years ago. She is the cofounder of VINE Sanctuary (formerly the Eastern Shore Sanctuary and Education Center), which currently provides shelter and care to almost 450 formerly farmed and otherwise exploited animals.

Lori Marino is a Senior Lecturer in Neuroscience and Behavioral Biology and a Faculty Affiliate of the Center for Ethics at Emory University. She is also the founder and Executive Director of the Kimmela Center for Animal Advocacy. She is the author of over 80 publications on dolphin and whale brain anatomy and evolution, comparative intelligence, and self-awareness. She serves as an expert witness and consultant on the effects of captivity on animals.

Clare Palmer is Professor of Philosophy at Texas A&M University. She is the author of three books, most recently *Animal Ethics in Context* (2010). She was the founding editor of the journal *Worldviews: Environment, Culture, Religion* and held the position of President of the International Society for Environmental Ethics from 2007 to 2010.

Lisa Rivera is Associate Professor of Philosophy at University Massachusetts, Boston. She works in the areas of moral and political philosophy and feminist philosophy. Her current research is concerned with the relationship between political membership and moral emotions, agency, and obligation.

Stephen R. Ross is Director of the Lester E. Fisher Center for the Study and Conservation of Apes at Lincoln Park Zoo in Chicago. In this role, he directs a multidisciplinary team focused on advancing the knowledge of ape biology, improving the care and management of captive apes, and conserving and protecting wild ape populations. He has studied primates for almost two decades in a range of settings, including research centers, sanctuaries, and zoos. For more than a decade, he has served as the Coordinator of the Chimpanzee Species Survival Plan (SSP), which manages the population of chimpanzees living in accredited zoos in North America. In 2008 he founded Project ChimpCARE, an initiative dedicated to helping chimpanzees, especially those living under private ownership as pets and performers.

Peter Sandøe is professor of bioethics at the University of Copenhagen. He is also the director of the Danish Centre for Bioethics and Risk Assessment (CeBRA), an interdisciplinary and cross-institutional research center founded

in 2000. From 1992 to 2012 he served as the Chairman of the Danish Ethical
Council for Animals. From 2000 to 2007 he served as President of the European
Society for Agricultural and Food Ethics. Since 2009 he has been honorary
Professor of Animal Ethics at the University of Nottingham. He is committed
to interdisciplinary work combining perspectives from natural science, social
sciences, and philosophy. He the coauthor of a number of tools for e-learning,
including Animal Ethics Dilemma (www.aedilemma.net). His books include
Ethics of Animal Use, coauthored with Stine B. Christiansen (Blackwell, 2008).

Robert Streiffer is an associate professor of philosophy and bioethics at the
University of Wisconsin–Madison. He also holds affiliate appointments in
Veterinary Medical Sciences, Agricultural and Applied Economics, and at the
Nelson Institute for Environmental Studies. Recent publications focus on the
use of human stem cells to create animal/human chimeras and the application
of genetic engineering to animals used in agriculture. Streiffer presently serves
on the UW Letters and Sciences' Animal Care and Use Committee, the UW All
Campus Animal Planning and Advisory Committee, and chairs the planning
committee for the UW Forum on Animal Research Ethics.

Introduction

LORI GRUEN ■

There has been very little philosophical attention paid to captivity given the shockingly large numbers of humans and nonhumans that are captives—in the United States in 2012, almost 7 million people were, in some form or other, caught in the "correctional" system and roughly 2 million of those were incarcerated; billions of animals are held captive (and then killed) in the food industry every year; hundreds of thousands of animals are kept in laboratories; thousands are in zoos and aquaria; millions of "pets" are captive in our homes. Given that there is a prima facie concern about denying individuals their freedom, the gap in the philosophical literature seems odd. There has been growing interest in the problem of human mass incarceration and the racial, political, and economic issues that it raises. In terms of nonhuman animals, for more than two decades concern for animal suffering and "animal rights" have been important topics for philosophers and animal studies scholars, as well as activists. But the ethical issues raised by human and nonhuman captivity itself have not been fully addressed. This volume begins to fill that gap.

Many institutions of captivity are largely invisible, hidden from sight and awareness. Most people don't know what prisons are in their area unless they work at one, were incarcerated there, or know someone who is incarcerated there. Unless one is forced to think about them, prisons remain somewhat anonymous structures and what goes on inside them is very rarely contemplated. Other than the most notorious prisons like Alcatraz, Attica, or Guantánamo Bay, most people can't name prisons, even those in their own state, let alone know how many prisoners are held in them.[1] Factory farms and laboratories are not places that can be readily located either, unless you work there, know someone who works there, or happen to see or be a part of a protest out front.

In contrast, some institutions of captivity are so normalized that it is hard to think of them in the same category as prisons or factory farms or laboratories. Pet-keeping and zoos are central parts of our culture. The Associations of Zoos and Aquariums has described zoos as "popular family fun" and boasts that "in 2012, the 222 zoos and aquariums accredited by the AZA attracted more than 181 million visitors. Approximately 50 million visitors were children, making accredited zoos and aquariums some of the best places for families to connect with nature and each other."[2] The accredited zoos held 751,931 animals. The American Pet Products Association estimates that 68 percent of US households have companion animals. According to their survey, over 83 million dogs and 95 million cats live in people's homes. But few think of the dogs and cats in their families as "captives," and if there was something objectionable about holding big cats, rhinos, hippopotamus, gorillas, and other wild animals in zoos, then so many people wouldn't subject their children to the experience of viewing them.

Whether captives are largely outside of our consciousness or right under our feet, the experiences of captivity demand further reflection. Though conditions of captivity vary widely for humans and for other animals, there are common ethical themes that imprisonment raises, for example, the value of liberty, the nature of autonomy, the meaning of dignity, and the impact of routine confinement on well-being, both physical and psychological. The essays that follow address these and other issues. While the emphasis in this volume is primarily on nonhuman animals, reflection on human incarceration is also included as it provides what is perhaps more immediately comprehensible and brings into sharp focus some of the ethical issues captivity raises for very different kinds of beings.

In Part One, those with expertise on specific forms of captivity discuss how and why that form emerged and then describe the particular conditions of captivity. Understanding how captivity is experienced by captives is important for a variety of reasons, not least of which is that knowing the specifics about captive conditions for particular individuals is essential for analyzing the ethics of captivity. Too often philosophers and others theorizing about captivity do so in the abstract or make claims that are too general. Given the wide variety of captive conditions and the variety of needs and interests that different types of captives have, understanding the particularities of captivity is necessary for determining whether or not a particular form of captivity is ever defensible. Lori Marino, a neuroscientist who has worked closely with whales and dolphins, and Catherine Doyle, director of science, research, and education at the Performing Animal Welfare Society and expert on elephants, both argue in their chapters that these large mammals cannot thrive in captivity. Other animals like dogs, for example, only exist because of captivity; as Alexandra Horowitz argues, "a dog who is not *species*-captive would not be a dog at all. And, too, to roam free, to live life without the attachment to humans, would be, for a domesticated species, more dangerous than keeping." Still others, such as chimpanzees, as Steve Ross argues, cannot be returned to the wild and can actually flourish in some captive conditions. Formerly farmed animals or animals from laboratories, like Albert the chicken discussed by Miriam Jones or Mrs. Bean the rabbit discussed by Margo DeMello, live in sanctuary, where their specific needs are tended to and they are provided with the most freedom captivity can provide. The last two chapters in Part One are written by individuals who themselves are or were captive. Five men who are currently incarcerated and who have been studying philosophy with me critically reflect on their experiences in a maximum security men's prison. The final chapter provides a slice of what life was like for Lauren Gazzola, an animal activist who served over three years in a federal women's prison.

In Part Two, philosophers and social theorists examine a range of ethical issues raised by captivity. The section begins with a discussion of a familiar captive, the cat. Considering whether the practice of routine confinement really is in the best interest of the cats, Clare Palmer and Peter Sandøe explore the variety of ways to understand well-being and the impact confinement has on the lives of cats. Most animals who live with humans or are regularly used by humans have been bred for specific purposes, and some suggest that domestication is the ultimate form of captivity. Alasdair Cochrane examines four positions on domestication and argues that domestication per se is not a harm. Of course, the uses that domesticated animals are put to is usually quite harmful, and Robert Streiffer suggests that the harm of confinement, though itself a tricky concept to analyze, should be taken into account in the overall assessment of the ethics of using other animals in research. There is a familiar justification for captivity, often invoked by zoos, that keeping animals captive can be a means to preserve species. Irus Braverman discusses this justification in the context of changing paradigms within conservation biology, as the distinction between captive populations and wild populations is getting harder to maintain. One form of captivity that is usually thought to be in the best interests of the captives is sanctuary. In her discussion, Karen Emmerman argues that sanctuary should be viewed as a form of restitution to the animals, but that it should never be seen as a full remedy for the wrongs that have been done to them by denying them their freedom. In my chapter, looking at zoos and prisons, I argue that it is possible to be held captive and to have one's dignity intact but only when captive environments are set up such that captor and captive are in a relationship of respect. In contrast, Lisa Rivera, who ends the section by focusing on human captives and the physical and psychological harms captivity exerts on them, examines the role that coercion plays in conditions of captivity and troubles the possibility that respect is ever possible: "Captivity depends on power but it is power of a special sort: The power to enforce the choice and action that the captor desires."

By exploring the various conditions of captivity and a range of issues raised by them, this volume provides a rich look into an obscured set of practices and the ethical issues they raise. But the volume is not meant to be comprehensive. It does not contain in-depth analyses of captive institutions like the prison industrial complex or concentrated animal feeding operations (CAFOs), for example. Nor does it survey all experiences of captivity. Many animals commonly seen in zoos or human captive conditions other than prisons are not included, and no disrespect is intended to the human refugees, victims of sex trafficking or the child slave trade, gorillas, giraffes, cheetahs, mice, turtles, birds, and many others whose story of captivity is not told in the pages that follow. Not every form of captivity is covered here either; people can be thought to be captive in disabled bodies, or in tyrannical political contexts, or by poverty. These are all topics that are worthy of further exploration, and I hope that this volume may serve to free up more discussions of the ethics of captivity.

NOTES

1. Data is kept and analyzed by the Bureau of Justice Statistics (www.bjs.gov/) See also (www.sentencingproject.org/).
2. The AZA website updates the statistics annually (www.aza.org/about-aza/).

CONDITIONS OF CAPTIVITY

Canis familiaris

Companion and Captive

ALEXANDRA HOROWITZ ■

The domestic dog, *Canis familiaris*, a species designed for tens of thousands of years by humans, is fundamentally held in captivity by humans. Through countless iterations of selective breeding, dogs have been shaped, essentially, to be dependent on their designers. One in three US households contains a dog, over 80 million dogs in all—largely, in this culture, kept for most of their days in a house or in an enclosed yard with or often without any persons or other dogs in the near vicinity. Their movement is restricted; their diet is regimented; their sexual impulses thwarted.

Yet to call dogs, subjects of gloriously overwrought sentimentalization by these self-same humans, "captive" seems at first pass ridiculous. For their free movement is restricted only for their safety, limited to the domicile and environs, as a child is reined by a parent; their diet may be regimented, but nourishment is provided to them daily; their sex hampered, but only so as to not overrun the neighborhood with more resultant puppies than there are persons to keep and feed them.

Dogs, thus, exemplify a characteristic tension when discussing the captivity of (typically wild) animals: between the limitations of captivity on the animals' lives and the freedoms that, paradoxically, captivity might make available. In addition, dogs, as domesticated animals, add another facet to this discussion. The dog is *constitutionally* captive. For domestication has changed the species sufficiently that there is no longer any true "wild" dog. The resultant *species*—not just individuals of the species—is held captive by its designers.

In this chapter these issues are explored, first through discussion of what it might mean to talk about "captivity" with dogs. The concept extends from the

Courtesy of Jo-Anne McArthur, *We Animals*.

very concrete—particular confinement measures imposed by pet-keeping—to the more abstract—the restrictions obliged by domestication. The effects of these captivities are then reviewed, by highlighting modes of interspecies interaction peculiar to the human-dog dyad. Finally, captivity's obverse, *freedom*, is considered with dogs.

STATES OF CAPTIVITY

When considering the "captivity of animals," most writers (e.g., Hediger 1964) are referring to *wild* animals—that is, species who predominantly live elsewhere and otherwise than with humans, and members of that species who are now confined. Indeed, though the nature of the captivity varies, some kind of *confinement* is a necessary element of a captive life. The confinement may be literal—as in a cage or pen—or more figurative—as with an uncaged animal who is nonetheless kept by humans.

By contrast, domestic dogs live *within* human society. There are no "wild" members of the species. There are "feral" dogs—recent descendants of domestic dogs who live around human society but are not kept by any individual or individuals; there are "free-ranging" dogs—those provisioned with food by, but living apart from humans; and there are "stray" dogs—those who lived with humans but have wandered away or been abandoned.[1] All are the same species, and humans are implicated, directly or historically, in their existence. Contrast this situation with that of dogs' closest genetic relation, *Canis lupus,* the gray wolf. While the wolf can be "tamed" or socialized, made manageable and able to live in provisional (if not guaranteed to be permanent) harmony with humans through long-term training and handling (Kubinyi, Virányi, and Miklósi 2007), no wolf voluntarily lives among humans. Some individual or small groups of wolves are, of course, held in captivity, in the traditional sense: in zoos and in preserves intent on supporting the perpetuation of the species (e.g., Wolf Park, in Indiana, and the Wolf Conservation Center, in New York). The only extant wild wolf packs in North America survive through the packs' maintenance of *distance* from human society, rather than living within it.

This difference between *Canis lupus* and *Canis familiaris* means that, in some sense, the subject of the discussion at hand is also changed: a discussion of "captivity" of wolves (as with most animals) typically refers to the state or condition of *individuals*; but with dogs an additional, and most prevalent, sense is of the *species*.

Thus, in considering the captivity of dogs, a two-pronged approach is due: discussing the nature of the species' situation (through domestication) and the nature of individual dogs' situations (through the confinement resulting from pet-keeping). With these explications in hand, we can ask what captivity entails for dogs. Is captivity possibly desirable? Is there even any other option for the dog?

DOMESTICATION

It is not too much of a stretch to say that dogs have been *designed* by humans. Changed in temperament, anatomy, and behavior, domestic dogs are inextricably intertwined with humans—at least, it is inextricable *for the dog.*

What does it mean to be domesticated? Etymology provides a hint: Samuel Johnson's 1755 dictionary defines the related *domestical* and *domestick* as, in part, "belonging to the house" (Johnson 1755). Domestic animals are those connected to, even a part of, a person's domicile—as opposed to those whose habitats are fundamentally not residential. Biologically, domestication is a variation on the evolutionary process of natural selection. The selective-breeding process that Darwin originally called "methodical" selection is now referred to as "artificial" selection (Darwin 1859).

Domestic dogs, and all domestic animals, are those whose breeding is controlled by human communities; these communities also provide nutrition and demarcate the territories—living spaces—of their charges (Clutton-Brock 1999). Under this "new regime" of human beings (Clutton-Brock 1999, 32), a population genetically isolated from their wild relatives is developed over many generations.

The dog family, *Canidae*, includes dozens of species, all terrestrial, social, and largely crepuscular and nocturnal in habit (Serpell 1996). The first two of these attributes appear to be contributory to being domesticatable, as they align with the attributes of the domesticator. Dogs, via a common ancestor they share with the wolf, were the first domesticated animals by thousands of years (Clutton-Brock 1999). Archaeological evidence dates dog domestication to approximately 14,000 years before the present. Found remains range from a tomb at Ein Mallaha, Israel, containing an adult human skeleton with a hand on the thorax of a puppy (Davis et al. 1978), to dog skeletons in trash heaps, implying their use as a food source. Canid mitochondrial DNA suggests a more distant split between ancestral wolves and dogs, pointing to a divergence between the majority wolf population and those who were to become dogs as long as 145,000 years ago (Vilá et al. 1997). We could call the latter wolves *proto-domesticators*, since they had themselves changed behaviorally in ways that would later encourage humans' interest (or merely tolerance) of them.

Theories of how early domestication happened abound, but most converge on a few salient points about the behavior of the early proto-domesticates: in particular, they must have had a changed fear threshold, enabling them to approach and interact with human communities. One prominent theory, consistent with the evidence to date, suggests that when humans became less nomadic and began to create fixed settlements, they also created piled food waste. These scraps-piles were, essentially, a new niche, full of usable food for opportunistic scavengers (Coppinger and Coppinger 2001). Wolves will scavenge as well as hunt (Mech and Boitani 2003), so those wolves who could overcome their fear of this potential predator, humans, would be able to exploit that niche. In this way, these ancestral wolves may have self-selected, with tamer wolves able to acquire the most food. Concurrently, humans may have tolerated, even taken in, some of the pups, allowing them to survive long enough to reproduce. Over many generations, a new species—dogs—began to emerge from those self-selected wolves (Coppinger and Coppinger 2001).

In the thousands of years hence, this new species, while still terrestrial and social, was further shaped by generations of artificial selection. Most recently, selection has taken the form of diversification of dogs into *breeds*—usually related dogs who have similar physical features and behavioral tendencies. In the late nineteenth and early twentieth centuries, breed "standards" arose, according to which dogs with traits conforming to a newly stated ideal were interbred and those who did not conform were not bred (Garber 1996). This phenomenon served to exaggerate the diversity of dogs' appearance, especially in size, head morphology, and communicative anatomy (such as tails and ears).

The resultant changes in today's dog are *physical*—of anatomy and especially superficial anatomy—and *behavioral*. Physically, the dog's brain volume is smaller, relative to head and skull size, than that of the wolf; indeed, a smaller brain is typical of domestic animals (Clutton-Brock 1999). Dog teeth are smaller and more compressed than their ancestors', a result of the foreshortening of the jawbone. Their skull shape changed to include a "stop," a more distinct forehead between the front of the face and the top of the skull. Dogs' eyes are more rounded and forward-facing (Clutton-Brock 1999), and their ears are often floppy rather than erect. The consequent appearance of the face, with some facial features reminiscent of the human face,[2] is a prototypic instance of the neotenous appearance of many domestic dogs (Hecht and Horowitz 2013). Dogs' coats show an unprecedented degree of variation for a single species, from brindle coloration, to single-color coats of silver, red, and black, as well as the piebald coloration. Similarly, dog tails are highly variable in shape and length, but notably less rigid than the ancestral wolves' tails. Hearing and vision are less acute than in wolves (Serpell 1996), and olfaction may be diminished as well (Horowitz, Hecht, and Dedrick 2013). Indeed, it has been proposed that domestication chiefly consists of suppressing the pre-domesticate's *Merkelt,* or "perceptual world." Sensory sensitivity, adaptive in a wild setting, is not favored—and selected against—in domestication (Hemmer 1990).

Behaviorally, as a result of the presumed founding trait of a raised fear threshold, dogs are more calm and less reactive than their wild forebears. The corresponding changes of the species' social and cognitive behaviors, begun in this slight way, are quite profound. Socially, while wolves live in family packs, domestic dogs do not pack. Neither stray dogs nor free-ranging or feral dogs form traditional social packs with a single breeding pair, although individual dogs may travel "together," in parallel. These dogs do not hunt cooperatively, as wolves do (Beck 2002). Instead, the dog is verily a member of a human social group: the natural environment for dogs is around other dogs *and people* (Horowitz 2009a; Miklósi 2007).[3]

Dogs are changed cognitively: for instance, dogs perform less well than wolves on physical problem-solving tasks, such as retrieving hidden food (Miklósi 2007). On the other hand, dogs excel at *social* cognitive tasks—that is, in understanding how to glean information from others (people or dogs). Their performance is not only higher than wolves' in this regard, it is higher than nonhuman primates'—especially in following human gaze (Agnetta, Hare, and Tomasello 2000) or pointing (Pettersson et al. 2011; Soproni et al. 2002), and in distinguishing levels of others' attention (Call et al. 2003; Horowitz 2009a; Schwab and Huber 2006). In fact, this social problem-solving skill may have displaced any physical problem-solving skill: just those abilities—attention, persistence, astuteness—that serve a wild animal well might have been replaced by a new skill: manipulating the environment by using humans as tools. Humans solve dogs' problems: opening closed refrigerators, cans of food, and locked doors.

This social-cognitive skill was enabled by a changed use of eye contact. For wolves, and most other social animals, eye contact is wielded as a threat: to stare is to assert dominance (Fox 1971). While useful, this prevents these animals from looking at each other for cues as to where their attention is and what they see and know. Dogs, however, do not shy from eye contact—and as people use eye contact to convey information, dogs have learned to glean that information as well. Just as a developing child learns to follow another person's gaze and use gaze-alternations to share and request, so does the dog (Horowitz 2009b).

Dogs mirror human infants in other ways: they show attachment behavior comparable to infants, responding differentially to their caregiver at reunion (Kubinyi, Virányi, and Miklósi 2007). Their behavioral flexibility in considering humans "conspecifics" may be due to a change in their social critical period: while wolf pups open their eyes at ten days old, and thus must be exposed to any nonconspecifics who are to be in their social world before that time, dogs' socialization window is approximately three months (Freedman,

King, and Elliot 1961; Kubinyi, Virányi, and Miklósi 2007). The result is dogs' ease at bonding to noncanid species introduced in that critical period.

Delineation of the far-reaching changes wrought by domestication of dogs indicates how inextricably bound they are to their domesticators. Their social group includes human beings, not just conspecifics. They are dependent on humans for food, territory, and protection. Their brain structure, and, as a correlate, cognition, has been altered. They no longer have the perceptual acuity to survive outside of human civilization. The very process of artificial selection holds dogs captive, tethered to persons in body and mind. As a species, consideration of the morality of keeping dogs captive is no longer relevant: without this captivity, domestic dogs would not exist.

While holding dogs captive—qua domesticates—has in some sense enabled their existence, it should be noted that recent artificial selection has also had grievous effects for many breeds. Standards of conformation themselves predispose members of dozens of breeds to inherit and pass down physical disorders (Asher et al. 2009). These disorders range from skeletal dysplasias in large breeds—bred to be large for large's sake, and too large to support their own weight—to spina bifida in the pug, a side effect of the gene for a tightly curled tail, required by the breed standard. Shar-Peis are prone to eye ulcerations as a result of human preference for protruding eyes, and the Cavalier King Charles spaniel may suffer the dramatic and grotesque disorder called sryingeomyelia, in which, because of human preference for a dog with a small head, the animals' brain grows too large for its skull. The result is brain swelling, neurological damage, and severe pain. Those breed members unlucky enough to be the genetic inheritors of these conditions are held captive by their own bodies. Humans have enabled this unfortunate circumstance.

PET-KEEPING

Moreover, within a domesticated captivity, there may be levels of confinement and restriction for the *individual* animal as a result of being owned by a person. These captivities may be physical, social, or sexual; the limitations sensory and dietary. To get a sense of these individual situations, we must consider the changing nature of pet-keeping, as far as it has been recorded through the ages. Some confinement methods have been used continuously, and others are specific to culture and time.

Pet-keeping was common in antiquity, although the specifics of the animals' lives with their owners are not known in detail. Some understanding of the reason for keeping pets and the dog-owner relationship is provided through epitaphs at gravesites (Bodson 2000), but this discovery method is quiet on the nature of the quotidian lives of the mourned pets. What is known of dogs is that they were originally kept to guard, herd, hunt, and as companions (Grier 2006). Upper classes and ruling classes are documented as providing their pets (including but not restricted to dogs) with lavish accommodation and life-style: sometimes taking them to bed, to the public baths, building them sepa-rate shelters, providing them stipends, and providing them space at the dinner table. Pups have been allowed to suckle at the breasts of humans in both monar-chies and in tribal societies (Serpell 1987). To be sure, this treatment should not be taken to represent a wholesale deification of dogs by the ordinary pet-owner. For instance, even as dog-breeding became a popular hobby, litters of unwanted puppies were routinely drowned, with only one puppy preserved for the bitch to suckle (Grier 2006).

To take an instance of the evolution of pet-keeping over a few centu-ries: American styles of dog-ownership have changed from a kind of benign neglect to a contemporary view of the dog that supports, as of 2013, a $50 bil-lion dog- and dog-product industry (American Pet Products Association 2013). The original settlers' practices were inherited from Europe, including keeping both companion and working dogs. In the nineteenth century, pet-keeping was a regular part of an American childhood, and with this, perhaps, the attitude toward the animals shifted slightly. Fewer were working dogs and more were kept for their looks or temperament (Grier 2006).

While the sight of dogs wandering along town streets was common, this century also saw the beginning of what was at once a curtailment of dogs' independent perambulations and a permission to share space in the owner's residence. Those animals who were considered "family dogs" were more often allowed *into* the house. Though dogs were usually restricted to a room or area, dog-training literature of the time advises to provide a dog with a "spot all his own"—"a corner or strip of old carpet or blanket" might suffice (Grier 2006, 65). Early twentieth-century advertisements for "dog beds" and even "dog couches," promoted as "beautifully finished in high grade lacquers" (Grier 2006, 309), demonstrate the evolution of this trend. In twenty-first-century America, the business of dog beds is booming, supporting the sale of multi-hundred-dollar beds with fashionable prints (Schaffer 2009). In addition, 50 percent of owners allow their dogs to join them in their beds (Chomel and Sun 2011).

Other quantifiable changes in American dog owners' behavior are visible in attitudes toward dog-walking and dog-feeding. For a country creating suburbs at a high rate, dog-keeping included having a (preferably fenced) yard in which the dog could roam. But as the population moved back city-ward, bringing their dogs with them, "dog walking" (itself a phrase not seen in prose before 1897 [OED 1989]) became a common activity. Subsequently, cities and munici-palities began developing dog "parks" or "runs," public areas where dogs could be brought by owners to interact with their owners and other dogs while off leash. These parks are usually fenced areas of one acre or more, with natural or artificial ground. The first park was opened in Berkeley, California, in 1979; there are now over 500 parks in American cities as well as estimates of a thousand more outside of cities (Trust for Public Land 2011).

Even more spectacularly, dog-keeping has grown a sizable industry committed to producing dog-specific food. While the proto-dog evolved by scavenging, and for most of human history dogs ate (some component of) what was left over after human consumption, "dog food" was invented by a company called "Spratt's" in 1860 (Grier 2006). While the public needed convincing that dogs needed their own food, they were eventually quite convinced: dog food is now a multi-billion-dollar annual industry (American Pet Products Association 2013).

Thus, the trend of American pet-keeping has been to provide dogs with some of the comforts and freedoms that their owners enjoy—beds, places to roam— as well as a diet worthy of a veritable "member of the family," as most owners describe them (Chomel and Sun 2011). On the other hand, much of typical contemporary dog-ownership behavior involves circumscription on the animal's liberties to roam and behave naturally. Dogs are decidedly *not* in a position of total freedom or self-determination.

For instance, ancient art and writings indicate that for at least the thousands of years these media portray, dogs were outfitted with collars and controlled with leashes. Wall-relief art from the ancient Near East from the first to second millennia BC show men holding dogs by short leashes attached to distinctive collars—wrapped rope or wound metal—worn on the neck (Johns 2008). *Statue of a dog*, a limestone representation of the same era, represents an alert, erect-eared Mesopotamian dog wearing a collar with a bell or tag on the chest (Pickeral 2008). Ancient Egyptian dogs, large-bodied guarding dogs, are depicted in art wearing spiked or decorated collars—such as one of "white leather decorated with pink and green insets and studs, featur(ing) a frieze of horses running around it" from the Tomb of Miherperi (1570–1320 BC) (Pickeral 2008, 30). The same approach held for ancient Roman and Greek dogs: military dogs were outfitted with spiked leather collars; favored dogs wore ornamented collars.

Presently, all American states mandate that dogs be leashed in public (dog parks excepted), and most owners appear to comply. Collars, or, increasingly, chest or head harnesses, serve to hold identifying tags and form an extension of the leash. In addition, muzzles, not attached to the leash but encaging the snout so as to limit the dog's ability to open his mouth widely, eat found objects, or bite, are regularly used on a minority of dogs. Indeed, in some municipalities, muzzles are required on dogs deemed "aggressive."

Leashes and other coupling apparatuses are thus, as ever, ubiquitous accoutrements for dogs in public. The dogs' ability to roam, to run, to investigate odors,
and to interact with other dogs or people is controlled by the person at the other
end of that leash. The leash and collar themselves serve as that control (or pre-
tense of control) over the animal, but also as marks of ownership of the animal.

Owned dogs are usually kept secured but geographically isolated from their
owners and from other social companionship during the day, while owners are
at work. This isolation may be inside the home, in a room in the house or apartment, or in a fenced yard or small dog run within a yard. In all events, the dogs'
movement is restricted to the domicile. The restriction on movement may be
further enforced by the practice, popular in dog-training programs, of keeping
domestic dogs in "crates"—cages—when an owner is away from the home and
at times also when the owner is at home (McConnell 2007). While dogs are
typically walked or let outside to relieve themselves, there has been an increase
in the popularity of "pee mats," which allow dogs to urinate inside. Those dogs
trained to pee on the mat may not leave the residence with regularity or often.

EFFECTS OF PET-KEEPING

In both the continuities and the discontinuities in dog-keeping practices across
eras, specific forms of individual captivities are in evidence. Here "captivity"
is used to speak of confinement and restrictive procedures. Clearly, that individual dogs are in many ways tethered to humans is a form of restriction. While
a leash may be used for public safety, as a form of control over the dog, or as
an assertion of ownership, it also serves to delineate the movement of the dog.

This restriction is more serious than it may first appear. For being attached
to humans—while certainly to the dog's advantage *as a species*—may be limit-
ing of the expression of the Umwelt *of the individual.* Subjected to a person's
decisions about everything from where to walk (down what routes, and when),
whom to approach (which dogs and people), and what to investigate (which
odors can be loitered on and which cannot), the dog has little independent
choice. These are not *abusive* constraints, to be sure; they are simply reduc-
tions of the dog's experience to what the person, and her sensibility, allows.
Conversely, while individual dogs have different "personal spaces," the social
distance around themselves that they try to maintain, the leash obliges close
proximity to a person while walking. This proximity is not always the most
comfortable or ideal location for the dog, as the considerable business of trying
to get a dog to properly "heel" attests (Horowitz 2009).

Importantly, a restriction on social interaction with other dogs can lead
to more difficult social interactions later in life. Furthermore, the typical

contemporary American dog is spayed or neutered,[4] a fact that reflects not only a national policy to prevent unwanted animal births, but also a national aversion to dog sexual practices. Mating among owned dogs is largely limited to breeders' forced pairings; rarely will "responsible" pet owners allow their dogs to breed. The topic of dog sex has all but disappeared from dog-training and dog-owning manuals: it is assumed that dogs will not be mating. While this is indeed responsible pet-ownership, it is a profound circumscription of what is, for all animals, an ordinary part of life and a significant part of social interaction with conspecifics.

Most interestingly, the very lifestyle of people who own dogs enforces isolation of the dogs. In writing about the condition of zoo animals, Hediger expresses concern for an animal's "isolation through captivity" (Hediger 1964). In typical contemporary dog-owning practices, owners risk creating "captivity through isolation." Left alone for much of their lives, dogs are socially captive: dependent on their owners, and unable to interact with other beings except in specific settings. Relatedly, "crating" a dog, while done with good intention, is still a confinement that will limit the sensory and social possibilities for that animal.

The United Kingdom's Farm Animal Welfare Council created, in 1965, a listing of the "Five Freedoms" that farm animals are due, with respect to their welfare during their lives. In the United States, the American Veterinary Medical Association has adapted these guidelines for animals kept in humane societies or shelters. They include freedom from hunger and thirst; from discomfort; from pain and disease; from fear and distress; and the freedom to express normal behaviors (Newbury et al. 2010). Certainly, few of these are violated by the average contemporary pet owner. However, the final freedom, expression of "normal behavior," is widely infringed upon by the very nature of typical pet-keeping practices. Leashes, harnessing, isolation, and curbing of social and sexual behavior and sensory exploration all prioritize a secondary motivation for the constraint over the experience of the animal. Leashes are used for their safety—even if they limit who or what the dog can smell. Workday isolation is quite customary—even if it is an extraordinary situation for any social animal to live in. The dog suffers our touching, our proximity, and our leaving him; endures restrictions on his movement, eating, and elimination. The domestic dog, as an individual, is in many ways held captive.

FREEDOM

Imagine the *least captive dog*. What would that dog be like? On the one hand, he would be freed of the confining devices typical of pet-keeping practices—the leash, the domicile restriction. He would have the liberty to smell what he would like, approach who he would like, and eat what he would like. Importantly, those breeds with severe physical disorders would be freed from their genetic destiny by ending the practices of inbreeding. On the other hand, a dog who is not *species*-captive would not be a dog at all. And, too, to roam free, to live life without the attachment to humans, would be, for a domesticated species, more dangerous than keeping. Indeed, dogs are so sociable that, let free, they will remain with their human "captors" (Serpell 1987). There is no "return to the wild" for this species, for there is no space for, condition of, or future for the wild domestic dog. "Freedom" in *this* sense has no relevance for animals so deeply domesticated.

The condition of being so "kept" is, thus, mitigated by being "a species who was selected to be kept." To that point, the most freedom for the dog, as the species appears today, would consist of letting the dog behave as he may, within the constraints of his speciesdom. It would be to let dogs do more than simply fulfill our requests for them: to *sit, stay, roll over, come, don't eat that, "leave it,"* as we bark at our charges. It would be to allow them to express their natural behaviors, even those we find disgusting, embarrassing, or even wrong. It would be to flourish in their relationship with humans, to acknowledge the "social gravity" of the dyadic relationship (Hearne 1999), and express their dogness within this relationship.

Just in the way that the sheep looks sheepish, Thelma Rowell has noted, because that is all we allow the domestic sheep to do—we do not give sheep a chance to do anything else (Despret 2005)—the dog is loyal yet limited because that is what we provide for him. He wags at our return because, with his tail, and his being locked in that room, there is little else to do when we return and unlock it. The dog sleeps all day because we give him nothing to be awake for. The dog's leash circumscribes who can be at the end of it. At death, the pieces of the dog left behind are the collar and tag: insufficient to represent the nobility of the neck they graced and body they jingled with. In life, we must find more apt ways to know dogs.

Notes

1. The literature is equivocal on the meaning and application of especially the former two designations, but in all cases, the animal described is still within the bounds of human society, though not the charge of a specific human being (Beck 2002; Cafazzo et al. 2009).
2. The resemblance to a human face is especially profound in some small breeds, such as the brachycephalic (broad- and short-headed) pug—greatly to the breed's deficit. The pug's short nose and flat face are linked to severe obstructions in breathing; and their bulbous eyes are prone to ulceration (Asher et al. 2009).

3. Indeed, it is now not a surprising revelation, as it might have been twenty years ago, that most dog owners—or guardians, as some see themselves—consider their animals to be "members of the family": just as it has been noted that pets began being given human names in the middle of last century (Brandes 2012), so too do many give their charges their surname.
4. Sterilization is widely required by animal shelters before, or as a condition of, adopting a shelter animal (Humane Society of the United States 2010).

REFERENCES

Agnetta, Bryan, Brian Hare, and Michael Tomasello. 2000. "Cues to Food Location That Domestic Dogs (*Canis familiaris*) of Different Ages Do and Do Not Use." *Animal Cognition* 3: 107–112.

American Pet Products Association. 2013. Accessed May 10, 2013. http://www.americanpetproducts.org/press_industrytrends.asp.

Asher, Lucy, Gillian Diesel, Jennifer F. Summers, Paul D. McGreevy, and Lisa M. Collins. 2009. "Inherited Defects in Pedigree Dogs. Part 1: Disorders Related to Breed Standards." *Veterinary Journal* 182: 402–411.

Beck, Alan M. 2002. *The Ecology of Stray Dogs: A Study of Free-Ranging Urban Animals.* West Lafayette, IN: NotaBell Books.

Bodson, Liliane. 2000. "Motivations for Pet-keeping in Ancient Greece and Rome: A Preliminary Survey." *Animals & Us: Exploring the Relationships Between People & Pets*, Anthony L. Podberscek, Elizabeth S. Paul, and James A. Serpell (eds.), 27–41. Cambridge: Cambridge University Press.

Brandes, Stanley. 2012. "Dear Rin Tin Tin: An Analysis of William Safire's Dog-Naming Survey from 1985." *Names* 60(1): 3–14.

Cafazzo, Simona, Paola Valsecchi, Claudio Fantini, and Eugenia Natoli. 2009. "Social Dynamics of a Group of Free-Ranging Domestic Dogs Living in a Suburban Environment." *Journal of Veterinary Behavior: Clinical Applications and Research* 4(2): 61.

Call, Josep, Juliane Bräuer, Juliane Kaminski, and Michael Tomasello. 2003. "Domestic Dogs (*Canis familiaris*) Are Sensitive to the Attentional State of Humans." *Journal of Comparative Psychology* 117: 257–263.

Chomel, Bruno B., and Ben Sun. 2011. "Zoonoses in the Bedroom." *Emerging Infectious Diseases* 17(2): 167–172.

Clutton-Brock, Juliet. 1999. *A Natural History of Domesticated Mammals.* Cambridge: Cambridge University Press.

Coppinger Ray, and Lorna Coppinger. 2001. *Dogs: A Startling New Understanding of Canine Origin, Behavior, and Evolution.* New York: Scribner.

Darwin, Charles. 1859. *On the Origin of Species.* London: John Murray.

Davis, Simon J. M., and François R. Valla. 1978. "Evidence for Domestication of the Dog 12,000 Years Ago in the Natufian of Israel." *Nature* 276: 608–610.

Despret, Vinciane. 2005. "Sheep Do Have Opinions." In *Making Things Public: Atmospheres of Democracy*, Bruno Latour and Peter Weibel (eds.), 360–368. Cambridge: MIT Press.

Fox, Michael W. 1971. *Behaviour of Wolves, Dogs and Related Canids*. New York: Harper and Row.

Freedman, Daniel G., John A. King, and Orville Elliot. 1961. "Critical Period in the Social Development of Dogs." *Science* 133: 1016–1017.

Garber, Marjorie. 1996. *Dog Love*. New York: Simon and Schuster.

Grier, Katherine C. 2006. *Pets in America: A History*. Orlando, FL: Harcourt.

Hearne, Vicki. 1999. "A Taxonomy of Knowing: Animals Captive, Free-Ranging, and at Liberty." In *Humans and Other Animals*, Arien Mack (ed.), 25–40. Columbus: Ohio State University Press.

Hecht, Julie, and Alexandra Horowitz. 2013. "Physical Prompts to Anthropomorphisms of the Domestic Dog (*Canis familiaris*)." *Journal of Veterinary Behavior: Clinical Applications and Research* 8: e30.

Hediger, Heini. 1964. *Wild Animals in Captivity: An Outline of the Biology of Zoological Gardens*. London: Dover.

Hemmer, Helmut. 1990. *Domestication: The Decline of Environmental Appreciation*. Cambridge: Cambridge University Press.

Horowitz, Alexandra. 2009a. "Attention to Attention in Domestic Dog (*Canis familiaris*) Dyadic Play." *Animal Cognition* 12: 107–118.

Horowitz, Alexandra. 2009b. *Inside of a Dog: What Dogs See, Smell, and Know*. New York: Scribner.

Horowitz, Alexandra, Julie Hecht, and Alexandra Dedrick. 2013. "Smelling More or Less: Investigating the Olfactory Experience of the Domestic Dog." *Learning and Motivation* 44: 207–217.

Humane Society of the United States. 2010. "Spay-Neuter by State." Accessed May 22, 2010. http://www.humanesociety.org/assets/pdfs/legislation/spayneuter_by_state.pdf.

Johns, Catherine. 2008. *Dogs: History, Myth, Art*. Cambridge: Harvard University Press.

Johnson, Samuel. 1755. *Dictionary of the English Language*. Accessed May 22, 2013. http://johnsonsdictionaryonline.com/?page_id=7070&i=637.

Kubinyi, Enikö, Zsófia Virányi, and Ádam Miklósi. 2007. "Comparative Social Cognition: From Wolf and Dog to Humans." *Comparative Cognition & Behavior Reviews* 2: 26–46.

McConnell, Patricia. 2007. *For the Love of a Dog: Understanding Emotion in You and Your Best Friend*. New York: Ballantine Books.

Mech, L. David, and Luigi Boitani, eds. 2003. *Wolves: Behavior, Ecology, and Conservation*. Chicago: University of Chicago Press.

Miklósi, Ádam. 2007. *Dog Behaviour, Evolution, and Cognition*. New York: Oxford University Press.

Newbury, Sandra, et al. 2010. "Guidelines for Standards of Care in Animal Shelters." Publication of the Association of Shelter Veterinarians.

Oxford English Dictionary. 2nd edition. 1989. Oxford: Oxford University Press.

Pettersson, Helene, Juliane Kaminski, Esther Herrmann, and Michael Tomasello. 2011. "Understanding of Human Communicative Motives in Domestic Dogs." *Applied Animal Behaviour Science* 133: 235–245.

Pickeral, Tamsin. 2008. *The Dog: 5000 Years of the Dog in Art*. London: Merrell.

Schaffer, Michael. 2009. *One Nation under Dog*. New York: Henry Holt.

Schwab, Christine, and Ludwig Huber. 2006. "Obey or Not Obey? Dogs (*Canis familiaris*) Behave Differently in Response to Attentional States of Their Owners." *Journal of Comparative Psychology* 120: 169–175.

Serpell, James A. 1987. "Pet Keeping in Non-Western Societies." *Anthrozoos* 1: 166–174.

Serpell, James A. 1996. *In the Company of Animals: A Study of Human-Animal Relationships*. Cambridge: Cambridge University Press.

Soproni, Krisztina, Ádam Miklósi, József Topál, and Vilmos Csányi. 2002. "Dogs' (*Canis familiaris*) Responsiveness to Human Pointing Gestures." *Journal of Comparative Psychology* 116: 27–34.

Trust for Public Land. 2011 "City Parks Facts Report." Accessed May 21, 2013. http://www.tpl.org.

Vilà, Carlos, Peter Savolainen, Jesús E. Maldonado, Isabel R. Amorim, John E. Rice, Rodney L. Honeycutt, Keith A. Crandall, Joakim Lundeberg, and Robert K. Wayne. 1997. "Multiple and Ancient Origins of the Domestic Dog." *Science* 276: 1687–1689.

2

Cetacean Captivity

LORI MARINO ∎

WHO ARE CETACEANS?

Cetaceans (dolphins and whales) are a diverse order of aquatic marine mammals comprising two modern suborders, the Odontoceti (toothed whales, dolphins, and porpoises) and the Mysticeti (the large rorqual and baleen whales). Cetaceans have been subjects of fascination and adulation by humans since ancient times (Marino 2007) likely because of their combination of physical beauty and elegance in a mysterious aquatic environment and their obvious intelligence, sociality, and curiosity. Indeed, many dolphins and whales have the second highest encephalization level (a measure of relative brain size) next to modern humans and significantly above even our closest primate relatives, the great apes (Marino 1998). Their cognitive and communicative abilities are prodigious (see Marino et al. 2008 for a review), and bottlenose dolphins are one of the few species to demonstrate human-like levels of self-awareness (Reiss and Marino 2001). We now know, as well, that cetaceans are among the most culturally sophisticated beings on the planet (Rendell and Whitehead 2001; Whitehead 2011).

With all that said, our relationship to cetaceans has been, at best, fraught with inconsistencies. Captivity represents one of the ways that humans have objectified and exploited cetaceans in the name of adulation. Humans have at various times, and still do today, both venerated and slaughtered cetaceans. White (2007) suggests that cetaceans are subject to such a wide range of treatments because they, more than any other animal, are the most similar and dissimilar to us at the same time. According to White, cetacean intelligence, self-awareness, emotionality, and social complexity mean that they, like us, experience life as persons. But they look and move very differently, live in an exotic milieu, lack clear facial expressions, communicate in unfamiliar modalities, and always seem to be smiling (although this is just an anatomical illusion). These differences make it challenging for humans to recognize the similarities to us and their ability to suffer like us, and, thus, make it easier to objectify and exploit them (Marino, 2013).

The history of cetacean captivity is the history of our simultaneous veneration and exploitation of cetaceans. The exploitation and abuses of cetaceans in captivity are, arguably, worse today for many cetaceans than ever before. Here is how it started.

HISTORY OF CETACEAN CAPTIVITY

Despite a long historical relationship with dolphins and other cetaceans (Aristotle is said to have observed and written on their behavior), one of the first documented cases of cetacean captivity and display derives from the 1860s, when circus mogul P. T. Barnum paid to have several beluga whales (*Delphinapterus leucas*) captured from the St. Lawrence River. They were shipped by train in boxes of seaweed and housed in Barnum's American Museum in small enclosures, where most of them died shortly afterwards (Mountain 2012). By the late 1870s, belugas and dolphins were being caught and supplied to aquariums and zoological gardens throughout the eastern United States, Europe, and Asia, where they were trained to perform (Rose 2009). The mortality rate during capture and confinement in these facilities was so high and the survival durations so short that it created a habitual revolving door of replacement by capture from the wild. Collectors expected the animals to die frequently, and they simply went about replacing their "stock" on a continual basis. Barnum himself started with two whales, and by the time his museum burned down in 1985, the ninth captive whale had died (*New York Tribune* 1861).

Another milestone in the history of cetacean captivity in the United States came in 1938 when a Hollywood film company, Marine Studios, built a seawater tank in Florida in which to film dolphins for movies. The place eventually became Marineland of Florida in the 1970s, the oldest operating cetacean park in the United States. The program's success led to the proliferation of dolphinariums across the world during the 1940s and 1950s, including the Miami Seaquarium and the first inland facility, Seven Seas Panorama in Chicago (Frontline 1997). By this time the public was generally accustomed to the idea of keeping dolphins and whales captive for amusement, and these early facilities were not afraid to promote this idea, marketing themselves as places of entertainment and distraction. But at the same time the public was also becoming aware of the prodigious abilities and intelligence of dolphins.

The major impetus for cetacean captivity and popularity came in the early to mid 1960s with the movie and TV series *Flipper*, about a friendly dolphin who saved humans from danger through his extraordinary cunning and anthropomorphic motivations. The show launched a dolphin frenzy with new dolphin facilities, paraphernalia, and products bursting forth globally. But there were no regulations for the welfare of the captive dolphins.

When *Flipper* ended in 1968 and the production was shut down, another pivotal point was reached when one of the dolphins' trainers, Ric O'Barry, reported that after the show was over and one of the dolphins, Kathy, was relegated to a small pool in the back of the studio, she became depressed and took her own life by holding her breath (O'Barry and Coulbourn 2000). That event changed O'Barry forever and launched his career as a tireless and unwithering activist for cetacean protection and freedom from captivity. His conversion mirrored the beginnings of public opinion against cetacean captivity, as the death toll at many hastily constructed facilities rose. Concurrently, the international campaign against whaling was mounting, and people were developing ethical and philosophical arguments against not only hunting whales and other marine mammals, but also keeping them in captivity.

With growing public concern several regulations were put into place to address cetacean welfare and protection. The Animal Welfare Act (AWA), which originated in 1964, provides for inspection of marine parks and other facilities holding captive marine mammals by government-employed veterinarians. But the AWA has been consistently criticized because actual inspections of parks happen infrequently and with little rigor.

The period of 1962–1970 saw some of the most egregious abuses of marine mammals as theme parks and aquaria scrambled to obtain one of the largest dolphins, the orca (*Orcinus orca*), or killer whale, for shows. During this period orca captures off British Columbia, Washington State, and California were completely unregulated. Capture is a "violent affair" (Rose 2009), and many orcas died during capture, suffocating in nets and drowning from immobilization. In August 1970 Ted Griffin and Don Goldsberry captured eighty orcas from the Washington southern resident population, leading to a devastating decline from which the orca population is still recovering. Four juveniles were accidentally killed. Public reports of these atrocities led to residents pushing for legislation to ban or control orca capture, and in 1971 Washington State passed regulating laws (Frontline 1997).

Among the orcas that were captured from the southern resident population in 1970 was a very young female named Tokitae (Lolita), who was transferred to the Miami Seaquarium, where she was housed with another orca, Hugo, captured earlier from the same pod, until his death in 1980. Lolita, who is now over forty-three years old, has remained the only orca in her tiny tank to this day.

She is the focus of intense animal advocacy efforts to rehabilitate and release her back into the same area she was captured from, where her pod, including her mother, lives to this day.

In 1972 more specific legislation, the Marine Mammal Protection Act (MMPA), was passed, forcing a number of the very worst of the dolphinariums to close. The MMPA, overseen by the National Marine Fisheries Service (NMFS), prohibits the taking of any marine mammals from US waters or by US citizens in international waters except by special permit. Permits are issued for the purposes of scientific work, public display, or strandings or accidental captures by fishermen (Marine Mammal Protection Act 1972). The grave results of the Washington orca captures eventually led to a total ban on capturing orcas from that state in 1976. At the same time, partly as a result of the "Save the Whales" campaign in the mid to late 1970s, the International Whaling Commission (IWC) banned whaling in international waters, but, in actual practice, it excluded dolphins and smaller cetaceans. There were also many legal loopholes for whaling nations. The MMPA provided a patina of protection for marine mammals and has been a positive force in many ways, but exceptions to the regulations and little oversight allowed for the marine theme park industry to operate essentially unfettered and without accountability.

Seeing the writing on the wall and the "green-leaning" zeitgeist of the day, marine mammal theme parks rebranded themselves as centers of education, science, and conservation. But while the public message had changed, the marine parks were still operating in a covert mindset that had the commercial interests of their facilities as the priority. The message seemed new and more ethically focused, but it was a superficial makeover at best.

Through the 1980s and early 1990s marine parks still took dolphins and whales from the wild for their facilities but drew increasing public ire for doing so. In 1989 the NMFS called for a voluntary moratorium on the capture of bottlenose dolphins (*Tursiops truncatus*) in the Gulf of Mexico and along the Atlantic coast primarily due to the uncertainty about how captures would affect wild populations (Rose, Parsons, and Farinato 2009). In 1990 SeaWorld contracted a team of orca hunters to capture three to six juvenile killer whales from Puget Sound. Marine mammal activists and the state attorney general at the time were able to ban transportation of captive whales in the State, and SeaWorld withdrew. Shortly thereafter, following a media firestorm, British Columbia banned orca captures (Frontline 1997). The last capture of a cetacean from US waters was in 1993, when the Shedd Aquarium took three Pacific white-sided dolphins (*Lagenorhynchus obliquidens*) from the coast of California for display. The public outcry put an end to this activity in the United States once and for all.

Since the moratorium marine parks have focused on captive breeding to maintain their populations for display. However, the infant mortality rate for

Courtesy of Jo-Anne McArthur, *We Animals*

captive cetaceans is generally too high to be self-sustaining (Rose 2004). This has led many captive facilities to argue for a return to wild captures. One particular example is the recent request to NMFS by the Georgia Aquarium to import eighteen wild-caught belugas from Russian seas. The captive beluga population is dwindling because these animals do not breed or survive well in captivity. Therefore, under the guise of education and conservation, the Georgia Aquarium, SeaWorld, and, ironically, the Shedd Aquarium are all driving an effort to bring these whales, who are already caught, into their facilities for public display. The request has been met with vociferous opposition from many marine mammal scientists, cetacean advocates, and much of the general public. If approved, this request would represent a full-circle return to outdated times when P. T. Barnum captured, exhibited, and caused the death of so many beluga whales.

CURRENT CAPTIVE CONDITIONS

At least nineteen cetacean species are currently held in captivity around the world; the most commonly held are orcas, beluga whales, bottlenose dolphins, and Pacific white-sided dolphins. The total number of captive bottlenose dolphins around the world is about 800, with the majority at popular tourist attractions in the United States, Mexico, and the Caribbean (Born Free Foundation n.d.). And because captive numbers are not sustainable, many facilities around the world regularly take individuals from the wild.

The ways in which dolphins and whales in captivity are exploited have expanded to increasingly more extravagant circus-like shows to swim-with-dolphin (SWD) programs to the burgeoning industry of dolphin-assisted therapy (DAT), in which dolphins are marketed as "therapeutic agents." Unlike these highly lucrative and growing commercial avenues, the use of captive cetaceans for scientific research has declined precipitously because of the untimely death of so many of the captive dolphins who were used in research throughout the 1980s to the early 2000s (see below). Moreover, the US Navy maintains several cetaceans and other marine mammals to conduct invasive research on them and deploy them in dangerous military situations. But not much is disclosed about these secretive projects.

Given that the overwhelming majority of dolphins and whales around the world are held captive for entertainment and recreation, I will focus here on the commercial venues: aquarium and theme park displays and shows, SWD programs, and DAT. Often these are found in the same facility and are offered as adjunct programs.

The public fascination with dolphins and whales continues to fuel the enthusiasm for visiting aquariums and theme parks. In the United States alone more than 50 million people visit captive facilities every year (Kestin 2004a). Few animals have the revenue-earning potential of dolphins and whales (Kestin 2004b). Shows have become increasingly commercialized, involving increasingly risky in-water contact between the animals and trainer/performers. As a result, there have been many injuries of trainers during these shows and rehearsals and several well-publicized deaths of both trainers and animals. One particularly pivotal incident occurred when a male orca, Tilikum, killed his trainer, Dawn Brancheau, at SeaWorld Orlando in 2010. Tilikum has been involved in the deaths of three humans over the years. Male orcas normally stay with their mother for a lifetime but Tilikum was taken from his family group in the wild when he was only three years old (Kirby 2012; Zimmerman 2010) and this maternal deprivation contributed to years of trauma and behavioral abnormalities. The deaths that Tilikum caused, as well as a number of other incidents at marine parks with orcas, have led to much public criticism of keeping orcas in captivity. Unfortunately, Tilikum and the orcas remain in confinement and marine parks like SeaWorld are fighting legally to maintain in-water work with them. Trainer lives continue to be put at considerable risk when working in the water with orcas, a species that has never injured a human in the wild but is responsible for multiple injuries and deaths in captivity.

It is apparently no longer satisfying to marine park visitors to simply watch dolphins and whales perform when they can get up close and personal with them in the water. Swim-with-dolphin (SWD) programs in captivity, where paying park customers interact and swim with dolphins in their tanks, emerged in the 1980s but have become a ubiquitous offering on the marine theme park circuit. SWD programs are enormously popular as the parks compete for customers. In 1990 there were only four SWD programs in the United States. but now there are as many as eighteen facilities offering dolphin "encounter" programs of one kind or another (Stewart and Marino 2009). SWD is also increasing worldwide, particularly in the Caribbean (Humane Society of the United States 2005).

Admission to these programs can range from $200 above general park admission fees to even $500 for "trainer of the day" sessions. The closer the visitors are allowed to get to the animals the higher the ticket price. Often these SWD attractions are touted as educational. Captive facilities claim that visitors learn about the behavior and protection of these animals during these activities and that this knowledge leads to an increase in conservation attitudes. But most of these facilities focus exclusively on husbandry and captive activities to the exclusion of information about the natural lives of dolphins and whales. And there is no evidence to support the claim that dolphin and whale shows or SWD attractions lead to greater or lasting knowledge about the animals or that visitors become more conservation-minded as a result (Marino et al. 2010; Stewart and Marino 2009). In addition, SWD programs can be dangerous for both humans and dolphins. There are numerous reports of swimmers being seriously injured by frustrated and aggressive dolphins in these programs. And exposure to humans can also increase susceptibility of dolphins to pathogens (Geraci and Ridgway 1991; Mazet, Hunt, and Ziccardi 2004).

Dolphin-assisted therapy (DAT) is actually just a type of SWD disguised as legitimate animal-assisted therapy in which dolphins are marketed as therapeutic agents for a variety of psychological and physical illnesses (Brakes and Williamson 2007). It began in the 1970s by Betsy Smith, who later denounced it publicly as exploitive. Children with autism and their needful parents are a strongly targeted population (Marino and Lilienfeld 2007a). Despite the many claims of this industry, there is no existing evidence that DAT has any therapeutic value (Humphries 2003; Marino and Lilienfeld 1998, 2007b). Actual therapy is treatment for a specific condition and, importantly, is verifiable by outcomes (improvement in some measure of the condition). No such criteria are applicable to DAT and, thus, there is no evidence that it meets even the minimal criteria for therapy.

DAT typically involves several sessions either swimming or interacting with captive dolphins often along with more conventional therapeutic tasks, such as puzzles and motor activities. The standard price of DAT, whose practitioners are not required by law to receive special training or certification, is exorbitant, reaching into the thousands of dollars. Thus, DAT has become a highly lucrative business with facilities all over the world, including the United States. DAT is not regulated by any health and safety standards for either humans or dolphins. Yet there are many risks to both humans and dolphins during DAT that include, but are not limited to, injury, disease transmission, and the potential loss of opportunities for real treatment (Marino 2011). Risks to swimmers and dolphins in DAT are the same for any SWD program. Moreover, the risks to participants in DAT are emotional. Often desperate parents of sick children are led to believe they will receive some kind of lasting improvement from DAT. When they return home to the same problems as before, the disappointment can be devastating, not to mention the financial cost and opportunity loss to engage more mainstream and efficacious treatments.

EFFECTS OF CAPTIVITY ON CETACEANS

Current captive conditions for cetaceans are certainly better than they were in Barnum's day, but despite the higher quality food, improved veterinary care, and advanced water filtration systems, the basic experience of captivity is the same for cetaceans today as it always was. Captivity for both wild-caught and captive-born cetaceans is devastating on several levels. And it is critically important to recognize that although some cetaceans fare better than others, *no cetaceans thrive in captivity*. The effects go beyond the serious welfare problems that plague individual animals when confined in tanks. And these larger effects are more insidious. One significant effect of keeping cetaceans in captivity is that it promotes perceptions of cetaceans that lead to further exploitation and abuse. There is a close ongoing connection between the global marine mammal display industry and dolphin slaughters such as those in Taiji, Japan (Batt 2013). In addition, the effects of removal of even small numbers of animals from a wild population for display can be more devastating than anticipated for the group (Lusseau 2007) because individuals within the group have differentiated social roles and the removal of key socially connected individuals could unravel the entire social network.

The scientific evidence for the damaging effects of captivity on individual dolphin and whale physical and psychological health is overwhelming. Captive cetaceans are considerably challenged by the constraints of their artificial enclosures (Couquiaud 2005). Confinement impacts not only physical freedom but social relationships, degrades autonomy through the imposition of enforced schedules of activity and behavior, causes boredom, induces frustration, and inhibits incentives and abilities to carry out natural behaviors such as hunting and traveling.

There is abundant evidence for stress, disease, and increased mortality in captive cetaceans as an inevitable outcome of confinement, loss of control, and deprivation in captive situations (Marino and Frohoff 2011). Captive cetaceans display physiological and behavioral abnormalities indicative of psychological distress and emotional disturbance. These include stereotypies, for example, repetitious maladaptive behaviors such as head-bobbing and pacing (Fowler 1978; Greenwood 1977), unresponsiveness, excessive submissiveness, hyper-sexual behavior (towards humans or other dolphins), self-inflicted physical trauma and mutilation (Sweeney 1988), stress-induced vomiting (Sweeney 1990), and excessive aggressiveness towards other dolphins and humans as has been seen in Tilikum and others (Stewart and Marino 2009).

The drivers of stress for captive dolphins and whales derive from every aspect of their existence, including capture and transportation from one facility to the next. The US Marine Mammal Inventory Report (2010) lists numerous stress-related disorders, such as ulcerative gastritis, perforating ulcer, cardio-genic shock, and psychogenic shock as "cause of death" in captive cetaceans, confirming that stress is a critical issue for captive marine mammals. Stress derives from many aspects of captivity, not the least of which is the social depri-vation associated with loss of one's natal group or transfer from one facility to another, housing with artificially constructed groups of dolphins, the taking of dependent juveniles from their mothers at early ages for transfer from one facil-ity to the next, the lack of space needed for successful conflict-resolution, loss of autonomy, and boredom.

Capture, handling, and confinement produce a demonstrable change in stress hormone levels similar to changes occurring during increased stress in humans (St. Aubin and Geraci 1988). And it is well established that chronic stress leads to immunosuppression and susceptibility to disease in marine mammals (St. Aubin and Geraci 1988; Noda et al. 2007; Spoon and Romano 2011). The result is high mortality rates for both captive-born and wild-caught cetaceans.

For orcas in particular captivity is catastrophic, as evidenced by their abnor-mal aggression towards humans and other whales and their very high mortality rates in captivity compared with their natural habitat. A recent review of orca health in captivity substantiates the many health risks by reporting two cases of deaths from mosquito-borne illnesses (St. Louis encephalitis and West Nile) in captive orcas. Unlike their wild counterparts, who are rarely stationary and spend a significant amount of time under water, captive orcas are often confined in pools too shallow for their body length and typically spend hours every day floating motionless on the surface, leaving them vulnerable to biting mosqui-toes and, therefore, a variety of blood-borne illnesses (Jett and Ventre 2012).

Moreover, most captive orcas are not provided shade from ultraviolet radiation and are often subject to its immunosuppressing effects (Jett and Ventre 2012). To add insult to injury, captive orcas typically suffer from dental problems associated with raking their teeth on gates and hard parts of their tank. Thus, their teeth are often drilled and left open to the air, exposing them to all kinds of bacteria (Jett and Ventre 2011). To combat infections they are given chronic doses of antibiotics that further reduce their immunity to diseases. Jett and Ventre (2011) suggest that this destructive cycle of poor welfare has long-term consequences that account for short life spans and high mortality for captive orcas.

Most captive orcas do not survive past the age of twenty years (Williams 2001). The natural average life span for male and female orcas is 29.2 and 50.2 years, respectively, with a maximum longevity of sixty and ninety years, respectively (Ford 2009; Ford, Ellis, and Balcomb 1994; Olesiuk, Bigg, and Ellis 1990; Wells and Scott 1990). DeMaster and Drevenak (1988) estimated the annual mortality rate for captive orcas at 7 percent, and two additional studies by Small and DeMaster (1995) and Woodley, Hannah, and Lavigne (1997) both estimated captive annual mortality rates at 6.2 percent (excluding calves), considerably higher than the 2.3 percent annual mortality rate figure for wild populations (DeMaster and Drevanek 1988).

Beluga whales seem to fare no better than orcas. Woodley, Hannah, and Lavigne (1997) report that beluga whales die prematurely in captivity. Although definitive life-span data have not yet been established for wild belugas, there is growing evidence that captive beluga life spans are significantly shorter than those in the wild. Wild beluga whales may live as long as fifty to sixty years (Stewart et al. 2006), but captive beluga whales routinely die before the age of thirty. Likewise, mortality rates for belugas in captivity are higher than in the wild (DeMaster and Drevanek 1988; Small and DeMaster 1995; Woodley et al. 1997). And, as mentioned above, the fact that the dwindling captive population has prompted some theme parks to capture and try to import more of them is evidence of the low survivorship and difficult breeding conditions for belugas in captivity.

Bottlenose dolphins do somewhat better in captivity than orcas and beluga whales but still suffer from stress-related diseases brought about by confinement and loss of autonomy. Only recently have survivorship statistics in captivity (6.4 percent) reached a level not statistically significantly different from that thought to exist in the wild (3.9 percent) (DeMaster and Drevenak 1988; Duffield and Wells 1991; Olesiuk, Bigg and Ellis 1990; Small and DeMaster 1995). The best estimate of average and maximum life span for captive and wild bottlenose dolphins is about 25 and 45 years, respectively (Small and DeMaster, 1995). But there are biases in these data that make it doubtful that bottlenose dolphins live as long in captivity as in the wild. Survivorship statistics from captive facilities often exclude periods of sharply increased mortality—those associated with capture and transfer. Bottlenose dolphins face a sixfold increase in risk of mortality immediately after capture from the wild and immediately after every transfer between facilities (Small and DeMaster 1995). According to Small and DeMaster (1995) the first sixty days of captivity should not be taken into account when calculating survival rates for captured individuals, since the mortality during this time is so high. Further, remote locations and many non-Western or developing countries were not included in these studies; hence it is likely that the worst of these facilities were omitted from these data. These biases can easily lead to artificially inflated survivorship data.

I personally experienced the toll captivity takes on dolphins with the life and untimely deaths of Presley and Tab, two young male dolphins housed at the New York Aquarium in Brooklyn. Presley and Tab were made famous inter-nationally by demonstrating that they recognized themselves in a mirror in a study Diana Reiss and I conducted. The study was the first to provide definitive evidence that at least one cetacean species, bottlenose dolphins, was capable of a complex level of self-awareness indicated by mirror self-recognition (Reiss and Marino 2001). But after all the media coverage died down the more impor-tant story, in my view, unfolded. Presley and Tab were captive born and thirteen and seventeen years old, respectively, when they were subjects in our study. Not long after our study, Presley and Tab were dead. Each of them was transferred to another facility and met an untimely death from two diseases related to stress and immune-system dysfunction. Presley succumbed to fungal encephalitis and Tab to gastroenteritis. Of course, they had other maladies, and all added up to a foreshortened life.

Presley and Tab are not alone in their fate. All of the dolphins who were subjects of the famed experiments by Lou Herman at Kewalo Basin, that is, Phoenix, Akeakamai, Hiapo, and Elele, died prematurely. A dolphin at another facility, Natua, who demonstrated a complex capacity for metacognition, that is, the ability to think about his own thoughts (Smith et al. 1995), was dead by the age of eighteen. In fact, none of these "research superstars" lived to the age of thirty, with four of them dying earlier than the average, not maximum, life span for *Tursiops*. These outcomes lead inevitably to the question: If captiv-ity involves state-of-the-art veterinary care, protection from external threats, and all the good fish one could eat, why don't these individuals live to their maximum life span? The only conclusion is that there is something inherently incompatible between cetacean well-being and captivity.

WHAT DOES THE FUTURE HOLD FOR CETACEANS?

The future for cetaceans in captivity is precarious. On the one hand there are increasing numbers of dolphinariums budding across the globe because the attractions these places offer are still very popular and lucrative. And as long as the public continues to make it profitable to keep dolphins and whales in captivity, it will continue. But at the same time there are forces working in opposition to cetacean captivity. The death of Dawn Brancheau at SeaWorld in 2010 drew an outpouring of media criticism, and the public has developed a more negative attitude towards orca captivity, if not cetacean captivity in general. Moreover, the incident has resulted in legal challenges and pressures for SeaWorld from the Occupational Safety and Health Administration. David Kirby's book *Death at SeaWorld* and the documentary *Blackfish* continue to contribute greatly to the public's awareness of the problems of orca captivity, and both send a disparaging and revealing message about SeaWorld and cetacean captivity in general.

Other efforts span the range from sidewalk protests to NGO-driven campaigns educating the public about the deleterious effects of captivity to the vanguard of advocacy—claiming personhood status and basic rights for cetaceans, including their having the right to life and liberty. Philosopher Tom White has spearheaded a number of important conference symposia on the issue of personhood in dolphins. He presents a cogent argument for personhood in dolphins based on the scientific evidence that they possess such psychological characteristics as autonomy, self-awareness, emotion, and strong social bonds. The fact that these symposia have attracted a lot of attention from the general scientific community, as well as the marine mammal community, suggests that the idea of personhood in dolphins is one we may be ready to embrace.

In May 2011, the nonprofit organization Whale and Dolphin Conservation (WDC) became the first NGO to sign the Declaration of Rights for Cetaceans: Whales and Dolphins (http://www.cetaceanrights.org/), a historic manifesto that lays out a list of principles promoting the right of cetaceans to life, liberty, and well-being. Currently the Nonhuman Rights Project (http://www.nonhumanrightsproject.org/) is working toward actual legal rights for members of species other than our own. The NhRP's mission is to change the common-law status of at least some nonhuman animals from mere "things," which lack the capacity to possess any legal right, to "persons," who possess such fundamental rights as bodily integrity and bodily liberty. The NhRP includes cetaceans on its list of potential candidates for legal personhood and will bring lawsuits to bear on this issue in the near future.

These are exciting times for cetacean advocacy and rights. Never before have concepts of rights and personhood for nonhuman animals been taken so seriously in this country. The marine mammal captivity industry is most certainly on the defensive and is losing ground. One can almost feel the tide going out on these abusive spectacles. It is a matter of time before this industry follows Barnum into the void.

REFERENCES

Aristotle. 1965–1991. *Historia Animalium (The History of Animals)*. Trans. A. L. Peck. Cambridge: Harvard University Press.

Batt E. 2013. "Dolphins Driven into Cove Heading for Highest Numbers in Four Years." Accessed on February 1, 2013. http://digitaljournal.com/article/342232.

Born Free Foundation. n.d. "Captive Whales and Dolphins." Accessed November 18, 2013. http://www.bornfree.org.uk/campaigns/zoo-check/captive-whales-dolphins/.

Brakes P., and C. Williamson. 2007. "Dolphin Assisted Therapy: Can You Put Your Faith in DAT?" Report for the Whale and Dolphin Conservation Society, October. Accessed November 18, 2013. http://www.wdcs.org/submissions_bin/datreport.pdf.

Couquiaud, L. 2005. "A Survey of the Environments of Cetaceans in Human Care." *Aquatic Mammals* 31(3): 279–280.

DeMaster, D. P., and J. K. Drevenak. 1988. "Survivorship Patterns in Three Species of Captive Cetaceans." *Marine Mammal Science* 4(4): 297–311.

Duffield, D. A., and R. S. Wells. 1991. "The Combined Application of Chromosome, Protein, and Molecular Data for Investigation of Social Unit Structure and Dynamics in *Tursiops truncates*." In A. R. Hoelzel (ed.), "*Genetic Ecology of Whales and Dolphins,*" special issue of *Reports of the International Whaling Commission* 13: 155–169.

Ford, J. K. B. 2009. "Killer Whale." In W. F. Perrin, B. Wursig, and J. G. M. Thewissen (eds.), *Encyclopedia of Marine Mammals*, 2nd ed., 650–657. Boston: Academic Press.

Ford, J. K. B., G. M. Ellis, and K. C. Balcomb. 1994. *Killer Whales: The Natural History and Genealogy of Orinus orca in British Columbia and Washington*. Seattle: University of Washington Press; Vancouver: UBC Press.

Fowler, M. E. 1978. "A Stereotyped Behavior Pattern in Dolphins." In M. E. Fowler (ed.), *Zoo and Wild Animal Medicine*, 33–34. Philadelphia: W.B. Saunders.

Frontline. 1997. "A Whale of a Business." Accessed March 1, 2013. http://www.pbs.org/wgbh/pages/frontline/shows/whales/man/mancron.html.

Geraci, J. R., and S. H. Ridgeway. 1991. "On Disease Transmission between Cetaceans and Humans." *Marine Mammal Science* 7(2): 191–194.

Greenwood, A. G. 1977. "A Stereotyped Behavior Pattern in Dolphins." *Aquatic Mammals* 5: 15–17.

Humphries, T. L. 2003. "Effectiveness of Dolphin-Assisted Therapy as a Behavioral Intervention for Young Children with Disabilities." *Bridges: Practice-Based Research Synthesis* 1: 1–9.

Jett, J., and J. Ventre. 2011. "Keto and Tilikum Express the Stress of Orca Captivity." Accessed on March 5, 2013. http://theorcaproject.wordpress.com/2011/01/20/keto-tilikum-express-stress-of-orca-captivity/.

Jett, J., and J. Ventre. 2012. "Orca Captivity (*Orcinus orca*) and Vulnerability to Mosquito-Transmitted Viruses." *Journal of Marine Animals and Their Ecology* 5(2): 9–16.

Kestin, S. 2004a. "Not a Perfect Picture: Part I of the Special Report 'Marine Attractions: Below the Surface.'" *Sun-Sentinel*. Accessed June 15, 2004. http://www.sun-sentinel.com/news/sfi-dolphins-parksdec31,30.791.1694 story.

Kestin, S. 2004b. "Captive Mammals Can Net Big Profits for Exhibitors: Part III of the Special Report 'Marine Attractions: Below the Surface.'" *Sun-Sentinel*. Accessed June

15, 2004. http://www.sun-sentinel.com/news/sfi-dolphins-parksdec31,30.791.1694 s
tory.

Kirby, D. 2012. *Death at SeaWorld: Shamu and the Dark Side of Killer Whales in Captivity*.
New York: St. Martin's Press.

Lusseau, D. 2007. "Evidence for Social Role in a Dolphin Social Network." *Evolution and
Ecology* 21: 357–366.

Marino, L. 1998. "A Comparison of Encephalization between Odontocete Cetaceans
and Anthropoid Primates." *Brain, Behavior, and Evolution* 51: 230–238.

Marino, L. 2007. "Dolphin Mythology". In M. Bekoff (ed.), *The Encyclopedia of
Human-Animal Relationships*, 491–495. Westport, CT: Greenwood.

Marino, L. 2011. "Dolphin Assisted Therapy: From Ancient Myth to Modern Snake
Oil." *Phi Kappa Phi Forum* 91(1): 4–6.

Marino, L. 2013. "Dolphins, Humans and Moral Inclusivity." In R. Corbey and A.
Lanjouw. (eds.), *The Politics of Species: Reshaping our Relationships with Other Animal*,
95–105. Cambridge: Cambridge University Press.

Marino, L., C. Butti, R. C. Connor, R. E. Fordyce, L. M. Herman, P. R. Hof, L. Lefebvre,
D. Lusseau, B. McCowan, E. A. Nimchinsky, A. A. Pack, J. S. Reidenberg, D. Reiss,
L. Rendell, M. D. Uhen, E. Van der Gucht, and H. Whitehead. 2008. "A Claim in
Search of Evidence: Reply to Manger's Thermogenesis Hypothesis of Cetacean Brain
Structure." *Biological Reviews of the Cambridge Philosophical Society* 83: 417–440.

Marino, L., and T. Frohoff. 2011. "Towards a New Paradigm of Non-captive Research
on Cetacean Cognition." *Public Library of Science ONE* 6(9): e24121. doi:10.1371/
journal.pone.0024121.

Marino, L., and S. Lilienfeld. 1998. "Dolphin-Assisted Therapy: Flawed Data, Flawed
Conclusions." *Anthrozoos* 11(4): 194–199.

Marino, L., S. O. Lilienfeld, R. Malamud, N. Nobis, and R. Broglio. 2010. "Do Zoos
and Aquariums Promote Attitude Change in Visitors? A Critical Evaluation of the
American Zoo and Aquarium Study." *Society and Animals* 18: 126–138.

Marino, L., and S. Lilienfeld. 2007a. "Dolphin Assisted Therapy for Autism and
Other Developmental Disorders: A Dangerous Fad." *Psychology in Intellectual
and Developmental Disabilities (Division 33), American Psychological Association*
33(2): 2–3.

Marino, L., and S. Lilienfeld. 2007b. "Dolphin Assisted Therapy: More Flawed Data,
More Flawed Conclusions." *Anthrozoos* 20: 239–249.

Mazet, J. A., T. D. Hunt, and M. H. Ziccardi. 2004. "Assessment of the Risk of Zoonotic
Disease Transmission to Marine Mammal Workers and the Public: Survey of
Occupational Risks." Final report prepared for United States Marine Mammal
Commission, Research Agreement Number K005486-01. Accessed November 18, 2013.
http://swfsc.noaa.gov/uploadedFiles/Divisions/PRD/Programs/Photogrammetry/
Marine_Mammal_Zoonoses_Final_Report-2.pdf.

Mountain, M. 2012. "How the Beluga Business Began." *Earth in Transition*.
September 5. Accessed March 1, 2013. http://www.earthintransition.org/2012/09/
how-the-beluga-business-began/.

New York Tribune. 1861. "The Whales." August 9. Accessed March 1, 2013. http://chnm.
gmu.edu/lostmuseum/lm/190/.

Noda, K., H. Akiyoshi, M. Aorki, T. Shimada, and F. Ohashi. 2007. "Relationship between Transportation Stress and Polymorphonuclear Functions in Bottlenose Dolphins (*Tursiops truncatus*)." *Journal of Veterinary Medical Science* 69: 379–383.

O'Barry, R., and K. Coulbourn. 2000. *Behind the Dolphin Smile*. Los Angeles: Renaissance Book.

Olesiuk, P., M. Bigg, and G. M. Ellis. 1990. "Life History and Population Dynamics of Resident Killer Whales (*Orcinus orca*) in the Coastal Waters of British Columbia and Washington State." *Reports of the International Whaling Commission Special Issue* 12: 209–244.

Reiss, D., and L. Marino. 2001. "Self-Recognition in the Bottlenose Dolphin: A Case of Cognitive Convergence." *Proceedings of the National Academy of Sciences USA* 98(10): 5937–5942.

Rendell, L. E., and H. Whitehead. 2001. "Culture in Whales and Dolphins." *Behavioural and Brain Sciences* 24: 309–324.

Rose, N. A. 2004. "Captive Cetaceans: The Science behind the Ethics." Paper presented to the European Cetacean Society 18th Annual Conference, Kolmården, Sweden.

Rose, N. A. 2009. "Do Marine Mammals Belong in Captivity in the 21st Century?" Accessed on April 3, 2013. http://www.humanesociety.org/issues/captive_marine/facts/do_marine_mammals_belong_in_captivity.html.

Rose, N. A., E. C. M., Parsons, & R. Farinato. 2009. *The case against marine mammals in captivity*. Washington, D.C.: Humane Society of the United States.

Small, R. J., and D. P. DeMaster. 1995. "Survival of Five Species of Captive Marine Mammals." *Marine Mammal Science* 11(2): 209–226.

Smith, J. D., J. Schull, J. Strote, K. McGee, R. Egnor, and L. Erb. 1995. "The Uncertain Response in the Bottlenosed Dolphin (*Tursiops truncatus*)." *Journal of Experimental Psychology: General* 124: 391–408.

Spoon, T. R., and T. A. Romano. 2011. "Neuroimmunological Response of Beluga Whales (*Delphinapterus leucas*) to Translocation and a Novel Social Environment." *Brain, Behavior and Immunity* 26(1): 122–131.

St. Aubin, D. J., and J. R. Geraci. 1988. "Capture and Handling Stress Suppresses Circulating Levels of Thyroxine (T4) and Triiodothyronine (T3) in Beluga Whales *Delphinapterus leucas*." *Physiological Zoology* 61(2): 170–175.

Stewart, R. E. A., and S. E. Campana, C. M. Jones, B. E. Stewart. 2006. "Bomb radiocarbon dating calibrates beluga (*Delphinapterus leucas*) age estimates." *Canadian Journal of Zoology* 84(12): 1840–1852.

Stewart, K. L., and L. Marino. 2009. "Dolphin-Human Interaction Programs: Policies, Problems, and Practical Alternatives." Policy paper for Animals and Society Institute.

Sweeney, J. C. 1988. "Specific Pathologic Behavior in Aquatic Mammals: Self-Inflicted Trauma." *Soundings: Newsletter of the International Marine Animal Trainers Association* 13(1): 7.

Sweeney, J. C. 1990. "Marine Mammal Behavioral Diagnostics." In L. A. Dierauf (ed.), *CRC Handbook of Marine Mammal Medicine: Health, Disease, and Rehabilitation*, 53–72. Boston: CRC Press.

US Marine Mammal Inventory Report. 2010. National Marine Fisheries Service, Office of Protected Resources.

Wells, R. S., and M. D. Scott. 1990. "Estimating Bottlenose Dolphin Population Parameters from Individual Identification and Capture-Release Techniques." In P. S. Hammond, S. A. Mizroch, and G. P. Donovan (eds.), "Individual Recognition of Cetaceans: Use of Photo-Identification and Other Techniques to Estimate Population Parameters," special issue of *Reports of the International Whaling Commission* 12:407–415.

White, T. I. 2007. *In Defense of Dolphins: The New Moral Frontier*. Oxford: Blackwell.

Whitehead, H. 2011. "The Culture of Whales and Dolphins." In P. Brakes and M. P. Simmonds (ed.), *Whales and Dolphins: Cognition, Culture, Conservation and Human Perceptions*, 149–165. London: Earthscan.

Williams, V. 2001. *Captive Orcas: Dying to Entertain You*. Chippenham, UK: Whale and Dolphin Conservation Society.

Woodley, T. H., J. L. Hannah, and D. M. Lavigne. 1997. "A Comparison of Survival Rates for Captive and Free-Ranging Killer Whales (*Orcinus orca*)." International Marine Mammal Association Inc. Draft Technical Report no 93-01.

Zimmerman, T. 2010. "The Killer in the Pool." *Outside*. Accessed November 18, 2013. http://www.outsideonline.com/outdoor-adventure/nature/The-Killer-in-the-Pool.html.

3

Captive Elephants

CATHERINE DOYLE ■

As values and attitudes toward nonhuman animals change, including attitudes about the ever-charismatic elephant, protests against circuses and other institutions that hold animals captive have markedly grown. Captive elephants have garnered particular attention, and municipalities worldwide have passed laws restricting the use of elephants in circuses, zoos, and religious processions. Contributing to these changing values is a growing body of scientific evidence of elephants' great intelligence, emotional natures, and profound social ties. With this evidence has come questions and controversy surrounding the welfare of elephants in different captive settings.

The tension between captive enterprises and a public that is increasingly better educated about elephants and their welfare has become obvious. As Dale Jamieson (1995) notes, "Conflict is the price of taking animals seriously" (69). Much debate about elephants centers on the circumstances of their captivity and the harm it does to them. Less consideration is given to elephants' capabilities and what captivity means to them as self-aware individuals. The key question becomes: Can captivity ever allow elephants to exercise their capabilities to the extent that they can fully realize their potential and truly be elephants?

ABOUT ELEPHANTS

Weighing 6,000–15,000 pounds and standing seven to thirteen feet high at shoulder (Shoshani 1991), elephants are the earth's largest extant land mammals, with impressively large brains equipped to meet the challenges of living in complex physical and social environments. Elephants share a surprising number of characteristics with humans, such as high intelligence, social complexity, long lives, long periods of infancy, and social learning of behaviors (Bates, Poole, and Byrne 2008; Lee 1991). They are known to use and even manufacture simple tools (Poole and Moss 2008) and have passed the mirror recognition test, which indicates recognition of self (Plotnik, de Waal, and Reiss 2006).

In nature, a complicated web of relationships forms elephants' social lives, radiating out from the mother-offspring bond to groups of multiple families to the greater population, which can number more than a thousand individuals (Poole and Granli 2009; Lee and Moss 2009). The matriarch, usually the oldest female, leads the family, in which the females remain together from birth until death; males disperse from their families at about age fourteen (Lee and Moss 2009). Elephants are on the move for about twenty hours a day and may travel seven to fourteen miles during that time (Sukumar 2003). Bonded elephants use a repertoire of long- and short-distance signaling to communicate with conspecifics who may be many miles away (Poole and Granli 2009).

Social complexity has resulted in elephants excelling at long-term spatial-temporal and social memory, and exhibiting behaviors indicating they may possess theory of mind (the capacity to understand that others see, feel, and know) (Bates et al. 2008; Poole and Moss 2008). Elephants are known to help injured or disabled individuals, and experiments suggest they may understand and respond empathetically to the death of a conspecific (Bates et al. 2008). In Africa, where poaching, culls, and habitat loss have decimated elephant populations and individuals witness the slaughter of their family members, elephants display symptoms associated with human post-traumatic stress disorder, such as hyperaggression and unpredictable asocial behavior (Bradshaw et al. 2005).

While the exact number of elephants held captive throughout the world is unknown, it is estimated that there are about 16,000 captive elephants in Asia (Dublin et al. 2006). Worldwide, there are approximately 1,200 elephants in zoos and 560 in circuses (Clubb and Mason 2002). The vast majority of elephants now in captivity were captured in the wild, and elephants continue to be taken from the wild for use in zoos, for tourism, and for religious purposes, even though wild populations are highly unstable at this time. The World Conservation Union (IUCN 2012a) labels Asian elephants as endangered, as populations have steadily decreased. Key threats are habitat loss and fragmentation and human-elephant conflict. African elephants, which can be found in greater numbers than in Asia (about 500,000 versus 50,000 in Asia), are labeled vulnerable (IUCN 2012b) though skyrocketing ivory poaching is a grave concern (TRAFFIC 2011).

HISTORY OF ELEPHANT CAPTIVITY

Elephants were "tamed" at least 4,600 years ago in the Indus Valley Civilization (Sukumar 2011; Saller and Gröning 1998). The means of controlling elephants included stockades, ropes, and spears (Sukumar 2011). Equipped with these simple accoutrements, humans were able to contain, dominate, and control elephants. These basic tools have not changed all that much over the years, and continue to be used in circuses, zoos, tourism, and traditional uses of elephants.

Once harnessed, the power and formidable presence of elephants was put to use in warfare. Elephants became a valued commodity: The more elephants a ruler owned, the greater his army and power. Beginning in 331 BCE, Alexander the Great used elephants in his campaigns to create one of the largest empires in the ancient world. Hannibal crossed the Alps into Italy with thirty-seven elephants in 218 BCE, but later found that elephants did not always win the day. He was defeated in 202 BCE, despite a regiment of eighty elephants (Wylie 1992; Alexander 2000). Elephants were not particularly effective in war, aside from the intimidation factor. Accounts describe them running amok and trampling soldiers on both sides in a panic, as they were hamstrung with axes, hit with flaming arrows, and bombarded with spears and javelins (Toynbee 1973).

In more modern warfare, elephants have been relegated to the role of transport. They were used in the First and Second World Wars, and as recently as the Vietnam War, to move military supplies. During the First World War an elephant named Jenny, from Hamburg's Hagenbeck Zoo, served the German army for two years, hauling military supplies and timber on the western front in France—her reward was a special ration of rye bread (Saller and Gröning 1998). During the latter part of the Vietnam War, American planes bombed and strafed elephants suspected of transporting provisions along the Ho Chi Minh Trail (Wylie, 1992; Scigliano 2002).

Perhaps the most well-known and grisly use of captive elephants was in the public spectacle of the Roman circuses, where thousands of wild and tame animals and captive humans were slaughtered over centuries. Elephants were provoked into bloody confrontations against other elephants, other nonhuman animals, and regiments of armed men (Toynbee 1973). In one account by Pliny, about twenty elephants were killed in one day by the Roman consul Pompey, eliciting a rare moment of pity from the audience when the elephants tried to escape the oncoming slaughter. The displeased crowd perceived the waving of the elephants' trunks and panicked bellows as pleas to save their lives. Pliny wrote that "the whole crowd wept and rose to its feet, cursing Pompey for his cruelty" (Toynbee 1973, 22). The Romans also used elephants in stately processions that are echoed in today's circuses when the elephants march into the ring.

The first known menageries to hold elephants were founded 2,900 years ago in Assyria and at a Phoenician zoo in Kalhu (Alexander 2000). Exclusive zoological gardens belonging to kings of Babylon and in the imperial court of China were said to house elephants, and in the thirteenth century Marco Polo described a large menagerie belonging to Kublai Khan in Shang-tu that held a variety of wild animals, including elephants (Mullan and Marvin 1987; Saller and Gröning 1998).

In the seventeenth and eighteenth centuries, menageries remained exclusive to the royal and powerful, who displayed elephants alongside other exotic animals, though their exhibition was more akin to circus acts. For example, an elephant captured in the Congo and held in the royal collection in Versailles from 1665 through 1681 reportedly entertained visitors by drinking wine and nimbly dipping bread into a bucket of soup. Royal menageries morphed into publicly run attractions, where elephants continued to be confined in impoverished conditions (Saller and Gröning 1998).

Around 1800, with the advent of the modern circus in England, elephants were mainly used as display animals and for giving rides (Saller and Gröning 1998; Mullan and Marvin 1987). They would remain a rarity in the United States and Europe until about the middle of the nineteenth century, when the trade in elephants from Asia and Africa escalated and the animals began to increasingly appear in circuses as performers. At about the same time, the first zoos began to appear and to display elephants as part of their collections (Saller and Gröning 1998).

Perhaps the most famous elephant is Jumbo, a male African elephant born in the French Sudan (now Mali). He was captured and spent two years at the Menagerie du Jardin des Plantes in Paris, until his transfer in 1865 to London's Zoological Gardens. Jumbo was used for exhibition and rides until he grew older and experienced his first musth, a period of heightened aggressiveness and sexual activity about which little was understood at the time. Jumbo could no longer be used for rides, but his great size attracted the famed showman P. T. Barnum. In 1881 the zoo sold Jumbo to Barnum for $10,000 and he was shipped to America for display in the circus. Angry Londoners came to the defense of Jumbo, flooding the zoo with irate letters; some accused the zoo of behaving like a slave trader (Saller and Gröning 1998; Chambers 2008). This may have been the first modern incidence of the public advocating on behalf of a captive elephant. The response calls to mind the disapproval of the Roman audience at Pompey's brutal slaughter of elephants. Though different places and times, the public expressed a certain affinity with elephants and displeasure with their poor treatment—though they may not have ended the harms.

By the turn of the twentieth century circuses had proliferated around the world and trained elephants were a major draw. They appeared en masse, with entire herds supplied from Asia and Africa. In 1887, Barnum, Bailey and Forepaugh combined to present an extravaganza at New York's Madison Square Garden that filled the ring with 160 elephants (Saller and Gröning

1998). Circuses today remain virtually unchanged in the display and treatment of elephants. The larger and more successful circuses boast greater numbers of elephants than less well-known circuses. But no matter the size of the circus, elephants are chained, intensively confined, and are forced to perform tricks taught through violent training methods. The instrument used to dominate and control elephants, the bullhook, has essentially remained the same over time.

THE MODERN ZOO

Early on, the public came to believe that a zoo was not a zoo without an elephant. Elizabeth Hanson (2002) in *Animal Attractions* states: "The elephant was a keystone of the collection. Most zoos considered the day that their first elephant arrived as the day they became 'real' zoos" (44). She describes how the Milwaukee Zoo, which was founded in the early 1890s, was not taken seriously until it received a donation of an elephant in 1906, and changed "from a joke into a serious matter for general public consideration" (44).

Elephants became more and more of a necessity for zoos if they were to compete with circuses and vaudeville acts using elephants, and even with other zoos. Paying customers supported the cost of maintaining these facilities and they wanted to see this star attraction. At the same time zoos were vying with one another to present the most impressive collections, the animals were confined in conditions so impoverished they "sometimes amounted to torture" (Saller and Gröning, 424). Even today, zoos continue to rely on elephants to attract customers and to satisfy the public's desire to see elephants, even though many, if not most elephants, are kept in deficient conditions that harm them physically and psychologically.

Some zoos presented circus-like performances that continued well into the 1980s (Elephants Doing Tricks 1983), and there remain vestiges of the performing elephant tradition found in some zoos today. Though these performances are framed as demonstrations of elephant husbandry and "natural" behaviors, elephants are all too often displayed sitting upright or standing on their hind legs, ridden by their keepers, and prompted to trumpet, squeal, and lift their trunks in a "salute" for the public's amusement.

Conditions did not start improving in zoos until later in the century, with the advent of more naturalistic enclosure designs (Hancocks 2001). However, elephants did not benefit in any meaningful way since their enclosures remained small, little or no attention was paid to social and psychological needs, and up until the 1990s it was common practice to physically restrain elephants with chains overnight, meaning they could spend fifteen or more hours a day immobilized indoors. This bad habit still exists in some zoos today, notably in developing countries but also in some modern zoos.

CURRENT CONDITIONS OF CAPTIVITY FOR ELEPHANTS

Zoos

In 2003, I was the plaintiff in a lawsuit that sought to enjoin the Los Angeles Zoo from separating two bonded elephant companions, Ruby, an African elephant, and Gita, an Asian, who had lived together for seventeen years. Before the case could be heard, the zoo trucked out Ruby in the middle of the night to the Knoxville Zoo in Tennessee. The lawsuit proceeded, and efforts to integrate Ruby with the other elephants at Knoxville were unsuccessful. In 2004, the mayor of Los Angeles ordered Ruby's return (Hahn 2004), though she was never physically reunited with Gita (they shared adjacent yards). Gita died in 2006, leaving Ruby a solitary elephant until 2007, when a sustained campaign succeeded in sending her to the Performing Animal Welfare Society (PAWS) sanctuary in San Andreas, California. Ruby lived as the gentle matriarch of the

Ruby, courtesy of Lisa Jeffries-Worgan, Performing Animal Welfare Society

sanctuary's African elephant group, roaming eighty acres of grassy hills and varied terrain until her death in 2011. The last time I saw her she was reaching up into a tree to pluck tasty acorns, something she could never have done at a zoo.

Ruby was not the first elephant to attract controversy or legal action, but her plight reignited the debate over the confinement of elephants in zoos, one that has been growing stronger over the last ten years around issues such as the separation of bonded females, lack of space, inadequate social groups, and coercive management methods. Fueling the debate was a meticulous report by animal welfare scientists Ros Clubb and Georgia Mason (2002) on conditions for elephants in European zoos. The Royal Society for the Prevention of Cruelty to Animals, which commissioned the report, concluded that elephants should be phased out of zoos due to inadequate conditions that cause elephants to suffer poor welfare and die early (RSPCA 2002). The Association of Zoos and Aquariums (AZA), a zoo industry trade group that accredits and promotes zoos, vehemently decried the report, using one statistical error to discredit the entire report. Yet another study published in the journal *Science* (Clubb et al. 2008) reported that female elephants in zoos are dying far earlier than those in wild populations, and that the effects of captivity are so profound that zoo-born Asian elephants' elevated adult mortality rates may be conferred during gestation or early infancy. The authors concluded: "Overall, bringing elephants into zoos profoundly impairs their viability. The effects of early experience, interzoo transfer and possibly maternal loss, plus the health and reproductive problems recorded in zoo elephants, suggest stress and/or obesity as likely causes" (1649). Health and reproductive problems include arthritis, foot disease, tuberculosis, acyclicity and pathologies of the reproductive tract (Clubb and Mason 2002).

The most hotly debated issue involves questions about how much space an elephant needs. It is a particularly important issue, as space affects elephants' health, social opportunities, and psychological well-being. Enclosure sizes in zoos are governed not by elephants' natural needs or by science, but by the resources that a zoo possesses in terms of land and funding. This usually translates to a *minimum* amount of space for elephants based on an arbitrary number set by the AZA or similar organizations. For example, current performance-based standards for AZA-accredited zoos allow an elephant to be confined in an area as small as 5,400 square feet outdoors—"significantly smaller than a baseball infield" (Berens 2012)—and 400 square feet indoors (AZA 2012). Small enclosures greatly inhibit movement and social group size. Currently, nearly a third of AZA-accredited zoos holding elephants have only two females, even though the Standards for the Care and Management of Elephants (AZA 2012) call for a minimum of three elephants.

Since 2000, zoos in North America have spent hundreds of millions of dollars to expand their exhibits and give elephants more space (In Defense of Animals 2011). While many expansions are a vast improvement over previous inadequate enclosures, most of the renovations provide elephants with just two or three acres, typically subdivided into a number of smaller yards. In many instances these zoos have plans to pack the exhibits with ten or more elephants. Despite the huge sums spent on these enclosures, there is no guarantee that elephant health and welfare will significantly improve. Unhealthy elephants do not breed well, nor do they thrive, hence the abbreviated life expectancy of elephants in zoos, where efforts to create a self-sustaining population of elephants are on a trajectory to failure (Berens 2012).

In addition to increased enclosure sizes, zoos are attempting to establish larger, multigenerational elephant groups to encourage breeding and shore up a dwindling captive population. But because the focus will be fixed on population management, elephant families and bonded individuals will remain subject to separation and interzoo transfers based on space constrictions and breeding initiatives that prioritize genetic management of the population over the best interests of the individual. Another effect on elephants is that zoos are pursuing highly valuable calves at any cost. The *Seattle Times* (Berens 2012) reported that the Woodland Park Zoo in Seattle has used invasive methods to artificially inseminate the female Chai an astonishing *112 times* in its quest for a calf. Calves are an enormous boon for zoos, as they are extremely popular with the public. An elephant calf can double a zoo's revenue and donations (Hancocks 2008).

The importation of elephants from free-living wild populations will be required by zoos, since captive breeding alone, even if it were to be successful, cannot create a self-sustaining population (Faust 2005a; 2005b; Faust, Thompson, and Earnhardt 2006). Not only will this bring more elephants into unnatural and inadequate conditions, it raises the ethical question of how zoos can knowingly subject elephants to conditions that historically have physically and psychologically debilitated them.

The management of elephants in zoos is another issue that has incited controversy both within and outside the zoo industry. This is due to the continued use of the antiquated free contact method, which is based on dominance and fear of physical punishment. In free contact, elephants have no choice but to comply with the trainer, for failure to do so will result in an aversive stimulus (e.g., hooking, prodding, or striking the elephant). The elephant may be hit or beaten to eliminate an undesirable behavior (Chadwick 1992; Hutchins 2008). At the core of this method is the bullhook (also called an ankus), a steel rod resembling a sharpened fireplace poker that elephants must learn to associate with pain. What is taken for obedience in elephants is "often only dread; and a sense of helplessness learned from punishments and restrictions" (Hancocks 2008, 264).

Keepers in zoos do not try to dominate other dangerous animals, nor do they venture into their enclosures holding a weapon for protection, yet this behavior is tolerated with elephants (Whittaker and Laule 2009). Approximately half the zoos and all circuses continue to use this problematic system.

The alternative system, protected contact, uses only positive reinforcement training and allows the elephant free choice in whether to participate in training sessions. A protective barrier separates trainer and elephants. When properly practiced, protected contact management ensures elephants are free from the threat of physical punishment (Kinzley 2006). This system allows keepers and veterinarians to safely provide required care, as they would for other dangerous wildlife (Whittaker and Laule 2009).

Many zoos have decided to end their elephant programs, and some have sent elephants to live out their lives in natural-habitat sanctuaries. Of AZA-accredited zoos, seventy-one currently hold elephants, and the number is expected to drop to around sixty (CLR Design 2010). Since 1998, eighteen zoos have closed their elephant exhibits, and another six have announced they will shut down or phase out their elephant programs. Whether zoos in other countries, where standards may be even lower and resources lacking, follow suit is yet to be seen.

Circuses

The use of wild animals in circuses has been controversial since the nineteenth century because of the cruelty associated with their confinement, treatment, and display. In the latter part of the twentieth century, with the burgeoning animal protection movements, circuses became a focal point for action (Beers 2006). Elephants have garnered particular attention. *Mother Jones* magazine (2011) published an exposé on a large US circus that found that elephants spend "most of their lives in chains or on trains, under constant threat of the bullhook—or ankus, the menacing tool used to control elephants" (Nelson 2011, 50).

Circuses of all sizes are on the move for as many as fifty weeks a year, as they travel from city to city, packing elephants into cramped trucks or train cars (Ensley 2012; Nelson 2011). Elephants are chained during travel, which virtually immobilizes the large animals, restricting them to just a few small and shuffling steps in any direction. *Mother Jones* reported that elephants in one circus routinely traveled twenty-six hours straight, with some travel times extending to seventy consecutive hours or more without a break. While traveling, the elephants are forced to stand in accumulating excrement and urine (Nelson 2011).

Training begins at about eighteen months of age for captive-born circus elephants, when the calves are forcibly removed from their mothers. The calf's every movement, instinct, and natural behavior becomes subject to discipline by handlers. The *Washington Post* (2009) published photographs of baby elephants bound with ropes, wrestled into difficult positions, and shocked with electric prods. They learn through fear of punishment to perform the unnatural tricks that circus consumers later applaud.

Training never ends for performing elephants. Handlers reinforce tricks and routines at the point of the bullhook, even though the elephants have performed these maneuvers hundreds of times. The bullhook is often embedded in sensitive areas of the elephant's skin, including inside the ear or mouth, behind the ears, in and around the anus, and in tender spots under the chin and around the feet. The hook and sharp tip of the instrument can cause lacerations and abrasions; an animal behaviorist for one large circus reported "an elephant dripping blood all over the arena floor during the show from being hooked" (Nelson 2011, 56).

Currently, there are about thirty-eight municipalities in the United States that have some form of restriction on performing wild animals. In 2013 Los Angeles became the largest US city to pass an ordinance restricting circuses, after the city council voted unanimously to ban the use of the bullhook (circuses claim they cannot perform without the device). This action is expected to encourage similar ordinances in even more cities. Worldwide, more than twenty countries have legislation that restrict the use of performing animals in circuses, and many have laws forbidding any performing exotic animals in circuses (LAAS 2012).

Sanctuaries

The difference between zoos and sanctuaries is not only a matter of dissimilar environments, but vastly different philosophies about captivity itself. Sanctuaries are convinced that elephants do not belong in captivity (Stewart 2013; Derby 2004). The late Pat Derby (2009), cofounder of the Performing Animal Welfare Society (PAWS), wrote that after accepting two aging Asian elephants at the sanctuary, Tammy and Annie, and removing the chains from their legs for the last time, she "knew we were committed to a program that was necessary but that, in our opinion, could never be ethically or morally justified" (201).

For those elephants already held captive, the philosophy of the elephant sanctuaries in the United States is to provide space, natural environments, social opportunities, and autonomy (Buckley 2009). Repatriation to the wild is not an option for these elephants for a variety of reasons, including that many suffer serious and enduring physical and psychological problems that were caused by the conditions in which they were originally confined.

Derby and her partner, Ed Stewart, cofounded PAWS in 1984 to rescue and care for captive wildlife, and later opened the 2,300-acre ARK 2000 facility in San Andreas, California, which currently cares for eleven elephants (six female Africans, three female Asians, and two male Asians), as well as lions, tigers, and bears (Performing Animal Welfare Society n.d.). The Elephant Sanctuary in Tennessee (TES) operates on 2,700 acres in Hohenwald and cares for twelve Asian and two African females (The Elephant Sanctuary n.d.). These facilities provide permanent homes for elephants rescued and released from zoos and circuses and allow them to roam pastures that are hundreds of times larger than the enclosures found in zoos. Elephants can navigate complex natural environments that offer deep lakes and ponds, varied topography, and natural vegetation for foraging (Hancocks 2008). Neither PAWS or TES use chains or bullhooks or seek to dominate and control the elephants, and neither sanctuary breeds, trades, or sells elephants. Both institutions are committed to the complete well-being of each individual elephant (Performing Animal Welfare Society n.d.; Kane and Forthman 2009).

Captivity in Asia

About 16,000 working elephants are found in a dozen countries in Asia, with the largest number in Burma, India, and Thailand. In some of these countries, they are used for logging in forests, begging, tourism, hauling goods, religious ceremonies, and elephant-back patrols to monitor protected areas or to mitigate human-elephant conflict. They can also be found in zoos and circuses (Sukumar 2008; Ghosh 2005; McNeely 1992; Working Elephant Programme of Asia n.d).

In some countries timber operations (legal and illegal) still use elephants. Lohanen (2002) states that after logging was banned in Thailand in 1989, some elephants were forced to work in illegal logging near or over the border in Burma. The elephants are often drugged with amphetamines so they work longer, and many step on land mines and are permanently crippled or die. No longer of use to the owner, these elephants will likely be killed for their meat.

Captive elephants across Asia have become more of an attraction for tourists. They are used for rides (treks) and circus-like shows that feature performing and painting elephants (a trained and not a natural behavior). Some elephants are trained to beg for money. According to reports, these elephants are overworked, routinely abused, chained for sixteen to twenty hours a day, and drugged for easier control (Ghosh 2005; Lohanen 2002). They suffer from a range of health problems including foot disease, bruised and torn legs from bearing chains, degenerative joint problems, neurotic repetitive behaviors, and blindness due to malnutrition (Ghosh 2005).

Elephants used for religious purposes in Asia are confined, often alone, and kept in temples, where they spend most of their lives in chained and solitary confinement. Many of the elegantly decorated elephants used in processions and festivals carry heavy howdahs on their backs that can cause pain and lead to arthritis (Ghosh 2005).

At least one facility in Thailand, the Elephant Nature Park, is promoting a more natural way of viewing the elephants it rescues and does not make them perform for tourists (Elephant Nature Park n.d.). Wildlife SOS in India has established a sanctuary for old and abused elephants, and the Cambodia Wildlife Sanctuary has taken in its first rescued elephants (Wildlife SOS n.d.; Tobias 2013). Even in these facilities elephants may be chained for prolonged periods of time, however, there is movement toward chain-free refuges.

EFFECTS OF CAPTIVITY ON ELEPHANTS

Most elephants in captivity were taken from the wild and placed in captive conditions that are the polar opposite of the natural physical and social environments to which they are adapted. A growing body of evidence suggests that elephants pay a high price for this rapid transition to captivity, whether in a zoo, a circus, or when being used for other purposes.

Conservation biologist Keith Lindsay (2008) suggests that elephants simply may not be able to cope with the limited spaces in which they are confined. In a statement to the Los Angeles City Council regarding its planned (and later constructed) elephant exhibit, he wrote:

> Studies of the home range sizes of Asian elephants have all shown spatial needs on the order of 100–200 km^2 at a minimum. By comparison, the 3.8 acres proposed for the new elephant exhibit…is roughly 10,000 times less than what we know elephants are shaped by evolution to cover. Elephants may be highly adaptable, but nothing is **that** adaptable, to cope with a reduction by four orders of magnitude in their living space as they are taken from nature to captivity.

A special report on elephants in zoos by Pulitzer Prize–winning investigative journalist Michael Berens of the *Seattle Times* (2012) appears to bear out Lindsay's conclusion. He relayed the following grim statistics:

> The Times did a first-of-its-kind analysis of 390 elephant fatalities at accredited U.S. zoos for the past 50 years. It found that most of the elephants died

from injury or disease linked to conditions of their captivity, from chronic foot problems caused by standing on hard surfaces to musculoskeletal disorders from inactivity caused by being penned or chained for days and weeks at a time.

Of the 321 elephant deaths for which *The Times* had records, half were dead by age twenty-three, more than a quarter of a century before their expected life spans of sixty to seventy years.

Berens found that for every elephant born in a zoo, on average another two die. At that rate, elephants in US zoos could be "demographically extinct" within the next fifty years because there will be too few reproductively viable females, according to zoo-industry research.

Elephants in zoos face a variety of problems that are linked to conditions of captivity, including obesity, abnormal repetitive behaviors (e.g., swaying, rocking, and head bobbing), birth complications, hyperaggression, and deadly foot and joint diseases. Reproductive problems are prevalent, with high rates of birth complications, stillbirths, and infertility (Clubb and Mason 2002). Berens (2012) reported that the infant mortality rate in zoos is nearly triple the rate in the wild. Foot disease and arthritis remain the leading causes of euthanasia in captive elephants (Fowler 2001), a product of captive conditions. Forcing elephants to live together in constricted spaces can result in stress, aggression, and injury. According to a 2005 survey of medical records for thirty-five zoos by In Defense of Animals, at least 28 percent of elephants were injured by a conspecific (Doyle and Roy 2006). Elephants in circuses share similar maladies to those afflicting elephants in zoos, caused by living in restricted spaces and by being forced to perform tricks that are stressful to their large bodies. Nearly 100 percent of adult elephants with one circus that holds a large number of the animals were found to be lame with foot disease or musculoskeletal disorders (Nelson 2011).

The coevolution of social complexity and high intelligence, while producing some impressive capabilities in elephants, has likely made them more capable of suffering in captivity, especially when held in socially inadequate situations (Veasey 2006). Elephants mostly confined in small, unrelated groups bear little semblance to those that live in large family groups and extended social networks in their natural habitats. Circuses, zoos, and private owners often keep elephants solitary, despite their highly social nature.

While no captive environment may be perfectly suitable for elephants, facilities such as sanctuaries attempt to mitigate some of the larger problems by providing spacious habitats with more opportunities for autonomous choice, including the ability to select social partners. The limitations of zoos, circuses, and other types of confinement, especially in terms of space, physical control (e.g., chaining), and breeding directives, greatly reduce or nullify choice and control for elephants.

Zoos claim that the benefits of confining elephants in peer-accredited facilities, as measured in terms of conservation, research, and education, outweigh the costs to the elephants in terms of diminished welfare (Hutchins et al. 2008). (Many circuses also claim to promote education and conservation.) This is contentious, especially since zoos do not intend to reintroduce elephants to the wild (Hutchins et al. 2008), but instead use elephants to support only zoo-captive conservation efforts. There is no evidence to support the education claims of zoos (Marino et al. 2010), and Stroud (2009) states that it is debatable whether elephants need to be sustained in captivity for any conservation purpose. The perceived "trade-offs" that elephants may appear to have in captivity (e.g., healthcare, food, security, elimination of predation) are illusory when considering that "illness, predation, or starvation are unlikely to be chronic episodes in the wild, whereas a general maladaptiveness of the individual to captivity are likely to present chronic welfare challenges" (Veasey 2006, 70).

An obvious tension exists between zoos' concrete interactions with elephants as individuals and zoos' focus on individuals only as a means to the "welfare" of the species. For example, Donahue and Trump (2006) write in *The Politics of Zoos*: "In the past, the AZA worried about member institutions with inadequate animal care standards. In the elephant case, *it sought to prevent individual zoos from caring too much about individual animals at the expense of the captive population*" (174). However, it is individual animals who possess welfare. When individual elephants suffer diminished welfare, as they do in most zoos, what follows is the widespread breakdown of attempts to establish a self-sustaining collection of captive elephants.

These perspectives on elephants fail to address the critical role of elephants' capabilities in their welfare. In *Elephants and Ethics*, Lori Alward (2008) draws on Martha Nussbaum's capabilities approach to ethical dilemmas to demonstrate that circuses are unsuited to elephants. Using the capabilities approach, one would not just ask whether an individual is satisfied or how many resources she is able to command, but "What is this person able to do and to be?" (Nussbaum 2000, 71). Alward writes:

> it is not sufficient to show that, say, an elephant has enough to eat and is free of disease to show that we have fulfilled our responsibilities to elephants. So, instead, we will ask what individual elephants in a given situation are able to do and to be, whether they are able to live fully elephantine lives. (Alward 2008, 216)

Alward determined that circuses cannot be made suitable, not only because circuses cannot allow elephants to express innate behaviors, but also because circuses force elephants to perform. However, she states that it is still a matter of contention whether elephants can exercise their capabilities in zoos. A careful review of Alward's list of central elephant functional capabilities shows that almost all of their capabilities go unmet in zoos and circuses. For example, elephants die prematurely in zoos, many suffer ill health due to captive conditions, they are unable to exercise certain natural behaviors due to restricted space, and they lack bodily integrity. It follows that zoos also are not suitable for elephants.

In nature, the complexity of everyday life for elephants requires critical decision-making, fluid social interactions with family members and mates, navigation in an ever-changing environment, and free agency that cannot be matched in captivity. By contrast, "the captive environment negates the possibilities of travel, kinship structure, roles within the group, group-based mental worlds, and constructs of cultural realities ... we know that it is precisely these types of mental processes that provide meaning for our human minds" (Savage-Rumbaugh et al. 2007, 12). Given current knowledge, there can be no ethical way to keep elephants, no matter what the alleged conservation justifications may be, because captivity cannot accommodate who elephants truly are and, just as important, who they can, and should, be allowed to become.

ACKNOWLEDGMENTS

My sincere thanks to Paul Waldau for his keen insights on this chapter and for his ceaseless encouragement. My appreciation to David Hancocks too for lending his fine editing skills and sharing his vast knowledge of elephants and the conditions of their captivity. Very special thanks to Lori Gruen for her editing expertise.

REFERENCES

Alexander, S. 2000. *The Astonishing Elephant*. New York: Random House.

Alward, Lori. 2008. "Why Circuses Are Unsuited to Elephants." In *Elephants and Ethics: Toward a Morality of Coexistence*, C. Wemmer and C. Christen (eds)., Baltimore: Johns Hopkins University Press.

Association of Zoos and Aquariums (AZA). 2012. "AZA Standards for Elephant Management and Care." Approved March 2011, revised April 2012. Accessed November 18, 2013. http://www.elephanttag.org/Professional/Revised_AZA_Standards_Elephant_Management_Care_April2012.pdf.

Bates, L. A., J. H. Poole, and R. W. Byrne. 2008. "Elephant Cognition." *Current Biology* 18: 544–546.

Beers, Diane. 2006. *For the Prevention of Cruelty: The History and Legacy of Animal Rights Activism in the United States*. Athens: Swallow Press/Ohio University Press.

Berens, Michael. 2012. "Elephants Are Dying Out in America's Zoos." *Seattle Times*, December 4. Accessed November 18, 2013. http://seattletimes.com/html/nation-world/2019809167_elephants02m.html.

Bradshaw, G. A., A. N. Schore, J. L. Brown, J. H. Poole, and C. J. Moss. 2005. "Elephant Breakdown." *Nature* 433: 807.

Buckley, Carol. 2009. "Sanctuary: A Fundamental Requirement of Wildlife Management." In *An Elephant In the Room: The Science and Well-Being of Elephants in Captivity*, D. L. Forthman, L. F. Kane, D. Hancocks, and P. f. Waldau (eds.), 191–197. North Grafton, MA: Tufts Center for Animals and Public Policy.

Chadwick, Douglas H. 1992. *The Fate of the Elephant*. San Francisco: Sierra Club Books.

Chambers, Paul. 2008. *Jumbo: This Being the True Story of the Greatest Elephant in the World*. Hanover, NH: Steerforth Press.

CLR Design. 2010. "Elephant Facilities Feasibility Study: Toronto Zoo." December 1. Accessed November 18, 2013. http://www.toronto.ca/legdocs/mmis/2011/zb/bgrd/backgroundfile-37875.pdf.

Clubb, R., and G. Mason. 2002. *A Review of the Welfare of Zoo Elephants in Europe*. Horsham, West Sussex, UK: RSPCA.

Clubb, R., M. Rowcliffe, P. Lee, K. U. Mar, C. Moss, and G. J. Mason. 2008. "Compromised Survivorship in Zoo Elephants." *Science* 12: 1649.

Derby, Pat. 2004. "Sanctuary vs. Zoo." September 13. Accessed November 18, 2013. http://www.pawsweb.org/documents/HUTCHINS_RESPONSE.pdf.

Derby, Pat. 2009. "Changes in Social and Biophysical Environment Yield Improved Physical and Psychological Health for Captive Elephants." In *An Elephant in the Room: The Science and Well-Being of Elephants in Captivity*, D. L. Forthman, L. F. Kane, D, Hancocks, and P. F. Waldau (eds.), 198–207. North Grafton, MA: Tufts Center for Animals and Public Policy.

Donahue, Jesse, and Eric Trump. 2006. *The Politics of Zoos: Exotic Animals and Their Protectors*. DeKalb: Northern Illinois University Press.

Doyle, C., and S. Roy. 2006. "Comments of In Defense of Animals on USDA Docket No. APHIS-2006-0044 'Captive Elephant Welfare.'" December 11. Accessed November 18, 2013. http://www.helpelephants.com/pdf/captive_elephant_welfare.pdf.

Dublin, Holly, Ajay A. Desai, Simon Hedges, Jean-Christophe Vié, Channa Bambaradeniya, and Alvin Lopez. 2006. "Elephant Range States Meeting. 24–26 January 2006, Kuala Lumpur, Malaysia, Report." World Conservation Union (IUCN) and Species Survival Commission (SSC). Accessed November 18, 2013. http://www.cites.org/common/prog/mike/0601AsERSM.pdf.

Elephant Nature Park. n.d. http://www.elephantnaturepark.org/.

Elephants Doing Tricks San Diego Wild Animal Park 1983. http://www.youtube.com/watch?v=K2g6fYP_fQ0

Ensley, Philip K. 2012. "Report to Determine Physical Condition and Suitability to Perform Following Inspection of Ringling Brothers and Barnum & Bailey Circus (RBBBC) at the Los Angeles Staples Center the Week of July 11–17, 2012." Commissioned by the Los Angeles Department of Animal Services.

Faust, Lisa. 2005a. "Technical Report on Demographic Analyses and Modeling of the North American Asian Elephant Population: Executive Summary." Unpublished report. Chicago: AZA Population Management Center, Lincoln Park Zoo.

Faust, Lisa. 2005b. "Technical Report on Demographic Analyses and Modeling of the North American African Elephant Population: Executive Summary." Unpublished report. Chicago: AZA Population Management Center, Lincoln Park Zoo.

Faust, L. J., S. D. Thompson, and J. M. Earnhardt. 2006. "Is Reversing the Decline of Asian Elephants in North American Zoos Possible? An Individual Based Modeling Approach." *Zoo Biology* 25: 201–218.

Fowler, Murray E. 2001. "An Overview of Foot Conditions in Asian and African Elephants." In *The Elephant's Foot*, B. Csuti, E. L. Sargent, and U. S. Bechert (eds.), 3–7. Ames: Iowa State University Press.

Ghosh, Rhea. 2005. *Gods in Chains*. New Delhi, India: Foundation Books.

Hancocks, David. 2001. *A Different Nature: The Paradoxical World of Zoos and Their Uncertain Future*. Berkeley: University of California Press.

Hancocks, David. 2008. "Most Zoos Do Not Deserve Elephants." In *Elephants and Ethics: Toward a Morality of Coexistence*, C. Wemmer and C. Christen (eds.), 259–283. Baltimore: Johns Hopkins University Press.

Hahn, James. 2004. Letter to John Lewis, General Manager of the Los Angeles Zoo. July 19. City of Los Angeles, California.

Hanson, Elizabeth. 2002. *Animal Attractions: Nature on Display in American Zoos*. Princeton, NJ: Princeton University Press.

Hutchins, M., B. Smith, and M. Keele. 2008. "Zoos as Responsible Stewards of Elephants." In *Elephants and Ethics: Toward a Morality of Coexistence*, C. Wemmer and C. Christen (eds.), 285–305. Baltimore: Johns Hopkins University Press.

In Defense of Animals. 2011. Press release: "2010–11 Top Ten Worst Zoos for Elephants." January 18. Accessed November 19, 2013. http://www.helpelephants.com/top_ten_worst_zoos_2010.html.

IUCN (World Conservation Union). 2012a. "Elephas maximus." The IUCN Red List of Threatened Species. Accessed November 19, 2013. http://www.iucnredlist.org/details/7140/0.

IUCN (World Conservation Union). 2012b. "Loxodonta africana." The IUCN Red List of Threatened Species. Accessed November 19, 2013. http://www.iucnredlist.org/details/12392/0.

Jamieson, Dale. 1995. "Wildlife Conservation and Individual Animal Welfare." In *Ethics on the Ark: Zoos, Animal Welfare and Wildlife Conservation*, B. G. Norton, M. Hutchins, E. F. Stevens, and T. L. Maple (eds.), 69–73. Washington, DC: Smithsonian Institution Press.

Kane, L. F., and D. L. Forthman. 2009. "Novel Strategies: Introduction." In *An Elephant in the Room: The Science and Well-Being of Elephants in Captivity*, D. L. Forthman, L. F. Kane, D. Hancocks, and P. F. Waldau (eds.), 190. North Grafton, MA: Tufts Center for Animals and Public Policy.

Kinzley, Colleen. 2006. "Right Here, Right Now." AZA *Communique*. February. Accessed November 19, 2013. http://www.idausa.org/wp-content/uploads/2013/05/Oakland-AZA-Communique.pdf.

LAAS (Los Angeles Animal Services). 2012. Report to the Board of Animals Services Commissioners. "Use of Exotic and Wild Animals, and/or Elephants in Performances by Traveling Shows Within the City of Los Angeles."

Lee, P. C. 1991. "Social Life." In *The Illustrated Encyclopedia of Elephants*, S. K. Eltringham, consultant, 48–63. New York: Crescent Books.

Lee, P. C., and C. J. Moss. 2009. "Welfare and Well-Being of Captive Elephants: Perspectives from Wild Elephant Life Histories." In *An Elephant In the Room: The Science and Well-Being of Elephants In Captivity*, D. L. Forthman, L. F. Kane, D. Hancocks, and P. F. Waldau (eds.), 22–38. North Grafton, MA: Tufts Center for Animals and Public Policy.

Lindsay, Keith. 2008. "Statement to Los Angeles City Council Regarding Elephants at L.A. Zoo." December 3.

Accessed November 19, 2013. http://helpbilly.org/facts.html.

Lohanen, Roger. 2002. "The Elephant Situation in Thailand and a Plea for Co-operation." In *Proceedings of the International Workshop on the Domesticated Asian Elephant*, I. Baker and M. Kashio (eds.). Food and Agriculture Organization of the United Nations. Accessed November 19, 2013. http://www.fao.org/docrep/005/ad031e/ad031e0r.htm.

Marino, L., S. O. Lilienfeld, R. Malamud, N. Nobis, and R. Broglio. 2010. "Do Zoos and Aquariums Promote Attitude Change in Visitors? A Critical Evaluation of the American Zoo and Aquarium Study." *Society and Animals* 18: 126–138.

McNeely, Jeffrey. 1992. "Elephants as Beasts of Burden." In *Elephants: Majestic Creatures of the Wild*, J. Shoshani. Emmaus (ed.), 149–151. PA: Rodale Press.

Mullan, B., and G. Marvin. 1987. *Zoo Culture*. Urbana: University of Illinois Press.

Nelson, Deborah. 2011. "The Cruelest Show On Earth." *Mother Jones*, November–December.

Nussbaum, M. 2000. *Women and human development: The capabilities approach*. Cambridge, England: Cambridge University Press.

Performing Animal Welfare Society. n.d. "About PAWS." www.pawsweb.org.

Plotnik, J. M., F. B. M. de Waal, and D. Reiss. 2006. "Self-Recognition in an Asian Elephant." *Proceedings of the National Academy of Sciences* 103: 17053–17057.

Poole, J. H., and P. Granli. 2009. "Mind and Movement: Meeting the Interests of Elephants." In *An Elephant in the Room: The Science and Well-Being of Elephants in Captivity*, D. L. Forthman, L. F. Kane, D. Hancocks, and P. F. Waldau (eds.), 2–21. North Grafton, MA: Tufts Center for Animals and Public Policy.

Poole, J. H., and C. J. Moss. 2008. "Elephant Sociality and Complexity." In *Elephants and Ethics: Toward a Morality of Coexistence*, C. Wemmer and C. Christen (eds.), 69–98. Baltimore, MD: Johns Hopkins University Press.

RSPCA. 2002. "Live Hard, Die Young: How Elephant Suffer in Zoos." Southwater, Horsham: RSPCA. Accessed November 18, 2013. http://www.idausa.org/wp-content/uploads/2013/05/Satellite-1.pdf.

Saller, M., and K. Gröning. (1998). *Elephants: A Cultural and Natural History*. Cologne: Konemann Verlagsgesellschaft.

Savage-Rumbaugh, S., K. Wamba, P. Wamba, and N. Wamba. 2007. "Welfare of Apes in Captive Environments: Comments on, and by, Specific Groups of Apes." *Journal of Applied Animal Welfare Science* 10: 7–19.

Scigliano, Eric. 2002. *Love, War and Circuses*. New York: Houghton Mifflin.

Shoshani, Jeheskel. 1991. "Anatomy and Physiology." In *The Illustrated Encyclopedia of Elephants*, S. K. Eltringham, consultant, 30–47. New York: Crescent Books.

Stewart, Ed. 2013. "No Ethical Way to Keep Elephants in Captivity." National Geographic News Watch, May 3. Accessed November 19, 2013. http://newswatch.nationalgeographic.com/2013/05/03/no-ethical-way-to-keep-elephants-in-captivity/

Stroud, Peter. 2009. "Tradition, Biology and Morality in Captive Elephant Management." In *An Elephant in the Room: The Science and Well-Being of Elephants in Captivity*, D. L. Forthman, L. F. Kane, D. Hancocks, and P. F. Waldau (eds.), 99–108. North Grafton, MA: Tufts Center for Animals and Public Policy.

Sukumar, Raman. 2003. *The Living Elephants: Evolutionary Ecology, Behavior and Conservation*. New York: Oxford University Press.

Sukumar, Raman. 2011. *The Story of Asia's Elephants*. Mumbai: Marg Foundation.

Tobias, Michael. 2013. "How the Life of a Chipmunk in Michigan Came to Save Elephants and a Million Acres in Cambodia." *Forbes*, February 21.

Toynbee, J. M. C. 1973. *Animals in Roman Life and Art*. Baltimore: Johns Hopkins University Press.

TRAFFIC. 2011. "2011: 'Annus horribilis' for African Elephants, says TRAFFIC." Accessed November 19, 2013. http://www.traffic.org/home/2011/12/29/2011-annus-horribilis-for-african-elephants-says-traffic.html.

Veasey, Jake. 2006. "Concepts in the Care and Welfare of Captive Elephants." *International Zoo Yearbook* 40: 63–79.

Whittaker, M., and G. Laule. 2009. "Protected Contact and Elephant Welfare." In *An Elephant in the Room: The Science and Well-Being of Elephants in Captivity*, D. L. Forthman, L. F. Kane, D. Hancocks, and P. F. Waldau (eds.), 181–188. North Grafton, MA: Tufts Center for Animals and Public Policy.

Wildlife SOS. "Elephant Haven." Accessed November 19, 2013. http://www.wildlifesos.org/rescue/elephants/sanctuary-haryana.

Working Elephant Programme of Asia. n.d. Accessed November 19, 2013. http://kotisivu.surffi.net/~heltel1/need.htm.

Wylie, K. C. 1992. "Elephants Used as War Machines." In *Elephants: Majestic Creatures of the Wild*, J. Shoshani (ed.), 146–148. Emmaus, PA: Rodale Press.

4

Captive Chimpanzees

STEPHEN R. ROSS ▪

The story of captive chimpanzees is a story of two species, barely a hairsbreadth apart in evolutionary time, engaged in a complex relationship. Without a doubt, one species, *Homo sapiens*, has held a dominant and controlling role, but the nature of the relationship transcends a simple and dyadic captor-captive representation. Long before scientific evidence of the genetic similarities between chimpanzees and humans came to light, the recognition of a unique and often troubling kinship were evident, adding layers of complex and often contradictory overtones to the relationship. The manner in which chimpanzees are housed and managed in captivity has often reflected the fluctuating and multifaceted ways they are perceived by humans. In this chapter, I will first discuss the primary characteristics of captive environments that affect chimpanzees. Within this context, I will describe the broad range of settings in which captive chimpanzees are housed in the United States, relating specifically to issues of their management, care, and ultimately their well-being. The focus of this chapter is very purposefully on captive chimpanzees in the United States where, even today, they exist in a dizzying array of housing circumstances, some unlike anywhere else in the world.

THE NEEDS OF CHIMPANZEES

The Social Environment

Providing captive chimpanzees with a rich, dynamic, and stable social environment is likely the single most important element in promoting chimpanzee well-being. Wild chimpanzees live in large social communities (Boesch and Boesch 2000) that can include over one hundred individuals (Mitani et al. 2000) who may rarely come together in a complete congregation, but who regularly associate as part of smaller groups of variable size and membership. Membership in chimpanzee groups is varied and may include newborns all the way up to seniors. While accurate age estimates for wild chimpanzees can be challenging, there are records of captive chimpanzees living into their seventies (Ross 2012) and as a result, individuals may share a varied and diverse set of relationships that extend back decades. Replicating this vast and diverse social structure is a lofty expectation for captive groups that live in substantially smaller areas, but the importance of a rich social life for captive chimpanzee welfare cannot be overstated.

In early life, absence of an appropriate social environment has profound consequences. In the wild, infants stay almost constantly with their mothers for upwards of five years (Pusey 1983) and thus it is no surprise that chimpanzees raised in social isolation suffer significant developmental detriments. Restrictively reared captive chimpanzees often develop a range of disorders and stereotyped behavior patterns such as rocking, self-sucking, and eye-poking (Davenport and Menzel 1963; Walsh et al. 1982) and seem to have a difficult time dealing with novel and challenging circumstances (Menzel 1964). These effects also manifest themselves later in life, as isolation-raised chimpanzees, even with substantial social experience through adolescence, continued to show abnormal social behavior patterns and general fearfulness (Turner et al. 1969). These effects extend to reproductive behavior and deficiencies in breeding and maternal competencies (Rogers and Davenport 1969).

Compared to these clear negative effects of impoverished social lives, evidence for the specific attributes of social groupings that are most important to chimpanzees is less obvious. For instance, the optimal size of a captive chimpanzee group is influenced by a wide range of factors including the available space, demographic makeup of the individuals, and their social experience. While there are accounts of chimpanzees living in groups of over forty individuals, most of the largest chimpanzee groups in existence today (primarily in sanctuary settings) do not reach thirty individuals. Baker et al. (2000) reported that chimpanzees housed in large groups may incur higher levels of minor wounding compared to smaller groups, but not more serious wounding. Though there is no empirical justification for specific group sizes, there is some common language in the various chimpanzee standards and guidelines. The AZA chimpanzee care manual suggests a target group size of three adult males and five adult females (Ross and McNary 2010), and a recent set of recommendations suggests a minimum group size of seven individuals (Working Group on the Use of Chimpanzees for NIH-Supported Research 2013). Importantly, both of these sets of guidelines recognize the importance of individual considerations in forming social groups of chimpanzees and also assert that larger groups provide the potential for even more dynamic and stimulating social environment.

The Physical Environment

As previously mentioned, the ability to house large and diverse social groups is directly tied to providing physical environments that can facilitate such groupings. One of the most frequently asked questions is how much space is needed to house chimpanzees. The answer is inexorably tied to a host of factors including but not limited to group size and composition, complexity of space, barrier types, placement and quantity of preferred elements and the location and quality of human interaction sites. Nonetheless, several attempts have been made to define the space requirements for chimpanzees from a regulatory standpoint. The table below shows the tremendous range of recommendations and demonstrates the diversity of opinion on what constitutes an appropriate physical environment for chimpanzees. Interestingly, Robert Gardner, an American zoologist, devised a set of standards for the housing of chimpanzees that rival many that appear over a hundred years later (Gardner 1896).

Human Influences

In addition to a captive chimpanzee's social and physical environment, there are several other factors that are likely to influence their psychological well-being.

REGULATORY SPACE RANGES FOR CAPTIVE CHIMPANZEES

Organization	Type	Space per chimpanzee (m²)[a]	Height (m)
Robert Garner (1896)	Recommendation	59	4.6
AAALAC/USDA (2011)	Minimum standard	2.3	2.1
Global Federation of Animal Sanctuaries (2010)	Minimum standard	58	6
Association of Zoos and Aquariums (2010)	Guideline	65	6.5
Working Group on the Use of Chimpanzees for NIH-supported Research (2013)	Recommendation	93	6.1
Pan African Sanctuary Alliance (Farmer et al., 2009)	Minimum standard	250	n/a

[a] Using group of ten as example for outdoor enclosure.

These may be termed the "management environment" or the manner in which human caretakers interact with the chimpanzee. Chimpanzees in captive settings likely interact with humans in a wide range of circumstances, and given their natural social nature and phylogenetic similarity to humans, it's not surprising that both positive and negative relationships can be formed and can influence the welfare of the chimpanzees.

The manner and frequency of human interactions can have different impacts on captive chimpanzees. In one study, researchers observed significantly more agonistic wounding in their laboratory-housed chimpanzee colony on weekdays than on weekends, and attribute this difference to staff presence and activity (Lambeth et al. 1997), which may agitate the chimpanzees. Direct and positive interactions with trusted human caregivers may foster positive relationships and result in beneficial outcomes; for example, unstructured positive interactions with lab-housed chimpanzees can result in lower rates of stereotypies as well as increased social grooming and observer-related affiliative behaviors (Bloomsmith et al. 1999; Baker 2004). Though this provides good evidence of the potentially enriching power of positive human interactions, there is also a risk of an interfering effect, such that even positively intended interactions can disrupt the social milieu of captive chimpanzees and potentially result in increased agonistic behavior and indicators of social anxiety (Chelluri et al., 2013). More structured human-chimpanzee interactions have often had positive effects. There is good evidence of the beneficial impact of positive-reinforcement training for chimpanzees (reviewed in Perlman et al. 2010) both in terms of its proximate behavioral effects and its facilitation of necessary veterinary treatment. Individuals who participated in training regimens tend to show enhanced social interaction (such as increased play behavior) not only during but also outside of training sessions. Likewise, innovative cognitive research with chimpanzees, involving everything from tool-use tasks to touchscreen interactions, has the potential to serve as an enrichment intervention to improve psychological well-being (reviewed in Ross 2010).

Choice and Control

One of the most significant constraints on captive chimpanzees is the lack of opportunities to control aspects of their daily lives. Allowing captive animals to make relevant choices in their environment has substantial potential to increase species-typical behavior and positively affect psychological well-being. However, the value of choice is inherently difficult to test and quantify, and for that reason there remains relatively scant empirical justification for the provision of choices. While chimpanzees who had control over a joystick-mediated task showed relatively little behavioral benefit compared to those without control (Bloomsmith et al. 2001), another study suggests that simply having the choice to access the outdoors can have a behavioral effect on zoo-housed chimpanzees (Kurtycz et al., in press) even if they don't opt for that choice.

WHERE CAPTIVE CHIMPANZEES LIVE

Chimpanzees are housed in as wide an array of settings as any exotic wildlife species held in captivity in the United States. For over a hundred years, chimpanzees have lived in laboratory and zoo settings, circuses and fairs, and more recently as pets, actors, and subsequently in dedicated sanctuaries. There are both evolutionary and sociopolitical explanations for the fact that only chimpanzees are subject to these diverse captive conditions, though neither by themselves can account for this variation.

Biologically, chimpanzees are likely the most robust of the great apes, historically ranging over a wider and more diverse range of habitats that other species. Partly because of the strong adaptive nature of chimpanzees, their numbers in captivity grew quickly in the early 1900s. First in zoos and laboratories, early breeding attempts allowed the population to grow. Their similarity to humans made them desirable subjects for scientific investigations, and as awareness of their physiological similarities grew, so did their application as models for human health. In a twist of cruel irony, the natural robust adaptivity that had allowed them to thrive across a wide range of conditions in Africa now facilitated their housing in entirely unsuitable conditions in captivity. Their similarity to humans also extended beyond their value as medical models and chimpanzees were recognized by the public as amusing human caricatures, and were thus trained to perform at circuses and fairs.

In addition to their natural adaptibility, a series of important regulatory events helped shape the course of history for captive chimpanzees in America. In 1973 the US Congress passed the Endangered Species Act to protect species that faced extinction, and three years later the Fish and Wildlife Service listed the chimpanzee as a "threatened" species. In 1989, chimpanzees were uplisted to "endangered" status but maintain the lesser "threatened" status for captive chimpanzees, primarily to facilitate their use for medical research. This highly unusual "split status" has been disputed as scientifically unjustified and will probably be eliminated, but to this point in time it has facilitated the wide range of uses of chimpanzees in the United States, including the ability to legally buy, trade, and own them.

Today, there are over 1,800 chimpanzees living in the United States, approximately three times as many as those living in their natural range country of

Tanzania, where Dr. Jane Goodall conducted her groundbreaking research. In 2009, Project ChimpCARE initiated a nationwide census of chimpanzees living in zoos, laboratories, sanctuary, and under private ownership, creating the most comprehensive database of the species (www.chimpcare.org). In the following sections, I describe the many settings in which chimpanzees have lived in the past and now live in the United States, and briefly describe their varied histories. Though many chimpanzees have personal histories that trace and overlap through these different settings, each setting represents a unique and prominent influence in the relationship between humans and captive chimpanzees.

CHIMPANZEES IN ZOOS

Keo was born somewhere in West Africa in 1958. He was imported to the United States before he turned one year old and transported to the Lincoln Park Zoo in Chicago, where he lived with a variety of other great apes. He entertained and delighted generations of zoo visitors, first as part of contrived "tea parties" through the 1960s and 1970s and then later, as a full-grown adult male in his artificial habitat. In 2004 he moved into his new facility, where he participated in cognitive touchscreen research and lived quietly with his small social group in an off-view enclosure until his death in 2013.

Keo, courtesy of Todd Rosenberg, Lincoln Park Zoo

For decades, chimpanzees represented an especially challenging exhibit species as a result of their similarity to humans. While some zoo visitors were attracted to them, others were put off by the uncanny anatomical and behavioral similarities. Whatever the reason, chimpanzees have remained a consistently popular exhibit animal over the last century. But the manner in which they have been housed has undergone a series of generational shifts in development that reflected societal attitudes toward wilderness in general and apes in particular (Coe and Maple 1987, 1996). Very early on, the great ape enclosure was typically a relatively barren, barred cage in which solitary dangerous adult animals would live out their lives on public display. Though scientific interest in great ape behavior and intelligence was already on the rise, the general public, and likely many zoo professionals, knew relatively little about the natural ecology of the species, and this lack of information impacted their care and management.

As industrial advancements produced more durable (and cleanable) materials, zoo exhibits evolved to what Coe and Maple (1996) describe as the "blue tile period" that likely extends through the most of first half of the 1900s. While the behavioral needs of chimpanzees remained largely unappreciated, social housing increased and the first captive breeding successes were achieved. In the 1970s exhibits began to be increasingly characterized by more complex, three-dimensional spaces and larger social groups. Lincoln Park Zoo's Lester Fisher Great Ape House opened in 1976 and, while making no attempt to appear "naturalistic" in aesthetic appearance, made great advances in providing a rich, functional environment for the resident chimpanzees. With vertically expansive dayrooms and a complex collection of ropes, platforms, and climbing towers, the facility was lauded as providing a high degree of behavioral choices for the apes. Nonetheless, chimpanzees here did not have access to outdoor space nor any naturalistic components to their environment.

The 1980s were characterized by a landscape immersion movement in which ape exhibits began to more closely resemble the natural habitats of chimpanzees. Zoo visitors were immersed in simulations of lush African forests that were argued to provide a more enhanced educational experience for visitors seeking to learn about the natural history of these species. While the more iconic of this immersion exhibits were built for gorillas, Detroit Zoo's expansive indoor-outdoor "Chimpanzees of Harambee" exhibit, opened in 1989, providing over two acres of outdoor space and two large, high dayrooms. Detroit and other zoo exhibits turned to the use of water moats to keep their chimpanzees separated from the viewing public. Though allowing larger, open-air expanses for the chimpanzees, water moats were unfortunately the cause of death for dozens of chimpanzees, and today, the Chimpanzee Species Survival Plan (SSP), a cooperative management program that manages the demographic and genetic health of the population as well as promoting individual well-being and functional group dynamics, recommends against their use for newly-designed exhibits.

Contemporary zoo design for chimpanzees continues to inch forward. The most modern exhibits such as Lincoln Park Zoo's Regenstein Center for African Apes (2004) and Houston Zoo's African Forest exhibit (2010) display large groups of chimpanzees in indoor-outdoor spaces that provide as much choice as possible to the residents. Today, thirty-four AZA-accredited zoos house approximately 260 chimpanzees. All are part of the Chimpanzee Species Survival Plan.

One of the most prevalent factors under study that is unique to the zoo environment was the effect of zoo visitors on chimpanzees. As I suggested earlier, research from the laboratory environment suggested that chimpanzees may be particularly susceptible to the influence of humans. Cook and Hosey (1995) collected data on the interactions between zoo-housed chimpanzees and human visitors and found that chimpanzee responses were only randomly associated with respect to human behavior. However, human responses associated significantly with the behavior of the chimpanzees, suggesting that chimpanzees were controlling rather than reacting to interactions with zoo visitors. Of course there are many documented cases of negative interactions with zoo visitors as well, notably aimed throwing of sod, feces, and even stones (Osvath 2009); however, broad evidence of a generalized stressful effect of zoo visitors remains absent in the literature. As with other ape species (Stoinski et al. 2012; Smith and Kuhar 2010; Kuhar 2008), there is growing consensus that well-designed zoo enclosures can greatly buffer any potential negative effect of zoo visitors.

The history of chimpanzees living in zoo environments is as long and varied as any exotic species in existence. Whether due to their active nature, obvious intelligence, or perceived role as a shadowy window into our own species history, chimpanzees remain among the most popular exhibit animals in zoos (Moss and Esson 2010). Just as zoos have evolved their principal objectives from purely exhibition to conservation, research, and education, so to have strategies used to display chimpanzees. Many accredited zoos play a significant role in funding conservation work. For instance, the Lester Fisher Center for the Study and Conservation of Apes at Lincoln Park Zoo provides long-term financial and administrative support to the Goualougo Triangle Ape Project, which is working to conserve wild chimpanzee populations in the Republic of Congo. Additionally, recent research points to chimpanzees as particularly able to have positive impacts on public perceptions on wildlife preservation and respect for natural ecosystems (Lukas and Ross in press). Chimpanzees in accredited zoos are managed by the SSP, which seeks to maintain a genetically and demographically healthy population of chimpanzees long into the future, so the question is likely less *if* chimpanzees will be in zoos in the future, than *how* they will be maintained.

LABORATORY SETTINGS

Drew was born at the Yerkes National Primate Research Center in Atlanta, Georgia. Before he was one year old, he received his chest tattoo of "629," indicating his institutional animal records ID, but by that time, he was already being hand-reared as part of a cohort of like-aged infants. Eventually he graduated from his peer group to live in a trio along the indoor-outdoor wing. He is not subjected to invasive biomedical studies but instead participates in a variety of less-invasive studies including neuroimaging investigations.

The use of chimpanzees in laboratory settings is a fiercely debated topic. However, it was not always this way, and for decades, the use of chimpanzees in a wide range of investigations simmered outside of public critique. Hundreds of chimpanzees have lived (and died) in research settings, and while the quality of housing and care they have been provided varied extensively, there is little doubt that we have learned as much about chimpanzees in laboratory settings as any other captive setting. Today the debate hinges on comparing apples and oranges: the potential benefits of knowledge versus the costs to chimpanzees. While zoo environments have evolved considerably in recent decades, change has been much slower in the laboratory environment.

The first scientific studies utilizing captive chimpanzees in the United States conducted by Robert Yerkes began in the 1920s. Yerkes recognized very early on the importance of care and housing of chimpanzees, not only for their intrinsic well-being, but for the facilitation of the chimpanzee's role as viable models of human physiology and psychology. In some of the earliest descriptions of captive care for chimpanzees, he provided detailed descriptions of chimpanzee requirements in terms of nutrition, space, husbandry, and veterinary care. He recognized the importance of basing the needs of captive chimpanzees upon their natural histories but also emphasized the importance of individualized care, and the inherent behavioral flexibility of this cognitively complex species.

If then, we were asked to sum up…the essentials of success, in keeping and breeding the higher primates, we should emphasize the following points: freedom, or reasonably spacious quarters; fresh air and sunshine, preferably coupled with marked variations in temperature; cleanliness of surroundings as well as of the body; clean and carefully prepared food in proper variety and quantity; a sufficient and regular supply of pure water; congenial species companionship and intelligent and sympathetic human companionship, which transcending the routine care of the animal, provides for the development of interest if not friendliness; and, finally, adequate resources and opportunity both in company and in isolation for work and play. Given these conditions of captive existence, primates originally healthful and normal should without difficulty be kept in good condition of body and mind and should naturally reproduce and success-fully rear their young. (Yerkes 1925, 241–242)

The degree to which these descriptions of essential captive care were met by early housing of captive chimpanzees is debatable. The majority of housing in this period was based on functional needs and hygiene, rather than the intrinsic species-typical behavioral and psychological needs we emphasize today.

Beginning in the 1940s there was considerable interest in using chimpanzees as models for human health, and scientists attempted to infect chimpanzees with diseases ranging from hepatitis to leprosy. These investigations of infec-tious disease had two substantial effects on the way chimpanzees were housed and managed. First, because of the infectious and potentially harmful nature of the agents being used in this research, housing for these chimpanzees became increasingly sterile and controlled. Sealed concrete walls and floors became the norm, and more chimpanzees were housed without any outdoor access at all. Second, the need for increased numbers of chimpanzees resulted in increased breeding and a steep increase in the laboratory chimpanzee population. During this time, many chimpanzees were removed from their mothers at birth to facil-itate research protocols and subsequently raised in nursery settings, where they have significant human influence on their development. While some chimpan-zees were almost exclusively hand-reared, others grew up in peer groups with like-aged conspecifics. We know much more today about the effects of limited maternal exposure, including detriments to future reproductive and maternal capabilities, and for a generation of chimpanzees, those handicaps had their origins during this period.

In 1981 the Centers for Disease Control and Prevention officially recognized acquired immunodeficiency syndrome (AIDS) as a significant health threat, and three years later, the first chimpanzees were experimentally infected with the associated human immunodeficiency virus (HIV). The NIH quickly moved to designate funds for the creation of the National Chimpanzee Breeding and Research Program in 1986 to facilitate the expansion of chimpanzees as an available research resource. The population in laboratory settings rose precipi-tously as a result of intensive breeding efforts and in anticipation of the need for chimpanzees to combat HIV/AIDS. By 1994 over 1,500 chimpanzees were housed in laboratory settings in the United States and there was rising con-cern about what to do with this growing population of chimpanzees, who can live for decades. In 1997, the Institute for Laboratory Animal Research (ILAR) published a report that concluded that there is a "moral responsibility" for the long-term care of chimpanzees used in research. Among the important recommendations in the report was a definitive rejection of euthanasia as a method of population control.

In 2000, the Chimpanzee Health, Improvement, Maintenance and Protection (CHIMP) Act was passed to provide means to fund a national sanctuary system for former research chimpanzees, and in 2002, the NIH selected Chimp Haven to build and operate the sanctuary system. In 2011 only 0.056 percent of active NIH-funded projects used chimpanzees, and in the face of continued public pressure to forgo the use of chimpanzees in invasive biomedical research, the NIH asked the Institute of Medicine (IOM) to study the necessity of chimpanzees for the advancement of human health research. The resulting IOM report (2011) asserted that "most current use of chimpanzees for biomedical research is unneccesary" and recommended that NIH should limit the use of chimpanzees. Furthermore, they recommended that those chimpanzees that are necessary for the decreasing research efforts need be housed in "ethologically appropriate physical and social environments," a previously undefined terminology.

While the IOM report set important precedent for the trajectory of chimpanzee use in invasive research, it left a number of important gaps in terms of implementation. So the NIH created a Working Group on the Use of Chimpanzees in NIH-Supported Research charged with providing advice on the implementation of the IOM recommendations (disclosure: the author was part of this working group). In late 2012 the Working Group provided their recommendations on, among other things, what constitutes "ethologically appropriate environments," which were characterized by:

- "sufficiently large, complex, multi-male, multi-female social groupings, ideally consisting of at least 7 individuals"
- "outdoor access year round"
- "the opportunity to climb at least 20 ft (6.1m) vertically"
- "foraging opportunities and diets that are varied, nutritious and challenging"
- "materials to construct nests on a daily basis"
- "relevant opportunities for choice and self-determination"
- "staff must include experienced and trained behaviorists, trainers and enrichment specialists"
- "at least 1000 ft^2 (93m^2) per individual."

In July 2013, the NIH responded by accepting virtually all of the Working Group's recommendations. The NIH opted to table a decision on the last item above, citing a lack of scientific consensus on space requirements as well as acknowledging the influence of the financial considerations tied to these standards. The decision marked a significant evolution of NIH's public stance on the future of chimpanzee use in biomedical research, and the manner in which the species is housed in research settings.

Proponents of chimpanzee-based biomedical research remain staunchly convinced that this species remains the best and, in some cases, the only viable model for critical human health crises facing this country. They point to advances in the housing of chimpanzees in the laboratory community and the security of an institutionalized and regulated standard of care. While housing and care of chimpanzees in research laboratories has unquestionably improved, many chimpanzee experts agree that the vast majority of chimpanzees living in laboratories are subject to environmental conditions that are unnatural and have potentially harmful long-term effects.

Nonetheless, the exponential acceleration of change in this area is staggering, even for proponents of ending invasive biomedical work with chimpanzees. Ideas thought to be unrealistic before the IOM report, such as the United States joining the rest of the world in ending invasive research with chimpanzees, now seems likely to come to pass. Concern has moved from ending the century-long use of chimpanzees as proxy for our species health issues, to the practical nature of how hundreds of chimpanzees can be transferred into retirement.

PERFORMERS, PETS, AND PRIVATE OWNERSHIP

Henry was born in the late 1980s, but no one is exactly sure where he came from. For the first ten years of his life, he was shuffled between roadside animal attractions until he was sold as a pet to a couple in central southeast Texas. He lived in the house with them until he bit someone and was returned to the animal dealer, who subsequently sold Henry again. For the next fifteen years, Henry lived in a small rusty cage in a residential garage. Given that he was not exhibited to the public, he virtually disappeared and was not subject to any oversight; thus he existed in squalid living conditions. He was fed soda and coffee and smoked cigarettes and was suffering from severe malnourishment when the Houston SPCA discovered and confiscated him in 2008. He was soon moved to Chimp Haven, where he continues his recovery and resocialization today.

Much less is known and documented about the lives of chimpanzees living as pets and entertainers. Until very recently, estimates of the number of privately owned chimpanzees ranged from just a few to many hundreds. Today, thanks to the Project ChimpCARE census, we have reasonably accurate estimates of the number of chimpanzees that live as pets, performers, and at unaccredited

Henry, courtesy of Amy Fultz, Chimp Haven

facilities (approximately 287 as of this writing). The variation in the circumstances of these chimpanzees varied far more than those in other settings such
as zoos or research settings. This can primarily be attributed to an "owner's"
general lack of understanding of chimpanzee needs in many of these settings as
well as an absence of any overarching standards of care and minimal oversight.
Those housing chimpanzees as pets have virtually no standards of care to which
they must adhere, and even those allowing public viewing of the chimpanzees
(such as circuses or roadside zoos) need only meet the minimum standards of
the USDA's exhibitor's permit.

   Chimpanzees owned as personal pets almost exclusively were born and bred at
one of the handful of breeders in the central United States. They were invariably
removed from their mother shortly after birth and subsequently hand-reared to
facilitate handling, a practice with well-documented long-term negative behavioral effects. The infants are usually sold (for approximately $35,000–$60,000)
to unprepared customers, many of whom "have always dreamed of having a pet
chimp" and likely have been heavily influenced by media portrayals of chimpanzees as cute and cuddly (Ross et al. 2011). Though a great deal of variation exists, the typical trajectory of the owner-chimp relationship follows this
course: the infant chimpanzee is loved and adored as a surrogate child, requiring care very similar to that needed by a human infant. Though the chimpanzee infant is often receiving attention, adoration, and contact, many of the key

developmental inputs are absent, and as a result, the seeds of developmental disorders are sown. Soon the chimpanzee becomes more mobile and active, and eventually destructive. Chimpanzee physical development progresses more rapidly than does human physical development, and it becomes increasingly difficult to use human-rearing tactics to control the infant. Eventually, the transition from child to pet takes place, and it becomes necessary to relegate the juvenile chimpanzee to a makeshift enclosure to control his or her natural exploratory tendencies. In the best of these unfortunate scenarios, chimpanzees are provided secure, outdoor facilities and enough care to keep them relatively healthy for the time being. Other pet chimpanzees are left to complete social isolation in a garage or basement, where they suffer physiological and psychological neglect. Many owners realize the error of their ways, sometimes through some form of delayed compassion but often because of financial burden, and the search for a better home begins in earnest. Others steadfastly cling to their belief that their love of the chimpanzee overshadows any potential benefit the chimpanzee might receive in a more appropriate environment. Though some ex-pet chimpanzees may find their way to a sanctuary setting, these chimpanzees are among the most difficult to resocialize because of the absence of appropriate exposure to other chimpanzees.

Chimpanzees have been used as "entertainers" in this country for over a hundred years. Some of the earliest recorded instances of chimpanzees are those housed as part of traveling circuses, which moved from city to city, housing a mobile menagerie of apes, elephants, tigers, and lions. Typically these chimpanzees were housed in meager settings consisting of steel-barred cages and little else, and few survived into adulthood. With the advent of moving pictures and later, television, chimpanzees became popular to a wider audience, often portrayed as silly caricatures of humans or, at best, sidekicks. Cheeta, of Tarzan fame, became one of the most recognizable chimpanzees to the American public, but many more were household names throughout the twentieth century. By the 1990s there were several colonies of chimpanzees maintained exclusively for filling the desire for trained chimpanzees for movies, television, print media, and advertisements.

Even today, most of the general public seems amused by the sight of a young chimpanzee dressed in human clothes and acting the fool. Recently however, there has been growing scrutiny on these practices based on two primary criticisms: animal welfare concerns and public perception concerns. Due to firsthand "undercover" accounts, there in increasing awareness of the use of aversive training techniques to train actor chimpanzees. During their training, young chimpanzees can be forced to essentially learn how not to behave in normal chimpanzee fashion, and in some cases, physical punishment and intimidation are the tools of the trade. These practices were brought to the forefront when chimpanzee trainers working on *Project X*, a movie about saving a chimpanzee from his role in the air force training program, were fined for physical abuse of a young chimpanzee actor on the set. Though monitoring programs exist to safeguard the care and training of animal actors on the set, there remains virtually no oversight of the more intensive training that goes on behind the scenes. The second criticism of the use of chimpanzees in entertainment stems from the public misperceptions that arise from inaccurate and often demeaning portrayals of this species. Ross et al. (2008) demonstrated that the public is less likely to consider chimpanzees to be endangered compared to other great apes, primarily because they are so often used in the entertainment industry. Showing chimpanzees in anthropomorphic settings such as office buildings and human residences creates the misperception and can influence people into thinking the species is not endangered or that chimpanzees would make good pets.

Over the past twenty years, the number of actor chimpanzees has diminished significantly, with dozens moving to sanctuary settings. In some cases, chimpanzees who have suffered physical abuse have difficulty adjusting to new settings but compared to pet chimpanzees who may have absolutely no exposure to other chimpanzees, actor chimpanzees appear to be easier to resocialize.

In a sad irony, the environments that likely have the worst long-term effects on chimpanzee behavior and well-being are the ones that are likely to be in existence for many years to come. Roadside zoos have little incentive to transfer away chimpanzees who, in many cases, are their biggest draw. Pet ownership of chimpanzees may someday be outlawed, but it would be doubtful if those regulations did not include "grandfather clauses" that would maintain these long-lived animals in their current situation for many more years. As I will describe next, sanctuaries (and also zoos) that have taken on the formidable charge to resocialize former pets and entertainers are subject to the challenges of dealing with long-lasting effects of solitary or human-centric early environments.

SANCTUARIES

Knuckles was born at a California entertainment compound in 1999 and was immediately identified as having developmental problems. He had motor control problems, muscle weakness, and difficulty moving around. Realizing the degree of special care he required, Knuckles was moved at the age of two to the Center for Great Apes, a sanctuary in central Florida that houses "special needs" chimpanzees. There he was diagnosed with cerebral palsy and was assigned to a team of occupational and physical therapists who help counter the effects of

this debilitating disease. Though Knuckles will always struggle with his handicap, the sanctuary is able to dedicate a diverse range of special care for him that
would be impossible in many other settings.

Chimpanzees sanctuaries have a much shorter history than zoos, labs, or
even entertainment venues such as circuses, primarily because sanctuaries are
by nature a response to a need created, to differing degrees, by those situations.
Simply put, while chimpanzees live in other settings for specific reasons (education, research, entertainment), chimpanzees exist in sanctuaries because of the
failure of those captive environments. Nonetheless, it would be an overstate-
ment to suggest that all sanctuary environments provide appropriate environments for captive chimpanzees.

Arguably, the first organized chimpanzee sanctuary to appear in the United
States was the Primate Foundation of Arizona (PFA), which was established in
1969 by Dr. Jo Fritz. Dr. Fritz had come into possession of a trio of young chimpanzees and housed them in her garage. Realizing her need for a more secure
location, she discovered an abandoned hydroelectric plant on a reservation in
Arizona. Large empty generator housing was fenced off, and from these beginnings grew a multitiered cage structure that housed up to eighty individuals
several decades later. In the mid-1980s, when funding for breeding colonies of
chimpanzees was available, PFA received funds to expand its outdoor housing
and became one of the seven NIH-funded primate centers.

Through the 1970s and 1980s, several other sanctuaries received chimpanzees from a variety of sources, including those moved from laboratories, zoos,
the entertainment industry, and the private pet trade. As biomedical research
centers reorganized and shut down, they were forced to transfer chimpanzees
to whoever would receive them. While some chimpanzees found their way to
long-term stable environments, others were relocated to sanctuaries where the
staff did not have the means or expertise to house a species as challenging as a
chimpanzee.

Many chimpanzees did not find sanctuary, however, and were instead relocated to other laboratory settings, and in some cases, worse conditions. Among
the most notorious of these labs was the Coulston Foundation in New Mexico,
which had the worst record of any lab in the history of the Animal Welfare Act.
In 1997, Dr. Carole Noon founded Save the Chimps with the intention of preventing the transfer of hundreds of former air force chimpanzees to Coulston.
She was successful, as Coulston was failing, and eventually Save the Chimps took
over the Coulston Foundation and all of the chimpanzees there. The chimpanzees were moved from New Mexico to Fort Peirce, Florida, where the sanctuary
is now home to over 200 chimpanzees, living on a series of three-acre islands.

In 2000, the federal government agreed to develop a national sanctuary
system for chimpanzees no longer needed in research programs, and Chimp

Haven received that contract. Chimp Haven was the brainchild of Dr. Linda Brent, an expert on the behavior and socialization of captive chimpanzees, Amy Fultz, and their associates who were then employees at the Southwest Biomedical Foundation in Texas. At Chimp Haven, chimpanzees experience settings that get closer to their natural environments than anywhere else in the country. Huge naturally forested habitats allow large social groups to roam and explore acres of territory. The chimpanzees also have indoor housing, reminiscent of laboratory enclosures, but importantly it is their choice if they want to be inside or outside. At Chimp Haven and other top-level sanctuaries, the focus is entirely on providing the highest level of captive care for the chimpanzees.

Most reputable chimpanzee sanctuaries insist that they are "in the business to go out of business." That is, that they are dedicated to the rescue and rehabilitation of chimpanzees from the laboratory, pet, and entertainment industry, and when these sources fade away, there will no longer be a need for sanctuaries. Unlike the cooperative breeding program in place at accredited zoos, sanctuaries practice reactive, rather than a prospective population management. Nonetheless, given the long life span of chimpanzees and the fact that today new chimpanzees are still being produced by dealers, we can expect the need for chimpanzee sanctuaries to extend at least another fifty years into the future. Given that prospect, the challenge facing sanctuaries is how to best prepare for that need and to ensure stable and sustainable organizations for the next half-century. Forty years ago the sanctuary community barely existed, but in the past decade hundreds of chimpanzees have moved to sanctuary settings, and there is considerable concern about how these settings can be maintained. Without the stability of robust, federal funding mechanism or the revenue-generating mechanism of public admission charges, sanctuaries rely heavily on fundraising and public support. The degree to which these organizations can meet these challenges and continue the important, and very expensive, prospect of caring for hundreds of chimpanzees remains to be seen.

CONCLUSION

Clearly, captive chimpanzees lead lives that differ substantially from those of their wild counterparts, and even the most ambitious captive environments will fail to approach the sheer size and complexity of this species' natural environment (Working Group 2013). That said, it is equally clear that the diversity of captive conditions in the United States alone makes it impractical to attempt to classify all captive chimpanzees as sharing a common experience. Comparing Henry, who spent a decade in a cage in which he could barely stand up, to Keo, who has experienced a wide diversity of zoo environments leading to his eventual modern setting, is an exercise in stark contrasts. Likewise, the emotional complexity and individual variation in temperament and behavior presents addition variation in assessing the manner in which captive conditions may affect this uniquely robust species. Drew may have adapted quite comfortably to his laboratory environment compared to Knuckles, who lives his life under the constant and dedicated care of sanctuary staff but suffers from developmental challenges.

Whether due to their longevity, scientific interest, or public fascination, chimpanzees will continue to exist in captive settings for many more decades. The challenge facing those charged with caring for them is to build from the long history of captive care—both successes and failures—to continually improve the captive environment for this complex species and create settings in which they can not only survive, but thrive.

REFERENCES

Association for Assessment and Accreditation of Laboratory Animal Care International. "Rules of Accreditation." Accessed March 19, 2013. http://www.aaalac.org/accreditation/rules.cfm.

Association of Zoos and Aquariums. "The Accreditation Standards and Related Policies." Accessed March 19, 2013. http://www.aza.org/uploadedFiles/Accreditation/AZA-Accreditation-Standards.pdf.

Baker, Kate C. 2004. "Benefits of Positive Human Interaction for Socially-Housed Chimpanzees." *Animal Welfare* 13(3): 239–245.

Baker, Kate C., Michael Seres, Filippo Aureli, and Frans de Waal. 2000. "Injury Risks among Chimpanzees in Three Housing Conditions." *American Journal of Primatology* 51(3): 161–175.

Bloomsmith, Mollie A., Kate C. Baker, Stephen K. Ross, and Susan P. Lambeth. 1999. "Comparing Animal Training to Non-training Human Interaction as Environmental Enrichment for Chimpanzees." *American Journal of Primatology* 49(1): 35–36.

Bloomsmith, Mollie A., and Susan P. Lambeth. 2001. "Videotapes as enrichment for Captive Chimpanzees (Pan troglodytes)." *Zoo Biology* 19(6): 541–551.

Boesch, Christophe, and Hedwige Boesch-Achermann. 2000. *The Chimpanzees of the Taï Forest: Behavioural Ecology and Evolution*. New York: Oxford University Press.

Chelluri, Gita I., Stephen R. Ross, and Katherine E. Wagner. 2013 "Behavioral Correlates and Welfare Implications of Informal Interactions between Caretakers and Zoo-Housed Chimpanzees and Gorillas." *Applied Animal Behaviour Science* 147: 306–315.

Coe, Jon C., and Gary H. Lee. 1996. "One-Hundred Years of Evolution in Great Ape Facilities in American zoos." In *Proceedings of the AZA 1995 Western Regional Conference*. Bethesda, MD: American Zoo and Aquarium Association.

Coe, Jon, and Terry Maple. 1987. "In Search of Eden: A Brief History of Great Ape Exhibits." *AAZPA Annual Proceedings*.

Cook, Shelley, and Geoffrey R. Hosey. 1995. "Interaction Sequences between Chimpanzees and Human Visitors at the zoo." *Zoo Biology* 14(5): 431–440.

Farmer, Kay H., Stephen Unwin, Deborah Cox, Doug Cress, D. Lucas, Barbara Cartwright, and Zeena Tooze. 2009. *Pan African Sanctuary Alliance (PASA) Operations Manual.* 1st ed. Portland, OR: PASA.

Garner, Richard L. 1896. *Gorillas & Chimpanzees.* London: Osgood, McIlvaine.

Global Federation of Animal Sanctuaries. "GFAS Standards of Excellence." Accessed March 19, 2013. http://www.sanctuaryfederation.org/gfas/for-sanctuaries/standards/.

Institute of Medicine. "Chimpanzees in Biomedical and Behavioral Research: Assessing the Necessity." Accessed March 19, 2013. http://iom.edu/Reports/2011/Chimpanzees-in-Biomedical-and-Behavioral-Research-Assessing-the-Necessity.aspx.

Kuhar, Christopher W. 2008. "Group Differences in Captive Gorillas' Reaction to Large Crowds." *Applied Animal Behaviour Science* 110(3–4): 377–385.

Kurtycz, Laura M., Katherine E. Wagner, and Stephen R. Ross. "Choice of Outdoor Access Affects Great Ape Behavior." *Journal of Applied Animal Welfare Science* (in press).

Lambeth, Susan P., Mollie A. Bloomsmith, and Patricia L. Alford. 1997 "Effects of Human Activity on Chimpanzee Wounding." *Zoo Biology* 16(4): 327–333.

Lukas, Kristen E., and Stephen R. Ross. "A Comparison of Visitor Knowledge and Attitudes towards African Apes before and after Exhibit Renovations." *Anthrozoos* (in press).

Menzel, Emil W. 1964. "Patterns of Responsiveness in Chimpanzees Reared through Infancy under Conditions of Environmental Restriction." *Psychological Research* 27(4): 337–365.

Mitani, John C., Thomas T. Struhsaker, and Jeremiah S. Lwanga. 2000. "Primate Community Dynamics in Old Growth Forest over 23.5 years at Ngogo, Kibale National Park, Uganda: Implications for Conservation and Census Methods." *International Journal of Primatology* 21(2): 269–286.

Moss, Andrew, and Maggie Esson. 2010. "Visitor Interest in Zoo Animals and the Implications for Collection Planning and Zoo Education Programmes." *Zoo Biology* 29(6): 715–731.

Osvath, Mathias. 2009. "Spontaneous Planning for Future Stone Throwing by a Male Chimpanzee." *Current Biology* 19(5): R190–R191.

Perlman, Jaine E., Victoria Horner, Mollie A. Bloomsmith, Susan P. Lambeth, and Steven J. Schapiro. 2010. "Positive Reinforcement Training, Social Learning, and Chimpanzee Welfare." In Elizabeth Lonsorf, Stephen R. Ross, Jane Goodall, and Tetsuro Matsuzawa (eds.), *The Mind of the Chimpanzee: Ecological and Experimental Perspectives,* 320–331. Chicago: University of Chicago Press.

Pusey, Anne E. 1983. "Mother-Offspring Relationships in Chimpanzees after Weaning." *Animal Behaviour* 31(2): 363–377.

Rogers, Charles M., and Richard K. Davenport. 1969. "Effects of Restricted Rearing on Sexual Behavior of Chimpanzees." *Developmental Psychology* 1(3): 200–204.

Ross, Stephen R. 2010. "How Cognitive Studies Help Shape Our Obligations for the Ethical Care of Chimpanzees." In Elizabeth Lonsorf, Stephen R. Ross, Jane Goodall, and Tetsuro Matsuzawa (eds.), *The Mind of the Chimpanzee: Ecological and Experimental Perspectives,* 309–319. Chicago: University of Chicago Press.

Ross, Stephen R. 2012. *North American Regional Chimpanzee Studbook.* Silver Springs, MD: Association of Zoos and Aquariums.

Ross, Stephen R., Sarah Calcutt, Steven J. Schapiro, and Jann Hau. 2011. "Space Use Selectivity by Chimpanzees and Gorillas in an Indoor-Outdoor Enclosure." *American Journal of Primatology* 73(2): 197–208.

Ross, Stephen R., Kristen E. Lukas, Elizabeth V. Lonsdorf, Tara S. Stoinski, Brian Hare, Robert Shumaker, and Jane Goodall. 2008. "Inappropriate Use and Portrayal of Chimpanzees." *Science* 319: 1487.

Ross, Stephen R., and Jennie McNary. 2010. "Chimpanzee (Pan troglodytes) Care Manual." Association of Zoos and Aquariums. Accessed November 19, 2013. http://www.aza. org/uploadedFiles/Animal_Care_and_Management/Husbandry,_Health,_and_ Welfare/Husbandry_and_Animal_Care/ChimpanzeeCareManual2010.pdf.

Ross, Stephen R., Vivian M. Vreeman, and Elizabeth V. Lonsdorf. 2011. "Specific Image Characteristics Influence Attitudes about Chimpanzee Conservation and Use as Pets." *PLoS ONE* 6(7).

Smith, Kathleen N., and Christopher W. Kuhar. 2010 "Siamangs (Hylobates syndactylus) and White-Cheeked Gibbons (Hylobates leucogenys) Show Few Behavioral Differences related to Zoo Attendance." *Journal of Applied Animal Welfare Science* 13(2): 154–163.

Stoinski, Tara S., Hannah F. Jaicks, and Lindsey A. Drayton. 2012. "Visitor Effects on the Behavior of Captive Western Lowland Gorillas: The Importance of Individual Differences in Examining Welfare." *Zoo Biology* 31(5): 586–599.

Turner, Corbett H., Richard K. Davenport Jr., and Charles M. Rogers. 1969. "The Effect of Early Deprivation on the Social Behavior of Adolescent Chimpanzees." *American Journal of Psychiatry* 125:1531–1536.

US Government Printing Office. "Chimpanzee Health Improvement, Maintenance, and Protection Act." Accessed March 21, 2013. http://www.gpo.gov/fdsys/pkg/ PLAW-106publ551/html/PLAW-106publ551.htm

US Department of Agriculture. "USDA Space Management Policy" Accessed March 19, 2013. http://www.ocio.usda.gov/sites/default/files/docs/2012/DR1620-002. htm.

Walsh, S., Claude A. Bramblett, and Patricia L. Alford. 1982. "A Vocabulary of Abnormal Behaviors in Restrictively Reared Chimpanzees." *American Journal of Primatology* 3(1–4): 315–319.

Working Group on the Use of Chimpanzees in NIH-Supported Research. "Report." Accessed March 19, 2013. http://dpcpsi.nih.gov/council/pdf/FNL_Report_WG_ Chimpanzees.pdf.

Yerkes, Robert M. 1925. *Almost Human*. New York: The Century Co.

5

Rabbits in Captivity

MARGO DEMELLO ■

Rabbits have been hunted for fur and for meat for thousands of years in Europe and Asia, but it wasn't until the Middle Ages that rabbits were domesticated. Those rabbits were kept in large pens for food and fur, and for hundreds of years bred on their own; later, their keepers selectively bred them for size, temperament, color, and other characteristics. By the early twentieth century, following the popularity of Gregor Mendel's work on the inheritance of traits, dozens of breeds of rabbits were created, primarily for the meat, fur, and newly developing show markets. Today, rabbits are purpose-bred to fulfill the needs of four primary industries: pets, meat, fur, and medical research. Unlike in the past, when rabbits were kept in pens, rabbits are now raised largely in cages.

In the United States, meat rabbit breeding is primarily a cottage industry, and typically takes place on backyard farms, unlike the massive factory farms that produce chickens or pigs for the table. Also unlike other meat producers, rabbit farmers are relatively unregulated—USDA inspectors only inspect rabbit production facilities when requested to do so by the operator. These federally inspected facilities sold two million rabbits, known as "fryers," for meat in 2001 (USDA 2002). Worldwide the total is about 800 million per year, primarily centered in France, Italy, and China, where rabbitries are much larger than in the United States.

Rabbits bred on meat farms live short, painful lives. Weaned at four weeks so that their mothers can be bred again (sometimes as soon as twenty-four hours after they gave birth), the baby rabbits live together in very small cages until they are slaughtered at twelve weeks. Breeding adults live their entire lives (about two years, as opposed to a pet rabbit's life expectancy of ten or more years) in solitary cages, which must be difficult for the rabbits since they are a social species, preferring to spend their time in the company of others. On top of the behavioral deprivation, living in small cages for one's entire life leads to disease, broken bones, damaged paws, and other problems. Once the rabbits are ready for slaughter, they may be shipped to a processing plant in small crates loaded onto trucks, during which many die from stress or injury prior to arrival.

Rabbits, like chickens, are not defined as livestock by the United States Department of Agriculture, which means they are exempt from the USDA's Humane Methods of Slaughter Act, which is meant to ensure that animals raised for meat are rendered insensitive to pain before they are slaughtered. Rabbits, then, can be killed while fully conscious, by breaking their necks, by hitting them with a blunt object, by decapitation, or by any other means.

The rabbit fur industry in the United States is the smallest of the industries that use rabbits for profit. Rabbit fur is not considered a luxury fur, and has never had the prestige of mink or sable. On the other hand, because it is cheap to produce, it is often considered a "fun" fur and is used on everything from cat toys to trim on cheap clothing aimed at young people with less disposable income. Today, most rabbit fur (and indeed, a large percentage of fur in general) used in American clothing and products is imported, primarily from China, although the number of rabbits killed for fur annually is not known. Wherever it is produced, rabbit fur is not a byproduct of the meat industry. Instead, fur is taken from rabbits who are slaughtered at six months, while rabbits killed for meat are killed much earlier, at three months. Rabbits raised for fur generally live packed tightly together in wire cages until they are slaughtered.

The pet rabbit industry is certainly the most benign of all of the industries that use rabbits for profit, in that it produces rabbits to be purchased as companions in families around the world. Unfortunately, like the other industries that produce animals for profit, rabbits suffer here as well.

Pet rabbits are either bred in small backyard rabbitries, or in large commercial operations, some of which could be called "rabbit mills." In either case, breeder rabbits are generally kept in solitary cages throughout their lives, being bred multiple times per year. Those living in the large-scale operations with annual profits over $500 must be licensed (and thus inspected) by the USDA, but these inspections are so infrequent that the facilities might as well be unregulated. Like puppies living in puppy mills, breeding does and bucks spend no social time with other rabbits, have no toys, and get no exercise. When they are no longer able to breed successfully, they are killed, or sometimes sold.

From the rabbitries, baby rabbits are transported via brokers or wholesalers to pet stores around the country, generally in large crowded trucks when the babies are four to six weeks old. Many rabbits die during transport (perhaps as many as 20 to 30 percent), and many die upon arrival at the pet store, due to the stress of the travel, the early age at which they were weaned, and the conditions at the store upon arrival (and the Animal Welfare Act does not cover the care of animals at pet stores).

The newest industry that uses rabbits is biomedical research and product testing. It wasn't until the mid-twentieth century that rabbits and other animals began to be purpose-bred specifically for laboratory use. Today, rabbits used in medical experimentation and product testing come from a handful of large laboratory animal suppliers that supply labs with millions of animals per year. Of the animals who must be reported to the USDA (rodents, birds, amphibians, and reptiles are excluded from reporting requirements), rabbits are the most commonly used laboratory animal in the United States, with 210,172 used in the United States in 2010 (USDA 2010). The number of rabbits—as well as many other animals—used in labs every year is dropping, as these animals are being replaced by nonanimal means as well as by genetically modified rodents.

While living in the lab, whether at a university, private testing facility, or government-run laboratory, rabbits typically lead lives of isolation. Because most are not surgically sterilized, they are kept alone in small, steel cages to prevent fighting and unwanted reproduction, and typically have nothing to play with and nothing to do. Rabbits, like other laboratory animals, are often observed engaging in stereotypic behaviors associated with emotional and psychological deprivation, such as bar licking, excessive grooming, or paw chewing, and sitting in a hunched position for hours at a time. The cages are too small to permit normal behaviors such as sitting up on hind legs, hopping, digging, and hiding. In addition, they often either undereat or overeat to counter their boredom; and many develop deformities in the spine and legs because they can't move freely in the tiny spaces.

On the other hand, some laboratories do provide environmental enrichment for their laboratory animals in order to try to meet the animals' psychological and physical needs as well as the requirements and recommendations of the Animal Welfare Act (which only *mandates* enrichment for primates and dogs, but *recommends* it for other animals). The USDA Animal Welfare Information Center provides resources for the voluntary enrichment of all animals. Suggestions for rabbits include social housing, the ability to forage and dig, and opportunities to run and play, and dozens of studies have been published on the benefits of enrichment for rabbits in the past fifteen years. Social living, for example, causes those stereotypic behaviors mentioned above to simply disappear (see for example Batchelor 1991, Boers et al. 2002, Fuentes and Newgren 2008, Heath and Scott 1990, Huls, Brooks, and Bean-Knudsen 1991, Love 1994, Podberscek, Blackshaw, and Beatie 1991, and Whary et al. 1993).

Adult male rabbits do tend to fight when living in groups, but some studies have found that neutering the males or, if that's not possible, letting them at least see and smell other rabbits from their single cages is more humane than keeping them in total isolation. The technicians at the University of British Columbia's Animal Care Center, which practices social housing, found that returning a rabbit to his or her group after surgery—rather than keeping the rabbit alone, as is standard practice—actually hastens the rabbit's recovery. "It is our experience that rabbits lie down beside a group member who is returning from a surgery and that this extra warmth and comfort hastens the recovery process," they wrote (Boers et al. 2002, 44).

The researchers at the Animal Care Center also recommend giving rabbits outdoor runs in which to play:

> The outdoor run allows the rabbits to indulge in "fast running," an activity that we frequently observe, particularly in young animals. A rabbit runs quickly to one end of the pen, stops and then runs quickly to the other. This may be repeated several times. We have never observed a special reason for this exercise, other than that the animals obviously enjoy it. (Boers et al. 2002, 45)

This is the very same play behavior that wild rabbits and domesticated rabbits living with "free range" have exhibited for centuries, and that people in the house rabbit community call "binkying," yet it is something that is usually denied to laboratory rabbits.

Some researchers have even investigated the effect of kind treatment for the rabbits, and have found that gentle handling, petting, playing, being talked to, and being given treats all help rabbits feel secure, develop a bond with their handlers, resist infection, and stay calm during unpleasant procedures. A strong bond with the animal also helps the technicians learn to notice the subtle changes in rabbit behavior (e.g., not eating) that can signal the beginning of an illness.

The rabbits living in the facilities at the University of British Columbia are certainly luckier than those at the vast majority of medical facilities. "We moved enrichment from an interesting research problem to the practical implementation a long time ago," says Dr. Jim Love, who leads the enrichment studies there. "That was possible primarily through the interest and the efforts of the technicians who wanted to make it work. I think that should be the goal of all enrichment studies, i.e. to get the results quickly to the animals" (personal interview; cited in Davis and DeMello, 301). Most research rabbits don't get to run, or leap, or spend a sleepy afternoon lying cheek to cheek with another rabbit, or enjoy the affectionate pats and chatter of a caring handler. Curiously, this may be one of the few instances in animal science research where the supposed experts—that is, the scientists—are learning what those who live with rabbits have known for a long time. Rabbits like to play, like to snuggle with other rabbits, like to be petted, and like to run and jump.

THE WILD RABBIT

Domesticated rabbits share the same genus and species (*Oryctolagus cuniculus*) as wild European rabbits, from whom they are descended and with whom they can still interbreed.

Unlike hares, cottontails, and other lagomorphs, who are solitary, European rabbits live in large warrens of dozens to hundreds of rabbits. Their social nature explains why European rabbits were domesticated but hares and cottontails were not. And while for hundreds of years, domesticated rabbits were often raised in groups, today rabbits raised for human use are almost always raised in solitary cages, away from contact with other rabbits (or other animals). For these highly social animals, living in such a bleak environment is both depressing and stressful.

In the wild, female rabbits spend hours digging the sophisticated warrens in which they live, while both males and females protect the warren, and the babies, against outsiders. Wild European rabbits spend much of their days foraging for food, hanging around with their friends and family members, grooming, "gossiping," mating, napping, playing, and fighting over territory. They play by jumping, running, and spinning—behaviors that are used to evade predators, but which are also fun for them, as our domesticated rabbits also "binky," either alone or with friends, when joyful.

Whether in the lab, in the rabbit mill, in the fur farm, in the backyard meat farm, or even in the majority of homes, these highly social, active, and playful animals are still kept in solitary cages, with little or no contact with others of their own kind, other animals, or even humans. Because of the way that this animal has been isolated, very little about their personalities, their needs, and desires is known to humans, and instead rabbits have been seen as passive, stupid, and dull creatures, which then justified their continued neglect and mistreatment. And the fact that rabbits do not vocalize—except in very rare circumstances—allows us to ignore them even further.

The fact that a species is unknown—as the rabbit is—means that we as humans can project all sorts of characteristics onto the animals that would deem them unworthy of protection. We can even project a trait of blankness on them; that is, because we don't understand the rabbit, we assume there is nothing to understand, that the rabbit is a creature with neither sentience nor subjectivity. And once we assume that, creating what in other species we would recognize as "suffering" becomes acceptable. Removed from sight and kept in small, bleak, inadequate cages, rabbits are "disappeared."

FREE-RUNNING RABBITS

I have been rescuing domestic rabbits through an organization called House Rabbit Society for twenty-three years. About twenty years ago, I decided to eliminate my cages, where I had previously been keeping my sanctuary rabbits, and let my rabbits live together in one large group, to try to mimic conditions found among their wild kin.

Over the course of a hot summer week in 1990, I created a large new outdoor play space which was connected to my home through a "rabbit door," and introduced the four dozen rabbits I had at that time to it, and to each other. Since that time, I have learned a great deal about domestic rabbit social behavior, much of which I have found echoed in the scant literature on wild rabbit social behavior.

My sanctuary rabbit population has fluctuated in number from a low of fifteen to a high of sixty-five since that time. They are mixed sexes, and all rabbits are spayed and neutered, either before they arrive or soon afterwards. In the different homes I've lived in, they have always had an indoor room in which to sleep and relax, and a large, secure, outdoor yard to play in, which they access either through a rabbit-sized door or, at one house, by the rabbits traveling up a ramp, through an open window, and down a ramp into the backyard. Eating is communal, and I feed the rabbits mornings and evenings. The rabbits typically arrive at my home individually, from animal shelters, or sometimes from meat facilities, laboratories, or as strays. Sometimes they arrive in groups from hoarding or neglect cases.

For example, I currently have survivors of three different hoarding cases living at my sanctuary right now: two are still with me from a group of over 1,600 rabbits living on a large property in Reno, Nevada, that Best Friends rescued many years ago, while about a dozen came from two cases, one involving a hundred rabbits, and the other over 350, from New Mexico, about three years ago. In all of the cases, the rabbits were feral, left to fend for themselves outside, with no food, no shelter, and very high mortality rates. Today the survivors are still relatively feral, and don't like to be handled or even touched. But they have food, shelter, comfortable beds, security, and best of all, friends with whom they no longer have to compete for basic resources.

Today most of the rabbits live in one big group in their own specially constructed wing of my house. Their room has a large human door (for me to use) that leads to an enclosed courtyard for safe outdoor play, and a rabbit-sized door that they can go in and out of as they like during the daytime. The court-yard is furnished with cardboard play structures and tubes, while their room has hammocks for them to relax on. Much like the wild rabbits from whom they are descended, the rabbits spend their days foraging for food in the courtyard, chewing on cardboard, lounging on their hammocks, and spending endless hours communing with each other—grooming, nuzzling, playing, "gossiping," or just hanging out. While these intraspecies relationships tend to mean that the rabbits will not bond with me (in fact, most will not even tolerate me touch-ing them), it is much more important to me that they experience the richness of rabbit-rabbit relationships.

FROM CAPTIVITY TO (RELATIVE) FREEDOM

Because of the conditions in which many of the rabbits I have rescued once lived, they face a number of challenges adapting to the new conditions at my sanctuary home, and I also face challenges in trying to create the best environ-ment for them. Because rabbits are social animals, housing them in a group situation is the most humane and enjoyable for the rabbits. It's also the easiest in terms of caring for a large herd.

Rabbits who spent their entire lives in cages haven't had contact with other rabbits or humans. Those who come from labs suffer from invasive and often painful contact with humans. The rabbits who end up in sanctuary, therefore, often have enormous psychological problems stemming from their lack of social contact and intellectual stimulation, as well as physical problems stem-ming from their lack of exercise and their intensive confinement. They tend to have weaker bones, weaker muscles, and poor motor coordination, so their mobility is often impaired and they need to be watched more closely to see that they thrive in their new environment.

In addition, rabbits living in laboratories are often in pathogen-free environ-ments, which means that they have not been exposed to the normal range of bacteria, viruses, and parasites that regular domestic rabbits encounter during their lives. They will be at greater risk for illness once they do become exposed to pathogens. My home is not a particularly clean one; besides the dozens of rabbits, I also live with dogs, cats, and a bird. So I have to be especially vigi-lant about keeping an eye out for signs of illness and need to treat those signs promptly.

Because of the lack of social contact, most of the unsocialized rabbits will often be extremely fearful, or very aggressive. I choose to take a hands-off approach in most cases, letting the rabbits find their own friends among the rabbit population, and I handle them as little as possible.

My first lab rabbit was Mama, an aggressive New Zealand rabbit with a large metal identification clip in her ear. Mama arrived at my house about twenty years ago with her three babies. Left over from an unknown experiment at a laboratory in Berkeley, Mama and her family had been sent to the local zoo to be used as snake food but were rescued by a zoo employee who happened to be a rabbit lover. She lived with me for three years until she died from myxomatosis—a horrible disease brought to Australia to solve Australia's "rabbit problem." Mama never did warm up to me; she remained aggressive and angry all the time she lived with me. However, she did make many rabbit friends, so I still consider the last few years of her life meaningful to her.

But sometimes even the possibility of having friends of one's own kind is too stressful for rabbits who have spent their entire lives in an isolated cage. These rabbits may present signs of trauma such as a thin appearance, poor hair quality, scars and wounds from fighting (or being bullied), a hunched posture, a lack of appetite, and an inability to relax completely. In these cases, I do intervene and provide these rabbits with a different environment to live in, where they may live with just one gentle rabbit, rather than a whole group.

In general, when a rabbit arrives who has lived in a captive situation where most or all of his or her life was beyond his or her control, I try to place as much control as possible back into the rabbit's paws, as it were. This gives them confidence and takes away some of their fear. That means that I try to give them the freedom to play where they want—during the day, they can play indoors or outdoors, in most any weather. Even when it snows, some of the bolder rabbits will venture outdoors to frolic in the fresh snow. They can nibble on hay throughout the day, they can lie wherever they like (as long as whoever is already there will let them), and they can play with whatever toys they like. They can modify their environment as they like—the cardboard and wood and wicker is theirs to tear apart any way they like, and rabbits can spend hours "decorating" their things to suit their desires.

Even the disabled rabbits that I live with are given as much freedom as possible; I have specially made carts that rabbits with little or no use of their rear legs can use to roll around the house, and I have seen their confidence soar once they begin using the cart. For instance, the first time I ever used a cart for a disabled rabbit was for a little Holland lop named Mrs. Bean. Mrs. Bean was paralyzed after being mishandled at an animal shelter and arrived at my house frustrated and full of rage. Worse yet, Mrs. Bean took her anger out on Hopper, a little bed-bound Dutch rabbit who I thought she could befriend, since he was disabled like her; instead, because she was so angry, she chewed on him constantly. Even though I tried to monitor their activities, I kept finding Hopper with scabs on his back and legs from Mrs. Bean's bites. What finally changed their relationship was when I purchased the cart for Mrs. Bean. Mrs. Bean took

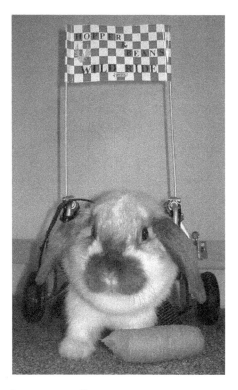

Mrs. Bean, courtesy of Margo DeMello

to it immediately, rolling around my house when I was home, and accompanying me to my job. At work, I would strap her into the cart and she spent the day visiting my coworkers and lounging with the office dog, Ty. As soon as Mrs. Bean got her freedom back, she began to soften in her behavior towards Hopper (whom she still slept with when not in the cart) and her chews and bites soon turned into licks.

Most importantly, freedom and control means that the rabbits can pick whatever friends they want. With friendship comes social support, and ultimately for most rabbits, that's what heals their trauma. Domestic rabbits who live with other rabbits often spend much of the day together—they'll eat together, sleep together, groom together, play together, even hop in the litter box at the same time to poop together.

Finally, like most people who live with companion animals, I talk to the rabbits. Rabbits who live in a lab or a rabbitry are rarely spoken to. We know that talking to nonhuman animals serves as a way to bond the human to the animal, to incorporate the animal into the human's social world, and allows for the human to talk *about* the animal as well, which is another way of making that animal family. Rabbits who do not live in a home with people are typically excluded from such communication, so talking to them is an important way of relating to them and interacting with them that feels good to the person, but also to the animal too. In addition, seeing and reading how rabbits communicate—with their ears, their noses, their tails, their bodies—and responding to their needs is a way to respect them. When we can understand, even to a limited extent, what rabbits are saying to us, we can then give them what they need, which will go a long way towards making them feel like their interests matter.

I also try to respond to rabbits in kind—by using their communication styles, as much as possible, to reach out to them on their own terms. I often lie on the ground to talk gently to Roxie, a big Californian rabbit who lives in my guest room because she's too fearful to live with the large group of rabbits. Lying on the rug in her room seems to soothe her, so I try to spend a few minutes every day on the rug with her.

STIMPY

Stimpy was a New Zealand rabbit—an albino rabbit, the most commonly used breed in laboratories around the world. Besides all the other factors that make rabbits popular "research tools" (like their short gestation cycle, gentle temperaments, the ease of drawing their blood, their sensitivity to teratogens, and the fact that they are induced ovulators), albino rabbits are especially popular because the lack of pigment in the eyes and lack of tear flow makes the eyes more sensitive to testing chemicals and products in the eyes.

Stimpy spent most of his life in a steel metal box in a Bay Area laboratory. I never found out the name of the lab; it was one of the conditions of his release—that the lab be kept anonymous. After the first year, his keepers judged his usefulness to be over. But rather than euthanize him, as is the usual practice, they decided to keep Stimpy indefinitely, in case they ever needed to use him again. He lived, alongside five other rabbits in three metal boxes just like his, in a darkened room, without contact with humans or other animals, for five more years.

An animal control officer ultimately found the rabbits in their dark steel boxes. Charging the facility with animal cruelty, she brought the rabbits to the local humane society, where they were picked up by two House Rabbit Society fosterers. Stimpy, who came to live with me, was the only survivor of the small group.

Stimpy had permanent muscle and nerve damage thanks to his lifetime of captivity and isolation and battled upper respiratory infections constantly, yet he lived with me for over three years. He had a large indoor cage that he shared with three other rabbits—two boys and a girl (all spayed and neutered)—and every day he went out into the backyard to chew on the grass, lounge in the sun, and dig holes in the dirt with his friends.

It's been a long time since Stimpy lived with me and since he died, when he was ten years old. I still remember the funny way he walked (rather than hopped), like an old hunched-back man, and the way his eyes were sort of hooded, and how poorly he could see. But I wonder now what it was like for him, when he first arrived at my house after all those years in the dark, and when he first got to see the sun. I lived in Davis, California, at the time, and it was sunny almost every day. The backyard was big and the grass was green and the rabbits loved going out to play every day. What could he possibly have thought about his new life, and his new friends, and the big blue sky and the soft green grass?

I wish now that I had spent more time watching Stimpy and paying attention as he transitioned from his life of isolation and horror—because it really must have been like a nightmare, every single day, living in that small cage in that dark room—to this vast new life full of birds and butterflies and bees. I was grateful that Stimpy got out, for sure, but didn't really think enough about how much it impacted him, and how enormously his life had changed. But I do know that it did.

Stimpy, like Mama before him, was lucky. He got out of the lab and was able, before he died, to run and jump, to groom another rabbit and be groomed, to taste grass and dig in the dirt, to feel the sun and sniff the breeze, to do rabbit things and feel rabbit pleasures. All the enrichment in the world won't provide rabbits living in laboratories, or in meat, fur, or pet rabbit facilities, with these pleasures.

RABBIT CAPTIVITY IN THE FUTURE

Thanks to the work of advocacy groups like House Rabbit Society, in the future, companion rabbits will be kept as house rabbits far more frequently than in the past. While it may not disappear, the "hutch rabbit" will become associated with ignorance and poverty, much like the backyard chained dog.

In biomedical research and product testing, the number of rabbits used will continue to drop, at least a bit, simply because alternative methods of testing will become more widely accepted and because mice and rats, exempt from the Animal Welfare Act, will be used in greater numbers.

While fur sales have been declining for years, especially on the high end of the trade, rabbit fur is the fastest growing segment of the global fur industry. Because rabbits are inexpensive to raise, rabbit fur products are considered "fun furs," and are used as trim on clothing, toys, or craft items, or are marketed towards younger consumers with limited spending power. Rabbits living on massive fur farms then, perhaps as many as a billion a year globally, will continue to suffer enormously as long as this market continues.

Finally, the world's appetite for rabbit meat is also growing. While in the United States rabbit meat was once a food item of the poor, it is now becoming a gourmet food, found in high-end restaurants. In addition, in recent years, as the local food and urban farming movements have taken off in North America, rabbits have found themselves at the center of these overlapping movements. Ironically, even while some Americans still struggle with eating "Peter Rabbit," others happily take classes where they learn to slaughter and butcher their own rabbit, which some are calling the "food of the future."

This, then, is the irony of the rabbit. At the same time that the house rabbit movement has emerged and picked up steam, with tens of thousands of people in North America (and around the world) realizing that rabbits are intelligent, loving, interesting companion animals who can share our homes and our lives the way other companion animals do, the locavore movement has also arrived, and with it the idea that the rabbit is the new superfood—small, easy to raise, apparently tasty, and easy to kill (thanks to the complete lack of federal or state regulation). Even as more rabbits gain freedom in our homes, more rabbits will find themselves caged in our yards, living their lives in small hutches until their three months are up, when they are slaughtered as the "new white meat."

REFERENCES

Batchelor, G. R. 1991. "Group Housing on Floor Pens and Environmental Enrichment In Sandy Lop Rabbits." *Animal Technology: Journal of the Institute of Animal Technicians* 42(2): 109–120.

Boers, K., et al. 2002. "Comfortable Quarters for Rabbits in Research Institutions." In *Comfortable Quarters for Laboratory Animals*, Viktor Reinhardt and Annie Reinhardt (eds.), 43–49. Washington, DC: Animal Welfare Institute.

Davis, Susan, and Margo DeMello. 2003. *Stories Rabbits Tell: A Natural and Cultural History of a Misunderstood Creature*. New York: Lantern Books.

Fuentes, Gabriela, and James Newgren. 2008. "Physiology and Clinical Pathology of Laboratory New Zealand White Rabbits Housed Individually and in Groups." *Journal of American Association for Laboratory Animal Science* 47(2): 35–38.

Heath, M., and E. Scott 1990. "Housing Rabbits the Unconventional Way." *Animal Technology: Journal of the Institute of Animal Technology* 41(1): 13–26.

Huls, W. L., D. L. Brooks, and D. Bean-Knudsen 1991. "Response of Adult New Zealand White Rabbits to Enrichment Objects and Paired Housing." *Laboratory Animal Science* 41(6): 609–612.

International Fur Trade Today. "We Are Fur." Accessed February 11, 2013.

Lebas, F., et al. 1997. *The Rabbit: Husbandry, Health, and Production*. Rome: Food and Agriculture Organization of the United Nations.

Love, J. 1994. "Group Housing: Meeting the Physical and Social Needs of the Laboratory Rabbit." *Laboratory Animal Science* 44: 5–11.

Podberscek, A. L., J. K. Blackshaw, and A. W. Beattie. 1991. "The Behavior of Group Penned and Individually Caged Laboratory Rabbits." *Applied Animal Behaviour Science* 28(4): 353–364.

United States Department of Agriculture Animal and Plant Health Inspection Service. 2010. "Animals Used in Research." Accessed February 11, 2013. http://www.aphis. usda.gov/animal_welfare/efoia/downloads/2010_Animals_Used_In_Research. pdf.

United States Department of Agriculture Animal and Plant Health Inspection Service. 2002. "Rabbit Industry Profile." Accessed February 11, 2013. http://www.aphis.usda. gov/animal_health/emergingissues/downloads/RabbitReport1.pdf.

Whary, M., R. Pepper, G. Borkowski, W. Lawrence, and F. Ferguson. 1993. "The Effects of Group Housing on the Research Use of the Laboratory Rabbit." *Laboratory Animal Science* 27: 330–341.

6

Captivity in the Context of a Sanctuary for Formerly Farmed Animals

MIRIAM JONES ■

ALBERT

Albert was a rooster who was born wild and lived wild on our grounds at VINE Sanctuary in Vermont. He slept up in one of the tallest pine trees on the property with about thirty other feral and wild birds, came down to eat and drink during the day, and generally lived exactly as he pleased. That all ended at some point in the second year of his life, when the people across the street threatened to murder him and his friends because they occasionally ventured into their yard. We held off the neighbors with a promise that we would have a stockade fence built within a couple of weeks. To keep Albert and about twelve other chickens safe until the fence was erected, we caught them and cooped them up in a small unused barn until the fence was complete. Unfortunately, during his time in the barn, Albert hurt his leg, and neither we nor the veterinarian could figure out what had happened; all we knew was that suddenly he was limping and could put no weight on the leg. We embarked upon a course of successive treatments, including wrapping his leg (no effect), giving him leg massages (no effect), and giving him cage rest (no effect). After about six weeks of cage rest we realized that if he was going to heal, it would not come from living in a cage. We decided to release him to the "sick bay," a quiet yard with just one other rooster—an older ex-cockfighter who doesn't bother too much with young upstarts anymore—and a few older and/or previously injured hens.

For the first two weeks, Albert did nothing but eat, drink, and sit, watchful, alongside the fence. When he walked, he limped, and it was increasingly clear that his leg was atrophying to a degree that would most likely be irreversible. Over time, Albert wandered about the yard more, and even interacted with some of the hens who lived there, but he was never the same as he had been when he was wild and living as he pleased with his wild friends. After a few months, we found Albert dead one morning in the coop. He had had no sickness or injury other than his chronic leg issue (which in most other birds is quickly overcome). He had not declined in any noticeable way, nor had his behavior changed in those few weeks. Moreover, he was young—a born-wild chicken who should have lived ten to fifteen years, easily. Why did he die? It was clear to me that once he finally accepted he would never walk well again— that he would never be free again—his life simply wasn't worth living, and so he died.

I begin with Albert because his particular situation reverses the normal order of things for us at VINE Sanctuary. Usually we accept animals from various captive situations and introduce them to lives that, while still technically captive for most of them, are as "free feeling" as we can make them. For the chickens in particular, the yards are large and include trees, bushes, shelters, rocks, and other things that they find interesting to explore, climb upon, or hide under. Every chicken yard has places that are free from snow in the winter and shaded from sun in the summer. We make sure all of the chickens have enough variety in their diets, treat their illnesses and injuries as they arise (and as we are able, as some chicken illnesses are mysterious to doctors and/or impervious to treatment), and otherwise we leave them alone. Way back when the egg factory farms were releasing spent hens to anyone who would pay for them, we found that even these individuals—arguably the most tormented of farmed animals in terms of both the length and the conditions of their captivity—are able to make the psychological journey from enslaved to free within a reasonable amount of time. VINE generally accepts animals who have been caged and offers them freedom; with Albert, that order was reversed. I am convinced that his death was related to his captivity.

Certainly, true freedom escapes almost all farmed or formerly farmed animals. We use the term "as free as possible" deliberately, as fences, enforced routines, involuntary medical procedures and regimes (including everything from forced sterilization to force feeding), and other impositions certainly do not comprise a free state of being for those on the receiving end. Those of us in the sanctuary movement routinely make decisions about the animals in our care (and under our control) that we, as ethical individuals, should find extremely problematic. How can one justify taking the reproductive ability away from another individual? How about taking the possibly-fertilized eggs of a broody hen, or penning up an active cow in a stall because she needs rest for an injury? The answer is simple: we justify these decisions because the alternatives are unacceptable. We live in a world that requires the rescue of members of certain species because other members of our own species will hurt and kill them if we don't; we do what we need to do, as ethically as possible, within the context of that reality. We also know—those of us who work with formerly farmed animals—that for most of them, survival on their own is an impossible goal. So-called broiler chickens, for example, are genetically engineered to reach slaughter weight at six weeks of age (i.e., when they are still babies), are bright white (not exactly easy to camouflage), have internal organs that cannot keep up with their massive preprogrammed weight gain, have legs that will not hold their weight once they reach a certain size, and have thin skin (the kind humans like to eat), which rips at the slightest provocation. They and most other farmed animals have no chance at all on their own, and so their only choices are death or captivity.

MAINTAINING CONTRADICTIONS

For these and other reasons, liberationist-oriented sanctuary workers such as myself continue to keep animals captive even while we deplore captivity. Given this troubling dichotomy—that is to say, given that we willingly do something in the smaller picture which we know to be unethical in the bigger one—we rely upon a combination of acquired knowledge and continuous observation to ensure that we do not stray from our self-defined purpose, which is to offer formerly farmed animals a chance to live life as much on their own terms as possible; to allow them to sustain a reasonable quality of life the conditions of which vary from species to species, type to type, and individual to individual. Acquired knowledge comes from a variety of sources, including accumulated information from veterinary visits, information shared with other sanctuary workers, as well as articles and books. Such knowledge is most helpful in times of injury or illness. Continuous observation, on the other hand, is a more powerful tool when ensuring that life in captivity resembles, to the furthest possible extent, life in freedom, for as many individuals as possible. It also helps us to ensure that life in captivity is meaningful for as many individuals as possible, as they themselves find meaning, even if their freedoms are restricted.

What does continuous observation entail? To start, the observer needs a baseline. Chickens of all types (whether "meat" or "egg") show interest in life by walking around, scratching at the ground, eating and drinking, making a wide variety of noises, flapping their wings and/or flying, exploring their environments, running after such things as eggs and bugs, laying eggs and/or getting broody (for some, that is to say—not all hens want babies), having sex (for some), climbing on various objects, expressing anger or distress at actions they find unacceptable (such as being picked up for medical care), sitting quietly next to one or more fellow birds, showing interest in new arrivals, and performing other, similar, behaviors. They need chicken companions of both sexes, space, interesting things to get under and climb over, a combination of sun and shade, clean food and water (warm in the winter and cool in the summer), and a clean shelter at night. These are baseline requirements that help inspire baseline positive behaviors. One need not ascribe any meaning to these behaviors to determine that they indicate a healthy, high-functioning chicken individual (as we know them to be today).

Once established, however, the baseline is challenged almost daily. Some chickens roam as many acres as you give them, while others deliberately choose to spend their time in small yards they could leave if they wished. Some chickens (usually roosters) prefer to spend most of their time alone—in sight of other birds, but alone—while others are very much group-oriented individuals. Some hens are as placid as the stereotypical New England complacent breeder of chicks, while others regularly get into physical spats with other hens. I've seen roosters whose companions are several hens, roosters whose companion is one other rooster, and roosters who don't do well with anyone much except very young birds. Most hens are excellent mothers, but we've had a few "crack hens" (as we affectionately call them) who abandon their babies within a month or two (presumably when they are tired of caring for them). Albert, who started this chapter, slept outside in a tree through the highest winds and biggest snows, while BooBoo, a fourteen-year-old mini rooster, prefers to sleep inside under the wings of some of the larger hens.

Over time, as individual differences become more pronounced, it becomes easier to return to the baseline in a more informed fashion and learn (in a visceral sense) some of the universal indicators of well-being and ill-being, all the way down to the question of whether or not a chicken is eating or drinking. Such knowledge is especially useful when chickens lose the use of their legs, such as when they contract Marek's disease. If they cannot move, but are still interested in the world around them and continue to eat and drink, we have no reason to conclude that life is not worth living for them, just as we would not conclude the same thing about a human paraplegic. Every year for the past thirteen years I have watched and learned from these individuals—thousands of them—with one primary purpose in mind: to ensure that their lives in captivity are as rich and meaningful to them as possible. I have no desire for these individuals to be my companions, nor are they my surrogate babies (sentiments I have heard from many otherwise well-intentioned people over the years); they are people in their own right who, through deliberate human actions, ended up being (*a*) born, (*b*) exploited, neglected, or otherwise harmed, and (*c*) brought to our sanctuary. All of these things happened against their will. But again—given the alternative, which is either continued suffering and/or exploitation or death—life in the "fake freedom" of a sanctuary is ethical and justified.

Taking a more comprehensive look at the alternative is critical if one claims that sanctuary is an improvement upon it. It isn't too hard to tell from the behaviors of chickens upon their arrival here what their lives used to be like in exploitative captivity situations. Hens from egg factories are the most notorious in terms of their Holocaust-survivor-style appearance and behaviors. Emaciated, pale, and almost completely featherless, these hens can barely walk when they first encounter actual dirt under their feet. They take one tentative step after another, which makes sense given that for eighteen months or so they've never left the confines of a cage. They are extremely cautious around the other birds, and in fact sometimes that caution never leaves them; this is magnified in their fear of humans. Over time, their halting steps become more graceful, and some of them have even ended up sleeping in the trees; that transition can take between a couple of weeks to a couple of years, given how horribly compromised by captivity they are when they arrive.[1]

More birds are arriving at sanctuaries from backyard bird situations, a problem that is growing as people come to learn that caring for chickens can be messy, labor-intensive, and expensive, not to mention the problem that occurs when people order chicks through the mail and find out that biology mandates the existence of at least a few roosters. These birds tend to be less afraid of other birds and/or humans. When they arrive in a group, they usually continue to affiliate with the other birds with whom they came—sometimes for a week or two, and sometimes forever. They generally have not been severely confined, so they have fewer psychic shackles to shed. However, the fact that they tend to resist exploring more than a very small area outside their coops tells us they have never known freedom and, now that they have relative freedom, they are afraid of it.

"Broiler" birds (those raised for flesh) who are liberated from farming situations tend to be afraid of humans for quite some time after their arrival here. Some among the current group of birds whom we rescued from a Yom Kippur ritual still shriek after several months of living at the sanctuary when we help lift them into the coops if they cannot make it on their own (although others of them are happy to be held). Cockfighting hens are the closest to feral chickens, even more so than the roosters (as the roosters have been handled by humans far more than the hens), and tend to take to the trees almost immediately.[2] The roosters, on the other hand, are usually quite gentle with humans, although their terror of other roosters influences their behavior for quite some time until they learn they are not rewarded for fighting other roosters.[3] The emotional commonality across all of these initial behaviors is fear. Chickens are a courageous species, on the whole, and adapt to extreme changes far better than humans do, but one can see their acquired fears in the ways they curtail their movements, in the choices they make (or do not make), and in other behaviors.

Birds from these and other situations eventually shed most of the fear-based behaviors they acquire during their captivity. Some behaviors, as those of the broilers, or of many former egg factory inmates who never feel comfortable around humans, never go away. Such behaviors include running away from us whenever we walk around the yards, screaming when we pick them up for various reasons, and either posturing as if to attack us, or actually attacking us. Because humans have been the ones who have hurt all of the animals who live here, the human caretakers never impose ourselves upon them. If the birds want relationships with us, we are happy to cultivate those relationships; when they want to keep their distance, so do we, and only in extreme situations do we force contact (e.g., when they want to sleep under a bush and we know they will most likely die from predation if they do). We provide them with as much space as possible (for the roosters in particular, far more than is recommended even by sanctuary folks); we provide them with the basic essentials for living a meaningful life in the context of being a chicken; and we leave them alone unless and until they make it clear they want some attention from us. We want them to feel they are living their own natural lives even though most of them can never do so because of the limitations foisted upon them by human scientists and farmers.

This approach to working with liberated, formerly farmed animals is not necessarily that taken by other sanctuaries. Many advocate and cultivate far more contact-intense relationships between human workers and animal "residents." Everyone in those sanctuary situations has a human name, everyone is handled by humans more than just for bare necessity, and none of the chickens are allowed to sleep in trees or otherwise (re)learn wild/feral behaviors. We at VINE do not condemn such approaches, but neither do we feel compelled to adopt them ourselves. We generally believe that, with chickens particularly, part of making a captive situation feel less captive is by allowing captives as great a degree of choice as possible within the context of captivity. Thus, except in cases of necessity, contact with humans is their choice, not ours.

All told, there are two primary things that make captivity in the context of sanctuary ethical. First is our continual observation of their behaviors, both upon their arrival and through their lifespan, which helps to ensure that their sanctuary-based captivity is as "free feeling" as possible. Second is our intentionality. We believe that in the context of an ideal world—one in which all animals were free to live their lives as they chose—our work would be unethical.

Regardless of how close we may feel to many of the individuals who pass through these figurative doors, we know that it would be better for most of them to have never existed, given how genetically altered and unhealthy chickens now are, and given that 99.9 percent of their counterparts will never know anything except exploitation, suffering, and untimely death during their tenure on this planet. Put simply, we know that what we do is not the same thing as providing actual freedom to the people who live here. It is this knowledge, on top of our watchfulness, that helps to ensure the animals who live here are as insulated from a captive state of being as possible.

Captivity that is imposed upon individuals for the sake of (animal) agriculture or other exploitative ventures, however, has no justification. Whether or not such enforced captivity (commonly and euphemistically referred to as "domestication") was ever necessary for our survival or otherwise ethical thousands of years ago when it began is a moot point—one to be argued about for the sake of entertainment or historical curiosity, perhaps, but certainly not germane to our world as it is today. The fact is that it is not necessary today, and in fact is counterproductive to an unhealthy world undergoing climate change. Beyond the question of necessity, however, rests another issue: the bizarre

Courtesy of Jo-Anne McArthur, *We Animals*

nature of captivity for food. The concept of farming animals—of breeding animals into captivity and keeping them there while they are used and/or until they are killed for their flesh or skin—is extremely odd when considered in the context of a world with no property lines, no national borders, and, in general, little to nothing in the way of ownership. So when did it begin? Who came up with the idea of domesticating nonhuman animals in the first place?

A SHORT HISTORY OF THE DOMESTICATION OF CHICKENS

While there is some dispute as to the exact origins of modern chickens (i.e., whether they all descended from the wild jungle fowl of Southeast Asia or whether they had multiple progenitors), most scientists believe they were first domesticated between 8,000 and 10,000 years ago (Potts 2012, 4). This timeline establishes chickens as one of the earliest animals to be domesticated, along with sheep and goats, who were domesticated around 10,000 years ago (Mench, 2009, 121). The first remains of domesticated chickens were found in what are now China and Pakistan, and date from 7,500 years ago (Potts 2012, 4). By 3000 BCE, domesticated chickens had been introduced in Russia, Turkey, and parts of eastern Europe; throughout most of Europe by 500 BCE; and to North America by about 1100 AD (Potts 2012, 4). Egypt in particular ramped up not only the domestication of the chicken, but also the industrialization of same; Smith and Daniel (2000, 14–16) describe enormous incubators capable of hatching 10,000 to 15,000 thousand chicks at once, heated by fires that were kept at a constant (and ideal) 105 degrees Fahrenheit. Their feats regarding the industrialization of chickens for their eggs and flesh were unmatched until fifty years ago, and were closely tied to the need to feed a large (and also captive) workforce that was busy building pyramids and other state-initiated projects.

Fast forward to the eighteenth and nineteenth centuries, when, in the United States and Europe particularly, the scientific revolution was gaining adherents among the class of "learned gentlemen" who, among other things, turned their attention to "the chicken" (Smith and Daniel 2000, 204). Given that, since their domestication, chickens had long been regarded as objects to use and/or dispose of as we wished, it is easy and natural to see how they became objects of interest to these amateur scientists. Breeding was especially popular, particularly as Asiatic breeds were imported from China (Smith and Daniel 2000, 205), and breeders soon were divided into two camps: those who bred chickens for show and fun, creating new breeds one after another, and those who bred them for business and profit. Those in the latter group eventually won out over the former; as Smith and Daniel (2000, 232) note,

By the end of the nineteenth century the national preoccupation with chickens had induced many farmers substantially to increase the size of their flocks and the proportion of their incomes derived from the sale of eggs and chickens. . . . Chickens that had ranged the barnyard and the farm found themselves confined in large outdoor areas, their activities and their output, once natural and uninhibited, now increasingly controlled.

Of course, one may strongly disagree that chickens' "output" was ever natural and uninhibited once humans took control of their lives, but the salient point here is that the captivity of chickens took a great leap forward in terms of intensity. It was only a matter of time before this happened; the joint demands of capitalism and human-centrism mandate that the trajectory of "progress" always moves toward more and bigger, all costs to everyone else be damned. It was inevitable, given this perspective, that someone would discover the incubator—that it would catch on (in the 1880s, in Petaluma, California, spurred by a farmer named Christopher Nisson)—and that increasing numbers of humans would take the process of creating baby chickens into their own hands as they had done with other aspects of chickens' lives (Smith and Daniel 2000, 235–236). Hens were no longer seen as thrifty God-fearing animals to be admired (even as they were held captive and killed at will), but rather as egg-churning machines who existed to turn a profit for their owners. This new approach to the farming of eggs took another giant leap forward during the Great Depression when people discovered that the rate of egg laying by chickens is related to light (Smith and Daniel 2000, 264). It was this discovery that propelled the captivity of chickens from the confinement of yards toward the captivity of cages.

In the 1950s and 1960s, Kimber Farms (yesterday's equivalent of Perdue Chicken) continued and accelerated the push toward the mechanization of chickens (Smith and Daniel 2000, 279). The work done by their geneticists to produce a hen who could lay far more eggs in a year than previous hens were able to do (250 for the "newly improved" hens, as opposed to 160 for the previous "models") may seem like a shocking deviation from humans' previous "relationship" with chickens, but in fact there was nothing surprising about it. While there might be a sort of romantic haze hovering over the breeding programs of the genteel amateur scientists of the Victorian era, that haze has everything to do with our own beliefs in our right to control and make captive individuals from other species, and nothing to do with the reality of the situation; the reality that dictates that once one justifies keeping animals captive, the only obstacles to further control are current levels of science and technology. In other words, our Victorian gentlemen would have been building artificial wombs and splicing spider genes into goats had those abilities been developed in their time. Kimber's contributions to the world of poultry spurred other developments as well, including the splitting of chickens into egg-laying and meat birds (Smith and Daniel 2000, 280), the "improvement" of meat birds such that they could be slaughtered as early as seven weeks of age (Smith and Daniel 2000, 282), and the futuristic factory-style slaughterhouses in which chickens are hung upside down by their feet, dunked in electrified water, run past whirring blades to have their throats cut, and bled out as they have their feathers plucked from them by mechanical fingers, often while they are still alive (Smith and Daniel 2000, 283).

It didn't take long for these developments to translate into an almost exponential growth in chicken-related "output." In 2012, egg producers the world over produced 65 million tons of eggs (Global Poultry Trends 2013), and chicken meat farmers produced 104.5 million tons of flesh (FAO 2012). Both of these figures are expected to rise in coming years. All of this, of course, was made possible by the initial acceptance of captivity as an ethical state of being. The vast underlying commonality among all of these ventures—from the great incubators of Egypt to the killing blades of Perdue—is the belief that it is ethically acceptable for humans to confine certain animals for our own purposes. But is it ever ethical to hold anyone captive?

CAN CAPTIVITY EVER BE AN ETHICAL CHOICE?

Most people who are animal liberationist in spirit get very simplistic when answering this question. We are speaking here of the actual lives of actual individuals: tens of billions of chickens, pigs, cows, sheep, goats, and many more nonhuman animal species who languish under the bonds of captivity. Countless billions of individuals from these species over the past several thousand years have seen their lives begin and end in captivity. They are not abstract theories bandied about, nor are they interesting ideas to trade over beer or coffee. Their lives—for we can all agree that they have lives, that they live and breathe, feel pain and fear, express a range of behaviors and emotional states, and so forth— are real and tangible. Therefore, what matters to them in the context of this particular debate (i.e., whether or not it is ethical to place nonhuman animals into captivity) are the actions we as humans take toward them. Emotions and ideas don't count for much when regarding the lives of actual individuals. For example, I may profess to love animals, but if I hurt them through my actions, my love means little.

Making this question of animal captivity more difficult for many humans are diverging opinions about such things as whether or not the sentience of creatures is significant when regarding their right to live life on their own terms, whether or not nonhuman animals possess culture and other supposedly "human" attributes (and whether the answer to this question matters in terms of their right to live free), and whether the reason for their captivity (i.e., for their sake or ours) is relevant to the fact of their captivity. Certainly, endless hours have been spent, and countless pages have been written, debating these and other questions. Many people tend to believe that the answers to these questions should hold all of the weight in this conversation; that is to say, such people tend to believe, for example, that proving that birds are intelligent (in the way most humans in the developed world have defined intelligence) should and will pave the way to more "humane" treatment of bird individuals. They tend to see this issue of animal captivity as complex, fraught with intricate layers, worthy of research followed by contemplation on said research followed by more studies and yet more contemplation.

I, however, being the cofounder of an animal sanctuary in Vermont, am on the front lines of animal care in a liberationist perspective. Over time, as I have observed chickens and many other formerly farmed animals, I have become increasingly stark in my beliefs and thinking about these issues. While I completely agree that life itself—the vast biosphere in which all living and nonliving beings interact in virtually infinite ways—is incomprehensibly complex, I have come to see that the ethics of our actions within that biosphere are not particularly complicated. After all, at this point in time, many humans agree that certain human-on-human actions are ethically objectionable (e.g., rape or child abuse) regardless of attempted justifications that rely upon cultural (or other) contexts, so why can we not agree that certain human-on-nonhuman actions are equally unsupportable?

Captivity for the sake of exploitation is one such unsupportable action. It is never ethical to place an individual of any species in captivity for any purpose other than the sole reason of protecting said individual. Moreover, it is unethical to place any individual in captivity if there exists another way to grant both freedom and a reasonable measure of safety to said individual. We must finally realize that chickens (and all other farmed animals) are individuals, people of other species, folks who, like everyone else on the planet, want to live their lives on their own terms within the boundaries of the ecosystems that have developed to support them. They no more choose captivity than individuals of the human species. It is time to allow people like Albert the freedom to live life on their own terms. As much as I love having the privilege of working and living around so many individuals of other species, it is more than time to put sanctuary workers like me out of commission by rendering obsolete the reasons for our work.

NOTES

1. It should be noted that hens from egg factories are almost impossible to rescue any longer, since owners of such factories don't want consumers to know how poorly they treat their "happy hens."

2. Feral chickens are increasingly common in many places, including Key West and New Orleans. They are descendants of domesticated chickens who have gotten free, been thrown out of their captive enclosures, or otherwise found themselves free to live in the unused spaces of human civilization.

3. For a complete explanation of the pioneering method VINE developed to rehabilitate fighting cocks, as well as other relevant information about cockfighting, please visit this URL: http://vine.bravebirds.org/projects/rooster-rehab/.

REFERENCES

FAO. 2012. Food Outlook: Global Market Analysis. Accessed December 9, 2013, http://www.fao.org/docrep/016/al993e/al993e00.pdf

Global Poultry Trends: World Egg Production Sets a Record Despite Slower Growth. Accessed December 9, 2013, http://www.thepoultrysite.com/articles/2653/global-poultry-trends-world-egg-production-sets-a-record-despite-slower-growth

Mench, J. A. 2009. "Behavior of Fowl and Other Domesticated Birds," In *The Ethology of Domestic Animals: An Introductory Text*, 2nd edn., Per Jensen (ed.). Oxfordshire, UK: CAB International, 121–136.

Potts, Annie. 2012. *Chicken*. London: Reaktion Books.

Smith, Page, and Charles Daniel. 2000. *The Chicken Book*. Athens: University of Georgia Press.

7

Life Behind Bars

JOHN BRYANT, JAMES DAVIS, DAVID HAYWOOD,
CLYDE MEIKLE, AND ANDRE PIERCE ■

Many people consider prisons necessary tools of punishment. We—poor African American (Ebony) men—consider them weapons of mass destruction. They are destructive to our families, whose economic hardship is often worsened in our absence. They are destructive to our children, who are placed at greater risk of succumbing to a host of social problems in our absence. They are destructive to our selves, because they are not designed to rehabilitate. Instead, prisons allow us to linger in a broken state. They are destructive to our communities in that they perpetuate the streets-to-prison, prison-to-streets, streets-to-prison pipeline.

We are experiencing the forces of this destruction today, but the destructive power has historical roots. After the constitutional end of slavery, prisons became a de facto form of slavery (Alexander, 2010). Through convict lease programs, former slave owners leased the labor of prisoners in southern states; around the country prisoners were forced to work on chain gangs to help build the country's infrastructure. In the middle to late twentieth century, the prison system of mass destruction was systematically deployed against men of color; this period marked a "racialization of crime" in which men of color were targeted and punished much more severely than whites for committing similar infractions. According to Douglas Massey (Massey, 2007), the war on crime (in the 1960s) and the war on drugs (in the 1980s) were essentially wars waged against poor Ebony men—us.

Massey argues that the rise in our incarceration rate did not necessarily correlate with rising crime rates. He suggests that poor men of color were incarcerated at such high rates due to racist policies and racial profiling. For the sake of argument, were we to assume that our high incarceration rate did correlate with high crime rates in communities of color, we nonetheless question the logic of fighting crime with destructive weapons rather than employing more effective methods such as drug rehabilitation programs, educational and economic opportunities, and job training and placement. That prisons are the weapon of choice belies a deeper, structural commitment, to keep poor black men as second-class citizens who are irredeemable and thus need to be removed from society for its own protection.

Though we ourselves made bad choices, we, like many rational people, believe that crime must be punished. However, we object to punitive captivity (prisons) that historically and presently are used against us as a form of discrimination while causing so much destruction to our families and communities. In this chapter we will discuss one of the central causes of criminal activities, describe the conditions of our captivity, and reflect on the ethical issues that mass incarceration raises.

SOCIAL FACTORS THAT LEAD TO CRIME AND INCARCERATION

There is a wide range of complex social factors that lead to crime and consequently incarceration. We will explore one of the root causes of crime as it relates to street culture. Street culture represents crime as a lifestyle. It is marked by drug dealing and drug use, gang and gun violence, and black-on-black crime. This street culture has been in the making for nearly four centuries—it began with slavery, was deepened further by structural racial discrimination and segregation, and has been maintained and reinforced through political, social, and economic disenfranchisement. Excluding people of color, particularly men of color, from three important institutions laid the foundation for street culture. First, there is exclusion from and discrimination in political institutions and electoral processes that prevent us from engaging in politics. Failure to have a voice in the political process means that our communities are unable to make elected officials aware of and take an interest in our specific community needs. Exclusion from and discrimination in educational institutions hinders our intellectual development, which in turn limits our ability to critically assess our conditions and develop courses of action to alter and improve our situations. Exclusion from and discrimination in the job market hinders us from earning money and accumulating wealth that could be passed on to our children. This limitation produces intergenerational poverty. Overall, our exclusion from and discrimination in political, social, educational, and economic institutions produces a group of people who are voiceless, intellectually stagnant, and impoverished. It is in this deteriorated and powerless state that crime is able to sprout roots. Due to our economic hardships, crime became a means to minimize economic suffering. Due to our poor intellectual development, we did not question or critically challenge our criminal thinking and values. Due to our disenfranchisement, we had no reason to believe that the resources needed to combat our deteriorated state would be forthcoming. Desensitization to the deterioration allows a street culture of crime to take hold.

Given that prison is the response to crime, our desensitization amounts to an acceptance of incarceration as part of street culture. We expect to go to prison. Once we internalize the streets-to-prison pipeline, and in the absence of institutions to counter the narrow and warped values reinforced in street culture, that culture defines and confines our worldviews and identities. The street culture also takes on a glamour and style that lure impressionable youth in our communities. For some readers this will sound like the logical theory of the cause of crime. For many urban poor, we are describing their reality—our reality.

THE CONDITIONS OF CONFINEMENT

Prisons are dominating structures that emasculate us upon our admission. The emasculation takes the form of an inspection of our genitals as well as a cavity search. In many cases we are having our bodies inspected by guards we see on a daily basis. It is hard to look a guard in the eye who has just performed a cavity search and not feel humiliated. Strip searches are routinely performed twice a year in addition to times when there are suspicions that a prisoner has contraband.

Some prisoners accept these degrading strip searches as a matter of routine. They have become desensitized to humiliation. Perhaps the lack of indignation results from being accustomed to domination. Many of us come from aggressive communities that have an increased police presence. The police tend to respond to aggression with equal, often indiscriminate, aggression. Many of us have experienced or witnessed excessive police force. It is possible that those prisoners who have grown to tolerate humiliation have done so due to exposure to domineering and humiliating police presence in their communities.

We caution that there is a danger of accepting domination. One risk is being crushed in spirit, allowing domineering prison practices to destroy or weaken our will. This in turn diminishes our sense of autonomy and, in the worst cases, causes our hopes and dreams to die. Our identities can be destroyed by having our individuality replaced with a number, an abstract enumeration that can cause us to lose our sense of humanity.

We choose to remain steadfast in quiet and dignified resistance to domination. We keep our spirits strong by exercising our autonomy to the extent we can without opening ourselves to severe punishment or physical force from guards. We keep our identities intact by not losing a sense of humanity, despite dehumanizing treatment. We define who we are on our own terms. While we can increase our tolerance for humiliation, we will never accept degrading treatment and emasculating strip searches as a matter of routine. By allowing ourselves to experience the humiliation, we are reminded of our inherent dignity.

After our initial humiliation upon being strip-searched when we enter prison, we lose all control of our lives. We will eat, bathe, and shave when told. We will be expected to follow direct orders, no matter how absurd or unfair. Noncompliance will be met with force. Although we have lost near total control of our bodies, we have made a conscious effort to maintain control of our minds. We pursue intellectual endeavors as a means of freedom—freedom of thought. We try not to allow our conscious space to be filled with unproductive prison concerns. We will not eat, dream, and breathe prison.

Privacy in prison is rare. We are housed either in a loud and crowded dormitory or in a cell with another person we probably don't know and may not like. A cell transfer is at the discretion of guards, and some guards will bluntly tell two quarrelling "cellies" that if they want a cell transfer, then fight it out. The implications being that if the guard is going to make a transfer, it will be to put the prisoner in "the hole"—or solitary confinement.

Our every movement is watched or recorded. As we walk through the halls, guards stare. As we eat, they hover. As we talk on the phone, they listen. When we are not under the steady gaze of a guard, we are being recorded by cameras. One prisoner described it as "stalking." We are never at ease at night knowing that every thirty minutes a guard is going to peer into our cells, blinding us with a flashlight. It is not that difficult to imagine what we experience. Just imagine while relaxing in the comfort and privacy of your bedroom, a police officer, or anyone really, suddenly shining a light in your bedroom window to watch you. Now imagine that happening all day and all night.

Our loss of privacy is coupled with the presence of constant noise. It seems that every minute of every day there is a toilet flushing or an announcement over the loudspeaker, or music blaring from someone's headphones, or the television blaring, or cell doors opening and closing, or the deafening sound of a smoke alarm triggered by steaming hot showers, or an unnecessarily loud conversation, or a rowdy or bored prisoner screaming out of his cell or across the dorm, or a guard's keys jingling as he make his rounds. The omnipresent noise is more than an inconvenience. It disturbs our meditations and chases away our private thoughts, replacing them with sonic clutter. In order to engage in introspection, to critically reflect, a certain degree of uninterrupted silence is necessary. The constant noise limits our thought and restricts our imagination.

The loss of privacy and incessant noise is worse in the dorms. Prisons with cells provide moments of silence and a semblance of privacy. If given a choice, many will opt to be transferred to a prison with cells. However, there is a trade-off. Although dorms afford us zero privacy and silence, they provide us greater privileges and freedom of movement. On the other hand, cells provide more privacy and silence but limited privileges and movement. Those of us who cherish our privacy choose the cell over the dorms. However, there is a danger to living in a six- by nine-foot concrete box.

Cell confinement can last up to twenty-three hours a day. The minimal human contact and companionship go against our nature as social beings. The resulting loneliness can be so overwhelming that it sometimes causes depression. The inability to find any relief from the loneliness, as well as the mind-numbing boredom, is perhaps equivalent to being trapped in a sinking ship without any possibility of escape. It produces anxiety and helplessness. When our cell door closes, we often have little to do as we watch our sanity burn and spirit sink.

Our cognitive function is challenged because of extremely limited intellectual stimulation. Though we are allowed a certain amount of reading material in our cells, the depressive environment tends to stifle intellectual curiosity. We simply become too tired and sullen to engage in intellectual pursuits. Simply put, we dwell in our cells, we are not actively using our minds, and in a very real sense, we are thus losing our minds.

The loneliness caused by prisons in general and prison cells in particular is exacerbated by the loss of intimacy and the loving touch of friends and family. There seem to be increasing restrictions on visits, while their duration times decrease. There has been a long effort to do away with conjugal and family extended visits. Hand-holding during visits has been limited to a brief embrace at the beginning and end of a visit. Because visits are so closely monitored, we cannot feel a sense of real intimacy. The loss of intimacy and loving touch causes further destruction of our mental and emotional health.

In such a disempowering prison environment, we tend to form prison identities to counter the negative forces and use them to maintain dignity and self-respect. While some prisoners take pride in their outcast identity, they are the rebels who refuse to conform or be controlled; other prison identities represent different sorts of values and aspirations. Prison identities include "hustler," "prison scholar," "convict," "jailhouse lawyer," and even "hostage."

The term "hustler" is used by prisoners who have business savvy. They pride themselves on being able to thrive in prison without the reliance on money orders from friends and family and without an institutional job. Such jobs are scarce and pay less than a dollar per day. The hustler's motto is "The hustle don't stop"—they hustled on the streets and they aren't going to stop because they are locked up.

"Prison scholars" are the intellectuals among the prison population. After years, if not decades, of steady pursuits of knowledge, they are capable of holding in-depth discussions on topics that span philosophy, religion, politics, international relations, economics, and history. It is common to see prison scholars holding "ciphers" (a group of people having an intellectual conversation) and "building" (engaging in an intellectual conversation) with other prisoners about a wide range of thought-provoking topics. By widening the worldviews of other prisoners and increasing their learning, prison scholars may have an indirect positive impact on our communities, by enabling prisoners to return more learned. Although prison scholars are in the minority, their "light" is bright enough to prevent prisons from becoming an abyss of total ignorance.

The term "hostage" expresses an open acknowledgment that the prisoner is being held against his will. However, this term may convey much more. It seems to imply that the prisoner refuses to legitimize the authority of the prison institution. Being a member of a historically oppressed minority group, perhaps the hostage sees prisons as an arm of the oppressive government.

The term "convict" represents an old-school prisoner mentality that was more hostile to prison guards and more willing to challenge their authority and defy the rules. The old-school prisoners usually were first incarcerated in the 1980s and 1990s. They have a code of ethics that forbids fraternizing with prison guards or, as they say, "jeffing with the police." The convict mentality is usually contrasted with the "inmate" mentality. Convicts consider inmates the worst kind of prisoner, because inmates tend to capitulate to oppressive prison rules. Convicts often suspect inmates of being snitches. The contrast between convicts and inmates usually comes into play when prison administrations enforce a needlessly oppressive rule or take away dwindling privileges. Convicts will bemoan that inmates will not challenge the rule either through legal action, the grievance system, or by force. Such conversations tend to then turn to nostalgic reminiscing of how convicts controlled the prisons "back in the day."

The convict code of ethics and "convicts" themselves are becoming a relic of the past. This is likely due to the price extracted from being a convict. Their hostility towards guards and defiance of the rules are increasingly met with equal hostility from the guards. This sometimes results in convicts being harassed and removed from the general population and placed in the hole or transferred to supermax facilities. Supermax prisons have a reputation for breaking the most hardened prisoner by exposing him to long isolation, very little human contact, and sensory deprivation. When convicts return, they try to become invisible to guards because they do not want any more trouble. In a sense, they have become "tamed."

While "convicts" and "jailhouse lawyers" may be specifically targeted to be broken in spirit to soften their militancy, this breaking process seems to be the unstated purpose of captivity. Common features of prison life are part of this breaking process—long isolation, sensory deprivation or sensory overload, and harassment by guards in the form of property confiscation, job termination, and bogus disciplinary reports. It requires a certain degree of callousness on the part of the guards. They seek to break us, but by treating us as less than human, they lose part of their humanity as well.

For better or worse, the breaking process has had its intended effects. Many of us have become pacified and comply with the rules. The price for breaking the rules has become too high. For example, a fistfight used to be sanctioned with a week or two in segregation. Now a fistfight is treated as a felony, earning the fighters additional years on their sentences, a two-year loss of contact visits, and a week or two in the "hole" and the loss of other privileges. To avoid such excessive punishment, many of us comply with the rules. What has resulted is a prison that is relatively safe from physical violence. We would go as far as to say that some prisons are just as safe as your average middle-class neighborhood. But while this breaking process may have broken us into compliance and greater safety, it does not serve as rehabilitation. While we may appear "good," in many cases we have not become "good." This is obvious given recidivism rates. Once we are released, most of us return to crime. To make us "good," we need to be rehabilitated.

Unfortunately, rehabilitation is not the primary goal in today's prison. The stated goal is safety and security. Maintaining safety and security usually translates into our basic human rights being violated or restricted in order to maintain an orderly prison. Because rehabilitation is not a primary goal, halfhearted efforts, when made, are doomed from the start. For example, a crash course in a drug program is often an approach used to rehabilitate. But there is no serious effort to provide intervention to reform a behavior that many of us took years, sometimes decades, learning and crafting.

Whenever the few rehabilitation services are being offered to the general prison population, "lifers" tend to be the group of prisoners that many believe should be excluded. The rationale proffered is that such programs and services would better benefit those prisoners who would be re-entering society in the near future. While this argument has merit on its face, a more in-depth analysis exposes the fallacy.

Consider the following: After the initial shock of having received a life sentence, many lifers come to begrudgingly accept prison as their home. As a coping mechanism, they tend to formulate a routine that serves to provide their new life a certain degree of order, even meaning. To have their routine disrupted is to disrupt their life; it is no small matter. Thus, to maintain their order, a lifer will try to avoid disruptive and impermissible behavior as much as possible, albeit many will still have certain vices. Their discipline, permanency, and relatively positive behavior are influential in setting the prison culture. Their manner of doing time has a certain wisdom that earns them the accolades of "knowing how to bid." It is not uncommon to see the less disciplined and inexperienced prisoners picking up cues from lifers on how to bid. Furthermore, there is a certain deference given to lifers because it is understood that prison is their home. Because they have a great potential on setting prison culture, it would seem logical to provide lifers rehabilitation programs. In setting a positive prison culture, lifers can indirectly influence the communities that 95 percent of prisoners will eventually be released into.

Any serious attempt at rehabilitation must necessarily address the street culture that many of us came from. Like any other culture, it consists of a code of ethics, a code of conduct, taboos, title seeking, social ranks, and a particular way of speaking. This culture must be understood if it is to be effectively challenged. Understanding this culture requires more than academic research or scientific studies, even if such research serves certain purposes. Street culture must be made intelligible by the very people who are a part of it. Those people who have crept, crawled, and preyed in the dark underworld where this culture germinated and grows. This would include former drug dealers, drug addicts, thieves, gang members, prostitutes, even murderers.

If rehabilitation were to become the purpose of captivity, there must be a social investment in ex-prisoners. This would help ensure our productive participation in society. The social investment would entail a provision of job skills suitable for the increasingly technological job market. As it stands, we are released in society, *if* we are released, unprepared to compete for jobs that require specialized skills and knowledge.

Further, being treated as undesirables on a federal, state, and social level sometimes causes us to internalize the stigmatization, hostility, and lack of respect. We can become the monsters we are perceived to be. Ex-prisoners must be provided with the social basis of self-respect that John Rawls argued all citizens of a just society are due (Rawls, 1971). There must be a public commitment to the idea that we do not lose our status as citizens with a conviction for a crime. We believe in a democratic society; a criminal conviction warrants punishment, not the forfeiture or suspension of one's citizenship or one's value as a human being. Without such a public commitment, our reassimilation will be met with resistance, we will be treated as second-class citizens, and it is not a far step back to the streets-to-prison pipeline.

ETHICAL INCARCERATION?

Can incarceration ever be ethical? Prisons are not places that are concerned with the good of the captive prisoners in their charge. As we noted, to maintain

safety and security, our basic human rights are curtailed, our freedom of movement is restricted, we are subject to collective punishment and arbitrary interference, we are isolated and socially deprived. This is not good for us.

Incarceration is contrary to our nature as complex social creatures with emotional and intellectual needs. Prison rules, even if they do have a rational justification, have an adverse effect on our psychological and emotional states. When
we are held in isolation our well-being is undermined. Our social needs are
constantly thwarted in prison. Here is one example: guards spend limited time
with prisoners. Intellectually, this is done to prevent undue familiarity between
the guards and us. But on an emotional and psychological level, this makes us
feel as though we are perceived as having an inherent "badness" or criminality
that is contagious or corrupting to guards. This separation has lasting impact.

Even policies that seem innocuous have adverse effects on our mental states.
A case in point would be the straight yellow lines on the hallway floors. We
know intellectually they are meant to provide orderly mass movement in the
hallways. This knowledge does not provide comfort because of what the yellow
lines signify on a subtle level. We tend to move through the hallways in large
groups, yet we must huddle together in a three-foot-wide walking space. The
guards tend to move through the hall usually singly or in pairs, yet they have
nearly triple the width that we are allotted to walk through. This inequality is,
of course, uncomfortable, but there is more. We are being herded, flanked by
guards, like cattle. We are made to feel like the "other" who must be separated
from the "decent" folks with whom we share the same space. The significance
of this use of space, though meant to provide order, creates psychic disorder. It
fosters hostility and distrust and creates an environment in which neither prisoners nor guards can be their best selves.

Since we are wards of the state, the prison is responsible for providing our
basic needs. We are clothed, fed, and sheltered without any financial cost to us.
The danger of being cared for in this way as an adult is that we can be infantilized and we become dependent. This dependency, at times, may become
pathological and can lead to recidivism. When some prisoners are released,
they have become "institutionalized" and have a tenuous sense of responsibility, agency, and autonomy. In this infantilized state, we find it difficult to care
for ourselves. Institutionalized ex-prisoners sometimes place themselves in
high-risk situations to increase their chances of being rearrested and returned
"home." Some prisoners are psychologically so damaged by prison they are
unable to live outside.

That prisons are not designed to promote well-being and in some cases actually create psychological disorders suggests to us that incarceration in prison
is not ethical. It is also unlikely, on simple utilitarian grounds, that the alleged
goods to society are actually greater than the costs and harms of incarceration.

But even though we believe that incarceration itself cannot be ethical, the treatment of prisoners can be.

First, ethical treatment must begin with an acknowledgment of our dignity and a commitment to maintaining it. We are generally viewed as second-class citizens because of our status as convicted felons. Making a genuine effort to acknowledge and maintain our dignity would promote a change in prison rules, policies, and practices that would take account of their effects on our well-being, self-respect, and psychological states.

Rehabilitation should be more widely available and address individual prisoner's specific needs. We do not all have drug problems. Some of us commit crime out of economic hardship. Others have distorted values. For those of us raised in violent communities, we have become desensitized to violence. Each of these conditions requires different rehabilitative methods. Treating drug addiction, providing job skills, critical thinking skills, and skills for developing empathy, for example, by allowing us to hear the pain and suffering we have caused our victims and their loved ones, will help prisoners and society more broadly.

Ethical treatment of those who are incarcerated would promote the maintenance of families in an effort to prevent criminal behavior from becoming intergenerational. Our absence from our children's lives, particularly our sons, tends to place them at greater risk of succumbing to the norms of street culture. Our absence from our families' lives tends to increase economic hardships that are often already acute. To ease this hardship, prisoners ought to be allowed to earn a decent wage, particularly from institutional jobs that have private contractors, so we can provide our families with some financial assistance.

We are the best advocates for our rehabilitation needs and thus we should be enfranchised. Denying prisoners the right to vote not only denies us a voice, but further distances us from civic engagement. A rehabilitated ex-prisoner who is politically active in his community has a certain insight into the needs of blighted communities, given that they were once the cause of part of the blight. Enfranchising us can translate into our being positive active members of our communities.

CONCLUSION

A society is made orderly by establishing laws that maintain peace and protect its members' property and rights. Unfortunately, there will always be those who transgress the law. When the law is transgressed, justice will be sought. Historically, and to the present day, justice has usually meant punishment in some form. A society does itself a disservice when it seeks justice solely in the form of retribution. Prisons are a form of retribution and they provide fertile ground for the further development of criminal behavior. It is in prison where we network with other criminals, share tricks of the crime trade, and become more clever criminals. Once released, we will be akin to a cancer that metastasizes, spreading our crime to any area we find opportunity.

We are under no delusion. We know it is our depravity that society needs protection from. But our deviant state is not an essential part of who we are. In most cases its origin comes for socioeconomic disadvantages. As John Locke noted, justice must be sought when people break the law, but the law should be clear and the punishment fair (Somerville and Santoni 1963). In present conditions, we think this would require avoiding retribution and an investment in rehabilitation. We also think there should be prevention by way of social and economic investment in blighted communities: investment in quality education, investment in job skill training, investment in programs that seek to reform criminal behavior and stop it before it starts. Justice is not served when people are left behind to decay in prison cells where criminality itself is refined and reinforced.

ACKNOWLEDGMENT

We are grateful to Lori Gruen.

REFERENCES

Alexander, M. 2010. *The New Jim Crow: Mass Incarceration in the Age of Colorblindness*. New York: New Press.
Massey, D. 2007. *Categorically Unequal: The American Stratification System*. New York: Russell Sage Foundation.
Rawls, J. 1971. *A Theory of Justice*. Cambridge: Harvard University Press.
Somerville, J., and R. Santoni. 1963. *Social and Political Philosophy*. New York: Anchor.

8

Political Captivity

LAUREN GAZZOLA ◼

ZEN PRISONER

Ms. Barone processed me in. She retrieved me from the waiting room where, throughout the next forty months, my steadfast visitors would wait to be granted entry, by way of a metal detector, to another room: sparse, with little more than rows of airport chairs and some vending machines, the only place where I could be seen in the flesh.

"Have you been in prison before?" Ms. Barone asked.
"Not really."
"You seem very calm."
And I was.

This surprised me too. I am not exactly known for my unflappability. Unexpected or unwelcome life changes big and small—to say nothing of mere fears of them—can whip me into a panicky lather, start me parading horribles, climbing a tree of terribles, unable to talk myself down. I hardly expected walking into prison to be a display of cool-headedness. I had anticipated panic. I had even dreamt about it.

Years before I'd had any inkling that I would one day do real time, I dreamed I was sentenced to serve twelve days in the county jail. I had taken my protesting a bit too far in some judge's opinion, and now he was going to give me a big enough taste of where that could land me so that I wouldn't stray that way again. As the bars closed me into a dank cell, decades of grime ground into its concrete floor, the bars an oily stain from untold faces and torsos and limbs pressed to and jutting through them, and my peripheral view narrowed, my heart raced—it felt like being buried alive. For twelve days I would be trapped in this box.

But now, wide awake, even as Ms. Barone led me into a cell very similar to the one in my dream, I was unfazed. Over the preceding three years, I'd had my home raided by the FBI, been arrested at gunpoint, sat through a Kafkaesque trial (twice, including a mistrial after an attorney fell seriously ill), been convicted of "terrorism," faced decades in prison, and lived on house arrest for eight months awaiting a space at the prison. Though I had never spent more than a few days in jail, by the time I self-surrendered to the Federal Correctional Institution (FCI) in Danbury, Connecticut, I was unruffled by most everything.

Still, I figured this was some kind of psychological defense—that when I actually walked past the razor wire and the electrified fence, below the guard towers and beyond the "free" world, not to emerge again for years, the veneer would crack. Seized by abject fear, I would need to concentrate—hard—on not hyperventilating. But there I was, cool as a cucumber.

It wouldn't last.

POLITICAL ACTIVITY

I landed in prison for reasons that people call *political*. Between 2001 and 2005, I was deeply involved in a grassroots animal rights campaign to close one of the world's largest and most notorious animal testing labs, Huntingdon Life Sciences (HLS). The campaign, Stop Huntingdon Animal Cruelty (SHAC), began after HLS was exposed in several undercover investigations that revealed horrific treatment of animals, repeated flouting of scientific protocols, drunkenness and drug-taking on the job, and other gross misconduct. Undercover investigators found animals sitting in their own congealed blood and feces, riddled with open sores and blisters, reeling in pain from forcibly swallowing, inhaling, or being slathered in chemicals. Lab technicians were recorded dissecting a conscious monkey, violently shaking and punching dogs in the face, and misdosing animals. In one video, an experimenter notes, "You can wipe your ass on that data." In another, a worker jabs a puppy with a needle over and over, complaining that the beagles being used are too young, so their veins are too small. In a harrowing encapsulation, an HLS employee described the animals as "rotting, but still alive."

These investigations sparked a passionate, relentless, global campaign to close HLS. Activists targeted the pillars of support for the lab—its investors, customers, service providers, and so on—demanding that these companies stop doing business with it. Across the United States and around the world, protestors levied every kind of pressure they could think of—both legal and illegal, from traditional pickets to creative pranks, from the humdrum to the humorous to the downright harassing. They held demonstrations at offices and homes, and hundreds of activists marched in regional and national protests. They wrote letters, staged phone blockades, and faxed black paper to corporations to use up the machines' ink. They entered offices shouting through megaphones and throwing leaflets. Anonymous activists set off stink bombs, broke windows, and launched cyberattacks against the computer networks of HLS and its affiliates. HLS employees received unsolicited magazine subscriptions and vegan pizzas, and their communities were plastered with "Do You Know Your Neighbor?" posters.

It worked. The targeted companies couldn't stand the pressure, and they were dumping Huntingdon in droves—among them, some of the largest corporations in the world, including Citibank, Merrill Lynch, and HSBC. The lab's share price plummeted, and it was kicked off the New York Stock Exchange, the OTC Bulletin Board, and the purgatory for poorly trading companies, the Pink Sheets. Senior company officials and lead experimenters resigned. HLS was on the verge of bankruptcy several times, saved only by the eleventh-hour efforts of major shareholders and even the UK government. At one point, the lab's largest investor and white knight, investment bank Stephens Inc., extended HLS a six-year, $33 million loan to keep it afloat—only to abandon the lab less than a year later. Stephens cut its losses, pulled the loan, and retreated in the face of the SHAC campaign.

My codefendants and I supported it all. We published a newsletter, researched and publicized HLS's business affiliates and employees, organized demonstrations and reported on other activists' protests, provided resources like flyers and event calendars, sent out action alerts, issued press releases, and published a website that was the news hub and central resource for the US arm of the campaign. The website became the centerpiece of our prosecution on domestic terrorism charges.

We were not shy. We encouraged campaigners to think outside the box, and we unabashedly supported any action that didn't injure anyone. When activists in Boston hid a putrid-smelling durian fruit in the office of HLS's insurance broker, we applauded. When the "Pirates for Animal Liberation" sank an HLS-affiliated bank executive's yacht, and topped it off by lowering the American flag in his yard and raising a pirate flag, we roared with laughter. When fourteen beagles were liberated from HLS, we cheered. We were brazen and unapologetic, sensational and hyperbolic. But we never crossed the line.

THE FIRST AMENDMENT 101

Neither I, nor any of my codefendants, were accused of participating in any independent illegal act. We hadn't vandalized property or hurt anyone; we hadn't even placed harassing phone calls, and the government did not claim that we had. Rather, our indictment alleged that we had engaged in a "conspiracy to physically disrupt the operations of HLS," and had thus violated the Animal Enterprise Protection Act,[1] committing the crime of "animal enterprise terrorism," through our encouragement of and reporting on legal and illegal protests against companies and individuals, such as HLS employees.[2]

The only activities the defendants had engaged in were speech and expressive activity (such as demonstrations). So the government needed to prove that, somehow, this expression added up to an illegal conspiracy. The boundaries of protected expression under the First Amendment are more expansive than most people realize. It is perfectly legal, for example, to give a speech advocating that people bomb the Pentagon in protest of US imperialism and military aggression. In fact, such a speech is constitutionally protected—that is, unless the party who wants to prohibit or punish particular expression can demonstrate that such protection should be removed, the lawsuit or prosecution will fail. In this way, speech is unlike other legal acts that can become illegal if they are taken in furtherance of a crime, such as purchasing ski masks for use in a bank robbery. Likewise, protesting outside people's homes in residential neighborhoods, publishing their home addresses on the Internet, and encouraging people to call, write, and protest those people is all protected expression. And the First Amendment protects an individual's right to be a member of a group that has both legal and illegal aims, as long as the individual herself does not commit unlawful acts. So the government's job in the SHAC 7 case, as we were dubbed, was to prove that our activity was not quintessential political speech, but instead unprotected and could therefore be criminalized.

First Amendment doctrine holds that speech is presumptively protected—that is, we will assume it is—unless it falls into one of a handful of "well-defined and narrowly limited" categories (*Chaplinsky v. New Hampshire*, 315 U.S. 568 1942:571–2.). And I do mean fall—the boundaries of the half-dozen or so categories of unprotected speech are constitutional cliffs, not slopes. Expression is either fully protected or it is unprotected; particular speech does not receive less protection as it increasingly resembles a type of unprotected speech. Moreover, repeated acts of protected expression do not add up to an unprotected whole; adding protected acts together is like adding zeros. In my case, the government argued that the speech on the SHAC USA website fell into two unprotected categories—incitement and true threats—and, thus, lost constitutional protection and could be criminalized.

The unprotected category of incitement defines when a speaker can be punished for advocating illegal conduct. In order for such advocacy to constitute incitement and lose First Amendment protection, it must be "directed to inciting or producing imminent lawless action and...likely to incite or produce such action," and "imminence" here means "immediate" (*Brandenburg v. Ohio*, 395 U.S. 444 1969: 447–48). In short, the speech must occur in a context in which there is no time or space for the listener to consider the advocacy and choose her actions, such as in the midst of a riot. In the SHAC 7 case, we argued that our speech clearly had not produced imminent lawlessness; indeed, we did not see how written words could *ever* constitute incitement.

Likewise, we argued that none of our speech constituted true threats, which courts have defined as "those statements where the speaker means to communicate a serious expression of an intent to commit an act of unlawful violence to a particular individual or group of individuals," and that act of violence is generally interpreted to mean physical harm (*Virginia v. Black*, 538 U.S. 343 2003: 359). The individuals protested by SHAC activists testified that the protests made them fear for their lives. We argued that this was never our intent, nor was it a reasonable fear, as we explicitly and repeatedly denounced physical injury, and no physical violence had occurred.

I believed fiercely in these First Amendment protections. For me, US free speech was the one redeeming feature in a country whose foreign and domestic policies generally, and increasingly, horrified me. When my codefendants and I were convicted, and even more so when we lost our appeal, I confronted the realpolitik that limits these ideal protections. After having been a pious believer in what is essentially an American religion, I would now be locked away for years for having practiced it.

"POLITICAL" CAPTIVITY

Still, it was months before I felt confined. Though the cell in which I spent my first few weeks looked similar to the one in my dream, being in it felt very different. The prison was overcrowded, and I was placed in the Special Housing Unit, or SHU (aka the Security Housing Unit, of recent Pelican Bay infamy). Three of us were stuffed into a cell clearly built to hold one person, and I found myself on a mattress on the gritty, sixty-five-year-old floor, my feet under the toilet if I stretched out. Someone could easily lose her mind locked in a space like this.

There I was, the most captive I had ever been, unable to go anywhere—not even to the other side of the cell, crammed as we were—with no way out for the foreseeable future, and, as I saw it, for no crime at all. Yet my first feeling was freedom; my first thought, "I don't have to do *anything*"—the word italicized in my mind. Even less than unflappability am I known for idleness. The walls holding me in mercifully kept the world—with its to-do lists and deadlines, its ringing phones and accumulating inboxes—out.

Feeling freedom in prison is a perverse luxury, one substantially less available to someone like Angie,[3] my first prison friend. When I met her, Angie had served twelve years of a thirty-year sentence for a drug conspiracy conviction. Her role? She had answered the phone and helped to facilitate her husband's purchase of a car that, unbeknownst to her, was used to transport drugs. The phone line was bugged. Angie pled guilty on her public defender's advice, because she was facing a life sentence. (Conspiracy law makes every actor responsible for the full conspiracy, including the entire quantity of drugs involved, even if the person did not know the extent of the conspiracy.) Though she is from Chicago, Angie was imprisoned in Connecticut, and her three children—now ages thirteen, eighteen, and twenty-two—had grown up without her. Her sister had died of cancer while Angie was in prison.

Or Elena.

From my journal:
March 21, 2008

Over the past week I have been so completely fed up with everyone and everything here, and this morning at work I got talking to Elena. She was telling me how she's lived her entire life in the US, but she's going to be deported back to Mexico, where she has no home, no family, doesn't know anyone, doesn't have an ID or a driver's license, and just plain doesn't know how to get on. Oh, and the state is trying to take her kids and put them in foster care. As I listened to her story, I told myself, "Shut up Lauren, stop feeling sorry for yourself."

What I found to be a respite, a sabbatical of sorts (at least at first), was hardly so for these women, whose lives had been upended and families torn apart by an inadvertent misfeasance, a lapse in judgment, or a desperate act; by overworked, underpaid lawyers and a legal system that is hardly an equal opportunity incarcerator; by addiction or economic status, race or an inconvenient birthplace—in short, because of fewer advantages in The Game of American Life.

June 15, 2007

There was a job fair today. Speakers came in and gave presentations on practical job skills, e.g. how to draft a résumé, how to act in a job interview (and some not-so-practical skills: one presenter talked about the different energy fields around men and women, because men generally carry a brief case at their sides, while women generally carry things in one arm, against their chests, thus cutting off the flow of energy. Um…ok). Dress for Success told us how to get office-appropriate clothing through them. I suppose some of the info could be useful to those who need it.

But the theme was "Initiative," and the front of the program read, "The only way to predict your future is to create it," and the whole event was like a sermon in the American myth of self-sufficiency, pull-yourself-up-by-your-bootstraps dogma, faith-in-individual-initiative claptrap. One big mystification of all the sociopolitical forces that profoundly shape our lives, seating responsibility for achieving (or failing to achieve) The American Dream squarely in the laps of the people at the biggest disadvantage of doing so. Get out of prison and go make your life great! If you don't, well, you have only yourself to blame.

But whatever. I suppose it's better to learn how to make a résumé than not to.

My story was from a different book entirely. Whatever miseries I endured in prison, I truly expected my criminal record and incarceration to do minimal permanent damage to my life. Indeed, they caused little disruption in the short term. No one was relying on me—no children, no aging parents, no ill family. I did not rely on public benefits, which I could have lost on account of my criminal record—thanks, of course, to my fortunate position in that benevolent, get-out-what-you-put-in, egalitarian force: The Free Market. I did not worry over my release; I would be going to my dad's house, where I could count on a roof over my head, food in the fridge, a loan (the car, some cash) as needed while I searched for a job—over which I also did not fret. With one fancy degree already under my belt, my post-prison job prospects seemed promising. I even planned to earn another fancy degree while in prison: a master's in First Amendment law. I had turned my prosecution into a graduate program! And, while I felt my conviction was unjust and unconstitutional, trial not exactly fair, the "process" not exactly "due," I couldn't exactly complain about having been railroaded. In the year and a half between my arrest and trial, our defense team had filed extensive pretrial briefing in an effort to dismantle the government's case. Throughout the case, including a three-and-a-half-week trial, I'd been represented by one of the leading free speech attorneys in the country. We had lost, of course, but he was working on a stellar appeal. In short, by virtue of my station in life—that is, due to pure luck—I was able to step off the stage and return in a later scene without any material injuries, only my psychological wounds in tow.

Of course, I am overgeneralizing. Some of the women I met in prison had committed heinous acts. And the Green Scare is not a fabrication—in recent years, animal rights and environmental activists have become the dissidents du jour for the US government (Potter, 2011). While we have fortunately faced less repression than many other social movements have historically endured, the unwarranted focus and heavy government hand is undeniable. Animal and eco-activists have been targeted with bogus prosecutions and enhanced sentences, our nonviolent property crimes and harassment made a priority while right-wing physical violence proliferates, and many people's lives have been profoundly impacted. Indeed, it was sheer luck that tragedy did not befall me while I was in prison—more than one of my codefendants lost family while incarcerated.

But there is much truth in these generalizations. Angie's and Elena's stories are legion. Rather than hardened criminals and sociopaths, the majority of the women I met in prison seemed to be victims—survivors, really—of a society that has its priorities all wrong. While I was perhaps "less guilty," in a technical sense, than someone who had sold drugs or immigrated illegally, it is a false distinction to call me a "political" prisoner and my fellow prisoners ordinary criminals. When we locate the "political" nature of captivity at whether the actor had an explicitly political motive, rather than at the point of criminalization or disadvantage, it conceals the irreducibly political nature of those social arrangements. The social choice to criminalize, rather than treat—or legalize—drug use, for example, is a political choice. Concentrating law enforcement on drug activity in low-income communities of color is a political choice. Excluding those with a criminal record from public benefits, such as housing and educational subsidies, and allowing employers to discriminate on the basis of criminal history, are political choices. Disenfranchising prisoners, parolees, and probationers is a political choice. There is deep political meaning to statistics that tell us that, though rates of drug use and sale are generally the same for all races, Black Americans are "disproportionately arrested, convicted, and incarcerated on drug charges" (Fellner 2009, 257; see also Alexander 2010). And it tells us something deeply political about our society that, most probably, the only way that I—a well-educated, middle-class, white girl—was going to end up in prison was to set out to deliberately fuck with the big boys.

A DAY AT DANBURY

All of which meant that, after the novelty of goofing off subsided, when the feeling of convalescence had long since been replaced by a deep, diffuse distress, it took quite a while before I could put a name to what I was feeling.

Oh, I could describe the emotions all right, and I seethed into my journal.

April 3, 2008

Waking up out of bed at 1:23 a.m., feeling like I'm going to explode. I am so. incredibly. fucking. angry. I have never felt anything remotely close to this fury for even a fraction of the time that it has now been boiling in me. The hatred that I feel is of a difference in kind—it is as though I have never felt hatred before. I am wishing for and envisioning destructive, murderous things. I want to punch walls. Crack skulls. I want this whole place to go up in a blazing inferno. I am a ticking time bomb. I now understand why people "go postal."

But I couldn't make sense of it. The fact of my imprisonment—the physical captivity, my absence from home, even the unconstitutional conviction—truly bothered me little. Certainly, I felt these things were unjust. But that didn't mean my time in prison had to be entirely agonizing and worthless. Notwithstanding my quickness to hit the panic button, in the end I generally make lemonade, and prison was no exception. Honestly, nothing to do but read, write, and work out didn't sound half bad to me. I had a master's degree to earn, novels to indulge, and bad TV to watch simply because I could. And I was determined to walk out of prison as ripped as Sarah Connor in *Terminator 2*. But Club Fed wasn't exactly panning out.

After a few weeks in the SHU, I was released onto the compound—a ring of two-story structures around a courtyard of sidewalks and grass. Most of these buildings are housing units, holding about one hundred prisoners each. There is also a dining hall, the Education Department, laundry facilities, a leisure library, a law library, the mailroom, a poor excuse for an infirmary, commissary, the lieutenant's office, administrative offices, and Recreation, which leads through a gymnasium out to a large yard behind the housing units on the eastern side of the compound. Danbury FCI was built in 1940 and is now a hodgepodge of newer and older architectural elements. The older housing units consist of cells, though they are never locked, and prisoners can move freely throughout the housing unit. The cells provide more privacy, control over lights, and some buffer against noise. The newer units, in which I was housed, are open dorms with cubicles. The cubicles are only as high as the bunk beds and, if you are assigned to a top bunk, as I was, you find yourself sleeping directly next to the person in the bed beside you, about an inch of space between your mattresses. I was under a fluorescent light that came on at 6:00 a.m. and was supposed to be turned off by an officer at 11:00 p.m., though it often stayed on well past that. No matter how many pillows and blankets and coats I piled over my eyes, I could not fall asleep until that light finally went out. And the noise, day and night, of one hundred women living in an open dorm, many of whom are less than respectful of communal space, is inescapable.

While the SHU is on twenty-three-hour-plus per day lockdown, the compound operates on a system of "controlled movement" focused around "ten-minute moves." Weekdays, between 7:30 a.m. and 3:30 p.m., prisoners can move from one place to another only during a ten-minute period, every hour on the half hour, when the doors are unlocked. You could, for example, go from your housing unit to Recreation. If you had finished doing your laundry at 2:00 p.m., you would have been waiting in the laundromat for the 2:30 move to return to your housing unit. You could run to the library for a book during a ten-minute move, but if you didn't check it out before the move ended, you'd be stuck at—physically locked in—the library for an hour, until the next move.

Monday through Friday, the housing units open around 6:30 a.m. for open movement—prisoners can eat breakfast, go to Recreation, the laundry, the mailroom, or run whatever prison errands demand their attention. At 7:30, work call is announced, and all prisoners are to report to their "assigned work assignments"—a redundancy that I found simultaneously amusing and irritating, and which, in my nearly three and a half years of listening to it, never got corrected. Doors are locked at 7:40—the end of the first ten-minute move.

Prisoners run the prison. They cook meals for both officers and prisoners; they staff the libraries and teach other prisoners who are earning GEDs; they mow lawns, shovel snow (often overnight), and haul trash; they become janitors and plumbers and electricians. Schedules vary in order to cover all the necessary work shifts. Some prisoners are up before dawn to prepare breakfast, while others work overnight at the power plant. And, though they are not required to be—when the Thirteenth Amendment declared, "Neither slavery nor involuntary servitude...shall exist within the United States," it pointedly excepted involuntary servitude "as punishment for a crime"—they are paid pennies (but required to purchase basic necessities like shampoo and toothpaste at inflated prices). Undoubtedly, despite the fact that the annual cost of housing a prisoner exceeds that of sending her to college, the United States' ability to incarcerate more than 2.2 million adults annually is due in no small part to enlisting prisoners in facilitating their own confinement.[4]

Controlled movement ends at 3:30 p.m., with the announcement of "recall," at which time all prisoners are to return to their housing units "in preparation for the four o'clock count," one of five daily counts of all 1,300 prisoners. The 4:00 p.m. count is a stand-up count. After count, housing units are opened one at a time for dinner, after which there is open movement until 9:30 recall for a 10:00 p.m. count. On weekends and holidays, housing unit doors open at 7:30 a.m., with open movement until 9:30 a.m. recall, an extra 10:00 a.m. stand-up count, lunch around 11:00 a.m., and open movement until 3:30 recall. At any time throughout the day, a "secure compound" may be called—if there is a fight, if a prisoner is being escorted from the SHU to another area, if there is a thunderstorm, and sometimes for reasons that you can't determine. When there is a secure compound, you are locked in wherever you were when the secure compound was called until it ends.

WHAT DOES OPPRESSION FEEL LIKE?

My captivity, in any meaningful sense, did not begin with walls. In a way, it was not really physical. But, as I settled into prison life, gaining nominally more movement within those walls—freedom of controlled movement, if you will— something else, something immaterial, began to squeeze itself around me. It was as if I'd been submerged in wet concrete, and it was slowly drying. Without any shackles or locks or bars at all, it held me captive.

It started at the most minute level.

May 20, 2007

I'm anxious about tomorrow. It's ridiculous, but everything here is a battle. Tomorrow, at commissary, I need to buy new sneakers. But I'm not sure whether they are leather or not, so I somehow need to find out before I buy them, cuz of course once the officer rings them up (which he'll do before he hands them to me) that's that, and he won't take them off my purchase without fight.

My anxiety was composed of these small things—the daily absurdities (January 21, 2008: "Yesterday, at dinner, I found metal in my food for the second time. I showed Officer Ploard, who told me, 'That tends to happen in a correctional environment.' I just stared at him, dumbfounded"); the constant disrespect (May 14, 2007: "'Ladies, shut up.' That's how Mr. DeMarco addressed us today at the start of 4:00 p.m. count"); the frustrations and hurdles to accomplishing the simplest things (I once got locked in the Education Department for two hours after I went there to sharpen a pencil and the compound was suddenly secured); the subtle and not-so-subtle reminders of power. "Danbury," as it was referred to by prisoners, was constantly making new rules, seemingly for the sake of doing so.

June 30, 2007

"Town Hall!! Town Hall!! A very important town hall!!"

Counselor Wilson was screaming her head off throughout the unit. We all crowded in near the officers' station for the prison version of collective governance—they command, we listen and comply.

"From now on, T-shirts worn under your khaki shirts must be tucked in." Very important indeed.

Shortly thereafter, this new rule was superseded by another new rule.

"Effective two weeks from today, you are to have both shirts tucked in, khaki shirts and T-shirts."

Counselor Wilson was not the only person who thought this was "very important." One day, I was filling a bottle at the water fountain in the Education building, where I worked as a GED tutor, when a prisoner walked by with her shirt untucked. "Whoa!!" said Dr. Jenkins, the head of the Education Department. "What are you doing? Tuck your shirt in. You're about to fall apart." "I will as soon as I get to my classroom," the woman responded, and continued walking. "No," Dr. Jenkins said, "now, in the bathroom," and he followed her. He came back saying, not entirely under his breath, "Whew! The things we have to deal with around here!" It was surreal. And it got better. About an hour later, Dr. Jenkins was "standing mainline" at lunch. As I walked past him, he was *still* talking about the shirt incident, telling another officer! As I told my journal, "I swear, you can't make this shit up. These people are caricatures of themselves."

"Mainline" is the prisoners' regular opportunity to speak with prison administrators. Different administrators on different days would stand in a line in the lunchroom, and we could approach them with various requests. It was a hit-or-miss system. Half the time it was productive. But the other half of the time, someone would write your name down and promise to follow up with you later, but you'd never hear from them. Or you'd be told to come back to mainline next week but, when you did, the administrator wouldn't be there. Or he or she hadn't gotten an answer for you as promised, and the same thing the week after that, and the week after that.

Tucking in our shirts was just the beginning (at least it was for me; no doubt "it" had begun long before I arrived). In a matter of a few months, a cascade of piecemeal rules took from us plants (small spider plants that we grew in water in plastic cups), all but two completed hobbycraft items (knitted, crocheted, and the like), then all completed hobbycraft items, decorations on our plastic coffee cups, fruit on commissary, then permission to take back fruit from the dining hall to our units, and visiting other prisoners in their cells or cubes. "No intercube visiting" meant you couldn't sit and chat, play cards, or share food with another prisoner in your living space—your "house." It also meant that I was once punished with "extra duty" (cleaning) for hugging a woman who was crying in her cube.

One day, a thick, red line of electrical tape appeared around the vending machines in the visiting room. Before this day, prisoners had been allowed to approach the machines with their visitors, select an item, and pay for it with money from their books that they had put on their prison ID cards. Now, this new, crimson mote made the vending machines "out of bounds". It was just far enough from the machines that you couldn't see what was in them, and your visitor had to read off each item to you. Whatever could be the purpose of this new rule? As far as anyone could tell, there had been no vending machine incidents. The machines didn't spin around like secret walls and let us out. I could only conclude that the new rule, like so many of the rules, existed for its own sake, an end in itself.

The unpredictability, frequent changes, and mounting deprivations piled on top of me, compressed my lungs, shortened my breath. My shoulders tensed and my stomach turned to lye. Why did I care so much? I never even had decorations on my coffee cup. I didn't have a plant, I don't crochet, and my friends mostly lived in other units, which had themselves been out of bounds since before I'd arrived, long before intercube visiting within units was banned. Most of this didn't change my daily life. Still, it—and much else that didn't seem to matter at all when I thought about it rationally—was driving me crazy.

March 19, 2008

March is officially the worst month here so far. Everyone says after your first year prison gets easier and time flies. For me, it's definitely the opposite. Things that are bearable in small and medium doses become increasingly unbearable after more than a year. It's just one thing after another here, and it's really starting to make me nuts. Case in point: they just keep picking things away because if they took them all at once, we might get worked up. One day I'm going to make a list of every miserable living condition, everything they've taken away from us, and every new rule they've implemented, just since I've been here. This is starting to feel like water torture. Drip. Drip. Drip.

It was hot. We were locked in concrete buildings with flat roofs, no shades on the windows, and barely a tree in sight. In the humid New England summers, the sun would bake those buildings, and they would trap the heat. I know people who live just a few miles from Danbury FCI, and their air conditioning rarely goes on. Though outside in the daytime can be brutal, there is enough airflow and it cools off enough at night that open windows will keep indoors comfortable. In prison, though, even when the temperature had dropped with the sun, the housing units were like ovens. Even with open windows and deafening, industrial fans, they would not cool down. I would wake up in pools of sweat and run my wrists under cold water in the bathroom. I would fill containers with ice (when our ice machine wasn't broken) and lay them over my heart and try to fall back asleep. And winter brought no relief—the thermostat in our unit didn't work, and in the four winters I was there it never got fixed, so the temperature soared. This dry heat came with a seasonal treat: bloody noses.

Another thing that drove me absolutely bonkers: you could never rely on things being open when they were supposed to be. You might, for example, need to go to the mailroom, which was supposed to be open in the morning until work call. A long line would form as soon as the unit doors opened, and you had better be in the front of that line, for, if they hadn't gotten to you by work call, you would not be mailing anything that day. You could have waited nearly an hour, but they'd abruptly lock the door and send you away. Frequently the mailroom wouldn't open at all—but no one would tell you that in advance. You would have hightailed it to the mailroom when the compound opened, having rushed to get dressed, skipped breakfast, not gone to the laundry, and then waited all morning in line only to have work call announced without the mailroom ever opening. And you would never know this until right before work call, because they never opened the mailroom at the same time—sometimes it opened at 6:30, sometimes it would not open until 7:25. You just had to wait and see.

Likewise, the law library. I spent many weekends in the law library, studying or working on my appeal, and I always wanted to get there as early as possible. I longed for big blocks of time in which to settle into my reading and writing, but they mostly eluded me. Prison is a bunch of interruptions. As soon as you get settled into something, it's time for lunch. After lunch, you have only a few hours before 3:30 p.m. recall and 4:00 p.m. count, which itself consists of about an hour of waiting around for officers to spend a few minutes counting. Then dinner. Then recall again. And the PA is always blaring, with some announcement or reprimand. Still, I did the best I could—for example, getting to the law library immediately after lunch on weekends. Not that it did me any good.

The compound officer—one officer designated daily to call the moves, secure the compound as needed, and instruct the other COs to open each unit upon its turn to go to the dining hall—was tasked with unlocking the law library after lunch and dinner. But he or she would often not show up. I would be standing there, along with the law library clerks who had arrived for work, waiting for the compound officer to spend half a second turning a key. We often waited over an hour. Other officers would walk by and refuse to unlock the door, though they had keys, because that was the compound officer's responsibility.

The lieutenant's office was a mere fifteen feet away, and the officers could see us waiting, but whenever we would ask them to open the door, they too would refuse.

Any time a prisoner pointed out to an officer how nonsensical something was, the officer's explanation was, "It's just like the real world." They would say this straight-faced, with no hint of irony, with even a touch of annoyance like, "Why are you complaining about something so obviously normal and reasonable?" The more they said it, the more I seriously doubted whether any of them had ever *been* in the real world. How could anyone think that this place was anything like broader society (except, of course, for the race and class inequities in the prisoner population, the overt and insidious oppression, and the fact that the whole thing only functions because of exploitation)? But this is how these people think. In prison, I was confronted with this type of thinking every single day.

With all of these, and many more, difficulties, I was more than a little distressed. Though I tried to keep things in perspective—even adopting a mantra, "Ignore, ignore, ignore," which I would repeat to myself every time my blood started to boil over some trivial thing—I was deeply affected by them. I felt as though I was constantly breathing in, but I never seemed to exhale, my lungs reaching capacity with each shallow breath, a balloon that would surely burst with just one more. My stomach shot geysers of acid up my throat all day long, and I envisioned a red sea in my belly, boiling with the rage I found increasingly difficult to keep at bay.

Worse, I could not seem to focus on anything, and I beat myself up over my slow progress on schoolwork. The saving grace of my captivity had been that it was only physical; I could transcend it by using my time productively. But I was being thwarted at every turn, seemingly by myself as much as by prison. It didn't make sense that my constant anxiety, my rage, or my slow progress could be attributed to prison inconveniences alone. They didn't beat us, I was never locked in a cell, I had frequent visitors, money on my books, and tons of support from the outside. Why couldn't I just ignore the ridiculousness and focus on what I wanted to accomplish? But I couldn't, and *that* is when I lost my freedom—when the prison bureaucracy soured my lemonade.

"SHE'S NOT BREATHING!"

Then there were the things that were not trivial, no matter how you looked at them. The toilets in my unit routinely backed up and septic water would flood the unit. We would have to pick everything up from under our beds, and the unit orderlies would spend hours pushing water and tampons and other refuse out the front door with push brooms while other prisoners repaired the plumbing. One time, when our toilets had been out of order for hours, we begged the officers to open the door to the unit next door so we could use the bathroom, but they wouldn't. Sometimes they just ignored our pleas. Sometimes they would say no and walk away. Sometimes they'd say yes—but they would walk away and never come back. According to the plumbers, my unit was at the end of the plumbing line, and whatever caused the clogs could have come from any of the seven housing units on that line. Nonetheless, my unit was often punished for the flood—as if living in a sewer wasn't punishment enough—with the loss of our TVs and microwaves.

Some things were downright scary. One night, a woman in my unit who had very high blood pressure was having trouble breathing. An officer came over and some prisoners started to take her up to Medical. I went for a walk and, when I came back nearly two hours later, she was still lying on her bed. I asked the officer why, and he said there was only one person from Medical on duty, and that he was in the SHU.

Another night was even more frightening.

May 9, 2008

Last night, in the middle of the night, a woman in my unit had a seizure. Lieutenant Wilson came and yelled at her, "Whining isn't going to get you anywhere!" Suddenly, Wilson yelled, "She's not breathing!" Only then did Wilson call someone from Medical—who was not even here, but at home. It took him 47 minutes to get here. I timed it. Fortunately, the woman started breathing on her own before then.

Despite my best efforts to stay sane in the face of so much that was irrelevant, absurd, or downright immoral, I felt like I was truly losing my mind, as if it was slowly disintegrating. And I was constantly on edge because I never knew what to expect and was always waiting for the other shoe to drop. I tried every constructive thing I could think of—I resolved to start each day anew, wrote affirmations to read to myself as needed, and vented to friends. I did yoga, walked for hours on the track, and watched sunsets, but nothing calmed me down. Some less constructive things at least kept me from exploding—I woke up from naps kicking my locker; I punched walls; I once threw a twenty-five-pound weight a dozen feet across the weight room—but they didn't fix the problem. In moments of forgetfulness, I tried seeing the prison psychologists, only to be immediately reminded that they are as institutionalized as everyone else who worked there. They implored me to accept my situation.

"You just need to realize that there's nothing you can do about it," one told me.

"*That's the problem*," I retorted. "If there was something I could do about it, I would go do it."

"Anger," I learned, from another shrink, "is what we call a 'secondary emotion.' It often indicates another, 'primary emotion,' like feeling disrespected."

I stared at this woman incredulously. "Being disrespected seems like a pretty good reason to be angry, if you ask me."

These people were useless.

I remember the moment when what I can only describe as my madness reached its pinnacle. I couldn't sleep. Once again, my anxiety was on a feedback loop, both fueling and feeding off itself, intensifying each time it washed over me. I got up and went to the front of my unit and stared out the small Plexiglas window in the door. The compound was bathed in fluorescent from the floodlights that forever hid the stars. For months, I had struggled to get control of my emotions and my disorganized thoughts, to no avail. "That's it," I said out loud, "I will never come out of this." I felt my mind had slipped past my reach; I would never get it back.

One day, I was in my GED class, sitting behind my teacher's desk, and the students were working. I had been very stressed as of late. The rage was rising in me, and clearly things were going to come to a head. I don't remember what set me off—my journal entry just says, "Went crazy. Got fired. Got unfired"— but it had me throwing books clear across the classroom, one after another— one! two! three!—like I had some good arm on me. I was on fire, seeing red, and I was about to throw bigger, heavier things. My boss, Mr. M., walked in and surveyed the scene. "You're going to have to find another job," he said, and walked away. I left the room and sat in a supply closet with the lights out.

The next day, after class, Mr. M came to talk to me. He told me I was not fired, but said that I really needed to learn how to cope. I bristled. "Coping" was becoming a charged concept for me. It meant not expressing my outrage, that the only place it would live was inside of me. To me, talking back to staff, crying, punching walls, and throwing books—in short, having a tantrum every now and again—*was* coping. It was a sane response to the crazy world in which I found myself, where no constructive effort seemed to make any difference. All of my attempts to address my frustrations—speaking up when I or others were treated badly, filing grievances, silly attempts at Zen living—had proved futile. And the shrinks were right: there was nothing I or any other prisoner could do about most of what we dealt with. (Sadly, there was little prisoner solidarity at Danbury, so collective action was not a realistic option.) As I saw it, all Mr.

M. was asking was that I cope in ways that were more socially acceptable, less disruptive to the smooth operation of Danbury FCI (and, at least on that occasion, to his class). I couldn't blame him. But I wasn't interested in making life any easier for my captors, even if in some ways it would have made my life easier as well. More to the point, I didn't think I could do it. My rage burned so hot, I didn't think I could simmer quietly; it would burn a hole right through me.

Interestingly, I had fewer tantrums once I justified them. My thoughts reorganized themselves, and the rage that fueled those periodic eruptions started to drain out of me. I still hated like never before, but thinking about that hatred and its expression as legitimate reactions to the way I and my fellow prisoners were treated lessened its unruliness. The realization came to me after one of my visits to a prison shrink. A few days after I saw him, Counselor Wilson called me into her office. The shrink had contacted Wilson after he and I had spoken and had relayed everything he and I had talked about. Apparently, confidentiality was not among his professional obligations. Counselor Wilson had some unsolicited advice for me: I should do what this guy suggested and join one of the prison support groups, rather than trying to deal with things in my "own selfish way."

At that moment, Counselor Wilson helped me more than she realized. Appalled that my private conversation with a therapist had been relayed to another officer, uninterested in baring my soul to staff and fellow prisoners who weren't my friends, and disgusted by this woman's patronizing, I heard in my head, "I am right, and you are wrong." I meant it less about the immediate conversation, and more about the entire sideshow in which I found myself. This place is evil, I thought. I am right about that, and they are wrong.

JEOPARDY

Late in my sentence, when I had only about a year left, I was finally able to put a name to my emotions. It came out, as on *Jeopardy*, in question form:

"What does oppression *feel* like?"

For years I had wondered why I was acting out when my material circumstances were tolerable. Trying to figure out why I couldn't accomplish what I'd set out to do, even when I wasn't constantly wishing to escape those walls. Captivity didn't bother me, I'd thought, so why was I freaking out?

Ultimately, my captivity was social and psychological, rather than physical or material (see chapter 15 in this volume). The walls that enclosed me were not so much physical structures that kept me from catching a bus home, as an arena in which irrational, unkind, unjust people controlled me. The loss of a plant I didn't have or a crocheted item I would never make were negligible material deprivations, but they were deeply meaningful psychological deprivations.

Shortly before I left prison, a new warden arrived with a new set of rules, among them that prisoners were only allowed to have two pairs of sweatpants. A friend of mine really thought we needed three, so she approached the warden at mainline and made her case. A few days later, a memo went around raising the allowable number of sweatpants to three.

> "See?" my friend said to me. "You just need to make these people think they have power over you and then you get what you want."
>
> "Is that what you want?" I asked her. "Because I'd rather not have the sweatpants."

CAPTIVITY IS POLITICAL

All captivity is political. Every time we lock someone up, that act is about one group having political power over another. This is true whether we are physically locking someone away or denying their autonomy, whether we are ourselves the captors or, more commonly, because our social arrangements create and reinforce inequality. And this is no less true when it comes to humans locking up nonhumans—whether it is to kill and eat them, to turn them into shoes, and jackets, and belts, or to pump them full of poisons or slice them up in the name of scientific "progress." Indeed, the most profoundly political act of captivity is for a group with power to use that power to determine the lives—even the very purpose—of others.

NOTES

1. In 2006, following our conviction, the Animal Enterprise Protection Act (AEPA) was substantially amended to criminalize even more activity and renamed the Animal Enterprise Terrorism Act (AETA).
2. I and three other defendants were also charged in five additional counts of the indictment, wherein portions of the activity that allegedly violated the AEPA were realleged. The 2006 amendment was, in part, intended to incorporate these separate counts into an "animal enterprise terrorism" charge.
3. Names and identifying details of some individuals have been changed.
4. According to the US Department of Justice, Bureau of Justice Statistics, "Correctional Populations in the United States, 2011" (November 2012).

References

Alexander, M. 2010. *The New Jim Crow: Mass Incarceration in the Age of Colorblindness*. New York: New Press.

Fellner, J. 2009. "Race, Drugs, and Law Enforcement in the United States." *Stanford Law & Policy Review* 20(2): 257–291.

Potter, W. 2011. *Green Is the New Red: An Insider's Account of a Social Movement under Siege*. San Francisco: City Lights.

CHALLENGES OF CAPTIVITY

9

For Their Own Good

Captive Cats and Routine Confinement

CLARE PALMER AND PETER SANDØE ∎

Cat owners in the United States, with increasing frequency and urgency, are being advised routinely to confine their cats indoors, and never to allow kittens outside at all. Both animal welfare organizations such as the Humane Society of the United States (HSUS) and more radical animal rights groups such as PETA agree in advocating that cats should be confined either wholly indoors, or with access only to a safe outdoor enclosure, all the time, for their entire lives. Until recently these views were strongly supported by the American Veterinary Medicine Association. However, in 2011 the association adopted a more moderate position that only "encourages veterinarians to educate clients and the public about the dangers associated with allowing cats free roam access to the outdoors" (AMVA 2011).

A central argument in favor of cat confinement, and the one on which we will focus in this chapter, maintains that confining cats—creating, as it were, "captive cats"—is what's *best for cats*. This is not the *only* argument promoting cat confinement; it's also often argued that outdoor cats can negatively impact wildlife, or be harmful to human interests. While these other arguments aren't the focus of this chapter, we will consider them later in the context of thinking through the broader ethical questions raised by cat confinement.

The argument that keeping cats confined is what's best for cats has two parts: the claim that roaming outdoors is highly dangerous to cats, and the claim that cats can be happy indoors. So the HSUS, for instance, claims both that "Allowing your cats to roam outdoors can significantly shorten their lives. Potentially deadly dangers...are constant threats to an outdoor cat" (HSUS 2013a) *and* that "Although many cats enjoy being outside, it's a myth that going outside is a requirement for feline happiness" (HSUS 2013b). PETA provides horror stories of outdoor cats burned with cooking grease and sold to laboratories, before concluding that "today's concrete jungles are far too dangerous for vulnerable, trusting little animals" and recommending "six steps to having a happy housecat" (PETA 2013). These claims are confidently and authoritatively asserted. But are they really plausible? What evidence is there to support such claims, and what ideas of "what's good for cats" are being presupposed here?

In this chapter, we'll examine these claims about routine cat confinement. By "routine confinement," we mean the idea that *all* cats should, *as a matter of routine*, be confined. (This does not mean that in specific circumstances there may not be good reasons to confine a particular cat, for example where the cat is anxious, or when the local outdoor environment contains major unavoidable hazards.) After outlining some important contextual issues, we'll explore the idea of "cat welfare." We'll point out that what constitutes "cat welfare" is contested, in several different ways. With this in mind, we'll look at what current research indicates about the lives of cats with free-roaming outdoor access, as opposed to the lives of cats that are confined indoors. What one concludes about whether these indoor/outdoor lives are "good for cats," we'll suggest, depends on what cat welfare is thought to be, how one weighs different elements of cat welfare, the circumstances in which particular cats are placed, and perhaps, even, on our ideas about what kind of being a cat actually is. But,

Courtesy of Susan Weingartner Photography

we'll conclude, even if it's possible to come to a clear view about what is in cats' interests, this does not necessarily tell us what to do ethically. Ethical decisions depend on what approach to ethical thinking we adopt (after all, we could think that cats have liberty rights, even if we also think liberty harms them) and how we weigh factors other than cat welfare (for instance, the welfare of cats' prey) in making such ethical decisions.

THE CONTEXT OF CONFINEMENT

The way in which humans live with companion cats in the industrialized world changed dramatically during the twentieth century; these changes made routine cat confinement feasible. Commercial cat food was first produced in the 1930s, and commercial cat litter in the 1950s; without these, the confinement of cats would be highly impractical. The latter part of the twentieth century also saw the growth of the idea that companion cats should routinely be spayed or neutered (an operation that was uncommon into the 1950s). In the United States, for instance, 80 percent of cats kept as companions are now neutered (Chu et al. 2009) and this number is growing. Neutering male cats is usually thought to be needed if cats are to be confined indoors in a normal home (and not in a cage as many male cats used for breeding are), since confined unneutered male cats are likely to manifest behaviors such as urine marking that make them difficult to live with. Since people also generally dislike living with female cats in heat, spaying female cats is often thought necessary too. For the purposes of this chapter, we'll assume that we're discussing the routine confinement of spayed or neutered cats; so we won't consider either the population issues generated by unneutered outdoor cats, nor the behavior of confined intact cats. Neutering is not the only surgical practice that has changed the way people live with cats; in some countries, significant numbers of cats are declawed—for instance, about 25 percent of cats in the United States (Patronek 2001). Declawing is a fairly significant surgery, involving amputation of at least ten of the cat's distal phalanges (the last bone in the toe) of the front paws, usually simultaneously, to prevent the cat scratching (furniture or people). This practice, again, makes living with cats indoors easier, but significantly changes the lives of the cats concerned.

The movement to confine cats is the culmination of a series of practices that have increasingly controlled the way cats live. And seen from a historical perspective, where cats were largely free to roam, the claim that routine confinement benefits cats themselves is not obvious. After all, confinement significantly reduces the space, variety, and forms of activity available to most cats. It removes them from the outdoor environments in which they evolved to become human companions, and entirely locates them in places typically designed around human convenience and comfort. It makes cats' dependence on human care and provision absolute in almost every sphere of their lives. And it closes off long-standing freedoms cats have had to adopt a second household, to completely relocate themselves in a different home, or to have no home at all. Many cat owners, especially in Europe, who object to the confinement of cats, make exactly these arguments: that confinement restricts cats' freedom and prevents them from roaming in the way cats always have.

The confinement of cats "for their own good" differentiates cats' situation both from the majority of cases of adult human confinement *and* most cases of animal confinement. In the human case, confinement normally requires special justification, based either on past harms committed or the deterrence of future harms. Adult human beings are not confined for their own good, unless they are judged to be in some way mentally incapable; the routine threats of going outdoors certainly do not justify adult human confinement. In the animal case, in contrast, special justifications for captivity are not usually seen as needed nor provided. Confinement may be for the use or convenience of the captor, for the benefit of other people, or in the service of a perceived greater good (such a breeding an endangered species). Animal confinement has grown as agriculture has intensified; in industrial farming, animals who would formerly have roamed outdoors now spend their entire lives confined within human structures. But the primary aim of *these* animal confinements has been to benefit people.

These just mentioned kinds of confinement contrast with the *paternalistic* move to confine companion cats indoors. We interpret paternalism here to mean a significant restriction on cats' freedom, without cats' consent or agreement (though of course, consent cannot be straightforwardly obtained from cats) in order to improve, or to protect their welfare.[1] This paternalistic argument runs something like this: Going outside is risky in a way cats can't understand or control; an indoor cat is a safe cat; it's in a cat's interests to be safe; so cats should be routinely confined.

Yet such claims about the confinement of companion cats raise questions. Is "indoors" really as safe as it may seem? How should "safety" be weighed against cats' freedom of movement? The first step in answering these questions is to think about what is in a cat's interest, that is, about the idea of *cat welfare*.

IDEAS OF CAT WELFARE

Ideas about cat welfare are highly contested. First, there are significant disagreements about how animal welfare in general should be understood, and what cat welfare in particular, should be taken to mean. Second, as Bradshaw and Casey (2007, 149) note, people's perceptions of companion animals affect what they believe to be in their animals' interests: "The ways in which owners treat their animals are profoundly influenced by their beliefs about how those animals evaluate the world around them; if any of those beliefs are inaccurate, the possibility arises that the animal may be treated in a way that the owner thinks is compatible with its welfare, but is actually detrimental." These factors together mean that understanding "what's good for cats" is a difficult task.

We'll start by outlining three prominent ideas of animal welfare. On the first view, what matters is an animal's inner subjective state—how it *feels*. Good welfare means "the absence of strong, negative emotional states that are often lumped together as 'suffering' and that include such states as pain, fear, frustration, deprivation, and in some species boredom" as well as "the presence of positive emotional states that are commonly called 'pleasure'" (Duncan 2005, 485). This is an essentially *hedonistic* view of welfare.

This hedonistic view is challenged by those who argue that whether animals are free to lead a full and natural life is wholly or additionally important to their welfare, "Animals, too, have natures—the pigness of the pig, the cowness of the cow, 'fish gotta swim, birds gotta fly'—which are as essential to their well-being as speech and assembly are to us" (Rollin 1993, 11). Here, Rollin suggests that animals' welfare partly, at least, depends on the animals being free to live in accordance with their "nature," usually understood in a species-specific way. It's not always clear on Rollin's account (or on other similar accounts) whether "living according to one's nature" is understood to be good for an animal's welfare in its own right (of course, it may *also* give the animal pleasure), or whether living according to his or her nature is good for the animal because it generally leads to more pleasant experiences. To avoid a collapse into hedonism, we'll here focus on the former view, on which being able to realize significant species-specific "natural" potentials and express natural behaviors is an essential element of a good life; we'll call this a "perfectionist" approach.

A third view of what constitutes animal welfare concerns the satisfaction of preferences or desires: essentially animals have good welfare when they get what they prefer or desire, and are not frustrated in doing so. This idea of what constitutes welfare is commonly accepted for humans: "for me, a good life is one in which my own considered, informed preferences are maximally satisfied" (Singer 2002). This account of preferences, though, raises interesting questions for *animal* welfare. First, there's some debate over what we should take a preference to be, and whether, to have a preference at all, one must be a language user—with the implication that few, if any, animals could have preferences at all (Frey 1980). However, most recent philosophical work at least accepts that we can make sense of "animal preferences"—that animals would rather be in some states than others, can make choices, and that it's reasonable to call these "preferences."

Singer's idea of preferences here, though, also maintains that preferences relevant to the good life should be "considered" and "informed." It's difficult to know how to apply these constraints on preferences to animals, since animals cannot reflect on their own preferences, nor can they straightforwardly be given relevant information that might change what they prefer. Yet the reasons Singer includes these constraints do seem relevant to animals, since they certainly could be ignorant of things that would change their preferences, and they could prefer things that are bad for them, and that would cause them, in the future, to be in states that they would not prefer. This raises some difficult questions about cat welfare, as we'll see.

These three accounts of welfare (and these aren't the only accounts of animal welfare) need not be completely exclusive. Someone could argue, for instance, that to have good welfare, a being must both have overall positive emotional states *and* must be free to perform natural behaviors. A hybrid view like this is, in principle, unproblematic. However, there may be cases where it's necessary to choose between one aspect of welfare and another—where performing natural behaviors might conflict with subjective feelings of pleasure, for instance. In such a case, it would be necessary to decide which element of welfare to prioritize.

Given these different accounts of welfare, then, what constitutes a *cat's* welfare can be construed in rather different ways. From a hedonistic perspective, there's no universal answer. Welfare will depend on specific circumstances, in terms of the way the cat's diet, environment, companions, health, and so on, affect the cat's subjective states of pain, pleasure, frustration, boredom, and stimulation. And since different cats may enjoy or dislike different things, this will vary between individuals. Welfare judgments here will also involve difficult calculations concerning how to weigh (for instance) definite current pleasures against small risks of severe future pains (for example, the pleasures of going outside versus the small chance of contracting a major disease).

From a perfectionist perspective, in order to assess cat welfare, we need instead to think about what constitutes "fulfilling natural potentials" and "natural behavior" for a cat, and to assess whether a particular cat is free to perform these natural behaviors. As Bradshaw and Casey (2007) argue, since cats are domesticated animals, identifying "natural behaviors" here may not be simple, but there are some very plausible candidates, such as scratching, hunting, pouncing, and various forms of territorial behavior.

In terms of a preference account of welfare, we would need to work out what individual cats do and do not prefer in order to understand their welfare. For some aspects of cats' lives, this could be approached by preference testing, where cats are given choices between different foods, toys, bedding, and so on (although such tests themselves are not without problems). However, other aspects of cats' lives will be more difficult to assess by preference tests; getting to "informed" preferences is not straightforward. As we'll argue later, it's problematic, for example, to conclude that a cat that has never been allowed outside could have an "informed preference" to remain indoors. In addition, there isn't a straightforward way of informing cats about the longer-term consequences of their preferences. This raises the possibility that we should think not only about cats' *actual* preferences, but also about their *hypothetical* preferences: what they *would* prefer, were they fully informed about risks and benefits. This, however, complicates this account of cat welfare, as we'll see.

These three accounts of welfare will often deliver the same verdict. A cat could easily have good welfare on all three measures. But equally, these accounts of welfare could diverge. A cat could have satisfied preferences, and be experiencing pleasure, but not be free to perform natural behaviors. Or a male cat could be performing natural behaviors—such as fighting another cat in his territory—and be satisfying his territorial preferences, but nonetheless be undergoing negative subjective states of pain or fear. So, we can't expect different accounts of welfare necessarily to converge on what to think about confining cats. And in fact, different understandings of welfare do appear to be one of the factors influencing the debate here.

But disagreement about what constitutes cat welfare doesn't end with different ideas of welfare. Even among those who accept similar interpretations of welfare, there are likely to be disagreements about how this is manifested in cats. For instance, even if two people agree that expressing natural behaviors is what's good for cats, they might still disagree about what actually constitutes cats' natural behaviors. For instance, as Clancy et al. (2003) note, cats have traditionally been understood as having independent or wild traits, and as Heath (2007) suggests, as "unsociable" and "aloof." If we think this is what cats are "naturally like" we might have an idea about their welfare that is different from PETA's description of cats as "vulnerable" and "trusting" kitties. Equally, two people who agree that subjective welfare is of primary importance could disagree on the substance of what *makes* for good subjective welfare—what actually gives cats pleasure, for instance. A focus on subjective welfare also raises questions about how one "trades off" positive and negative subjective experiences in welfare terms. For instance, does a cat that's roaming in a rich but risky outdoor environment and is painfully stung by a bee have better subjective welfare than a stressed, confined cat that's safe from external threats such as painful bee stings? (These questions are not after all unique to cats; similar questions are raised in terms of human welfare.) So deciding whether keeping cats confined is what's best for cats, then, depends—among other things—both on what's thought to *constitute* cat welfare, and on how one thinks this welfare is *actually manifested* in cats.

Having outlined these basic, and contrasting, ideas about what cat welfare actually is, we'll now move on to look at what research suggests the lives of cats both with free-roaming outdoor access, or kept wholly indoors, might be like. We can then think about how to interpret cat roaming and cat confinement in terms of cat welfare.

OUTDOOR ACCESS

What's meant by "outdoor access" varies considerably. Some cats have constant, free-roaming outdoor access. Others have outdoor access only for periods of the day, or only during the daytime (Clancy et al. [2003] found that of the cats allowed out, 97.1 percent were kept in at night). Some cats are confined by high fencing within a garden, but are not supervised there. Yet other cats have very restricted freedoms: for instance, always being kept on leashes outside. We'll take "outside access" here to mean unsupervised activity outdoors for at least a couple of hours a day, though "outside" may include a fenced yard.

There are significant cultural differences in terms of outdoor access for cats. In the United Kingdom (though figures are imprecise) more than 75 percent of cats have outdoor access. In the United States, however, only a minority of cats has unrestricted access to the outdoors. One study of 256 US households surveyed from 1993 to 2003 found that only 17 percent of cats had unrestricted outdoor access, and 50 percent of cats were kept indoors all the time (Bernstein 2007).

What are the lives of companion cats with outdoor access like? Cats usually establish a "home range," an area that they frequently patrol, and may have a smaller area, their "territory," that they "defend against encroachment from conspecifics" (Voith and Borchelt 1986). They mark their range by spraying urine, rubbing against objects, and scratching bark, leaving visual signs (Feldman 1994). While outdoors, they may run and climb, hide or perch, hunt rodents, birds, reptiles, and insects, and defecate and bury their feces, preferably in areas of loose soil. As recent research at the University of Georgia reveals, some cats also visit second homes (NPR 2012). Although few formal studies of the behavior of outdoor companion cats exist, it also seems likely that going outside allows cats to develop skills, behaviors, and ways of problem-solving that they would not be able to develop indoors (certainly, similar arguments are made for the benefits of unsupervised outdoor play by children—see research discussed in Valentine and McKendrick 1997).

Cats with outdoor access also face hazards. Some come from other animals: raptors, uncontrolled dogs, and in some places, coyote predation (Grubbs and Kausmann 2009). Unlike indoor-only cats, outdoor cats are also likely to encounter alien cats, with the potential for fighting, biting, and in the longer term for infectious disease including feline immunodeficiency virus (FIV) and feline leukemia virus (FeLV). There's no effective vaccine for FIV, and although cats can live well for many years with the virus, it can ultimately be fatal. However, FIV is fairly difficult to catch, and the major risk is for unneutered male cats who may sustain deep bites while fighting. FeLV is more easily transmitted, but an effective vaccine is available for outdoor cats.

The greatest hazard for cats with outdoor access, almost everywhere, is traffic. Exact statistics on the incidence of cats having road traffic accidents (RTAs) are difficult to find. Rochlitz (2003, 587) in a study carried out in Cambridge, UK, found that of 980 cats with outdoor access, brought to a small group of veterinary practices for reasons other than a road traffic accident (RTA), 12 percent had been in an RTA in the past. This study found that age, sex, and time of day were very significant factors in risk for RTAs (being young, male, nonpedigree, and out at night created greatest risk). Rochlitz (2004, 391) also found the mortality rate of owned cats in RTAs in Cambridge to be 21 percent (including cats found dead at the scene; of those owned cats who made it alive to the vet after a RTA, 13.7 percent died). However, we don't have good statistics on what percentage of outdoor companion cats actually suffer an RTA in the first place.

These factors taken together show that cats with outdoor access have both plentiful opportunities and significant risks. We don't know what the combined risks of disease, being hit by cars, and being attacked by other animals actually are to companion cats; and in any case, such risks will vary significantly, based on age, sex, whether the cat goes out at night, whether the cat lives near a busy road, whether there are local predators, and so on. Statistics on the life expectancy of cats with outdoor access are strongly disputed, though there's general agreement that on average, these cats live shorter lives than cats confined indoors.

So: cats allowed to go outdoors inevitably face hazards including traffic, "stranger danger," and infectious disease; but they also move in a rich and stimulating environment. How does this compare with the lives of "captive cats"?

INDOOR CONFINEMENT

Just as cats' outdoor contexts vary substantially, so may the contexts of indoor cats. Some confined cats may have a previous history of roaming; others may never have been outside. Some cats may be confined in large houses; others may be in studio apartments. Some may share their home with other people or animals most of the time; others live mostly solitary lives. Whatever their circumstances, though, one idea that's widely thought to be obvious is that indoor-only cats are safer and face fewer hazards than outdoor cats. But indoor cats do also face hazards, although some of these are more "slow-burn" than the hazards that outdoor cats meet.

First: accidents happen to indoor as well as outdoor cats: they can be scalded, they can have falls, and they can be poisoned. Rochlitz (2007) reports the Blue Cross in London as recording that household accidents were the second most common reason that kittens and puppies were brought into their hospital. However, this risk is not really relevant here, since cats with outdoor access usually come inside, so they will face these risks too. We're primarily interested here in special risks that face indoor-only cats.

Indoor confinement itself presents higher risks of certain diseases. Some (but not all) studies suggest that indoor cats are at greater risk of feline urologic syndrome, hyperthyroidism, and serious dental disease (Buffington 2002, Rochlitz 2007). Other recent studies—for example, Slingerland et al. (2007, 251)—report that "the outdoor/indoor status of the cat appeared to have a significant influence on the risk of developing DM (diabetes mellitus) with the risk being significantly lower in cats that spent time roaming outdoors." Being indoors also raises the likelihood of obesity, which generates further health risks (Sandøe, Corr, and Palmer 2013). In addition, a recent Danish study (Bjørnvad et al. 2011) of indoor-confined, adult, neutered cats found that due to lack of exercise, some indoor cats are in a state called "skinny fat." As with some physically inactive people, due to a decrease in lean body mass, these cats have a relatively high level of body fat despite what appears to be a healthy body weight. And as in the human case, "skinny fat" can lead to diabetes and other serious health problems.

So confined cats don't live in a risk-free environment, in terms of either accident or disease, although as far as threats of sudden death and incurable disease go, the indoor environment is, overall, less risky. But the confined nature of the indoor environment also raises other difficulties.

One of these occurs when cats, especially cats that do not get along well, are confined together in small spaces. Research suggests that while cats frequently tolerate being housed with their mother or siblings, living with an unrelated cat can be highly stressful, and doing so increases the likelihood of cats developing urinary tract infections and expressing what are called "problem behaviors"— that is, "inappropriate elimination," urine spraying, aggression towards people or other animals, and scratching. (See Bradshaw and Casey 2007.) Salman et al. (2000) report that "the presence of at least one other pet in the household appeared to be strikingly associated with an increase in feline relinquishments for behavioral reasons." In fact, several studies, most recently Amat et al (2009), suggest that—in general—cats without outdoor access show significantly more "problem behaviors" than those able to go outdoors. Although these behaviors may signify stress, by "problem" here is meant a problem for the *owner*, not the cat directly. However, Salman et al. (2000) found that behavioral problems are the second most frequently offered reason for feline relinquishment at animal shelters; and in the case of cats, a high percentage of relinquishments end in euthanasia.

A final worry about the indoor-only life concerns "behavioral restriction," when "Captive conditions are...too impoverished (i.e. barren, without appropriate stimuli or substrates) or too small, to allow animals to perform natural behavior patterns that they would display in more natural settings" (Mason and Burn 2011, 98). How far indoor cats are likely to undergo behavioral restriction depends on how much space they have, how this space is arranged, and what activities cats' owners engage in as substitutes for behaviors cats would be able to perform outside. If cats have places to hide, climb, run and scratch, regularly changed moving toys that allow them to jump and pounce, and other forms of stimulation, for example based on clicker training, then they are much less likely to undergo behavioral restriction. However, many owners have limited time and space to dedicate to their indoor cats; and this can lead to cats' frustration and boredom.

COMPARATIVE CAT WELFARE

This brief review of evidence (and there is not much) about the comparative lives of indoor-only/outdoor-access cats raises many questions about whether confinement indoors—creating "captive cats"—actually is for their own good.

From a hedonistic welfare perspective, no *general* answer is possible. Each cat should be taken individually, to consider what indoor and outdoor environments are available, what seems to give the cat pleasure, what creates states of fear or frustration, what experiences the cat has already had, and what experiences the cat is likely to forgo. So, a lively, inquisitive cat, used to outdoor access, located in a relatively benign external environment, with only a small amount of space indoors, is likely to be better off going outdoors. The converse may be true of a cat that's timid, has never been outdoors, and that lives in a large house near a busy road. Since the benefits and risks cats' environments present are to some degree open to manipulation, however, they should not be taken entirely as given. Indoor environments can be adapted to better satisfy indoor cats; threats from the outside can be reduced, for instance by vaccinations against disease, by keeping cats in at night, and by fencing in yards. So, taking this into account, the confinement of cats for their own good, on this view of "good," could be justified in some cases, but not in others. It seems very implausible that, on a hedonistic view, *routine* confinement could be justified.

If cats' welfare is judged wholly or largely by the freedom to fulfill natural potentials and to express natural behaviors, it's likely that, in most cases, having outdoor access will create better welfare than confinement. Many behaviors that studies suggest are natural to cats cannot straightforwardly be carried out indoors, or—like urine spraying—would be very unwelcome there. Adaptations of indoor environments may accommodate some natural behaviors: scratching on a scratching post, for instance. But indoor cats will, in almost all cases, have much smaller territories than those with outdoor access, will be able to exercise less, and will have their predatory behaviors considerably curtailed, even if toys are provided. They will never gain the learning experiences that flow from dealing with complex and unpredictable environments. While from other welfare perspectives this may not matter (since indoor cats will permanently be confined indoors, they will not need these skills for their future welfare), from a perfectionist view, at least some of these skills are manifestations of natural potentials that it's good for cats to express. So, from a perfectionist perspective, outdoor access looks as though it will normally give cats better welfare.

Perhaps the most difficult issues here are raised by preference-based approaches to welfare. Clearly, some cats with experience of the outdoors desire to go out: they scratch at doors, try to slip through them, and vocalize noisily. In these circumstances, important preferences are being frustrated. Cats that have never been outside, but that can see through a window, may also desire to go out. But some indoor-only cats may have no preference to go out, not knowing that there's anything else to choose, nor that they are missing anything. Indeed, faced with the prospect of going outside, an indoor cat may display fearful or indifferent behavior. These cats either don't positively desire to go outside, or actively desire not to go out. Achieving such states seems to be the goal of urging owners always to keep cats inside: cats won't miss what they've never had. So, does this mean, from a preference perspective, that these indoor cats have good welfare?

The main problem that's raised here concerns whether the preferences of indoor cats that don't want to go out are "considered" or "informed." A case could be made for saying that they are not—rather, they may be seen as "adaptive" or "deformed." Although these terms can be used in different ways, in the human case "adaptive preferences" are usually characterized as preferences "produced through indoctrination, psychological manipulation, and the denial of autonomy" (Bartky 1990, 42) in the context of unjust and oppressive background conditions. Nussbaum (2007, 343) extends this idea to some animal preferences, maintaining that "animals, too, can learn submissive or fear-induced preferences." While the case of cats is obviously much less complex than the case of humans, nonetheless a version of this argument might be applied to indoor-only cats. Having always been denied outdoor access, their preferences may have adapted to their circumstances, though this could not be described as a choice. This resembles a scenario Regan (1984) describes:

> If I were to raise my son in a comfortable cage, in isolation from other human contact, though seeing to it that his basic biological needs were satisfied, and if, in all of my dealings with him, I went to considerable trouble to insure [sic] that he experienced no unnecessary pain, then I could not be faulted on the grounds that I was hurting him. However, I would have quite obviously harmed him and this in a most grievous way. How lame would be my retort that my son "didn't know what he was missing" and so wasn't harmed by me. That he doesn't know what he's missing is part of the harm I have done to him. (Regan 1984, 97)

We can't be confident, then, that the actual preferences of indoor cats to stay inside really reflect what's best for them on a preference account of welfare; these may be distorted, adaptive preferences. This suggests we should, also, consider indoor cats' *hypothetical* preferences: what they would prefer, had they experience of both outdoor access and the indoor life. What answer we give here, though, will depend on what we think will best serve cats' welfare; so this throws us back to the question of what we conclude constitutes cat welfare in the first place. Equally, we can't be confident that outdoor cats' preferences to go outdoors should count as "informed" either. Even if cats are experienced with traffic and predators, they can't understand the risks they face (for instance) from disease; perhaps we need to think about hypothetical preferences here, too. So, this leaves us in a confusing position. Some cats have actual preferences to go outside, others to remain inside. Hypothetically, we might conclude that some cats would prefer to go outside, were they "fully informed"; while others, with full information, would prefer to stay inside. But one thing that does emerge here is that whatever we might conclude in any particular case, a preference account of welfare does not clearly support the *routine* confinement of cats.

In fact, none of these three accounts of cat welfare, given the evidence, *clearly* supports the position that cats should be routinely confined for their own good. The "natural behavior" account of welfare tends to the view that it's better for cats if they are *not* confined, and are free to express important natural behaviors. However, even on this view if a sufficiently spacious and enriched indoor environment could be created, cats may be able to express enough natural behavior to have good welfare. A subjectivist view of welfare would not support routine confinement, but would accept that it may be best for a cat's welfare on some occasions; and a preference account, likewise, would not support routine confinement, though (depending on what view one takes of hypothetical and adaptive preferences) it's likely to be what's best for particular cats on many particular occasions.

So far, we've focused on the relationship between cat confinement and welfare. But even if we establish that, in some particular case, confinement is not in a cat's interests (or otherwise) this alone would not tell us what to do; for this, we need to think about the broader ethical context in which cat welfare is situated.

ETHICS AND CAT CONFINEMENT

In order to work out what we should actually *do* in any particular case, cats' welfare must be thought through in the context of a broader ethical framework, which includes the welfare of other affected individuals, and other potentially significant values, and that may include values, principles, and concerns that are not about promotion of welfare. However, for the sake of brevity we'll confine ourselves to considering two contrasting theoretical approaches here: a rights-based view, such as that recently proposed by Donaldson and Kymlicka (2012); and a broadly welfarist and consequentialist approach, one that aims at maximizing overall welfare (including, but not restricted to, cats' welfare). (For a fuller overview of positions in animal ethics see Palmer and Sandøe 2011.)

Donaldson and Kymlicka (2012) argue that while all sentient animals have certain basic rights, companion cats—as domesticated animals brought into our homes—should be understood as *co-citizens*, with specific rights that attach to this status. These rights include a negative right not to be restrained or confined, and a positive right to mobility. On this view, at first sight at least, we should not confine cats; doing so would be a serious rights infringement. However, this needs closer scrutiny. Central to this rights account is that an individual's rights should not be violated to benefit others. But this does not rule out a *paternalistic* argument, where rights are infringed in order to benefit that very same individual. And while it's highly implausible that a paternalistic argument could justify *routine* overriding of cats' liberty and mobility rights, there could be some cases where, even on a liberty-rights view, paternalistic confinement could be justified, and an individual cat be confined for his or her own good.

What could count as acceptable paternalism here, though, will again depend on how cat welfare is understood. Donaldson and Kymlicka (2012, 127) are wary of similar paternalistic claims in the human case: "Historically, people with disabilities or mental illness have been confined in ways that far exceed an acceptable paternalism. This should make us wary of calls for confinement/

restraint that are alleged to be in the interests of the person being subject to restriction." And certainly, as we've maintained in this chapter, it's not clear that confinement is always, or usually, in the interests of the cat being subject to restriction. If we are working within a framework that includes liberty rights, a clear-cut justification for confinement would be needed before infringing on cats' liberty for paternalistic reasons.

However, Donaldson and Kymlicka also argue that, in terms of making overall judgments about confining cats, we need to take into account the effect they have on other sentient animals, through predation. This shifts the ground from what's essentially a *paternalistic* argument to a *deterrence* argument, where the aim is to deter attacks by cats on other sentient individuals.

It's worth noting here that the most recent study, based on filming by cats carrying "kitty cams," shows that only 44 percent of cats with outdoor access actually hunted (although it's possible that the presence of even nonhunting cats in the ecosystem may affect wildlife) (Loyd et al. 2013). So not every outdoor cat is a significant threat to the welfare or liberty of others. However, as Donaldson and Kymlicka (2012, 150) note, cats "are unable to self regulate when it comes to respecting the basic liberties of others." For this reason, they suggest belling and supervising cats outdoors to prevent predation. Yet while, as studies show, belling probably does have some effect on predation (Ruxton, Thomas, and Wright 2002; Woods, McDonald, and Harris, 2003), belled cats remain successful predators. And supervision of cats while outdoors will in most cases be either impractical or significantly restrictive. So it may be that to protect the liberties of prey animals, on this view, cats should be confined, not because it's in their interests, but to prevent other sentient animals from being harmed.

Although Donaldson and Kymlicka argue that the basic liberties of prey animals need to be respected, and thus cat predation restrained, this *need* not follow from a rights-based view. They maintain that allowing cats to hunt is "not much better than killing the birds and mice ourselves" (2012, 150). But this claim is surely too strong. If a person killed birds and mice directly, on a view on which animals are rights-holders, that person would violate the animals' rights. But there's a difference between someone killing a mouse him- or herself, and his or her cat killing a mouse. While it is possible for someone to violate another being's rights by directly using an animal as a weapon (for instance, in the case of giving a command to "kill!" to a trained attack dog), cat predation is rather different. Cats don't predate on human command, and they are not agents for their owners. A cat that kills a mouse does not violate the mouse's right to life because cats are not moral agents; they do not (in our view) have the capacities required to be held morally responsible for their actions. But if cats are confined to prevent them killing mice, their liberty rights do seem to be violated.

It might be argued, though, that in a rights framework that includes sentient animals, we have duties to *assist* sentient animals (or even, that they have positive rights to assistance). So we should assist cats' prey, by confining cats. However—although there is not space to develop this argument in detail here—this opens up a variety of problems. It implies that cats' negative rights not to be confined are secondary to other animals' positive rights to be assisted, or that duties to assist should be prioritized over basic liberty rights. Yet negative rights such as those not to be confined are normally thought to have priority in conflict cases. Second, it appears to imply that we have general duties to intervene in predation, unless another argument is made that picks cats out from other kinds of predators (perhaps on the basis of our responsibility for cats' presence). Even Donaldson and Kymlicka (2012, 245) do not think that *all* predation should be prevented; for instance, where certain animal populations become too high, they suggest that we may "foster habitat conditions allowing for population dispersal and the re-emergence of predators or competitors." So a rights framework does not seem to justify the *routine* confinement of cats, though it allows for some paternalistic confinements where the benefits to the confined cat are clear-cut; and (given certain controversial additional theoretical arguments) confinements of some cats to protect other sentient animals.

Let's turn to the second ethical approach here: a consequentialist one. Here the goal is to bring about best outcomes in terms of welfare (other versions of this approach could include consequences such as impacts on biodiversity), taking into account all the beings affected by the confinement (or otherwise) of cats—including people and other sentient animals. Should cats be confined, on this approach? Obviously, the answer to this question will depend not only on cats, but on what consequences for all those concerned is taken to be. One thing that does seem clear, however, is that if it can be argued that it's in a cat's interests to be confined, then there's unlikely to be any countervailing argument. It's very unlikely that confining a cat, when it's in the cat's interests, is going to significantly diminish the morally relevant consequences for humans or other animals. The difficulties here arise in cases where confining a cat does *not* seem obviously to be in the cat's interests, but it is in human interests or in the interests of other living beings. Suppose, for instance, that there's a cat that appears to get great pleasure from the outdoors, behaves as though he desires to go out, and performs natural behaviors and fulfills potentials while outside—including much successful predation. On every account of welfare, outdoor access rather than confinement appears to be in the interests of this cat.

But on this consequentialist approach, we should also take other factors into account. Free-roaming cats can affect human welfare. They can upset and annoy those who live nearby, for example, by digging, hunting, defecating, urine spraying, and leaving their footprints on cars. Their hunting behaviors may also threaten conservation values, which may be seen as a problematic consequence in its own right, and cause distress to conservationists. Outdoor cats may also carry diseases, such as toxoplasmosis and cat-scratch disease that can significantly affect human welfare (understood in any sense). So these concerns must be weighed against what's in the cat's interests.

A consequentialist approach should also take into account the effects of the cat's predation on its prey. And predation seems problematic to the prey on at least two accounts of welfare. On a hedonistic approach to welfare, the cat is likely to cause a significant amount of suffering and negative welfare for the prey, especially if the cat is a successful hunter. This may well outweigh the negative experiences (or the reduction in positive experiences) that confinement would cause the cat—even though the cats that hunt the most may well be those for whom confinement is most subjectively traumatic. Similar conclusions seem likely for a preference-based view: the outdoor, hunting-oriented preferences of the cat don't obviously outweigh the preferences of the prey to go on living.

These factors all suggest that, working with a broader ethical framework, there are reasons to confine more cats than is suggested by just looking at what's "good for cats" alone. In many cases—depending on what we take welfare to mean—cats themselves would do better with relatively unrestricted outdoor access. But at least some cats' outdoor access may cause problems for other people, and for wildlife. This is likely to lead us to conclude that we should confine some cats, not because it's in their interests, but because it's in the interests of others. Nonetheless, this still does not take us to a commitment to *routine* confinement. None of the views of welfare, combined with any of the ethical theories we've considered, recommend that all cats should be confined, all the time, for their own good—or for the good of others.

SOME CONCLUSIONS

We began by exploring the widespread and confidently asserted paternalistic claims that keeping cats confined in our homes—making "captive cats"—may be in cats' own interests. We've argued that there are many different interpretations of what constitute cats' interests, and that cats themselves have very different experiences and live in very different circumstances. There certainly are significant hazards for cats outdoors; but indoor cats face often underestimated risks from disease, stressful and unsuitable environments, and owner reactions caused by "problem behaviors." Consequently, general claims that routine confinement is in cats' interests seem implausible. At best, confinement may be in *some* cats' interests; and on accounts of welfare that emphasize natural behavior and fulfillment of natural potential, confinement may be in very few or *no* cats' interests.

However, cats' interests are not the only relevant factor in terms of broader ethical decision-making about cats. On some ethical views, for instance, we need to take into account the interests of the sentient animals on which outdoor cats prey, the value of protecting populations of wild animals which may be affected by cats and the people to whom outdoor cats cause distress. This may lead us to conclude that some cats, at least, should be confined even when it's *not* in their interests, and when they would be better off having outdoor access.

However, the idea of confining cats when it's not in their interests seems to raise the question whether, in such cases, cats should be kept at all. But that it would be better for a particular cat to go outside does not mean that the alternative—life inside—is necessarily bad; just that, for this cat, it is not the best life possible. The cat *may* still have reasonable welfare indoors, on any measure of welfare. In addition, before deciding that a cat should not be kept indoors, we would need to consider what the alternatives are for that particular cat. Cats living long term in a "no-kill" shelter waiting for adoption are likely to be better-off in a studio apartment than a cage, even if they would be better off still with outdoor access. However: if an indoor environment is too small, and for whatever reason cannot be made sufficiently stimulating, such that a cat is unhappy, frustrated, or cannot perform natural behaviors, then there's a strong prima facie argument against keeping the cat. This argument is particularly compelling for those who are sympathetic to perfectionist theories of animal welfare: DeGrazia (2011, 763), for instance, argues that if cats must be kept indoors, they should not be kept at all. We're familiar with such arguments in the context of zoos, though often in zoo cases, we are dealing with animals whom we could have avoided breeding in the first place, as opposed to—as is frequently the case with cats—animals already in existence that need adoption.

Whatever is concluded about when it's acceptable for cats to live wholly confined lives, we have argued here that such confinement should *not be routine*, on the grounds that confinement is what's good for cats. Although this claim is confidently and widely repeated, we suggest that it should be revisited and reconsidered. Confinement is good for some cats in some places at some times. But confinement is no universal prescription for good cat welfare.

ACKNOWLEDGMENTS

The authors are grateful to Sara Kondrup for help in searching for literature for this chapter, to Ayoe Hoff and Lori Gruen for useful comments on an earlier version of the manuscript, and to Sandra Corr for helpful discussions on cat welfare and health.

NOTE

1. This is a version of the conditions of paternalism outlined by Dworkin (2010). We should also note here that some breeding cats are confined (like agricultural animals) to secure efficient production. We don't have space to consider this issue here, but it's worth noting that if domestic house cats are very widely neutered and confined, intensive breeding might increase in order to maintain the supply of suitable companion cats.

REFERENCES

Amat, M., J. L. R. de la Torree, J. Fatjo, V. M. Mariotti, S. Van Wijk, and X. Manteca. 2009. "Potential risk Factor Associated with Feline Behavior Problems." *Applied Animal Behaviour Science* 121: 134–139.

American Medical Veterinary Association (AMVA). 2011. "Revised Policy on Free-Roaming, Owned Cats." Accessed November 21, 2013. https://www.avma.org/About/Governance/Documents/Resolution7.pdf.

Bartky, Sandra L. 1990. "Narcissism, Femininity, and Alienation." In *Femininity and Domination: Studies in the Phenomenology of Oppression*, Sandra Lee Bartky (ed.), 33–44. New York: Routledge.

Bernstein, Penny. 2007. "The Human-Cat Relationship." In *The Welfare of Cats*, Irene Rochlitz (ed.), 47–90. Dordrecht: Springer.

Bjørnvad, C. R., D. H. Nielsen, J. Armstrong, F. McEvoy, K. M. Hølmkjær, K. S. Jensen, G. F. Pedersen, and A. T. Kristensen. 2011. "Evaluation of a Nine-Point Body Condition Scoring System in Physically Inactive Pet Cats." *American Journal of Veterinary Research* 72(4): 433–437.

Bradshaw, J., and R. Casey. 2007. "Anthropomorphism and Anthropocentrism as Influences on the Quality Of life of Companion Animals." *Animal Welfare* 16(S): 149–154.

Buffington, C. A. T. 2002. "External and Internal Influences on Disease Risks in Cats." *Journal of the American Medical Veterinary Association* 220(7): 994–1002.

Chu, Karyen, Wendy Anderson, and Micha Rieser. 2009. "Population Characteristics and Neuter Status of Cats Living in Households in the United States." *Journal of the American Veterinary Medical Association* 234(8): 1023–1030.

Clancy, Elizabeth, Antony S. Moore, and Elizabeth R. Bertone. 2003. "Evaluation of Cat and Owner Characteristics and their Relationships to Outdoor Access of Owned Cats." *Journal of the American Veterinary Association* 222(11): 1541–1545.

DeGrazia, David. 2011. "The Ethics of Confining Animals: From Farms to Zoos to Human Homes." In *The Oxford Handbook of Animal Ethics*, Tom Beauchamp and R. G. Frey (eds.), 738–768. Oxford: Oxford University Press.

Donaldson, Sue and Will Kymlicka. 2012. *Zoopolis: A Political Theory of Animal Rights*. New York: Oxford University Press.

Duncan, Ian. 2005. "Science Based Assessment of Animal Welfare: Farm animals." *Revue Scientifique et Technique* 24(2): 483–492.

Dworkin, Gerald. 2010. "Paternalism." In *The Stanford Encyclopedia of Philosophy* (Summer 2010 edition), Edward Zalta (ed.). Accessed November 21, 2013. http://plato.stanford.edu/archives/sum2010/entries/paternalism/.

Feldman, H.N. 1994. "Methods of Scent Marking in the Domestic Cat." *Canadian Journal of Zoology* 72: 1093–1099.

Frey, R. G. 1980. *Interests and Rights: The Case against Animals*. Oxford: Clarendon Press.

Grubbs, S. E., and P. R, Krausman. 2009. "Observations of Coyote-Cat Interactions." *Journal of Wildlife Management* 73(5): 683–685.

Heath, S. 2007. "Behavior Problems and Welfare." In *The Welfare of Cats*, Irene Rochlitz (ed.), 91–118. Dordrecht: Springer.

Humane Society of the United States (HSUS). 2013a. "Home, Sweet Home: Bringing an Outside Cat In." October 2. Accessed November 21, 2013. http://www.humanesociety.org/animals/cats/tips/bringing_outside_cat_indoors.html.

Humane Society of the United States (HSUS). 2013b. "How to Keep Your Cat Happy Indoors." July 31. Accessed November 21, 2013. http://www.humanesociety.org/animals/cats/tips/cat_happy_indoors.html.

Loyd, Kerrie, Sonia Hernandez, John Carroll, Kyler Abernathy, and Greg Marshall. 2013. "Quantifying Free-Roaming Domestic Cat Predation Using Animal Borne Video Cameras." *Biological Conservation* 160: 183–189.

Mason, G., and C. Burn. 2011. "Behavioural Restriction." In *Animal Welfare*, 2nd ed., M. C. Appleby, J. A. Mench, A. Olsson, and B. O. Hughes (eds.), 98–119. Wallingford, Oxfordshire: CABI.

National Public Radio (NPR). 2012. "Kitty Cam Reveals the Secret Life of Roaming Cats." August 10. Accessed November 21, 2013. http://www.npr.org/2012/08/10/158589981/kitty-cam-reveals-the-secret-life-of-roaming-cats.

Nussbaum, Martha. 2007. *Frontiers of Justice*. Oxford: Oxford University Press.

Palmer, Clare, and Peter Sandøe. 2011. "Animal Ethics." In *Animal Welfare*, 2nd ed., M. C. Appleby, J. A. Mench, I. A. S. Olsson, and B. O. Hughes (eds.), 1–12. Wallingford, Oxfordshire: CABI.

Patronek, G. J. 2001. "Assessment of Claims of Short- and Long-Term Complications Associated with Onychectomy in cats." *Journal of the American Veterinary Medical Association* 219(7): 932–7.

People for the Ethical Treatment of Animals (PETA). 2013. "Why All Cats Should Be Indoor Cats." Accessed November 21, 2013. http://www.peta.org/living/companion-animals/indoor-cats.aspx.

Regan, Tom. 1984. *The Case for Animal Rights*. Berkeley: University of California Press.

Rochlitz, Irene. 2003. "Study of Factors That May Dispose Domestic Cats to Road Traffic Accidents: Part 1." *Veterinary Record* 153(18): 549–553.

Rochlitz, Irene. 2004. "Clinical Study of Cats Injured and Killed in Road Traffic Accidents in Cambridgeshire." *Journal of Small Animal Practice* 45: 390–394.

Rochlitz, Irene. 2007. "Housing and Welfare." In *The Welfare of Cats*, Irene Rochlitz (ed.), 177–204. Dordrecht: Springer.

Rollin, B. E. 1993. "Animal Production and the New Social Ethic for Animals." In *Food Animal Well-Being*, Conference Proceedings and Deliberations, Purdue Research Foundation (ed.), 3–13. West Lafayette, IN: USDA and Purdue University Office of Agricultural Research Programs.

Ruxton, G. D., S. Thomas, and J. Wright. 2002. "Bells Reduce Predation by Domestic Cats (*Felis catus*)." *Journal of Zoology* 256(1): 81–83.

Salman, M, J. Hutchison, R. Ruch-Gallie, L. Kogan, J. New, P. Kass, and J. Scarlett. 2000. "Behavioral Reasons for Relinquishment of Dogs and Cats to 12 Shelters." *Journal of Applied Animal Welfare Science* 3(2): 93–106.

Sandøe, P., S. Corr, and C. Palmer. 2013. Forthcoming. "Fat Companions: Understanding the Welfare Effects of Obesity in Cats and Dogs." In *Dilemmas in Animal Welfare*, M. Appleby, D. Weary, and P. Sandøe (eds.). Wallingford, Oxfordshire: CABI.

Singer, P. 2002. "A Response to Martha Nussbaum". http://www.utilitarianism.net/singer/by/20021113.htm

Slingerland, L. I., V. V. Fazilova, E. A. Plantinga, H. S. Kooistra, and A. C. Beynen. 2007. "Indoor Confinement and Physical Inactivity Rather Than the Proportion of Dry Food Are Risk Factors in the Development of Feline Type 2 Diabetes Mellitus." *Veterinary Journal* 179(2): 247–253

Valentine, G., and J. McKendrick. 1997. "Children's Outdoor Play: Exploring Parental Concerns about Children's Safety and the Changing Nature of Childhood." *Geoforum* 28(2): 219–235

Voith, Victoria, and Peter Borchelt. 1986. "Social Behavior of Domestic Cats." *Continuing Education* 8(9): 637–646. http://expeng.anr.msu.edu/sites/animalwelfare/files/Social_Behavior_1_%28Voith,_1986%29.pdf.

Woods, Michael, Robbie A. McDonald, and Stephen Harris. 2003. "Predation of Wildlife by Domestic Cats *Felix catus* in Great Britain." *Mammal Review* 33(2): 174–188.

10

Born in Chains?

The Ethics of Animal Domestication

ALASDAIR COCHRANE ■

The forms of animal captivity that cause the most public controversy are undoubtedly those involving wild animals. Many feel deeply uncomfortable about holding majestic wild animals in captivity; whether it be killer whales and dolphins in sea life parks, chimpanzees and other great apes in zoos and wildlife parks, or elephants and bears in circuses. But while the captivity of wild animals undoubtedly poses pressing ethical problems, the vast majority of captive animals are in fact members of *domesticated* species. The companion animals in our homes, the food animals in our farms, and the research animals in our laboratories have not only been bred specifically to be held captive, but they have also been bred for quite particular traits in order to make them more amenable to captivity. As such, if we are to conduct a rounded assessment of the ethics of captivity, it is absolutely vital that we have an assessment of the ethics of animal domestication.

This chapter identifies four positions on the ethics of domestication, each of which conceives of domesticated animals—and their captivity—in a different way. The first position, found in the work of certain environmental ethicists, is that domestication is morally problematic insofar as it creates unnatural "living artifacts" who are stunted and inferior versions of their wild ancestors. The second position, by way of contrast, sees nothing unnatural about domestication, but instead sees it as a benign process that animals themselves pursued as a successful strategy for survival. The third position can be found in the work of "abolitionist" animal rights scholars, and claims that domestication is unethical in view of the fact that it reduces animals essentially to "slaves," who are totally dependent upon humans for every aspect of their well-being. The final position agrees that domestication makes animals dependent, but argues that they can still lead flourishing lives if we acknowledge certain "special" obligations towards them, perhaps even involving the recognition of their "citizenship."

This chapter is organized by critically evaluating each of these positions systematically. It finds each of them wanting: none properly describes the ethical problems posed by domestication, and none properly resolves them. After these candidate positions having been considered, at the end of the chapter an alternative position on animal domestication is briefly sketched. This position does not conceive of domesticated animals as in any way different from other animals (not artifacts, not strategists, not slaves, not citizens). Instead, it simply asks us to conceive of and to treat domesticated animals like any other: as individual sentient creatures with interests of their own. This understanding, it claims, offers the best means by which to deal with the moral problems posed by domestication. It also implies that while we have no obligation to end domestication, or to stop holding all domesticated animals captive, we do have a pressing obligation to eradicate and overhaul those institutions and practices that ensure that domesticated animals lead short lives full of suffering.

Before getting to this analysis, however, a crucial problem remains unaddressed. Just what does this chapter mean by domestication? And in turn, which animals count as domesticated, and which do not?

WHO ARE DOMESTICATED ANIMALS?

Some claim that domestication can either be understood as primarily "biological" or as primarily "sociological" (Swart and Keulartz 2011; Anderson 1997). While the former focuses on the physiological changes to the animals that take place through processes of separation and breeding, the latter focuses more on the patterns of dependency and domination that are entailed. One way in which this difference can be illustrated is by thinking about the examples of animals in sea life parks, zoos, wildlife parks, and circuses mentioned above. Under a strictly biological understanding, these animals would not be regarded as domesticated, for they possess the same physiological characteristics as their conspecifics in the wild. However, if one adopts a sociological definition of domestication then these animals certainly are domesticated, dependent as they are on human beings for their care and well-being (Swart and Keulartz 2011; Anderson 1997).

This chapter will adopt a conception of domestication that sees both biological *and* sociological changes as intrinsic to the process. Having biological change as part of the conception is in keeping with the ordinary understanding of the term: physiological changes and differences are usually considered a necessary part of labeling an animal "domesticated"; and captivity and domestication are not usually regarded as coterminous. Nonetheless, a plausible conception of domestication cannot focus solely on the biological changes entailed, for it must also be acknowledged that the process involves a massive transformation in the *relations* between the humans and animals involved.

The focus of this chapter will thus be those processes whereby animals are separated from their wild conspecifics, who are tamed and bred, and who then develop certain physiological differences from their ancestors (Clutton-Brock 1989, 7). How should we assess those processes ethically?

DOMESTICATED ANIMALS AS "ARTIFACTS"

Some environmental ethicists have claimed that the domestication of animals is a moral wrong. On this view, domesticated animals are "unnatural," "lack integrity," and should be "eliminated" (Rodman 1977, 101; Rolston III 1991, 67). For these thinkers, the moral problem with domestication is that it is emblematic of humanity's desire to control and shape nature to its own ends: it transforms natural entities into "artifacts." While J. Baird Callicott has since changed his mind about domesticated animals, his earlier views really do capture the spirit of this environmentalist critique of domestication extremely well:

> They (domesticated animals) are living artefacts, but artefacts neverthe-less, and they constitute yet another mode of extension of the works of man into the ecosystem. From the perspective of the land ethic a herd of cattle, sheep, or pigs is as much or more of a ruinous blight on the land-scape as a fleet of four-wheel-drive off-road vehicles. (Callicott 1995, 50)

For Rodman, Rolston III, and Callicott (once), domestication is morally wrong insofar as it transforms natural entities into man-made "things."

However, this position is extremely implausible. In the main, it is hard to dis-cern precisely what is morally wrong with the transformation of natural entities into man-made artifacts. After all, the implicit assumption behind this thinking is that what is natural must be considered morally good and worth preserving as it exists presently. But not everything that exists should exist, at least in its present form. For example, some natural entities—like harmful viruses—can and ought to be viewed as bad and worth changing or even eradicating. The transformation of harmful natural entities into helpful man-made artifacts—such as the use of the vaccinia virus in the smallpox vaccine—ought to be regarded as a moral good rather than a bad.

Moreover, it is not just the transformation of harmful natural entities that must be considered morally permissible. We must of course remember that in order to survive and live minimally decent lives, human beings must transform all sorts of natural material into artifacts: stone, wood, and plants must be transformed into tools, shelter, and clothes, for example. Once again, it seems absurd to view such processes as morally problematic, let alone impermissible.

Finally, it is also possible to regard certain transformations of *animals* as morally good rather than bad. For example, selective breeding or genetic interventions may allow us to create animals who are resistant to certain diseases—such as hens who are resistant to Marek's disease, or pigs without malignant hyperthermia (Sandøe, Holtug, and Simonsen 1996, 18). It is very difficult to explain why transformations of animals that actually improve and enhance the well-being of the animals involved should be considered morally problematic.

However, even if we concede for the sake of argument that what is natural is always worth preserving as it exists presently, that still does not mean that the domestication of animals is morally problematic. After all, it is hard to definitively judge whether domestication is natural or unnatural. For one, some might argue that there is nothing more natural than a species doing that which expands its ecological niche and survival opportunities, as humans did when the processes of domesticating animals began some 9,000 years ago. Furthermore, and as we will explore more in the next section, there are many who believe that domestication was not something enforced upon animals against their will. Instead, these thinkers claim that the closer interaction with humans that led to domestication was a "natural" evolutionary strategy to deal with the fluctuating environmental conditions of the time (Budiansky 1997).

DOMESTICATED ANIMALS AS "STRATEGISTS"

A second important position on animal domestication does not regard the process as unnatural at all. Writers like Stephen Budiansky have put forward the view that domestication involved a "cooperative evolution of our species in a mutual strategy for survival" (Budiansky 1997, 14). Budiansky claims that the ancestors of today's domesticated animals were "opportunists": members of those species best adapted to deal with the dramatic environmental changes at the end of the Pleistocene (Budiansky 1997, 74). According to this view, it was those species that were able to move into new territory and adapt to these new conditions successfully that did best during these tumultuous times. This context provided a powerful force for the selection of neotenic (juvenile) traits within these species: curiosity, ability to learn and adapt, a lack of fear of new situations, and also a willingness to associate with other species (Budiansky 1997, 77). Crucially, these traits were also those that led certain animals to approach human settlements, prevented humans from turning these animals away, and in turn led to these animals being held captive (Budiansky 1997, 80).

Put simply, Budiansky's claim is that the human-animal social interactions that facilitated the separating, taming, and eventual breeding of certain types of animal were the result of natural evolutionary forces. On this view, domestication and the captivity of domesticated animals were not processes dominated by humans and imposed upon animals. Rather, the process of neotenization began quite naturally because of evolutionary pressures, and has been furthered through selective breeding by humans.

Budiansky's account of domestication is certainly controversial. Nevertheless, this is not the place to assess its validity, which is better undertaken by scholars with relevant expertise. What this section asks, instead, is what this account means for the ethics of domestication. Assuming that domestication was not imposed upon animals, but was shaped by natural evolutionary forces, what does that mean for us as we confront domesticated animals here and now? For Budiansky, it means that domestication can be regarded as morally benign on the basis that it provides mutual benefits for both humans and animals (Budiansky 1997, 165; Bokonyi 1989, 22). Domesticated animals benefit from the protection and care they receive from being held captive, while humans benefit from the labor, skins, flesh, milk, eggs, and so on of the animals involved.

However, it is not immediately clear that animals themselves have necessarily benefited from domestication in the way that Budiansky assumes. Budiansky's claim rests in part on an analysis of how domesticated animals have performed in terms of species population:

> From an evolutionary point of view, the answer is undeniable.... Domestic dogs, sheep, goats, cattle, and horses far outnumber their wild counterparts. The global populations of sheep and cattle today each exceed one billion; their wild counterparts teeter on the brink of extinction. (Budiansky 1997, 61)

But this way of assessing the benefit of domestication for animals is implausible. If domesticated animals have benefited, then we need to be able to locate an improvement in their well-being: an improvement in how their lives fare. In particular, we need to look at how the process affects *individual lives*, rather than species populations. And of course it does not matter to any individual cow or sheep that they are part of a huge number of other cows and sheep. The success of their domesticated kind is of absolutely no concern to them, and does not appear to impact on their own personal well-being in any obvious way.

But Budiansky also thinks that domesticated animals benefit individually. Indeed, he argues that domestication and the captivity it entails benefit animals by allowing them to lead better lives than they would possess if they were wild: "Freedom from predators, from starvation, and from parasites are not advantages to be dismissed casually" (Budiansky 1997, 144). However, there are two flaws with this argument. First of all, it is unclear why the comparison with the life of a wild animal is relevant to the attribution of benefit to a domesticated animal. Once again, benefit suggests that an individual's well-being is improved in some way. And yet it is hard to see why any domesticated animal's well-being is improved because she has higher levels of well-being compared to a wild animal. For we are talking about real domesticated animals here: individuals who have *always* been domesticated; creatures who were *never* themselves wild. As such, the comparison with wild animals seems irrelevant.

Second, even if we think we *can* judge domesticated animals' lives by a comparison with the lives of wild animals, it is unlikely that the well-being of domesticated animals necessarily comes out on top. After all, the vast majority of domesticated animals are bred for industrialized farming, and it is quite wrong to assume that these animals necessarily have lives of higher well-being than those of wild animals. For example, take Budiansky's claim that domesticated animals benefit by being protected from predation. Such a claim is bizarre in respect to most domesticated animals who are bred for intensive farming: human beings are their predators! Furthermore, the lives of those domesticated animals are cut drastically short compared to those of many wild animals. A small number of farmed animals might be lucky enough to survive for a few years, but for most their life span will be much shorter. Indeed, for many male calves, their lifespan will usually just be a day or two, and for many male chicks it will just be a minute or two.

Budiansky responds to this obvious point by arguing that the slaughter of animals can be reconciled with compassion and even "reverence" for animals if we understand that "in our practice of agriculture we are part of nature" (Budiansky 1997, 161). But this type of response seems to rely on a dubious "fetishization" of nature. Even if agriculture is "natural," that does not mean that it and all of its component parts are thereby morally permissible. Indeed, it is hard to take seriously the idea that many of the practices of intensive agriculture—the rape rack, the farrowing crate, live export, the use of growth-promoting drugs, genetic manipulation, and so on—are either natural or morally benign.

Perhaps a better point in favor of the view that domestication benefits animals is to point out that if it were not for domestication, domesticated animals simply would not exist. For as was pointed out above, it is not as if these animals would exist in some other "wild" form if they were not domesticated; if they were not domesticated, then they would not exist at all. By creating them, perhaps domestication benefits domesticated animals.

While such a claim seems intuitively plausible, there is a key problem with it. The problem is that it assumes that existence is necessarily a benefit to domesticated animals. Unfortunately, that is not true. As was discussed above, most domesticated animals are bred for intensive farming. And intensive farming necessarily creates short, frustrated and painful lives for the animals involved. Indeed, for many of these animals, the frustration and suffering endured is so intense that it is perfectly reasonable to conclude that existence is of no benefit to them whatsoever.

In sum, this section has argued that even if we accept Budiansky's account of the processes of domestication, this does not mean that we should accept his ethical conclusions about it. It is implausible to suggest that animals necessarily benefit from their domestication.

DOMESTICATED ANIMALS AS "SLAVES"

The third position on the ethics of domestication recognizes that serious harm is inflicted upon many domesticated animals. In fact, "abolitionist" animal rights theorists see domestication as *necessarily* harmful to the animals involved in virtue of the fact that it necessarily renders those animals dependent and captive (Francione 2012; Bryant 1990, 10). For such thinkers, all forms of animal captivity are morally wrong, and since domestication necessarily renders animals captive, it must also be wrong. Gary Francione, the leading proponent of abolitionist animal rights theory, offers the following analysis:

> Domestic animals are neither a real or full part of our world or of the non-human world. They exist forever in a netherworld of vulnerability, dependent on us for everything and at risk from an environment that they do not really understand. We have bred them to be compliant and servile, or to have characteristics that are actually harmful to them but are pleasing to us. (Francione 2012)

On this view, because domesticated animals lead such harmful lives, they ought to be phased out of existence (Francione 2012; Bryant 1990, 9). This of course does not mean that all currently existing domesticated animals must be eliminated. The proposal is rather to protect the basic interests of those that currently exist in the world, but to prevent their reproduction. This policy would guarantee that no future animal would suffer the lack of freedom and harm entailed by domestication.

This section will critique the abolitionist position by arguing that domestication does not necessarily lead to impoverished, harmful, and wrongful lives for the animals created. This, of course, is not to say that animals are never harmed by domestication, as Budiansky's analysis seems to imply. Domestication can obviously be harmful to individual animals in a number of ways. As pointed out above, if animals are bred for use in intensive farming or for other practices that cause serious suffering, then quite clearly they are harmed by their domestication. Second, even if Budiansky's account of domestication as a natural phenomenon "chosen" by animals themselves is correct in general terms, it will not be correct for every single instance of domestication or attempted domestication. That is to say, sometimes humans have attempted and still do attempt to domesticate animals by capturing them forcibly from the wild. Clearly, such practices are incredibly distressing for the animals involved and those left behind, causing harm to both. Third, domestication involves selective breeding, and often such breeding is forced upon animals against their will. For example, dairy cows are usually impregnated through artificial insemination: the cow is restrained in a so-called rape rack, has her uterus positioned via an arm up the rectum, and then semen is inserted via an instrument penetrated into the vagina. It seems only reasonable to surmise that this process causes distress to the cows involved. Finally, the selective breeding of domesticated animals to produce certain traits often leads to disabilities and other abnormalities that mean those animals have fewer opportunities for well-being than other members of their species. For example, many breeds of dog suffer from a range of health problems as a direct result of being bred for size, looks, or other traits. Such problems include skin conditions, immunity problems, blood disorders, neurological disorders, heart diseases and other organ failures, increased propensities for cancer, and all sorts of orthopedic problems (BBC News 2008).

And yet none of these examples show that domestication is *necessarily* harmful to animals. For example, it is quite possible to produce domesticated animals without using them in intensive agriculture, without capturing them from the wild, without using coercive breeding methods, and without producing abnormalities that reduce their opportunities for well-being. Not all domesticated animals have their lives blighted by these kinds of harms. Nevertheless, abolitionists maintain that the lives of *all* domesticated animals are necessarily impoverished. Why is that?

Abolitionists claim that the physiological changes that domesticated animals have been subjected to have rendered them "servile" and "dependent." As described above, selective breeding has resulted in the *neotonization* of domesticated animals: the retention of juvenile traits such as low aggression, playfulness, and cute features into adulthood (Donaldson and Kymlicka 2011, 83). These physiological changes have had important effects on these animals' ability to look after themselves independently. Indeed, the claim of the abolitionists is that these changes mean that domesticated animals necessarily become "stunted" versions of their wild ancestors, reliant as they are on human care for every aspect of their well-being.

The problem with this argument, of course, is that all animals, including human beings, are dependent beings to some extent (Donaldson and Kymlicka 2011, 83; Arneil 2009; Dolgert 2010; Swart 2005, 257). Writing in a different context, Barbara Arneil has pointed out:

> we are all in various ways and to different degrees both dependent on others and independent, depending on the particular stage we are at in the life cycle as well as the degree to which the world is structured to respond to some variations better than others. (Arneil 2009, 234)

It is thus hard to see why the lives of domesticated animals are impoverished simply because they are dependent. For that would imply that all of us, including humans, necessarily lead diminished lives.

At this stage, perhaps the abolitionist might concede that we are all dependent beings, but respond that the level of dependence endured by domesticated animals is of a quite different order. Indeed, abolitionists might point out that unlike other animals, domesticated animals are dependent on others for nearly every aspect of their well-being and also for all of their lives.

But once again there are good reasons to doubt this analysis. Domesticated animals are not the pathetic dependents that the abolitionist picture paints. Many domesticated animals can look after themselves, and can secure their own interests, even without human assistance. There are many examples of domesticated animals going feral and leading decent lives with little or no human assistance: thriving populations of feral cats, dogs, goats, horses, pigs, and so on are all evidence of this. Furthermore, it would also be quite wrong to say that captive domesticated animals are unable to exercise any control over their own lives. All of us who live with companion animals can tell you their important preferences concerning food, exercise, company, and the like, as well as the actions they themselves take to satisfy those preferences. It seems clear enough that many domesticated animals can protect many of their important interests quite independently.

Of course, the abolitionist might acknowledge that some domesticated animals, such as our pets, can pursue certain of their interests independently, but nevertheless press the point that these same animals are *captives*, and hence are essentially *slaves*. For example, companion animals may have small degrees of freedom in their lives, but that does not detract from the simple fact that such freedom is held at the whim of their masters. In the language of republican political theory, we might say that like slaves, companion animals are necessarily *dominated*, and this explains the ethical problem with many forms of domestication (Pettit 1999).

But again this analysis is flawed. While comparing companion animals to human slaves has a good deal of rhetorical power, it glosses over some important differences between the two. The reason that we find the kinds of domination involved in slavery to be so morally egregious comes down to the intrinsic importance of autonomy to human well-being. Even if a slave is happy or granted certain freedoms, her condition is still harmful and wrongful in virtue of the fact that she lacks *ultimate* control of her life. In Rawlsian terms, she is unable to frame, revise, and pursue her own conception of the good (Rawls 1993, 72). This of course does not mean that humans must be totally independent in order to lead decent lives. As pointed out above, that would be ludicrous. But it does mean that for most humans, being in control of fundamental choices regarding family, employment, religious belief, and so on are central to living well. The requirements of a decent life for domesticated animals, however, are quite different in this regard. The majority of nonhuman animals lack the ability to frame, revise, and pursue their own conceptions of the good. They thus also lack that intrinsic interest in having ultimate control over their own lives (Cochrane 2009). As such, while dominating humans through slavery is necessarily harmful, dominating animals through holding them captive as pets is not.

But perhaps there is still reason to hold onto the idea that domesticated animals' lives are harmful. For example, suppose that we decided to domesticate a group of *human beings*: selectively breeding them for juvenile traits in order that they become more docile and dependent upon us. Surely the right conclusion in this scenario is that these humans would be harmed by being bred in such a way, and thus that such selective breeding would be wrong. If correct, consistency surely demands the same conclusion in respect to domesticated animals.

In response to this objection, we might just say that our intuitions are wrong about this case: humans would not be harmed by being created with such reduced capacities. After all, had they not been so created, then they would not exist at all. As such, since the action benefits them overall, that same action cannot be said to harm them (Parfit 1984, ch. 16). The difficulty with this analysis, however, is that it adopts an overly simplistic and implausible account of harm. It is in fact sometimes possible to be harmed by an action even if that same act benefits you overall (Woodward 1986; Cochrane 2012, 122). Consider, for example, a man imprisoned in a Nazi concentration camp whose experience enriched his character to such an extent that it actually made his life better overall than it would have been if he had not been imprisoned. All of us would agree that he was impermissibly harmed by his imprisonment (Harman

2004, 99). As such, it is not implausible to argue that even though animals (and humans) benefit overall from their domestication, they are nevertheless still harmed by it.

And yet even if we adopt this more sophisticated understanding of harm, it still does not lead to the conclusion that the creation of domesticated animals— or indeed humans—necessarily harms them. To explain, the idea of humans becoming domesticated is not quite as shocking and outrageous as it might at first appear. Indeed, a common view in evolutionary theory is that humans are already domesticated—and that the evolutionary story of humans is one of neotonization (Gould 2008). To emphasize the point, it is worth reflecting on the fact that humans are essentially neotenized chimps: possessing reduced heads, teeth, jaws, and bones; and also exhibiting reduced aggression, increased desire to play and learn, increased sociality, and increased sexuality (Donaldson and Kymlicka 2011, 85). Of course, it might well be that these developments in human beings have made us more dependent as individuals. But it is hard to believe that we have thereby been harmed by them. Indeed, the development of these traits is usually considered to be extremely positive in the case of humans (Donaldson and Kymlicka 2011, 86). Perhaps then, the processes by which certain animals have evolved to be more social, less aggressive, and so on, can also be viewed positively. Or at the very least, perhaps they can be considered harmless.

In sum, the abolitionist claims that domesticated animals are often harmed by their domestication, and that domesticated animals are dependent beings, are both true. But the claim that their dependence necessarily leads to them being harmed cannot be upheld. We thus have good reason to reject the abolitionist conclusion that they all ought to be phased out of existence.

DOMESTICATED ANIMALS AS "CITIZENS"

The final position on domestication agrees that phasing domesticated animals out of existence is quite unnecessary. It also agrees that domesticated captive animals *can* lead decent and flourishing lives. In fact, thinkers belonging to this final group argue that in order to ensure decent lives for domesticated animals, we need to recognize that we have quite special and distinctive obligations towards them. This position claims that it is necessary to pay close attention to the unique *relational* position domesticated animals are in.

Clare Palmer, a proponent of this relational understanding of our obligations to domesticated animals, argues that our obligations to wild animals and domesticated animals are quite different: we have positive obligations of care and assistance to domesticated animals that we do not ordinarily have to wild animals (Palmer 2010; 2011). Such obligations are owed to domesticated animals, she claims, because we are responsible both for their existence and for their dependence upon us. Indeed, Palmer claims that we have made domesticated animals dependent on us in two important ways: through their captivity; but also through the physiological and behavioral changes that we have induced in them (Palmer 2010, 92). Wild animals, by contrast, are not dependent upon us, and so are not ordinarily owed obligations of care and assistance. However, that changes if wild animals suffer because of actions or events that human beings are responsible for. A good example of this would be the suffering caused when humans destroy the habitats of wild animals. In cases where human responsibility can be attributed, we do indeed have remedial duties of care and assistance to those wild animals (Palmer 2010; 2011).

While Palmer's recognition of the strong and important obligations we have to domesticated animals is admirable, the justification she provides for them is less convincing. After all, it relies upon a fundamental ethical distinction between domesticated animals and wild animals that is hard to sustain. For one, the picture that Palmer paints of the differences in capacities between wild and domesticated animals is exaggerated. As outlined above, we should not fall into the trap of thinking that all wild animals are completely independent beings able to secure their basic interests without assistance, and all domesticated animals are pathetic dependents reliant on humans for everything. Dependency is something shared by all sentient creatures and is a matter of degree. Indeed, Jac Swart has argued that the difference between wild and domesticated animals should not be measured by the differing degrees of dependence they possess, but by what they are dependent upon. Most domesticated animals are characterized by a dependent relationship with human society; whereas wild animals are mainly characterized by a dependent relationship with wild nature (Swart 2005, 257). Given this, it seems wrong to assert that special obligations are owed to domesticated animals because they are dependent and none are owed to wild ones because they are independent.

Of course, it is necessary to recall that Palmer also thinks that causal responsibility is crucial for accounting for the differences in obligations owed to wild and domesticated animals. Since *we caused* domesticated animals to exist and thus also caused their dependency, special obligations of care and assistance are owed to them. Because we are not responsible for the existence and dependency of wild animals, on the other hand, no such obligations are owed to them. That changes, of course, if we are somehow responsible for their suffering. Palmer supports this position by giving the example of discovering a population of starving human beings on Venus who have suffered from crop failure due to some natural catastrophe. Palmer argues that while it is plausible to say we have strong negative duties towards these Venusians, such as not to steal their remaining crops, we have no positive duty to assist them since we are not responsible for their plight (Palmer 2010, 86–87).

The problem with this view is that it is not at all clear that positive duties are not owed to the Venusians in the example—and hence why such duties cannot also be owed to wild animals. Indeed, many would argue that in the Venusian example positive obligations are owed simply because of the suffering involved, and that any assessment of causal responsibility is quite irrelevant (Singer 1972; Unger 1996). And it does seem right that if we know of their suffering and can do something about it, then leaving the Venusians to starve to death is morally abhorrent.

In fact, Palmer seems to recognize as much and suggests that we *do* have special duties to assist human beings who are suffering from natural or accidental catastrophes. Crucially, however, she argues that these duties emerge out of membership of a common group: the human community (Palmer 2010, 121). Because wild animals are not part of this relevant group, however, when they suffer from natural catastrophes and the like, no obligations of care and assistance are generated.

And yet it is unclear why membership of the human community is necessary to generate such obligations. Crucially, we need a reason why bare humanity is morally relevant in this way. After all, membership in the human species is just a biological characteristic, such as skin color or height and thus seems an implausible basis for the attribution of special responsibilities. Perhaps it might be claimed that all humans possess some morally relevant characteristics not possessed by any nonhuman, such as reason, language-use, or moral autonomy. But of course animal rights scholars have successfully shown that there is no special ingredient possessed by all and only human beings: for example, some nonhuman animals have rational capacities that far outstrip those of some human beings (Dombrowski 1997). Hence Palmer's claim that wild animals are not owed special duties of care and assistance because they are not members of the relevant group is extremely problematic.

Sue Donaldson and Will Kymlicka have provided an alternative relational theory of animal rights that recognizes that positive obligations of care and assistance are owed to wild animals, irrespective of whether or not we are causally responsible for their suffering (Donaldson and Kymlicka 2011, 208). But in spite of that difference, Donaldson and Kymlicka share Palmer's view that the relational position of domesticated animals generates different and more extensive duties towards them. Indeed, they claim that in order for domesticated animals to be able to lead decent lives they should actually be awarded rights of *citizenship*. These rights go beyond the universal rights that they claim are shared by all sentient creatures, and recognize that domesticated animals are members of our political communities. For Donaldson and Kymlicka, there are three crucial rights of citizenship belonging to domesticated animals:

> residency (this is their home, they belong here), inclusion in the sovereign people (their interests count in determining the public good), and agency (they should be able to shape the rules of cooperation). (Donaldson and Kymlicka 2011, 101)

While Donaldson and Kymlicka's theory is to be applauded for recognizing the important and demanding obligations we have to both domesticated and wild animals, there are once again reasons to be concerned about the way in which this approach separates wild and domesticated animals, and their respective rights. Political communities have long used citizenship as a means to differentiate rights on relational grounds, and historical and current practice reveals the inherent danger in these practices: there is always a tendency to award too few rights—or deny rights altogether—to those individuals who are not currently in a close relational position. The worry is that Donaldson and Kymlicka's theory has the potential to repeat this problem in the context of animals.

The basic difficulty is that it remains unclear why wild animals should be denied the rights of citizenship identified above. Consider, for example, the right of residency. This right must be grounded in animals' interest in a safe and secure habitat. But this is an interest that *all* animals share, including wild ones. It just so happens that what a safe and secure habitat consists of will sometimes vary for different animals: for domesticated animals, their safe and secure habitat is (usually) alongside human communities; and for many wild animals it is (usually) in wild habitats. Given that shared interest, it seems plausible that *all* animals possess this right to safe and secure residency.

Consider also the right to have one's interests counted in the public good. It is unclear why only domesticated animals should have that right. Since wild animals have basic interests which can be affected by human political decisions in profound ways, it seems crucial that wild animals are also protected in that right.

And finally, consider the right to political agency. Donaldson and Kymlicka argue that the fact that animals have more limited rational capacities does not mean that they ought to be denied political agency. In fact, they point out quite rightly that their more limited rationality makes them particularly vulnerable to being left out of the policymaking process. As such, they advocate that the interests of domesticated animals ought to be represented by proxies or "collaborators" in much the same way as the interests of children and the severely mentally disabled are included (104). But it is unclear why these collaborators should not also represent the interests of wild animals in this way. After all, given their distance from us, their interests are even more likely to be left out of policy deliberations. As such, it seems reasonable that wild animals also ought to enjoy the right to political agency, on Donaldson and Kymlicka's own terms (Cochrane 2013).

The accounts of what we owe to domesticated animals put forward by Palmer and by Donaldson and Kymlicka have important merits. They recognize that domestication and captivity do not necessarily harm animals. But they also recognize that we have important obligations to domesticated animals in order to ensure that they can lead decent lives. And yet grounding our obligations to domesticated animals on the basis of their relational "closeness" to us has important—and problematic—implications for nondomesticated animals. As argued above, it effectively relegates them to an inferior and diminished level of protection that is unwarranted.

CONCLUSION: DOMESTICATED ANIMALS AS "ANIMALS"

This chapter has evaluated the four leading positions on the ethics of domestication and has found them all to be problematic. The environmentalist critique that domestication is wrongful because it changes what is natural into artifacts is implausible: not only is the creation of artifacts out of nature necessary and often benign, but processes of domestication can coherently be thought of as natural. Budiansky and others plausibly claim that domestication is a natural process, but wrongfully conclude that domesticated animals have necessarily benefited from the process rendering it morally unproblematic. The abolitionist critique rightly recognizes that serious harms can be inflicted by processes of domestication, but unjustifiably concludes that domestication and captivity are necessarily harmful to all animals. The relational approaches of Palmer and of Donaldson and Kymlicka are to be applauded for recognizing the real harms that domestication can cause while also accepting that it is possible for domesticated captive animals to lead decent and flourishing lives. However, in so doing these theories make a problematic ethical distinction between wild and domesticated animals, which can lead to the former failing to receive their proper entitlements.

What is required, then, is an approach which recognizes that domesticated captive animals can lead decent and flourishing lives, but does not do so by diminishing our important obligations to wild animals. I want to claim that an approach that can do this is one that simply treats domesticated animals as *animals*. That is to say, we should not regard domesticated animals as strange and exotic creatures who require an entirely unique ethical framework. Domesticated animals are not artifacts, strategists, slaves, or citizens; they are simply animals. They are sentient creatures with basic interests like any other. And it is an assessment of their *individual* interests that ought to determine our treatment of them.

To be clear, such an approach is not proposing identical treatment for all animals. It is not saying that that all animals have exactly the same rights in all the same situations. That would clearly be absurd. Different obligations are owed to different animals in different contexts. But crucially, the specification of what is owed to animals is properly made through a consideration of *all* relevant interests and factors, and not simply by appeal to whether the animal is wild or domesticated, free or captive. For example, consider the case of a domesticated captive goldfish and wild mountain gorilla. Clearly it would be quite wrong to say that they had exactly the same set of rights. And yet surely it is also wrong to say—as relational theories must—that the goldfish has stronger and more extensive entitlements because of her closer relational position. The proper analysis seems to be that the gorilla ordinarily has stronger and more extensive rights. And that is because other factors outweigh the importance of relational position in this case. For example, the sophisticated cognitive capacities of the gorilla surely mean that her interests are weightier and more complex than those of a goldfish. Furthermore, the endangered status of gorillas might also count in favor of granting the gorilla more stringent rights to certain goods.

The point is not that relational position is of no importance in assigning rights; it is simply that it is just one consideration out of very many that needs to be taken into account. And without doubt, the most crucial consideration is an assessment of the interests of the creature involved and their relative strength, not whether the animal is domesticated. As such, the basic interests of domesticated animals should be the primary focus in determining how we ought to relate to them.

So what implications does this approach have for how we ought to treat domesticated animals? First of all, there is no obligation to eradicate all domesticated animals, nor to phase them out of existence. Domesticated animals are not harmed simply because they have been created by human beings, nor are they harmed because they are dependent. Furthermore, and contrary to the view of abolitionists, domesticated animals are not harmed simply because the majority of them are held captive. Domestication is not the same as human slavery, and domesticated animals who are held captive can lead good lives, provided that their basic interests are satisfied.

Second, while we have no obligation to phase domesticated animals out of existence, we do have an obligation not to deliberately attempt to create new domesticated species. Separating members of species from their wild conspecifics and deliberately breeding them causes considerable suffering and harm to the animals involved and is impermissible as such.

Third, and most importantly, we also have an obligation to massively overhaul those institutions and practices that create and use domesticated animals. This includes an obligation not to create domesticated animals via harmful breeding practices, such as coerced mating or insemination via the rape rack. It also entails a duty not to breed animals in ways that result in harmful disabilities, diseases, and other health conditions in the created animals. More broadly, however, it also involves putting an end to the routine suffering and killing that domesticated animals endure in contemporary farms, laboratories, and so many other contexts. The vast majority of domesticated animals are created to endure short miserable lives for the sake of often trivial benefits to human beings. If we are to take the interests of domesticated animals at all seriously, such practices must end.

There is no doubt that domestication creates "man-made" and dependent animals, who are often held captive. Nevertheless, these features of the process are not in themselves morally problematic. The real problem of contemporary animal domestication as it is currently instituted is the immense suffering and diminished opportunities that it involves. Fortunately, such harms are not intrinsic to domestication: we have both the ability and the duty to eradicate them.

REFERENCES

Anderson, Kay. 1997. "A Walk on the Wild Side: A Critical Geography of Domestication." *Progress in Human Geography* 21: 463–485.

Arneil, Barbara. 2009. "Disability, Self-Image and Modern Political Theory." *Political Theory* 37: 218–242.

BBC News. 2008. "Pedigree Dogs Plagued by Disease." August 19. Accessed November 21, 2013. http://news.bbc.co.uk/1/hi/uk/7569064.stm.

Bokonyi, Sandor. 1989. "Definitions of Animal Domestication." In *The Walking Larder: Patterns of Domestication, Pastoralism and Predation*, Juliet Clutton-Brock (ed.), 22–27. London: Unwin Hyman.

Bryant, John. 1990. *Fettered Kingdoms*. Rev. ed. Winchester: Fox Press.

Budiansky, Stephen. 1997. *The Covenant of the Wild: Why Animals Chose Domestication*. London: Phoenix.

Callicott, James Baird. 1995. "Animal Liberation: A Triangular Affair." In *Environmental Ethics*, Robert Elliot (ed.), 29–59. Oxford: Oxford University Press.

Clutton-Brock, Juliet. 1989. Introduction to *The Walking Larder: Patterns of Domestication, Pastoralism and Predation*, Juliet Clutton-Brock (ed.), 7–21. London: Unwin Hyman.

Cochrane, Alasdair. 2009. "Do Animals Have an Interest in Liberty?" *Political Studies* 57: 660–679.

Cochrane, Alasdair. 2012. *Animal Rights without Liberation*. New York: Columbia University Press.

Cochrane, Alasdair. 2013. "Cosmozoopolis: The Case against Group-Differentiated Animal Rights." *Law, Ethics and Philosophy* 1: 127–141.

Dolgert, Stefan. 2010. "Species of Disability: Response to Arneil." *Political Theory* 38: 859–869.

Dombrowski, Daniel. 1997. *Babies and Beasts: The Argument from Marginal Cases*. Urbana: University of Illinois Press.

Donaldson, Sue, and Will Kymlicka. 2011. *Zoopolis: A Political Theory of Animal Rights*. Oxford: Oxford University Press.

Francione, Gary. 2012. "'Pets': The Inherent Problems of Domestication." July 31. Accessed November 21, 2013. http://www.abolitionistapproach.com/pets-the-inherent-problems-of-domestication/#.UaMlSKJJM08.

Gould, Stephen Jay. 2008. "A Biological Homage to Mickey Mouse." *Ecotone* 4: 333–340.

Harman, Elizabeth. 2004. "Can We Harm and Benefit in Creating?" *Philosophical Perspectives* 18: 89–113.

Palmer, Clare. 2010. *Animal Ethics in Context*. New York: Columbia University Press.

Palmer, Clare. 2011. "The Moral Relevance of the Distinction between Wild and Domesticated Animals." In *The Oxford Handbook of Animal Ethics*, Tom L. Beauchamp and R. G. Frey (eds.), 701–725. Oxford: Oxford University Press.

Parfit, Derek. 1984. *Reasons and Persons*. Oxford: Clarendon Press.

Pettit, Phillip. 1999. *Republicanism: A Theory of Freedom and Government*. Oxford: Oxford University Press.

Rawls, John. 1993. *Political Liberalism*. New York: Columbia University Press.

Rodman, John. 1977. "The Liberation of Nature." *Inquiry* 20: 83–131.

Rolston, Holmes, III. 1991. "Environmental Ethics: Values in and Duties to the Natural World." In *The Broken Circle: Ecology, Economics, Ethics*, F. Herbert Bormann and Stephen R. Kellert (eds.), 73–96. New Haven: Yale University Press.

Sandøe, P., N. Holtug, and H. B. Simonsen. 1996. "Ethical Limits to Domestication." *Journal of Agricultural and Environmental Ethics* 9: 114–122.

Singer, Peter. 1972. "Famine, Affluence, and Morality." *Philosophy and Public Affairs* 1: 229–243.

Swart, Jac A. A. 2005. "Care for the Wild: An Integrative View on Wild and Domesticated Animals." *Environmental Values* 14: 251–263.

Swart, Jac A. A., and J. Keulartz. 2011. "Wild Animals in Our Backyard: A Contextual Approach to the Intrinsic Value of Animals." *Acta Biotheretica* 59: 185–200.

Unger, Peter. 1996. *Living High and Letting Die: Our Illusion of Innocence*. Oxford: Oxford University Press.

Woodward, James. 1986. "The Non-Identity Problem." *Ethics* 96: 804–831.

11

The Confinement of Animals Used in Laboratory Research

Conceptual and Ethical Issues

ROBERT STREIFFER ■

THE ETHICAL RELATIONSHIP BETWEEN EXTRA-RESEARCH CONFINEMENT AND RESEARCH

Discussions about the ethics of research involving (nonhuman) animals usually focus on the significance of the knowledge produced by the research and on the harms caused by research procedures performed upon the animal subjects. For animals used in laboratory research, though, these procedures typically occupy only a small portion of their lives compared to the time they spend confined in their cages while not actively involved in research.[1] Here I discuss several conceptual and ethical issues raised by the confinement of laboratory animals. How should "confinement" be analyzed? Are the ethical costs and benefits of confinement relevant to the ethical evaluation of the later research in which the animals are used? In what ways are animal's interests instrumentally related to their being confined? Do they have an intrinsic interest in liberty that is frustrated by confinement per se? And, finally, what are the ethical implications of the ways in which confinement is or is not related to animals' interests?

Answering these questions is in service of addressing the practical question of whether the ways in which animals are typically confined for research are morally prohibited, merely permitted, or required. Reaching a conclusion about this question would require addressing several complicated issues that are beyond the scope of this paper, including what kind and degree of moral status do animals have; do they have rights and if so, with what content and weight; what is the correct account of their welfare; how harmful are the different kinds of confinement to them; how much could their conditions be improved and at what cost; how valuable is the research in which they are used and what are the opportunity costs of funding it? My goals here are more modest: exploring the relationship between the ethics of confinement and the ethics of research, clarifying some of the conceptual issues involved in analyzing confinement, and exploring the kinds of intrinsic and instrumental relationships confinement bears to the interests of animals.

Despite the ubiquity of extra-research confinement, some commentators appear to believe that its ethical evaluation is irrelevant to the ethical evaluation of particular kinds of animal research. For example, in their discussion of how Institutional Animal Care and Use Committees (IACUCs) should review protocols using animals to study sleep-disordered breathing, Joseph Kemnitz and Nancy Schulz-Darken (2009) discuss the need for IACUCs to evaluate whether research procedures that cause pain, distress, or death are justified by the value of the data being collected, but they do not address the possibility that the ethical costs and benefits of confining the animals while not undergoing research are relevant to the ethics of the research itself. In a recent defense of the use of nonhuman primates for stroke research, Sughrue et al. (2009) mention the issue of the confinement of animals prior to experimentation, but then conclude, solely on the basis of a comparison of benefits to humans as compared to the harms of stroke induction to the monkeys, that the research is justified. That is, in their ethical evaluation of the stroke research, they give no consideration whatsoever to the ethical evaluation of the preexperimentation confinement, even though the experiment itself "is generally terminated after a brief recovery period (7–10 days)" and so occupies only a tiny portion of the animal's life compared to the preexperimentation confinement (2009, 8).

This could simply be an oversight, but it could instead suggest a considered view according to which the ethical evaluation of a certain bit of research is independent of the ethical costs and benefits of the extra-research confinement that the animals experience prior to that research. Of course, confinement is often a part of the research procedures themselves (e.g., behavioral research that involves confining a mouse to a Morris water maze), and some research is research on the effects of confinement; in such cases, the ethical costs and benefit of the confinement are obviously relevant to the ethical evaluation of the research.[2] But according to what I will refer to as the "Strong Independence Thesis," these are the only situations in which the ethics of confinement are relevant to the ethics of the research.

Why might one think that the Strong Independence Thesis is true? One argument might begin by noting that the researchers are typically not assigned institutional responsibility for the conditions under which the animals are kept while not undergoing research procedures. This institutional responsibility is typically assigned to the IACUC, the facility managers, the veterinarians, and the animal care staff. A proponent of the Strong Independence Thesis might then make an argument by analogy: holding the researcher responsible for the extra-research housing conditions is analogous to holding a surgeon accountable for the conditions of the hospital room in which the patient waits for or recovers from the surgery. But it isn't the surgeon who is responsible for those conditions; rather, it is the hospital staff and those who oversee them.

This argument, though, is unsuccessful, and the analogy, properly understood, supports the opposite conclusion. Pre- and postoperative conditions can affect the risks of surgery, and when they do, they are relevant when ethically evaluating the surgery itself. Suppose that hospital A and hospital B are alike except that A has a substantially lower rate of postoperative infections because of its superior recovery room cleaning procedures. It could be the case that the risk/benefit ratio of surgery in hospital A makes the surgery ethical to perform in A, whereas the risk/benefit ratio of surgery in hospital B makes the surgery unethical to perform in B, even though surgeons aren't institutionally responsible for cleaning the recovery rooms. When factors affect the risks of surgery, those factors are relevant to the ethical evaluation of the surgery regardless of whether the surgeons are assigned institutional responsibility for them.

In the case of lab animal research, many negative aspects of the ways in which animals are routinely confined have been identified as potentially affecting the risks and benefits of the research. The animal care literature routinely repeats the mantra that research results and, hence, the prospects for benefit from animal research can be undermined by uncontrolled sources of pain, stress, or ill-health due to the conditions in which the animals are confined. (See, e.g., Wolfensohn and Lloyd 2013, 39; Russell 2002, 1; and Coleman et al. 2012, 153.) Examples are numerous: many routine situations have been identified as causing stress and undermining animals' well-being (Morgan and Tromborg 2007; Balcombe, Barnard, and Sandusky 2004; Reinhardt 2004); improving the conditions in which rats and rabbits are confined improves their recovery after certain kinds of surgery (Will et al. 1977; De Vos-Korthals and Van Hof 1985); psychosocial stressors related to housing have been shown to influence the immune systems of nonhuman primates (Coe 1993). Hence, the Strong Independence Thesis is false.

Someone initially attracted to the Strong Independence Thesis might concede that, when extra-research confinement has effects on the risks and benefits of the research, it is relevant, but maintain nonetheless that it is relevant *only* when it has such effects. They might thus endorse the Weak Independence Thesis: the ethical costs and benefits of confinement are morally relevant to the ethical evaluation of the research to the extent that, and only to the extent that, the confinement affects the risks or benefits of the research.

The Weak Independence View avoids the objection to the Strong Independence View, but, depending on how broadly or narrowly we construe what counts as research, it is either subject to its own objection or it construes research so broadly that the antecedent confinement of animals for the purpose of making them available for later research itself counts as part of the research. Although my focus here is on laboratory animal research, this is clearest in the case of field research.

Suppose that a researcher wants to take various measurements of wild animals living in a remote region. The research will involve trapping the animals, taking the measurements, and then releasing the animals. Let us suppose that the research is important enough to justify the minor discomfort experienced by the animals when taking the measurements. However, because of the remoteness of the region, the traps the researchers must use can be checked only once a week and some of the animals will suffer a great deal if confined in these traps for so long. Finally, let us suppose that the particular parameters that the researcher is measuring are unaffected by this suffering, and that the suffering does not make the animals any more susceptible to harms resulting from the measuring procedure. Thus, the suffering of the animals does not affect the risks or benefits of the research *procedures* themselves. It is nonetheless clear that the suffering caused by the confinement is relevant to ethically evaluating the research itself: if the suffering is sufficiently great, and the research itself sufficiently trivial, then the research will not be ethical.

If what counts as research is very narrowly construed to consist only of the research procedures themselves, to the exclusion of the confinement prior to the measurements, then this is a counterexample to the Weak Independence View. But the proponent of the Weak Independence View could say that there is more to research than just its procedures. In particular, the capture and the confinement of the animals prior to the procedures are also part of the research. Hence, any ethical costs or benefits of the captivity ipso facto affect the ethical costs and benefits of the research and so the Weak Independence View implies the (correct) conclusion that they are relevant.

But now imagine two further cases. In the second, the researcher hires a local who is familiar with the area to do the trapping. And in the third, because several researchers are engaged in this type of research, a local entrepreneur starts a business that estimates demand, preemptively traps a suitable number of animals, lets the researchers take the measurements for a fee, and then returns the animals to their native environment.

In the second case, the ethical evaluation of the trapping is still clearly relevant to the ethical evaluation of the research. What about the third case? There are of course moral differences between (a) your hiring someone else to perform an activity for you and (b) your being a consumer in a market the suppliers of which perform that activity for many different consumers. However, it is not at all plausible to suppose that those differences make the ethical evaluation of the activity irrelevant when mediated by the market (as in (b)) when it *is* relevant when done more directly by others on your behalf (as in (a)). (For general discussion of consumer responsibility, see Schwartz 2010, Brinkmann 2004, and Harrison et al. 2005.) So, if the ethical costs and benefits are ethically relevant to the research in the second case, as they are, then they are also ethically relevant to the research in the third case. How is this conclusion to be accommodated by the Weak Independence View?

In the second case, the proponent of the Weak Independence View might, with some plausibility, avoid implying a false conclusion by maintaining that, once the local is hired, the local effectively becomes part of the research team and so the trapping counts as part of the research. This becomes much less plausible in the third case, however, and even if it could be maintained, this would just mean that in any research in which animals are antecedently confined for the purpose of being made available for later research, the confinement is itself part of the research, and so its ethical evaluation is relevant according to the Weak Independence View. Thus, either the Weak Independence View is subject to counterexample, or it must endorse a very expansive understanding of what counts as research, an understanding that includes captivity prior to the conduct of the research procedures themselves when the captivity will be for the purpose of making the animals available for later research. I conclude, then, that in research where the subjects are antecedently confined for the purpose of being made available for later research, the ethical evaluation of that confinement is relevant to the ethical evaluation of the research itself.

Switching from field research back to lab animal research, it is clear that the third field research case is analogous to the norm in lab animal research: researchers typically buy animals from commercial animal breeders or use ones that are owned by the research facility in which they work. Since confinement for the purpose of being used in later research is a ubiquitous aspect of the lives of almost all research animals, its ethical relevance is important to consider when ethically evaluating the later research for which those animals are being confined.

THE DEFINITION OF CONFINEMENT

It is clear that animals used in laboratory research are normally confined, but it will be helpful to clarify the concept of confinement and to briefly explore its relation to the concept of captivity.

Consider a few examples. A business executive is confined during a flight, but is not a captive. Similarly, a baby in a crib is confined, but is not a captive. A prisoner in his cell is confined, and is also a captive. Confinement and captivity both seem to involve external limits on an individual's freedom of movement. Confinement seems to involve external limitations on the individual's freedom to move from one place to another. Captivity seems to involve confinement along with the additional exercise of dominion over the individual.

It might be objected that it is no less true of the baby than it is of the prisoner that others exercise dominion over them above and beyond the mere fact of confinement, and yet the prisoner is a captive while the baby is not. The obvious possible ways of drawing a distinction between these two situations fail. First, it could be said that the confinement of the baby is done for her own interests whereas the confinement of the prisoner is done for the good of others. But even if imprisonment were done for the good of the prisoner, the prisoner would still be a captive. Second, it could be said that the prisoner was captured, whereas the baby was not. But many captive animals are born in captivity and so were never captured. Third, it could be said that confinement supplants the autonomy of the prisoner but does not supplant the autonomy of the baby, who has no autonomy. But a baby who has been kidnapped is a captive, and yet has no autonomy. Given that my focus is on confinement (which is conceptually prior to captivity anyway), there is no need to press for a fully adequate account of captivity.

There is a further problem: not all external limitations on an individual's freedom of movement constitute confinement. Someone who locks the door to his house places an external limitation on the freedom of movement of those outside, but does not confine them. He *merely* excludes them. Consider what I will call the North Pole / South Pole example: imagine an individual standing at the North Pole with a high circular wall a few feet away from him, surrounding him completely and over which he cannot escape. Now imagine the wall moving away from the individual, getting longer to accommodate the larger circumference of the earth. The wall keeps moving until it moves past the equator, then starts getting shorter, until, finally, it forms a small circle around the South Pole.

At the start, the individual is confined. At the end, he is no longer confined, although he is *merely* excluded from the South Pole. This suggests that the distinction between being confined and being merely excluded is one of degree. Confinement and exclusion are both species of a larger metaphysical genus, which I will refer to simply as *restrictions*.[3]

The situation described in the North Pole / South Pole example seems different from what I will call the Covered North Pole / South Pole example. As before, imagine the wall encircling the person, but also imagine a roof of wire mesh over the person, connecting the walls. The walls move away from the person and the roof gets larger. At the end, the roof covers the entirety of the globe except for a small portion around the South Pole. Even at this point, it seems right to say that the individual is still confined to the (very large) room, and yet his movement is subject to the same restriction in this case as it was in the North Pole / South Pole example since, with or without the roof, the wall was impassable. I think that the presence of the roof in the Covered North Pole / South Pole example makes salient that, even at the end of the example, the area accessible to the individual under the roof is still much smaller than the area from which the individual is excluded, which now is understood as including the area up away from the surface of the earth (viz., the rest of the universe). Because the former is smaller than the latter, we say that the individual is confined. At the end of the North Pole / South Pole example, we find salient a different comparison, that between the area of the earth's surface that is accessible and the area of the earth's surface that is inaccessible. Because the former is not smaller than the latter, we judge that the individual is not confined.

This linguistic fact of context sensitivity—that in different linguistic contexts, different comparisons can be relevant to the truth-conditions of utterances of sentences of the form "X is confined" and "X is not confined"—means that, when making or interpreting claims about confinement, we must be careful to make clear which comparison is being invoked. The comparison is between the size of the subregion of a larger area to which the individual has access as compared to size of the subregion of the larger area from which the individual is excluded, but which area counts as "the larger area" may vary from context to context.

Compare: assertions of sentences of the form "X is tall" express different propositions in different linguistic contexts, depending on the comparison class the speaker is implicitly invoking. If the context determines that the relevant comparison class is that of jockeys, "Alfred is tall" expresses the proposition that Alfred is taller than most jockeys, and that proposition might be true. But if the context determines that the relevant comparison class is that of basketball players, then the sentence expresses the proposition that Alfred is taller than most basketball players, and that proposition might be false. In each case, the comparison is one between the individual's height and the height of most members of a comparison class, but which class counts as the relevant comparison class may vary from context to context. So Alfred can accurately be labeled "tall" in one linguistic context and yet be accurately labeled "not tall" in another linguistic context, without any change in his height. (See Stanley 2000 for discussion on this kind of context sensitivity generally.)

So not only is the difference between confinement and mere exclusion one of degree, but one and the same restriction can be accurately labeled "confinement" in one linguistic context and yet be accurately labeled "not confinement" in another. Thus, when someone utters a sentence of the form "X is confined," the proposition that the sentence expresses varies from linguistic context to linguistic context, and is more complicated than the surface form of the sentence suggests.

I propose that, if linguistic context L determines that A is the relevant area, then the proposition that a sentence of the form "X is confined" expresses in L is the proposition that (a) there are external obstacles that prevent X from leaving a subregion of A, R, and (b) R is smaller than the subregion of A from which X is excluded.[4] The subregion is sometimes specified explicitly, as when someone says, "The baby is confined to the crib."

Given this context sensitivity, is there even such a thing as confinement simpliciter? After all, there is no such thing as being tall simpliciter; there are only more specific properties such as being 5 foot 6 inches tall and relational properties such as being taller than Joe or being taller than most basketball players. But an account of confinement simpliciter can be constructed out of the account just outlined via existential generalization: X is confined simpliciter if and only if there is an area A such that (a) there are external obstacles that prevent X from leaving a subregion of A, R, and (b) R is smaller than the subregion of A from which X is excluded.

As will become clear in the next section, there is an interplay between the correct understanding of confinement, proposed analyses of other relevant concepts such as freedom and liberty, and proposed ethical principles about the relevance of such concepts to the issue of laboratory animal confinement.

THE ETHICAL EVALUATION OF RESTRICTIONS

Metaphysical and Conceptual Ground Clearing

If confinement simpliciter is properly understood in the way I suggest, then confinement simpliciter has no ethical relevance to the issue of laboratory animal research. The animals currently in cages are confined simpliciter, but so are we all. For every organism on earth, there is an area, namely, the universe, such that (a) there are external obstacles (e.g., gravitational forces, lack of oxygen) that prevent that organism from leaving a subregion of the universe, the Milky Way, and (b) the Milky Way is smaller than the subregion of the universe from which the organism is excluded. But is a person who utters "That animal is confined" while pointing to an animal in a cage in a laboratory ever asserting a proposition whose truth is guaranteed by the fact that the animal is confined to the Milky Way? Presumably not. Rather, she is asserting something like the proposition that there are external obstacles (viz., a cage) that prevent the animal from leaving the area inside his cage and that area is much, much smaller than the area of the earth from which the animal is excluded. So if this is the right understanding of confinement simpliciter, it is never what is at issue in disputes about the ethics of confinement.

This also means that depriving animals of what we might call "liberty per se" or "liberty in the broadest sense," understood simply as being free of any and all external constraints on one's freedom to move from one place to another, is ethically irrelevant to the task at hand. None of us is at liberty in the broadest sense. Discussions about confinement or liberty without explicit qualifications as well as discussions ostensibly about confinement or liberty per se will need to be reinterpreted if they are to be relevant.

Often, I suspect, people ostensibly talking about confinement simpliciter really mean to be distinguishing between one's access being restricted to a particular area and the conditions within that area, and referring to the former rather than the latter. For example, James Rachels, in discussing the confinement of hens to battery cages, distinguishes between harms that result from "the type of confinement" and harms that result "from the bare fact that the birds are confined" (1989, 212). This language suggests that Rachels is saying that harms can result from confinement simpliciter, but Rachels then clarifies that the latter kind of harm includes the birds' not being able to stretch their wings. This harm results not from the bare fact that the birds are confined but rather from the bare fact that the birds are confined *to small cages*. The former kind of harm includes the discomfort of sitting on wire, sloping floors, which results from what the cages are like on the inside. Confinement simpliciter or confinement per se is clearly not what is at issue here.

Moreover, as I argued above in the North Pole / South Pole example, the distinction between confinement and being merely excluded is one of degree. More strongly, the Covered North Pole / South Pole example shows that one and the same restriction can be accurately labeled "confinement" in one linguistic context and yet be accurately labeled "mere exclusion" in another. Thus, whatever ethical issues arise from confinement arise more fundamentally from the restriction on the individual's freedom to move from one area to another, regardless of whether that restriction constitutes confinement or not. Since the individual in the North Pole / South Pole example has no more access to the rest of the universe than does the individual in the Covered North Pole / South Pole example, the presence of the roof is ethically irrelevant (assuming it has no effects on anything other than access). This suggests that there is no intrinsic ethical difference between being confined and being merely excluded and that it is correct to draw a conclusion about one if, but also only if, it is also correct to draw the same conclusion about the other, assuming all other ethically relevant factors are held fixed. This is not to deny the common-sense belief that confining someone is usually more morally problematic than merely excluding someone, but it does mean that some *further* morally relevant difference will need to generally hold to explain why (e.g., compared to merely excluding, confining is generally easier to avoid or generally accompanied by a worse motive) (Bennett 1995, 75–76).

Restrictions' Instrumental Relationships to Well-Being

The ways in which a particular restriction is related to well-being will depend both on the details of the restriction and on the correct view of well-being. Theories of animal well-being, like theories of well-being generally, can be classified into three categories. (Animal well-being is also discussed in chapter 9 in this volume. Also see Appleby and Sandøe 2002. For discussion of many of the complications, see DeGrazia 1996, 211–257.) Mentalistic theories hold that well-being is constituted by the overall balance of positive mental states—for example, joy, happiness, and pleasure—over negative mental states—for example, pain, distress, and sadness—experienced by the individual. Desire-satisfaction theories hold that well-being is constituted by the overall balance of the satisfaction of desires over the frustration of desires.[5] Finally, objective list theories hold that well-being is constituted by the realization within the individual's life of objective value that can include positive mental states and the satisfaction of desires, but which also go beyond these two categories. Two popular objective list views with regard to animals are health views and natural function views. On a health view, being free of injury, illness, and disease is a component of well-being, regardless of whether the ill-health would affect the animal's mental states or desire-satisfaction (Broom 1991). Natural function views vary in how they specify the additional component of well-being. Some identify it as the exercise of species-typical behaviors; others as the exercise of species-specific behaviors; still others as the exercise of natural capabilities or capacities. They all agree, though, that a mouse who can burrow into a substrate or a monkey mother who can nurse her baby has a life that goes better in a way, even setting aside any impact these activities might have on the animal's subjective mental states or the fulfillment of the animal's desires (Taylor 1986; Nussbaum 2004; Jamieson 1985).

The restrictions to which laboratory animals are typically subjected are instrumentally related to the most uncontroversial aspects of their well-being, their experiences of positive and negative mental states. On the positive side, the restrictions typically enable veterinary care and the provision of a nutritionally adequate diet, protect the animals from the agonistic behavior of conspecifics and from such natural threats as bad weather, predators, and parasites, and enable a relatively painless death. (I say only "typically" because in some research, animals are intentionally or inadvertently not provided with these benefits.) On the negative side, the restrictions often involve the production of negative mental states such as boredom, discomfort, fear, isolation, and frustration, prevent animals from engaging in numerous enjoyable activities that require access to more space, more conspecifics, or more natural habitats, and allow them to be exposed to research procedures that themselves cause pain and suffering (Reinhardt 2004; Wemelsfelder 1990; Russell 2002; Balcombe, Barnard, and Sandusky 2004; Morgan and Tromborg 2007). While there is controversy about the magnitude and the frequency of these harms and benefits, and, of course, whether we are justified in or prohibited from imposing the harms on laboratory animals, it would be unreasonable to deny that they are morally relevant to ethically evaluating the ways in which laboratory animals are typically restricted. It should also be agreed upon by all sides that where improvements can be made to the benefit/harm ratio of restrictions at reasonable cost (including both financial and nonfinancial factors), we are morally required to do so.

The effects of restrictions and their attendant conditions on the positive and negative mental states of laboratory animals mentioned above are generally relevant to well-being on any plausible view. But certain effects are instrumentally related to animal well-being only on natural functioning views that some find implausible. Alasdair Cochrane, referring to the species-typical behavior of fights among stags for mates and territory, says, "It seems nonsensical to suppose that the losers of such fights who often suffer painful and life-threatening injuries have lives that go well for themselves" (Cochrane 2009, 672). Such putative counterexamples, though, are not probative: something's being a constituent of an individual's well-being is compatible with its attainment being accompanied by other effects that are harmful such that, on balance, the individual is worse off.

Moreover, just as some mentalistic and desire-satisfaction theorists exclude certain positive mental states or the satisfaction of certain desires (e.g., the pleasures and desires of an evil sadistic torturer) from being constituents of well-being, so too do some natural function theorists exclude the exercise of certain natural functions. Martha Nussbaum, for example, is clear on this point with regard to human well-being, and extends it to her view of animal well-being:

In the human case, the capabilities view does not attempt to extract norms directly from some facts about human nature. We should know what we can about the innate capacities of human beings, and this information is valuable, in telling us what our opportunities are and what our dangers might be. But we must begin by evaluating the innate powers of human beings, asking which ones are the good ones, the ones which are central to the notion of a decently flourishing human life, a life with dignity. . . . Thus, a no-evaluation view, which extracts norms directly from observation of animal's characteristic ways of life, is probably not going to be a helpful way of promoting the good of animals. (2004, 310–311)

Rather than fighting stags, the most decisive case would be one in which a restriction prevents the exercise of a valuable natural behavior but which has no effects at all on the animal's mental states, desire-satisfaction, or any other putative elements of animal welfare. If, in such a case, the animal's well-being is unaffected, then this would be a counterexample to the natural functioning view. Clear cases of this kind are difficult to find, though. As David DeGrazia notes: "In most cases, confinement that significantly interferes with an animal's ability to exercise her natural capacities also causes her to suffer, entailing unambiguous harm" (2011, 740).

DeGrazia suggests that this controversy is of little practical importance precisely because of the overlap just noted. If the different theories largely overlap in their classification of confinement as harmful or not, then, DeGrazia says, "our ability to address most practical situations involving confinement of animals need not await the outcome of this contest between mental statism [which for DeGrazia includes both mentalistic and desire-based theories as I have categorized them] and objective list accounts of well-being" (2011, 740). But this is too quick: the most plausible objective list theories don't include natural functioning *at the expense of* including mentalistic or desire-satisfaction components; rather, they include them *in addition to* some of those components. For any view of animal well-being to be plausible, it must at the bare minimum allow that negative mental states (desire-frustrations are more controversial) are negative constituents of well-being independently of their relationship to species-typical behavior. This means that confinement that both causes negative mental states and also prevents species-typical behavior will be categorized as causing a greater degree of harm according to any plausible natural function view than according to a mentalistic theory, assuming the theories are the same in other respects. On most views about the ethics of animal research, this has the potential to make a significant difference because, on most views, it is not enough to decide whether the animals are harmed; the magnitude of the harms is also ethically relevant.

Restrictions' Intrinsic Relationships to Well-Being

Are restrictions intrinsically related to animal well-being? On mentalistic theories, the answer is clear: since a restriction is itself neither a positive nor a negative mental state, it can only have an instrumental relationship to well-being.

It is tempting to make a similar argument with respect to desire-satisfaction theories: a restriction can of course satisfy or frustrate desires, but it is a category mistake to say that it itself is the satisfaction or frustration of a desire and so it can only have an instrumental relationship to well-being on desire-satisfaction theories. But the desire-satisfaction theorist could allow that states of affairs that the individual desires intrinsically—as ends in themselves—are constituents of that individual's welfare, even though what is desired is not itself a satisfied desire. For example, if Jill desires to be a great artist, and she desires this as an end in itself rather than merely instrumentally (say, because she thinks it would secure her a good income), then her being a great artist could, according to the desire-satisfaction theorist, be a constituent of Jill's well-being. And this is so even though her being a great artist is not a satisfied desire; rather, it is what satisfies her desire.

There is a well-established literature on the preferences animals have about their restrictions and its conditions. For example, Marian Stamp Dawkins (1978) reports that hens demonstrate a clear preference for larger cages over smaller cages, grass floors over wire floors, and, interestingly, smaller cages with grass floors over larger cages with wire floors. She does not explore the question of whether those preferences are intrinsic or instrumental to some further goal, but research on the motivational drives of animals long ago undermined the simplistic view that animals are only fundamentally motivated by hunger, pain, and sex. Harry Harlow, Margaret Harlow, and Donald Meyer found that rhesus macaques liked to solve mechanical puzzles simply out of curiosity, concluding that "the performance of the task provided intrinsic reward" (1950, 84). A desire to engage in "intrinsic exploration," exploratory behavior that is not further motivated by other goals, is well documented in a wide variety of species (Hughes 1997). Wood-Gush and Vestergaard (1989) discuss how several species of agricultural animals desire to engage in intrinsic exploration and how this desire is often frustrated by the animal's being restricted to a monotonous environment. It's not clear that an animal would desire to be at liberty in the broadest sense, but that is fully compatible with an animal's having an intrinsic desire to not be restricted *to this or that particular area*. A desire-satisfaction theorist should thus acknowledge the possibility that animals can have an intrinsic interest in being free of certain restrictions.

On an objective list view, if something on the list is intrinsically antithetical to being restricted in certain ways, then those restrictions are intrinsically inimical to well-being. As already mentioned, an objective list view can encompass a desire-satisfaction view and so, for the reasons already mentioned, can allow that animals can have an intrinsic interest in being free of certain restrictions. Would the additional items on the list ground additional interests intrinsically frustrated by restrictions? Health views would ground only additional *instrumental* interests, as restrictions are only causally related to health. The situation with other objective list views, such as natural function views, is more complicated, as explained below.

Natural function theorists sometimes include liberty or freedom as a constituent of well-being for autonomous animals on the grounds that, very roughly, liberty is necessary for the exercise of autonomy, a species-typical behavior. Other objective list theorists might also want, for independent reasons, to include liberty or freedom as a constituent of well-being for autonomous animals. Cochrane (who rejects natural function views) argues that autonomy—which he understands as "the capacity to reason and reflect on [one's] desires, and change them in relation to one's values and conception of the good"—grounds an intrinsic interest in liberty (2009, 665). Similarly, Lori Gruen argues that autonomy—which she understands as the ability "to follow one's own wants and desires, interests and dreams, and not simply those that are imposed from the outside, or those which are internal but outside of control like addictions"—grounds an intrinsic interest in liberty (2011a, 148).

Cochrane (without citing any evidence) asserts that, apart from great apes and cetaceans, no animals possess the metacognitive capacities to reflect upon their own desires and values, and so concludes that most animals lack autonomy (2009, 667–668). Gruen agrees with Cochrane that few animals possess the metacognitive capacities required by his conception of autonomy, but argues that many animals are autonomous in her sense on the grounds that many animals make their own choices about "what to do, when to do it, and who to do it with" (2011a, 148–150).

Gruen may be right that many animals satisfy her conception, but it is more robust than she realizes. Consider Harry Frankfurt's assertion (made without citing any evidence) that animals are "wantons," individuals that have desires that motivate their actions but who have no second-order desires to be moved or to not be moved by their first-order desires (1971, 11). Wantons can deliberate about how to best satisfy their desires, but they cannot critically reflect on whether their desires are as they want them to be. If animals are wantons, they can engage in the various activities Gruen cites and yet, because their desires are outside of their control, they are analogous to addicts and so do not satisfy Gruen's conception of autonomy.

Even though Gruen rejects the idea that autonomy requires second-order desires, her own conception of autonomy may commit her to that idea unless she can give an alternative account of why the desires of animals with only first-order desires do not count as being "internal but outside of control." Although much of the research on metacognition in animals has returned positive findings, some scientists have concluded that the research methodologies are not yet sufficiently refined to distinguish between behaviors that are best explained by first-order cognition and behaviors that are best explained by metacognition (Smith et al. 2008; Smith 2009; Crystal and Foote 2009). It thus seems premature to make broad generalizations in this area.

Suppose, though, for the sake of discussion, that an animal is autonomous. Both Cochrane and Gruen would conclude that this grounds, for that animal, an intrinsic interest in liberty. Neither Cochrane nor Gruen hold the implausible view that *every* restriction is incompatible with this intrinsic interest (Cochrane 2009, 666; Gruen 2011a, 149), so this can't be an intrinsic interest in liberty per se. Perhaps instead the conclusion is that autonomous individuals have an intrinsic interest in *specific* liberties. Gruen says, "If other animals can be thought to be autonomous agents, then it makes sense to say that their liberty *to act in the ways that they choose within their species-typical behavioral repertoires* is valuable as such" (2011a, 150, emphasis added). Cochrane says that the way in which Truman, of *The Truman Show*, was not well-off was not that he was unhappy or that he had his desires frustrated (since he was happy and his desires were satisfied), but rather that "he was unable to frame and pursue *his own* life plans" (2009, 666, emphasis in the original). These suggest that the specific liberty in which autonomous individuals have an intrinsic interest just is the freedom to exercise their autonomy.

This seems plausible, but notice that the concept of "freedom" is no longer doing any independent work.[6] To clarify this, suppose that an individual is capable of feeling pleasure and so has an intrinsic interest in experiencing pleasure. It is also true that this individual has an intrinsic interest in being free to experience pleasure. But it does not follow that the individual also has an intrinsic interest in freedom or that the intrinsic interest in being free to experience pleasure carries moral weight over and above the intrinsic interest in experiencing pleasure. Rather, the only intrinsic interest at issue is the intrinsic interest in pleasure itself. Similarly with autonomy: what is at issue is not an intrinsic interest in freedom, but rather an intrinsic interest in autonomy.

Now, if *captivity* is defined as confinement accompanied by additional elements of domination, as inconclusively discussed earlier, then captivity necessarily frustrates an autonomous individual's interest in autonomy. Thus, an autonomous individual does have an intrinsic interest in not being a captive. *Restrictions*, though, are not necessarily incompatible with the exercise of autonomy and so have only instrumental relationships to an autonomous individual's interest in autonomy.

CONCLUSION

I have argued that the ethical evaluation of the confinement experienced by laboratory animals is relevant to the ethical evaluation of the research for which they are being confined. A proper conceptual analysis of confinement suggests that the concept of a restriction is more fundamental than the narrower concept of confinement and also that what really matters in discussions about the confinement of laboratory animals is not the bare fact that they are restricted, but rather the more particular facts about the kinds of restrictions to which they are subjected.

On any plausible view of animal welfare, these kinds of restrictions are instrumentally related to the well-being of laboratory animals in morally relevant ways. These instrumental relationships exhaust the ways in which restrictions benefit or harm animals on mentalistic views of animal well-being. Adding health as a constituent of animal well-being does not generate any additional intrinsic relationships. On desire-satisfaction views and objective list views that encompass desire-satisfaction views, animals can have an intrinsic interest in being free of certain restrictions, but this will depend on what they desire noninstrumentally. Although some objective list theorists have evaluated confinement through the lens of an interest in liberty, I have argued that it is more perspicuous to frame that discussion directly in terms of an interest in exercising one's autonomy. In assessing the magnitude of the various welfare effects of restrictions on laboratory animals, which view of animal welfare is correct has the potential to make a tremendous difference, even if the different views largely overlap in classifying restrictions as harmful or not. The resolution of continuing controversies about the proper understanding of animal welfare and the distribution and moral significance of higher-order cognitive capacities will help clarify many of these issues. Regardless of how these particular issues are resolved, discussions about the ethics of confinement should play a larger role in discussions about the ethics of laboratory animal research.

ACKNOWLEDGMENTS

Thanks to Paul Kelleher, Alan Rubel, Samuel Streiffer, and Lori Gruen for many helpful discussions and comments. Some text and ideas were originally published as part of a response to Gruen 2011b.

NOTES

1. Field research and veterinary research on client-owned animals, although often involving brief periods of confinement, are obviously different in this respect. These account for only a small proportion of the animals used in research, though, and so my focus here is on laboratory animal research.
2. The Morris water maze, a circular pool of water containing a hidden resting platform, is widely used to test spatial learning in mice and rats (Vorhees and Williams 2006).

3. Using the language of species and genus to describe this relationship was suggested to me by a talk on an unrelated topic by Luca Ferrero.

4. It should also be added that even if the obstacles don't prevent X from leaving R, it is enough if they would prevent X from leaving R were X to try to leave. This raises the question, though, of how hard X must try. An individual surrounded by a fence would normally be confined, but being surrounded by a very low fence that one is simply too lazy to jump over doesn't count as confinement. More generally, most fences limit one's freedom in a way that is overridable if the person devotes enough time and energy to the matter. How challenging an obstacle must be in order for it to amount to confinement will vary from linguistic context to linguistic context, but this will matter little for our purposes: for laboratory animals, escape is impossible no matter how hard were they to try.

5. Desire-satisfaction theories are typically subdivided into actual desire satisfaction theories and idealized desire satisfaction theories. Idealized desire-satisfaction theories are typically found to have more plausible implications for particular cases but, arguably, collapse into objective-list theories. See Griffin 1989, 17.

6. Ronald Dworkin makes a similar argument in response to those who claim that there is a right to liberty: "If we have a right to basic liberties not because they are cases in which the commodity of liberty is somehow especially at stake, but because an assault on basic liberties injures us or demeans us in some way that goes beyond its impact on liberty, then what we have a right to is not liberty at all, but to the values or interests or standing that this particular constraint defeats" (1978, 271).

References

Appleby, Michael, and Peter Sandøe. 2002. "Philosophical Debate on the Nature of Well-Being." *Animal Welfare* 11: 283–294.

Balcombe, Jonathan P., Neal D. Barnard, and Chad Sandusky. 2004. "Laboratory Routines Cause Animal Stress." *Journal of the American Association for Laboratory Animal Science* 43(6): 42–51.

Bennett, Jonathan. 1995. *The Act Itself.* Oxford: Clarendeon Press.

Brinkmann, Johannes. 2004. "Looking at Consumer Behavior in a Moral Perspective." *Journal of Business Ethics* 51(2) (May 1): 129–141.

Broom, David. 1991. "Animal Welfare: Concepts and Measurement." *Journal of Animal Science* 69: 4167–4175.

Cochrane, Alasdair. 2009. "Do Animals Have an Interest in Liberty?" *Political Studies* 57(3) (October): 660–679.

Coe, Christopher L. 1993. "Psychosocial Factors and Immunity in Nonhuman Primates: A Review." *Psychosomatic Medicine* 55(3): 298–308.

Coleman, Kristine, Mollie Bloomsmith, Carolyn Crockett, James Weed, and Steven Schapiro. 2012. "Behavioral Management, Enrichment, and Psychological Well-being of Laboratory Nonhuman Primates." In *Nonhuman Primates in Biomedical Research: Biology and Management*, 2nd ed., Christian Abee, Keith Mansfield, Suzette Tardif, and Timothy Morris (eds.), 1:149–176. London: Elsevier.

Crystal, Jonathon D., and Allison L. Foote. 2009. "Metacognition in Animals." *Comparative Cognitive Behavioral Research* 4: 1–16.

Dawkins, Marian. 1978. "Welfare and the Structure of a Battery Cage: Size and Cage Floor Preferences in Domestic Hens." *British Veterinary Journal* 134(5): 469–475.

De Vos-Korthals, W. H., and M. W. Van Hof. 1985. "Residual Visuomotor Behaviour after Bilateral Removal of the Occipital Lobe in the Rabbit." *Behavioural Brain Research* 15(3): 205–209.

DeGrazia, David. 1996. *Taking Animals Seriously: Mental Life and Moral Status*. Cambridge: Cambridge University Press.

DeGrazia, David. 2011. "The Ethics of Confining Animals." In *The Oxford Handbook of Animal Ethics*, Tom L. Beauchamp and R. G. Frey (eds.), 738–768. Oxford: Oxford University Press.

Dworkin, Ronald. 1978. "What Rights Do We Have?" In *Taking Rights Seriously*, by Ronald Dworkin, 266–278. Cambridge: Harvard University Press.

Frankfurt, Harry. 1971. "Freedom of the Will and the Concept of a Person." *Journal of Philosophy* 68(1): 5–20.

Griffin, James. 1989. *Well-Being: Its Meaning, Measurement, and Moral Importance*. Oxford: Oxford University Press.

Gruen, Lori. 2011a. *Ethics and Animals: An Introduction*. Cambridge Applied Ethics. Cambridge: Cambridge University Press.

Gruen, Lori. 2011b. "The Ethics of Captivity." *On the Human Forum*. Accessed November 21, 2013. http://onthehuman.org/2011/06/the-ethics-of-captivity/.

Harlow, Harry, Margaret Harlow, and Donald Meyer. 1950. "Learning Motivated by a Manipulation Drive." *Journal of Experimental Psychology* 40: 228–234.

Harrison, Rob, Terry Newholm, and Deirdre Shaw, eds. 2005. *The Ethical Consumer*. London: Sage Publications.

Hughes, Robert N. 1997. "Intrinsic Exploration in Animals: Motives and Measurement." *Behavioural Processes* 41(3) (December): 213–226.

Jamieson, Dale. 1985. "Against Zoos." In *In Defense of Animals*, Peter Singer (ed.), 108–117. Oxford: Basil Blackwell.

Kemnitz, Joseph W., and Nancy Schultz-Darken. 2009. "An IACUC Perspective on Animal Models of Sleep-Disordered Breathing." *ILAR Journal* 50(3): 312–313.

Morgan, Kathleen N., and Chris T. Tromborg. 2007. "Sources of Stress in Captivity." *Applied Animal Behaviour Science* 102(3–4) (February): 262–302.

Nussbaum, Martha. 2004. "Beyond 'Compassion and Humanity': Justice for Nonhuman Animals." In *Animal Rights: Current Debates and New Directions*, Cass Sunstein and Martha Nussbaum (eds.), 299–320. Oxford: Oxford University Press.

Rachels, James. 1989. "Do Animals Have a Right to Liberty." In *Animal Rights and Human Obligations*, 2nd ed., Tom Regan and Peter Singer (eds.), 205–223. Englewood Cliffs, NJ: Prentice-Hall.

Reinhardt, V. 2004. "Common Husbandry-Related Variables in Biomedical Research with Animals." *Laboratory Animals* 38(3) (July 1): 213–235. doi:10.1258/002367704323133600.

Russell, William M. S. 2002. "The Ill-Effects of Uncomfortable Quarters." In *Comfortable Quarters for Laboratory Animals*, 9th ed., Victor Reinhardt and Annie Reinhardt (eds.), 1–5. Washington, DC: Animal Welfare Institute.

Schwartz, David T. 2010. *Consuming Choices: Ethics in a Global Consumer Age*. Lanham, MD: Rowman & Littlefield.

Smith, J. David. 2009. "The Study of Animal Metacognition." *Trends in Cognitive Sciences* 13(9) (September): 389–396.

Smith, J. David, Michael J. Beran, Justin J. Couchman, and Mariana V. C. Coutinho. 2008. "The Comparative Study of Metacognition: Sharper Paradigms, Safer Inferences." *Psychonomic Bulletin & Review* 15(4) (August): 679–691. doi:10.3758/PBR.15.4.679.

Stanley, Jason. 2000. "Context and Logical Form." *Linguistics and Philosophy* 23(4): 391–434.

Sughrue, Michael E., J. Mocco, Willam J. Mack, Andrew F. Ducruet, Ricardo J. Komotar, Ruth L. Fischbach, Thomas E. Martin, and E. Sander Connolly. 2009. "Bioethical Considerations in Translational Research: Primate Stroke." *American Journal of Bioethics* 9(5) (May 14): 3–12.

Taylor, Paul W. 1986. *Respect for Nature: A Theory of Environmental Ethics*. Princeton: Princeton University Press.

Vorhees, Charles V, and Michael T. Williams. 2006. "Morris Water Maze: Procedures for Assessing Spatial and Related Forms of Learning and Memory." *Nature Protocols* 1(2) (July): 848–858.

Wemelsfelder, Francoise. 1990. "Boredom and Lab Animal Welfare." In *The Experimental Animal in Biomedical Research*, Bernard Rollin M. Lynne Kessell (eds.), 1:243–272. Boca Raton: CRC Press.

Will, Bruno E., Mark R. Rosenzweig, Edward L. Bennett, Marie Hebert, and Hiromi Morimoto. 1977. "Relatively Brief Environmental Enrichment Aids Recovery of Learning Capacity and Alters Brain Measures after Postweaning Brain Lesions in Rats." *Journal of Comparative and Physiological Psychology* 91(1): 33–50.

Wolfensohn, Sarah, and Maggie Lloyd. 2013. *Handbook of Laboratory Animal Management and Welfare*. 4th ed. Oxford: Wiley-Blackwell.

Wood-Gush, D. G. M., and K. Vestergaard. 1989. "Exploratory Behavior and the Welfare of Intensively Kept Animals." *Journal of Agricultural Ethics* 2(2): 161–169.

12

Captive for Life

Conserving Extinct in the Wild Species through Ex Situ Breeding

IRUS BRAVERMAN ■

Are there "fates worse than death," to use Kurt Vonnegut's title? Is captivity one such fate? This chapter examines these questions through the lens of conservation biology's ex situ models of captive management—and captive breeding in particular—for wild animals, and especially for species that have been designated as Critically Endangered or as Extinct in the Wild. Drawing on interviews with leading conservation biologists, the chapter describes the erosion of the distinctions between species management in captivity and conservation in wild nature, often referred to among conservationists as ex situ and in situ conservation. The chapter examines situations in which the extinction, or the near extinction, of a species in the wild is imminent and a captive breeding program is initiated, typically by zoos, to ensure this species' survival. I also describe the International Union for the Conservation of Nature's (IUCN) Red List and IUCN's emerging One Plan approach for integrated management of wild and captive populations.

Because freestanding wilderness areas absent human management are increasingly rare, the binary between wilderness and captivity—and between in situ and ex situ conservation—is somewhat outmoded. In place of these bifurcations, what emerges is a continuum between different (and increasing) levels of management. This chapter considers some of the complex political questions that surface with such an intensified management of life.

WHY IN SITU VERSUS EX SITU CONSERVATION?

Initially adopted from other disciplines to indicate the importance of place for the utility of conservation management of plants (Braverman 2014), in the 1980s the in situ / ex situ terminology gained traction within the emerging science of conservation biology as a convenient replacement for the emotionally loaded terms "nature," "wild," and "captivity." This new terminology has been used broadly by zoo experts, who encounter resistance from both animal rights and animal welfare activists for holding animals in captivity (Donahue and Trump 2006, Jensen and Tweedy-Holmes 2007). In place of the negative associations of the term "captivity," the term *ex situ* highlights the scientific characterization of this work as part of conservation. In the words of wildlife manager Evan Blumer, former director of The Wilds in Ohio: whereas "the terminology began with this binary of captive versus wild," it "then got broadened and softened by bringing the Latin into it with in situ and ex situ" (interview).

The in situ / ex situ terminology—in its Latin form in particular—also figures prominently in what is arguably the most important legal text on biodiversity conservation: the 1992 Convention on Biological Diversity (CBD)—an international treaty signed by 193 countries. Article 8 of the CBD—entitled "In Situ Conservation"—establishes that "Each Contracting Party shall, as far as possible and as appropriate: (a) Establish a system of protected areas or areas where special measures need to be taken to conserve biological diversity; . . . (d) Promote the protection of ecosystems, natural habitats and the maintenance of viable populations of species in natural surroundings" (United Nations CBD 1992a). Under the title "Ex Situ Conservation," Article 9 of the CBD establishes that "Each Contracting Party shall, as far as possible and as appropriate, and predominantly for the purpose of complementing in-situ measures: (a) Adopt measures for the ex-situ conservation of components of biological diversity, preferably in the country of origin of such components" (United Nations CBD 1992b).

Clearly, whereas in situ nature conservation is defined by many conservation biologists as the ultimate goal of conservation, ex situ is constrained in that it must be executed "predominantly for the purpose of complementing in-situ measures," as mentioned above. This hierarchical understanding of the relationship between in situ and ex situ conservation is not only the law "on the books," but is also how many conservationists define and experience their work, as I have discovered in the numerous interviews conducted for this project. Such preferential treatment is founded upon the belief that there can, in fact, be a place that is more "inside" nature, which may then be compared with a place that is "outside" of nature by measuring their relative placement on a fixed and linear in situ/ex situ continuum. Put differently, the current definition of conservation still depends on the bifurcation between in situ and ex situ and the prioritization of a predetermined vision of in situ over ex situ conservation.

The effects of the in/ex situ paradigm are apparent in the various definitions by leading conservation organizations. For example, according to IUCN's Red List definitions, an animal that is Extinct in the Wild is defined as "non-conserved," even if it still lives in captivity (IUCN 2012a). In the words of Onnie Byers of the IUCN: "Real conservation is [defined as] self-sustaining populations in nature. If a species in total is only in captivity, they call that 'not conserved'" (interview). Existing conservation practices thus manage nonhuman species differently based on their linear placement along the continuum between "in" and "out" of nature. Is such a linear framework practical in a messy world that requires careful management decisions? Furthermore, is it ethical?

ZOOS AS EX SITU CONSERVATION INSTITUTIONS

In the 1970s, a system of national and international legal codes came into effect that dramatically limited the ability of zoos to take certain wild animals from their habitats. To survive, zoos needed to find a way to (re)produce animals other than by their translocation from the wild into captivity. In the late 1970s, animal programs—and especially Species Survival Plans and Taxon Advisory Groups—were set up by the Association of Zoos and Aquariums (AZA) to collectively manage their breeding across accredited zoo facilities in the US. The initial purpose of these programs was to create a sustainable population of certain species within zoos. Distributed among zoos across the country, it was unavoidable that managed animal populations would quickly succumb to inbreeding without frequent, carefully planned contraception and transfers for breeding. In order to create such sustainable populations, zoos realized, they must exchange animals between them—effectively establishing an insular ecosystem that I have referred to as "zooland" (Braverman 2012). Animal programs "thus serve as control towers for the movement of zoo animals between accredited zoos" (Braverman 2012, 162).

In 2011, AZA's animal programs administered 303 species and subspecies. Parallel to the American system, animal programs also came to existence in Europe (European Endangered Species Programme) and Australasia. The World Association of Zoos and Aquariums currently manages eleven taxa on a global scale through Global Species Management Programs (GSMPs) (Dick, interview). In 1995, more than three thousand vertebrate species were bred in zoos and other captive breeding facilities (Koontz 1995, 132). From a genetic standpoint, however, the task of orchestrating such reproductions and the ethical dilemmas at stake have proven to be considerably more challenging than zoo experts may have anticipated (Braverman 2012, 159–185).

Within the course of just one decade (into the 1990s), the focus of zoo animal programs shifted from sustainability within ex situ populations to the conservation of in situ populations. Accredited zoos (which, admittedly, encompass a small minority of zoos in North America, see Braverman 2012) were reconceived as a modern Noah's ark: sustaining threatened species until they could be reintroduced "back into the wild" (Foose 1986). At one time, zoos and aquariums argued that breeding animals in captivity for eventual reintroduction to the wild would become the defining rationale for their continued social relevance and future existence (Reading and Miller 2010).

The interplay between genetics and captive breeding became the foundation for the emergence of conservation biology in the 1980s as the science of modern species conservation. "Among other changes," these scholars note, "conservation biology marked a shift in the management of living collections away from displays only and toward population management designed to sustain genetically diverse, demographically stable, and viable captive populations…that were to serve as assurance colonies should wild populations go extinct" (2011, 39; see also Soulé et al. 1986; Dickie, Bonner, and West 2007, 224). Christoph Schwitzer, Primate Specialist Group vice chair at the Species Survival Commission of the IUCN and head of research at the Bristol Zoo, says along these lines, "My view on things is that ex situ is a very important tool, and will become much more important in the future for species conservation planning and species conservation action" (interview). Finally, Paul Pearce-Kelly of the Zoological Society of London remarks, similarly, that "if [many species] are going to survive—not be conserved, but survive—they're going to need ex situ support" (interview).

Captive breeding has become a recognized strategy of ex situ conservation largely because of its potential to create a captive reserve for endangered or even extinct wild animals. Such insurance or assurance populations—and it is interesting to note that whereas assurance implies *in the inevitable event* that something happens, insurance implies *in case* something happens—are typically bred in zoos with an eye toward their conspecifics in the wild, but with minimal (if any) actual genetic exchange with such wild populations. Increasingly, however, zoo experts are questioning the effectiveness of such isolated ex situ breeding for conservation. Some have argued along these lines that "there are far too many endangered species and not nearly enough space to breed them all in captivity and, in many cases, far too little habitat remaining in which to reintroduce them. In addition, reintroduction programs are difficult and expensive, and they amount to treating the symptoms of species loss rather than the causes" (Hutchins, Smith, and Allard 2008, 515; Snyder et al. 1996). As a result of these realizations, many zoo experts have become wary of the "zoos as arks" metaphor (Soulé et al. 1986), once again focusing on the sustainability of zoo populations within zoos.

The refocus of zoos on the sustainability of zoo animal populations is arguably the reason for the emergence of AZA's 2010 Action Plan. This plan, which took effect in fall 2012, classifies all AZA animal programs into three categories based on their sustainability within North American zoos: green, which are demographically sustainable for one hundred years at least; yellow, which are potentially sustainable; and red, which are unsustainable for having less than fifty individuals. Whereas green and yellow programs are prioritized by the AZA for collective management, red programs are to be phased out or, in the zoo experts' language, "bred to extinction." In 2011, there were thirty green, 278 yellow, and 240 red programs (Braverman 2012, 180–181). This plan has potentially significant effects on conservation by zoos because, as I have pointed out, "many of the red coded species are not only underrepresented in zoos (*ex situ*) but are also endangered in the wild (*in situ*)" (183). In effect, AZA's new priorities for ex situ breeding arguably conflict with the central goal of in situ species conservation, where the more vulnerable a species is, it is typically assigned a higher priority. To what extent this plan will in fact redefine the breeding focus of animal programs in North American zoos is yet to be seen. Nonetheless, many—including American and European zoo experts I interviewed for this project—view it as an odd and counterintuitive decision by the AZA.

In recent years, zoo scientists have been calling into question even the focus on isolated sustainability within zoo animal populations. In his 2013 article, "Achieving True Sustainability of Zoo Populations," population biologist Robert Lacy of the Brookfield Zoo points out that "Zoos were once reliant on harvest from the wild to populate their exhibits; in the past few decades zoos proudly and appropriately shifted away from reliance on continued wild collection to breeding of closed populations; perhaps we need now to move to a third era of thinking about the best way to care for species assurance populations" (Lacy 2013, 20). I will soon return to the third era proposed by Lacy, which I see as intimately interconnected with IUCN's One Plan approach. Before doing so, however, I would like to discuss what is arguably a core concept driving the discourse of conservation biology, both inside and outside zoos: extinction. Within this broad concept, the category that brings out the ethical underpinnings of the various approaches toward conservation and nonhuman animals is IUCN's Red List category of Extinct in the Wild.

EXTINCT IN THE WILD

Many conservation biologists would probably agree that the most urgent challenge for conservation is the rapid disappearance of natural habitat and wildlife

(Balmford, Mace, and Ginsburg 1998)—specifically, that "25 percent of all mammals, 12 percent of birds and more than a third of amphibians are threatened with extinction" (Holst and Dickie 2007, 23). Kent Redford and colleagues explain along these lines that "Conservation biology was founded with a focus on the *plight of species* by a group of scientists that included representatives of the zoo and botanical garden communities" (2012, 1157; my emphasis). This species-oriented approach defines conservation biology's goal as preventing the extinction of species with an orientation toward crisis intervention. "Extinction was the middle name of conservation biology, and preventing extinctions was seen as the new discipline's major aim," Redford and others claim in another article (Redford et al. 2011, 39; see also Mace et al. 2008). The extinction paradigm focuses on numerical counts of rare and threatened species, what Michael Soulé and colleagues refer to as "manifest demographic or numerical minimalism" (2003). Redford and his colleagues explain that "This trend is still evident in the fact that successful conservation is defined by many conservation biologists with reference to minimum population sizes, minimum areas, and minimally sufficient sets of sites" (2011, 40).

IUCN's Red List is the epitome of conservation biology's focus on extinction and its negative projections. From the Red List's overview: "The introduction in 1994 of a scientifically rigorous approach to determine risks of extinction that is applicable to all species, has become a world standard" (IUCN 2012b). The Red List classifies taxa into eight categories: Extinct, Extinct in the Wild, Critically Endangered, Endangered, Vulnerable, Lower Risk, Data Deficient, and Not Evaluated (IUCN 1994). A quantitative population viability analysis (PVA) is performed in many cases to estimate "the extinction probability of a taxon or population." The general aim of this listing system is "to provide an explicit, objective framework for the classification of species according to their extinction risk" (IUCN 1994; for more about PVA's see Braverman, draft).

Specifically, the Red List defines Extinct in the Wild as follows: "A taxon is Extinct in the Wild when it is known only to survive in cultivation, in captivity or as a naturalised population (or populations) well outside the past range." Schwitzer of the IUCN explains that "there's a distinction between Extinct, which is basically gone (and we are very, very careful with assigning this status to anything).... And then there's Extinct in the Wild, which simply means that all the animals are in captivity somewhere, whether in a zoo or in a reserve, it doesn't matter—but it's not in the wild" (interview).

Currently, the IUCN lists thirty-two species as Extinct in the Wild (IUCN 2013). Père David's deer is the first example I would like to consider here. According to the IUCN: "The species became Extinct in the Wild due to habitat loss and hunting. The size of the reintroduced population was only 120 in 1993, although it has increased to over 2,000 since that time.... The present re-introduced populations are contained within enclosures and are essentially still subject to captive management" (Zhigang and Harris 2008).

Amphibians and partulid snails arguably have the highest number of species representatives on the Extinct in the Wild list. Kevin Zippel, director of IUCN's Amphibian Ark project, tells me in an interview:

> When the amphibian extinction crisis came to light and we realized how many species were in such dire need and how relatively few resources they needed to be saved, suddenly the ark metaphor became useful once again. We literally have species that are Extinct in the Wild, existing on the planet only for the very fact that they exist in captivity.... We are literally functioning as an ark. But, for me, it is not so much an ark metaphor as it is a fleet of life rafts all around the planet, each working with their own particular species.

Of the thirty-two species listed as Extinct in the Wild, eleven are partulid snails (Figure 12.1). According to the Red List, native partulid species began rapidly disappearing from their habitats in French Polynesia after the intentional introduction of the carnivorous snail *Euglandina rosea* into this area in the late 1980s as a way to control the numbers of the giant African land snail (*Achatina fulica*) that was previously introduced as biological control over "pest" populations. By 1992, few partulid snail species were left on the islands. This genus is currently maintained in captivity in a global breeding program. "It's not a zoo saving them, not a museum, but it's all of us working together," Paul Pearce-Kelly of the Zoological Society of London and coordinator of the Partulid Global Species Management Programme tells me. "You try to make the best you can through a very difficult path that we're on." "There's no question that if one didn't intervene to the degree we are, there'll be a lot of species lost, even beyond what there already is," Pearce-Kelly continues. "If we have the ability to try and keep things as healthy as possible, then we have the obligation," he concludes (interview). According to the Bristol Zoo, "Currently twenty Partula species have been saved from extinction by zoos and Universities; fifteen are classified as extinct in the wild and five are critically endangered" (NewsWatch 2010).

Still, many conservation biologists view ex situ breeding first and foremost as a tool for promoting the goals of in situ conservation. The central idea behind these efforts is that once nature is restored, or once a population has strengthened itself, the vulnerable species can be reintroduced "back into the wild." For example, certain conservation biologists have argued in the context of amphibians that "Maintenance of assurance populations in captivity may be

Partulid snails at the London Zoo, courtesy of Irus Braverman

the only route to survival for hundreds of species of amphibian, until a future point where chytrid is, if ever, eradicated from, or controlled in, the environment" (Dickie, Bonner, and West 2007, 224). Robert Loftin argues along these lines: "In cases with truly no alternative to extinction in the wild, taking the remnant into captivity for the purpose of augmenting the population through captive breeding is justified." "The difficulty," he adds, "is to discern when this is and is not the case" (1995, 165).

Although the technological capacities for maintaining Extinct in the Wild species in captivity may be available, some have raised concerns about whether those should in fact be used. Just because we can breed animals in captivity for reintroduction, does that mean we should (Reading and Miller 2010, 103)? Is reintroduction just a human endeavor to "redecorate nature," as Marc Bekoff (2000) has suggested, and as such ought to be severely limited, if not curtailed? Robert Loftin has argued in response that humans have already redecorated nature extensively through global and local species extinctions and introductions (1995), hence reintroduction is merely a redecoration of a redecoration. The Extinct in the Wild designation surfaces some of the nuanced differences between conservation biologists on the ethical questions regarding the proper relationship between captivity and nature and between ex situ and in situ conservation.

In an interview, Zippel of the Amphibian Ark depicts his model for bridg-
ing the existing tensions between the in situ and ex situ approaches, which
again clearly prioritizes in situ through its privileged treatment of in situ
experts:

> The Amphibian Ark [has created] an objective process to evaluate which
> species needs what kind of help, and uses the expertise of the in situ peo-
> ple to determine that. We don't even involve the ex situ people in species
> selection. [We] just have the in situ people develop the list: these species
> need to have assurance populations in captivity, these species need to have
> head-starting programs, but these ones need to be protected in the field,
> these ones need research in the field, these ones need mass breeding to
> counter overcollection. So we've got seven or ten different categories of
> conservation intervention…and then [we] hand them to the ex situ folks.
> (interview)

The relationship between experts of ex situ and in situ conservation is,
clearly, fraught with tensions and emotions. The case of the California condor
demonstrates the heightened emotions at stake in the struggle between captive
breeding and extinction. Here is how the episode unfolded, in the words of
leading zoo expert William Conway:

> I was on the special committee put together by American Ornithological
> Union and the National Audubon Society some years ago to decide
> whether it made sense to take condors into captivity. There was a very
> large and vocal group of critics saying, "No, no, no! Better dead than bred!"
> Well, we met at length in California, and I wrote much of the program, and
> we said, "We have no choice: if we leave them out there, they will be dead."
> They said, "Fine." We didn't agree with that. When we finally got down to
> twenty-two birds, we took them into captivity.

The Audubon Society opposed placing the condor in captivity. One of its
members, bird leader and ornithologist Rich Stallcup, articulated the issues
at stake:

> But must we still try to conceal the guilt of condor spoilage? Must we bur-
> den and demean the doomed skymasters with electronic trinkets, then
> imprison them in boxes and demand that they reproduce? Or can we just
> say, "Yes, el condor, we blew it long ago, we're sorry. Fly, stay as long as you
> can, and then die with the dignity that has always been yours." (Golden
> Gate Birder 2013)

This approach is very much in line with Tom Regan's argument that "the general policy regarding wilderness would be precisely what the preservationists want—namely, let it be!... Were we to show proper respect for the rights of the individuals who make up the biotic community, would not the community be preserved? And is not that what the more holistic, systems-minded environmentalists want?" (Regan 1983, 363). According to Regan, the requirement that individual organisms be sacrificed for the whole is a type of "environmental fascism" (362). "The rights view is a view about the moral rights of individuals," he says. "Species are not individuals, and the rights view does not recognize the moral rights of species to anything, including survival" (359). Similarly, Robert Loftin argues that "Breeding animals in captivity is in some sense breeding the wild out of the animal" (1995, 169) and quotes David Brower: "A [California condor] is only five percent bone and feathers. Ninety-five per cent of condor is place" (178).

In 1986, the Audubon Society filed a lawsuit against the Fish and Wildlife Service's decision to take the last remaining condors into captivity, claiming that it violated the Administrative Procedure Act, the Endangered Species Act, and the National Environmental Policy Act. Their preliminary request for injunction barring the capture of the wild condor was granted, but reversed on appeal. The United States Court of Appeals in the District of Columbia ruled in 1986: "We believe that the Wildlife Service's decision to capture the remaining wild condors was manifestly defensible" (*National Audubon Society v. Fish & Wildlife Service*, 801 F.2d 405 [DC Circuit 1986], at 408).

Père David's deer, the Wyoming toad, and certain partulid snails are thus kept alive in captivity. The California condor, on the other hand, has been reintroduced "back" into the wild "and now we have over 300 and they are breeding in Arizona and California" (Conway, interview). Unfortunately, many similarly threatened species have not fared as well. For example, although all parties agreed at the time that the last remaining Northern white rhinos were insecure in Kenya because of poaching threats, they could not agree on the measures to be taken. "It was an absolutely classic tale of disaster," IUCN officer Mark Stanley-Price tells me in an interview, lamenting that the inability to bridge the divides between all the concerned parties and officials consigned the Northern white rhino to extinction.

Animal welfare advocates typically adopt a more nuanced approach to the dead-or-bred debate between zoos and animal rights activists. Chris Draper, senior scientific researcher for the Born Free Foundation, defines himself as an animal welfarist. The following is his position on the merits of ex situ breeding. "If there is a justification to do something like that, to really take the last individuals in," he tells me, "it should be with the view of getting them the hell out of there as quickly as possible" (interview). Although he is focused on the welfare of individual animals (which he assumes to be severely compromised in many captive settings), Draper still sees the point in taking animals into captivity, provided that they are on the brink of extinction, that they can be properly cared for, and that they will promptly be returned to their places of origin. But this is rarely possible, as I show shortly.

Clearly, the debate between extinction and captivity raises difficult questions. "Do we have any responsibility to try to prevent extinction…even if doing so in some way mentally or physically 'harms' individual animals? How to balance the welfare and rights of individual animals against the value of captive breeding to reintroduction programs and our obligations to sustain populations, species, and ecological communities and processes?" (Norton 1995). Michael Hutchins and colleagues describe this as "issues of individual animal welfare versus overall species and ecosystem conservation" (2003, 964). At times, actions designed to benefit populations will conflict with the interests of individual animals held in captivity (Wuichet and Norton 1995).

CAPTIVE—FOR LIFE?

For many conservationists, the ethical assessment of captivity depends on the existence of a wild "out there" into which species can be released. It is generally assumed, then, that while the species might be extinct, its natural habitat, however degraded, continues to exist. But what if the species habitat no longer exists for the last of its specimens to return back to? Are conservationists still ethically obligated to save it, or are they now prohibited from doing so? In the words of Robert Loftin: what happens when animals are "all dressed up but [with] no place to go" (Loftin 1995, 177)? The recent dramatic changes in ecosystems thus raise the following question more urgently than ever before: should humans save nonhuman species that can exist *only* in captivity?

The response of the zoo experts I interviewed for this project was uniform: save them first—you never know what will happen later. In the words of Christoph Schwitzer: "[T]here is an inherent value in saving every single species. I just don't want my children to grow up without blue-eyed black lemurs, or anything like that—even if it's some odd frog species, or a mosquito. I want them to be able to experience these, and that's my motivation" (interview). "It is better to have the species in captivity than not to have it at all," Robert Loftin argues similarly (1995, 165). "Conditions could conceivably change," he adds, "more habitat might become available, public attitudes might shift, or environmental contamination might decrease. Unlikely as these scenarios are for some animals, at the very least keeping the biological species in existence in some form, even in a cage, keeps some future alternatives open to some extent."

Draper disagrees: "There's no point catching the last individuals into captivity without doing something to restore their habitat in the wild," He says, explaining that:

> Let's take a hopefully hypothetical situation where there is no polar ice cap on the planet. What do we do with the polar bears that are in captivity at that point?...I will be probably ruthlessly honest here and say that it doesn't matter, because under current management they're not going to breed to sustainable numbers, and they're going to be extinct in captivity anyway....Let's not be distracted by the glitz and glamour of the snazzy captive stuff. For the long run, it's going to be little more than a costly diversion.

The focus on extinction thus pits the pro- and anticaptivity communities against one another, with animal welfarists sitting on the fence. Yet these "crisis" scenarios and solutions are limited in that they are projections in a mode of last resort. Koen Margodt asks along these lines: "Is it better to vanish in the wild than to lead a rich life in captivity?... Would it be more desirable to die free rather than to live in captivity?" She responds: "Fortunately, the actual picture is not such a black-and-white one" (Margodt 2010, 30). Similarly, I argue that conservationists can and should find a way around the "bred or dead" dichotomy. Some conservation biologists propose that emerging population management approaches, such as the One Plan approach, are attempting precisely that.

THE ONE PLAN APPROACH

Diseases that increasingly threaten wildlife populations and intensifying effects of climate change have led certain conservation biologists to assert that there is no longer a way around intense wildlife management across the board. "The view that species can be effectively conserved with minimal management simply by creating large areas of natural habitat no longer holds true," Redford and others have claimed. "Humans will likely never be able to stop managing species in order to maintain the richness and diversity we hold in such esteem" (Redford, Jensen, and Breheny 2012, 1157–1158).

Since 2010, a few scientists at IUCN's Conservation Breeding Specialist Group (CBSG) have been advocating an approach that mitigates the extremities of in situ versus ex situ and extinction versus captive breeding through what they have coined as the "One Plan" approach (for an earlier account, see WAZA 2005). This approach was officially proposed to the IUCN World Conservation Congress and to the European Association of Zoos and Aquaria

Conservation Committee in 2012. According to CBSG chair Onnie Byers, "The One Plan approach proposes integrated species conservation planning, which considers all populations of the species—both inside and outside their natural range—under all conditions of management, involving all responsible parties, and engaging all available resources" (interview). Beyond captivating, breeding, and reintroducing animals from species that are on the brink of extinction, the One Plan approach argues for the importance of an integrative management across human and nonhuman populations that brings all the actants and experts around one table.

Population biologists Robert Lacy and Jonathan Ballou are the minds behind metapopulation models that enable such integrative management of populations. Lacy cautions that many of the zoos' "most valued and often irreplaceable breeding programs are not projected to meet demographic and genetic goals designed to ensure that the populations persist." Specifically, he claims that the one-hundred-year goal for sustainable management of zoo animal populations is not only arbitrary but also insufficient, as it does not consider what will happen after those one hundred years are over. Lacy concludes that "our measures of 'sustainability' are measuring success toward goals that are actually counter to true sustainability" (Lacy 2013, 20). Furthermore, Lacy claims that because closed population will always lose genetic diversity, "for zoo populations to be truly sustainable, they cannot be maintained indefinitely as static, closed populations, but must instead be managed as a dynamic component of a metapopulation that includes wild populations and perhaps also less intensively managed populations in semi-wild environments" (Lacy 2013, 22). Managing ex situ populations alone is not species conservation, Lacy states. "Rather than seeing zoo populations as last resort insurance to prevent species loss when all else fails in the field," he says, "zoo populations would be managed as an integral component of ongoing conservation success" (2013, 24). The idea, then, is that instead of the previous disconnected units of management for wild and captive populations, a unified and more effective form of management should emerge (for more on this model see Braverman, draft; for other forms of integrated population management, see Shea et al. 1998). As Lacy explains in our interview: "No longer can the zoo world operate differently from a national park. The captive populations are most likely not viable on their own . . . and the wild population certainly is not viable on its own, either. We have to be working in partnership because we need each other."

Such an integrated *inter situ* approach is already taking place on the ground (Braverman, draft). For example, the African penguin has been in steep decline for the last couple of decades—down from several million breeding pairs at the turn of the last century to twenty-five thousand breeding pairs in 2013. This drastic decline, Schwitzer explains, is not only due to overfishing, but also due to global climate change and the resulting changes in ocean currents that have led to an ecological mismatch between the penguins and their prey: the fish have moved east to places where there are no penguin colonies. In Schwitzer's words

> When they nest and have chicks, penguins can only swim for about twenty kilometers to find fish. So if the fish is further away from the nesting colony than twenty kilometers, then the whole system breaks down and the chicks starve, which is what is currently happening. So we are saying: if the mountain doesn't come to the prophet, we need to bring the prophet to the mountain. We are trying to bring the penguins to the fish.

To do so, Schwitzer and others needed to figure out a way to overcome "breeding site fidelity"—namely, a penguin, when it becomes sexually mature, always goes back to where it hatched to start breeding there. Schwitzer presents the most recent solution:

> We are taking away these starving chicks from the colonies, we are hand-rearing them in captivity…and when they are nice and fat, we chuck them back in, and we bolster the wild population by doing that. But we don't bring them back to where they came from, at least not all of them…. They are all banded, with flipper bands, and we can see which one goes where…. [E]ventually, we would like to use zoo-bred penguins, at least eggs from penguins in European and North American zoos, and bring [them] back to South Africa, hatch them…and then use these to bolster the wild population, too…. We want to know that this works, in case the wild population further crashes down. We want to be able to use the several thousand strong zoo population to actually bring that wild population back. (interview)

Under the One Plan approach, in situ and ex situ conservation projects are codependent and reciprocal; they also enable animal transfers between various sites for the sake of conservation. As species population management becomes holistic, the lines between in situ and ex situ conservation are effectively blurred. Some conservation biologists believe this to be an inevitable and positive change: "zoos have contributed a set of approaches to species management that are being integrated with those from field conservation to create hybrid forms of species management better suited to present-day conditions" (Redford, Jensen, and Breheny 2012, 1157). According to its proponents, such a flexible negotiation of in situ and ex situ incentives will foster proactive modes of conservation that will eventually relieve the current narrow focus on extinction (for other views, especially ones that caution about the political economical effects of such integrative approaches, see Braverman, draft).

REASSESSING IN SITU VERSUS EX SITU

I have shown that the relationship between captive and wild populations is complex, illuminating the problems of bifurcated definitions such as nature/captive and in/ex situ. The intensified management of animal populations in nature reserves as well as in other typically perceived "wild" sites calls into serious question the ability to depict something as purely in situ or ex situ conservation in the first place. Certain conservation experts have proposed, for example, the establishment of extractive reserves (Conway 1999; Redford, Brandon, and Sanderson 1998), which entail designating a natural habitat and managing it for animal production, including surveys of the habitat, the species present, ecological interactions, and the movement of animals in both directions—from the reserve to zoo populations and vice versa—to improve the genetic diversity of the individual populations (Dickie, Bonner, and West 2007, 228). Would such extrative reserves be sites of wild nature or of captivity, of in situ or ex situ?

Hamish Currie of the South African nonprofit organization Back to Africa explains some of the problems that have resulted from the rigid application of what he calls the "old school" definitions of in situ and ex situ. In his words, "There are very few places left that are actually really wild. So whether you like it or not, you have to manage wildlife." "We still talk 'in situ,' and 'ex situ,'" he continues, but "in fact,…in most scenarios you are managing animals" (interview). Currie also points to the disparity between the world of zoo scientists and academics and the realities of animal management in Africa. In his words,

> Too many people—too many academics, too many people working in zoos—sort of think 'well these are captive animals and then there's the wild.' They think of this vast continent of Africa where animals are running around, moving vast distances, all the genetic exchange is taking place—and that's the wild. What they don't realize is that it's now being sort of boiled down to smaller and smaller pockets, and within those pockets animals might have to be managed. (interview)

Zoo expert William Conway provides an even more sweeping critique, this time of the term "original habitat," which has been used frequently in describing in situ operations. In his words, the whole business of in situ and ex situ are artificial concepts....Habitats are moving and changing, climate is changing. Animal populations in the past have been able to adapt to these changes, sometimes. [But] lots of time they couldn't and became extinct before humans came around. That's why we don't have giant sloths and mammoths. There used to be mammoths 11,000 years ago in the Bronx; 18,000 years ago there were polar bears in the south of France. That's not so long [ago]. So [the term] "original habitat" depends on how original you want to be....[W]e usually apply the same sort of meaning we do to history: history is since we were here, and "original" is the way it was when we remember it. But it doesn't necessarily mean it was here in the day of the dinosaurs. So these terms have to be taken with great deal of flexibility. (interview)

Nature and its implied originality are thus understood by many conservationists to be relative and flexible concepts that greatly depend on human definitions: "Original is the way it was when we remember it," in Conway's words. Nonetheless, others such as Draper insist that, "When I hear about ex situ conservation I think that there needs to be a clear divide between if it happens in Bronx Zoo and Regent's Park; or if it happens in their place of origin." These narratives and many others illuminate the current challenges that conservationists face in their attempt to adequately consider temporal benchmarks, the non-linear or immanent nature of ecological complexes, and the criteria by which humans might evaluate emergent or novel ecologies. In one of many examples for such nuanced practices, Soulé and colleagues have suggested that the current implementation of environmental laws and policies generally ignores what they call "interspecific effects," mistakenly focusing on recovery goals that are "autecological, short term, and numerically and spatially minimalistic" (Soulé et al. 2003)

CONCLUSION

Until very recently, the existence of the modern has depended on an ideal conception of nature; it relied on the animal's status as wild, exotic, and other (Braverman 2012, 30–49). Moreover, without such a wild, free, and timeless nature, captivity could have no meaning. Indeed, the perception of nature advanced by modern zoos in the latter part of the twentieth century has thus been one of a Nature that is untouched by humans—the ultimate other of the zoo's captivity. Captivity defines the very possibility of nature precisely by being its opposite, without which nature cannot exist. The modern institution of captivity has, in other words, evolved hand in hand with the modern institution of wilderness and alongside the ethics of modern conservation that effectively manage and also exacerbate this divide.

This chapter has drawn on multiple interviews with conservation experts to question the still powerful modern divide between in situ and ex situ conservation. Prompted by the ecological challenges that face today's world, some conservationists are starting to question the validity of the in situ and ex situ paradigms of conservation, which lie within the broader schisms of nature versus human and wild versus captive animals. I have discussed current efforts by certain conservation biologists to bridge the in/ex situ divide through the One Plan approach. Parallel efforts to bridge in situ and ex situ conservation are increasingly mushrooming in the conservation world through projects of re-wilding (Lorimer 2013), reconciliation ecologies (Rosenzweig 2003), and "land sharing" versus "land sparing" debates in Europe (Green 2005).

Finally, I have hinted toward the possibility of abandoning the "in" and "out" paradigm that has so characterized modern conservation narratives in favor of an understanding of conservation that focuses on a more dynamic and less predetermined understanding of ecosystems and populations. Such a holistic model breaks with the bifurcations of modern conservation to offer relational configurations of managing wild life (Braverman, draft). The shift to integrated forms of conservation admittedly triggers a host of novel ethical questions and concerns that go to the very heart of the definition of conservation. Some of the questions raised by conservation biologists and explored in this chapter were: Should we conserve species without a real prospect of releasing them "back"? How will we decide which species to manage for life, and which should be left to "fly" on their own? And, more broadly, what are the emerging motivations and criteria for a more dynamic and relational form of conservation?

ACKNOWLEDGEMENTS

I would like to thank Lori Gruen, Jack Schlegel, and Gregor Harvey for their comments and editorial advice.

REFERENCES

Balmford, Andrew, Georgina M. Mace, and Joshua R. Ginsberg. 1998. *Conservation in a Changing World*. Cambridge: Cambridge University Press.

Bekoff, Marc. 2000. "Redecorating Nature: Reflections on Science, Holism, Community, Reconciliation, Spirit, Compassion, and Love." *Human Ecology Review* 7: 59–67.

Braverman, Irus. 2012. *Zooland: The Institution of Captivity*. Stanford: Stanford University Press.

Braverman, Irus. 2014. "Conservation without Nature: The Trouble with In Situ versus Ex Situ Conservation." *Geoforum* 51: 47–57.

Braverman, Irus. *Wild Life: The Nature of* In Situ *and* Ex Situ *Management* (draft, under review).

Conway, William. 1999. "The Changing Role of Zoos in the 21st Century." Paper presented at the Annual Conference of the World Zoo Organization, Pretoria, South Africa, October 18.

Dickie, Lesley A., Jeffrey P. Bonner, and Chris D. West. 2007. "In Situ and Ex Situ Conservation: Blurring the Boundaries between Zoos and the Wild." In *Zoos in the 21st Century: Catalysts for Conservation?*, Alexandra Zimmermann, Matthew Hatchwell, Lesley A. Dickie, and Chris West (eds.), 220–235. Cambridge: Cambridge University Press.

Donahue, Jesse, and Erik Trump. 2006. *The Politics of Zoos: Exotic Animals and Their Protectors*. DeKalb: Northern Illinois University Press.

Foose, Thomas J. 1986. "Riders of the Last Ark: The Role of Captive Breeding in Conservation Strategies." In *The Last Extinction*, Lee Kaufman and Kenneth Mallory (eds.), 141–165. Cambridge: MIT Press.

Golden Gate Birder. 2013. "The Condor Recovery Debate, 30 Years Later." February 7. Accessed April 18, 2013. http://www.goldengateaudubon.org/blog-posts/the-condor-recovery-debate-30-years-later/.

Green, Rhys E. 2005. "Farming and the Fate of Wild Nature." *Science* 307: 550–555.

Holst, Bengt, and Lesley A. Dickie. 2007. "How Do National and International Regulations and Policies Influence the Role of Zoos and Aquariums in Conservation?" In *Zoos in the 21st Century: Catalysts for Conservation?*, Alexandra Zimmermann, Matthew Hatchwell, Lesley A. Dickie, and Chris West (eds.), 22–35. Cambridge: Cambridge University Press.

Hutchins, Michael, Brandie Smith, and Ruth Allard. 2008. "In Defense of Zoos and Aquariums: The Ethical Basis for Keeping Wild Animals in Captivity." In *The Animal Ethics Reader*, Susan Armstrong and Richard Botzler (eds.), 513–521. London: Routledge.

International Union for the Conservation of Nature (IUCN). 1994. "1994 Categories & Criteria (version 2.3)." Accessed April 18, 2013. http://www.iucnredlist.org/static/categories_criteria_2_3#categories.

International Union for the Conservation of Nature (IUCN). 2012a. *The IUCN Red List of Threatened Species. Version 2012.2.* Accessed January 21, 2013. http://www.iucnredlist.org.

International Union for the Conservation of Nature (IUCN). 2012b. "Red List Overview." *The IUCN Red List of Threatened Species. Version 2012.2.* Accessed April 18, 2013. http://www.iucnredlist.org/about/red-list-overview#introduction.

International Union for the Conservation of Nature (IUCN). 2013. "The IUCN Red List of Threatened Species." Search under "Animalia" and "Extinct in the Wild." Accessed April 18, 2013. http://www.iucnredlist.org/search.

Jensen, Derrick, and Karen Tweedy-Holmes. 2007. *Thought to Exist in the Wild: Awakening from the Nightmare of Zoos*. Santa Cruz, CA: Novice Unheard.

Koontz, Fred. 1995. "Wild Animal Acquisition Ethics for Zoo Biologists." In *Ethics on the Ark*, Bryan G. Norton, Michael Hutchins, Elizabeth F. Stevens, and Terry L. Maple (eds.), 127–145. Washington, DC: Smithsonian Institution Press.

Lacy, Robert C. 2013. "Achieving True Sustainability of Zoo Populations." *Zoo Biology* 32(1): 19–26.

Loftin, Robert. 1995. "Captive Breeding of Endangered Species." In *Ethics on the Ark: Zoos, Animal Welfare and Wildlife Conservation*, Bryan G. Norton, Michael Hutchins, Elizabeth F. Stevens, and Terry L. Maple (eds.), 164–180. Washington, DC: Smithsonian Institution Press.

Lorimer, Jamie. 2013. "Wild Experiments at the Oostvaardersplassen: Rethinking Environmentalism in the Anthropocene." Draft. Cited with permission.

Mace, Georgina M., Nigel J. Collar, Kevin J. Gaston, Craig Hilton-Taylor, H. Resit Akçakaya, Nigel Leader-Williams, Eleanor Jane Milner-Gulland, and Simon N. Stuart. 2008. "Quantification of Extinction Risk: IUCN's System for Classifying Threatened Species." *Conservation Biology* 22(6): 1424–1442.

Margodt, Koen. 2010. "Zoos as Welfare Arks? Reflections on an Ethical Course for Zoos." In *Metamorphoses of the Zoo: Animal Encounter after Noah*, Ralph R. Acampora (ed.). Plymouth: Lexington Books.

NewsWatch, "Bristol Zoo breeds world's last Partula faba snails," posted by David Braun of National Geographic, April 16, 2010. http://newswatch.nationalgeographic.com/2010/04/16/bristol_zoo_breeds_worlds_last/.

Norton, Bryan. 1995. "Caring for Nature: A Broader Look at Animal Stewardship." In *Ethics on the Ark: Zoos, Animal Welfare and Wildlife Conservation*, Bryan G. Norton, Michael Hutchins, Elizabeth F. Stevens, and Terry L. Maple (eds.), 102–121. Washington, DC: Smithsonian Institution Press.

Reading, Richard R., and Brian J. Miller. 2010. "Captive Breeding Ethics." In *Encyclopedia of Animal Rights and Animal Welfare*, 2nd ed., Marc Bekoff (ed.), 101–104. Santa Barbara, CA: Greenwood.

Redford, Kent H., George Amato, Jonathan Baillie, Pablo Beldomenico, Elizabeth L. Bennett, Nancy Clum, Robert Cook, et al. 2011. "What Does It Mean to Successfully Conserve a (Vertebrate) Species?" *BioScience* 61(1): 39–48.

Redford, Kent H., Katrina Brandon, and Steven Sanderson. 1998. *Parks in Peril: People, Politics, and Protected Areas*. Washington, DC: Island Press.

Redford Kent H., Deborah B. Jensen, and James J. Breheny. 2012. "Integrating the Captive and the Wild." *Science* 338: 1157–1158.

Regan, Tom. 1983. *The Case for Animal Rights*. Berkeley: University of California Press.

Rosenzweig, Michael L. 2003. *Win-Win Ecology: How the Earth's Species Can Survive in the Midst of Human Enterprise*. Oxford: Oxford University Press.

Shea, Katriona, and the NCEAS Working Group. 1998. "Management of Populations in Conservation, Harvesting and Control." *Trends in Ecology and Evolution* 13: 371–375.

Snyder, Noel F. R., Scott R. Derrickson, Steven R. Bessinger, James W. Wiley, Thomas B. Smith, William D. Toone, and Brian Miller. 1996. "Limitations of Captive Breeding in Endangered Species Recovery." *Conservation Biology* 10: 338–348.

Soulé, Michael, William Conway, Tom Foose, and Michael Gilpin. 1986. "The Millennium Ark: How Long a Voyage, How Many Staterooms, How Many Passengers?" *Zoo Biology* 5: 101–113.

Soulé, Michael E., James A. Estes, Joel Berger, and Carlos Martinez Del Rio. 2003. "Ecological Effectiveness: Conservation Goals for Interactive Species." *Conservation Biology* 17: 1238–1250.

United Nations. 1992a. "Article 8: In-situ Conservation." Convention on Biological Diversity, Rio de Janeiro, Brazil, June 5, pp. 6–7. United Nations Treaty Collection. Accessed January 27, 2013. http://treaties.un.org/Pages/CTCTreaties. aspx?id=27&subid=A&lang=en.

United Nations. 1992b. "Article 9: Ex-situ Conservation." Convention on Biological Diversity, Rio de Janeiro, Brazil, June 5, p. 7. United Nations Treaty Collection. Accessed January 27, 2013. http://treaties.un.org/Pages/CTCTreaties. aspx?id=27&subid=A&lang=en.

World Association of Zoos and Aquariums (WAZA). 2005. *Building a Future for Wildlife: The World Zoo and Aquarium Conservation Strategy*. Berne, Switzerland: WAZA Executive Office.

Wuichet, John, and Bryan Norton. 1995. "Differing Conceptions of Animal Welfare." In *Ethics on the Ark: Zoos, Animal Welfare and Wildlife Conservation*, Bryan G. Norton, Michael Hutchins, Elizabeth F. Stevens, and Terry L. Maple (eds.), 232–252. Washington, DC: Smithsonian Institution Press.

Zhigang, Jiang, and R. B. Harris. 2008. *"Elaphurus davidianus." IUCN Red List of Threatened Species. Version 2012.2*. Accessed April 18 2013. www.iucnredlist.org.

INTERVIEWS

Blumer, Evan. Former director, The Wilds; Board member, Conservation Breeding Specialist Group, IUCN. February 18, 2013.

Byers, Onnie. Chair, Conservation Breeding Specialist Group, IUCN. August 1, 2012.

Conway, William. Former director, Bronx Zoo; Former president of the Wildlife Conservation Society. January 28, 2013.

Currie, Hamish. Director, Back to Africa. January 10, 2013.

Dick, Gerald. Executive director, World Association of Zoos and Aquariums. July 16, 2013.

Draper, Chris. Senior scientific researcher, Born Free Foundation. April 2, 2013.

Pearce-Kelly, Paul. Senior curator of invertebrates, lower vertebrates and research, Zoological Society of London. March 14, 2013.

Lacy, Robert. Population biologist, Chicago Zoological Society (Brookfield Zoo). July 31, 2012.

Schwitzer, Christoph. Vice chair, Primate Specialist Group, Species Survival Commission of the IUCN; Head of research, Bristol Zoo. April 5 and 13, 2013.

Stanley-Price, Mark. Former director, Jersey Zoo; WildCRU researcher; Board member, Conservation Breeding Specialist Group, IUCN. March 12, 2013.

Zippel, Kevin. Program director, Amphibian Ark. August 3, 2012.

13

Sanctuary, Not Remedy

The Problem of Captivity and the Need for Moral Repair

KAREN S. EMMERMAN ▪

Two years ago, I had the privilege of meeting the chimpanzees residing at Chimpanzee Sanctuary Northwest in Cle Elum, Washington. Annie, Burrito, Foxie, Jamie, Jody, Missy, and Negra—known as the Cle Elum Seven, all survivors of biomedical research—spend their days eating, tickling one another, and playing in their individual ways. Although the sanctuary is generally closed to the public and these chimpanzees are not "on display," friends and guests are occasionally invited, and I was lucky enough to accompany a friend of the sanctuary on a visit. We raided the local supermarket for dark leafy greens and bags of walnuts still in their shells, then drove the stretch of Interstate 90 that leads out of urban Seattle into beautiful pine-laden mountains still bearing the remnants of winter in their snow-dusted peaks.

As we approached the sanctuary, I was filled with anticipatory excitement. This was an honor, a rare experience, an opportunity to interact with chimpanzees outside of a zoo environment. When we arrived at the sanctuary, the first thing I saw was a barren, small, metal cage, a reminder of the chimpanzees' previous living quarters. Seeing the cage brought me back to thinking about why these chimpanzees were there in the first place, thus shifting my mood from anticipatory excitement to something more like species shame.

After a crash course in chimpanzee etiquette, we went into a small area where we could visit with the chimpanzees on the other side of the tall, chain-linked fence. Gradually, several of the chimpanzees approached the fence, enjoyed the snacks we had brought them, and interacted with us in their unique ways. Jamie checked out our footwear, Burrito hung around on the fence being sociable and goofy, and Jody spat water at us from her cheeks. Having never seen a chimpanzee in person, I was struck by how large and powerful they are, and how each is an individual with her own personality and preferences. I found myself contemplating how capable of forgiveness they must be. For, even though the caregivers at the sanctuary were not responsible for their prior suffering, the chimpanzees would have every reason to show scorn and mistrust for humans.

I left the sanctuary feeling more conflicted than I had anticipated feeling. Certainly, I was in awe of these animals and thrilled to have met them. They felt like new friends; I knew I would always care about them and want to support their well-being. I felt joy that their time in biomedical research labs was over and delighted that they had made their way into sanctuary. After these emotions settled down, however, I could not stop asking myself the same question repeatedly: Is this really the best we can do for them?

Since then, I have been mulling over the question of how captivity might complicate our efforts to make things right again for nonhuman animals who have suffered in service of human interests. This chapter is an effort to begin to answer that question. I argue that keeping nonhuman animals in lifelong captivity, even in the very best sanctuaries, is morally problematic. In the public's conscience, sighs of relief are common when we hear an animal has made her way to sanctuary. This relief often translates into a sense that the moral work is

Missy, courtesy of Chimpanzee Sanctuary Northwest

done with respect to that animal; that the moral universe has righted itself again and we can turn our attention elsewhere. I want to push against this tendency to think of sanctuary as the last stop in the moral work needed to counter the harm humans cause animals. I suggest that where captivity is a necessary part of our efforts to make things right again, restitution is rarely possible. Rather than viewing sanctuaries as sites of restitution, we should view them as part of the work of moral repair. This insight is important, I argue, because it should be reflected in our thinking about how we adjudicate interanimal conflicts of interest in the first place. We cannot allow humans' interests to trump animals' interests with the justification that we can compensate the animals by eventually providing them with sanctuary.

Many dedicated people who work in sanctuaries know this all too well, but policymakers and the general public seem to adhere to Paul Taylor's notion that careful attention to restitution helps us avoid "a burden of eternal guilt" (Taylor 1986, 306) and think of sanctuaries as doing that restitutive work. I want to submit this perspective to scrutiny. I begin with a discussion of the important ethical impetus to rectify past harms by providing restitution.

INTERANIMAL CONFLICTS AND THE POSSIBILITY OF RESTITUTION

Our moral norms include the insight that rectifying past harms ought to involve providing restitution to those harmed. Restitution can take a number of forms, but compensatory restitution is a particularly important part of ethical life. When someone is harmed, we hope to make her whole again or at least to provide her with compensation commensurate with her losses. In interhuman morality there are many ways to "make it up" to those who have suffered at our hands. These can range from significant material payouts to a lovely bouquet of flowers depending on the degree and nature of the harm as well as on the relationship between the parties. Efforts at restitution are an important part of showing respect for those harmed. By offering restitution we acknowledge that they matter (as groups or individuals) and that the harms done were real and warrant the effort required to redress them. Those responsible for the harm can demonstrate respect for their victims by acknowledging their responsibility and expending effort on the victims' behalf. Restitution functions to compensate the victim but also to enable the party responsible to make amends and move on.

Given that human beings rely on billions of animals a year to fulfill their interests in food, clothing, entertainment, and biomedical research, it is unsurprising and inevitable that conflicts regularly occur between humans' and animals' interests (I call these "interanimal conflicts"). When we adjudicate these conflicts in favor of humans' interests, animals often suffer considerable harm. Though moral philosophers have been working on interanimal conflicts of interest for decades, making restitution to nonhumans harmed in service of human interests has not been a topic of much discussion in their work. This is not entirely surprising given the dominant approach to interanimal conflicts. This approach involves proposing systems for determining what kinds of interests have priority in conflict adjudication. Generally, these systems argue for a particular prioritization scheme (either by ranking the kinds of interests at stake or by presenting a hierarchy of parties to whom the interests belong). It is up to the moral agent to assess priority according to the scheme and adjudicate the conflict correctly. For most theorists working on interanimal conflicts the moral deliberation ends here. Having correctly assessed the weight of the various interests at stake, the moral agent can move on to other endeavors content with the knowledge that the right thing was done. There is no recognition that our adjudication may have resulted in moral remainders—work left unfinished or unresolved, leaving harms that have not been addressed (Walker 1995). Thus, it is rare for these adjudication schemes to include discussions of making restitution to those we have harmed as a result of our interest-weighing.

Taylor's work in *Respect for Nature* is an exception. Though *Respect for Nature* was published in 1986 and much has happened in the fields of environmental and animal ethics since then, I begin with Taylor because he was one of the very few philosophers to insist on restitution for animals harmed in service of human interests. Taylor argued that humans have a duty to make restitution any time we harm wild animals and plants. He suggested that compensatory restitution is crucial for showing respect for the lives and well-being of the living things we harm in the course of pursuing our own lives. Taylor further averred that restitution, when properly undertaken, means "we need not bear a burden of eternal guilt because we have used them—and will continue to use them—for our own ends. There is a way to make amends" (Taylor 1986, 306). Taylor has a demanding view regarding human obligations to nonhumans. At the same time, he recognizes that human interests will sometimes trump animal interests. Built into Taylor's adjudication scheme is the recognition that accurately assessing which interests should prevail is not sufficient for fully discharging our moral obligations.[1] When we purposely do harm to nonhumans' interests, we must make restitution.

Taylor's principle of restitutive justice requires that when we sacrifice the interests of wild animals (and plants) we must "bring about an amount of good that is comparable (as far as can be reasonably estimated) to the amount of evil to be compensated for" (1986, 305). He also notes that "the greater the harm done, the greater the compensation required." My sense of Taylor's principle of restitutive justice is that he has in mind the sort of process whereby we harm animals' interests and then seek to make compensation of some sort, thus permitting ourselves to walk away from the situation feeling as though we have made things right again; our moral work with respect to the animals we have harmed is complete. He says that when we can respond to harmed individuals we must return them "to a condition in which they can pursue their good as well as they did before the injustice was done to them." Taylor is aware that this may be difficult, noting that compensation may take a holistic form when individual compensation is not possible (1986, 188). Still, he clearly thinks that restitution is about compensating the harmed animal so that she is made whole (or as close to whole as possible) and then setting aside our guilty feelings (as much as possible). We often think of restitution in this way; as a singular act or series of acts of some finite duration at the end of which the party who committed the wrong (or her representatives) has adequately compensated the party who was harmed. Whether or not restitution must work this way is a topic I do not take up here. But this seems to be how Taylor thinks of it even as he acknowledges that there are limits to such efforts (1986, 206), and, as I have noted, sanctuaries are considered in this way by most people who are not intimately familiar with their work.

Extending the ethical impetus to rectify past wrongs through restitution to nonhumans is an important signifier of taking animals' interests seriously because it shows respect for their moral worth. Yet I worry that careful consideration of efforts at restitutive justice in the interanimal realm reveals significant limitations on the possibility of actually making restitution to animals. These limitations are particularly evident in cases where permanent captivity is a necessary feature of the restitutive efforts. I turn now to a brief discussion of the sites where interanimal efforts at restitution take place.

SANCTUARIES AS SITES OF RESTITUTION

It is common for people to believe that sanctuaries provide restitution to animals for harms they have suffered at human hands. This belief is reflected in the public discourse around sanctuaries as well as in some animal welfare campaigns. For example, the New England Anti-Vivisection Society has a campaign called "Project R&R: Release and Restitution for Chimpanzees" aimed at ending the use of chimpanzees in biomedical research and providing the chimpanzees with "permanent release and restitution in sanctuaries" (NEAVS n.d. a). The heading on Project R&R's "Sanctuaries/Facilities" page is "Sanctuaries: Restitution for a Fortunate Few" (NEAVS n.d. b). The belief that sanctuaries provide restitution is prevalent enough that policymakers may justify harms to animals with the idea that restitution through sanctuary is possible. Thinking along these lines may have been in play in the National Institute of Health's (NIH) decision to release all but fifty of their chimpanzees to sanctuaries. (See chapter 4 in this volume for more discussion of this decision.) The remaining fifty will be in reserve in the event that they are needed for research purposes. Given that the NIH stipulated that this part of their decision would be reconsidered every five years, it is reasonable to wonder if the possibility that the animals could make their way to sanctuaries, thus compensating them for their loss, was a factor in their decision. Whether or not that was the case in this specific example, the belief that sanctuaries provide restitution for animals very likely plays a role in various policy decisions regarding interanimal conflicts of interest.

There are other sites where these efforts are arguably undertaken: wildlife rehabilitation centers, ecological restoration projects, domestic animal rescue organizations, and shelters to name a few. I focus on sanctuaries in particular because they involve permanent captivity for the animals we seek to help, whereas these other institutions may not. Captivity of some sort is a necessary part of life in a sanctuary for it is captivity that ensures safety for both animals and humans. There are, of course, different kinds of sanctuaries serving different kinds of animals. I will narrow my discussion to sanctuaries serving wild animals rather than domesticated and farmed animals. I do not want to gloss over potentially important differences in how animals respond to life in captivity by treating sanctuaries as a homogenized group.[2]

Before proceeding with the discussion about sanctuaries, it is worth saying a word about zoos. There are two reasons for this: first, zoos often position themselves as sites of interanimal restitution and, second, some people talk as though there is a bright line to be drawn between well-run zoos and sanctuaries. In thinking through the problem of captivity for animals in sanctuaries we will see that some of the difficulties they face are similar to those animals face in well-run zoos. This is important to notice since these similarities are often glossed over by those who propose sanctuaries as sites of restitution. I will revisit this issue in the following section.

Many zoos position themselves as, in some sense, doing the work of restitution. For, part of the justification they offer for their existence is that some members of particular species must be kept captive (and bred) in zoos in order to protect the species against extinction. Many zoos profess to be engaged in the vital work of educating the public about wild habitat destruction and the dangers of species extinction. Whether or not zoos succeed in this part of their mission is a subject of some debate (Braverman 2013, 89; Marino et al. 2010; Hutchins et al. 2008; Jamieson 2002a, 169; 2002b). Irus Braverman quotes one zoo curator as saying, "The animals are deprived of their individual freedom in order to save the rest of their species and even their entire habitat" (2013, 87).

Some zoos position themselves as providing a space where humans can correct and make restitution for the catastrophic consequences of the impact of our choices on wild animals and their habitats. As Ralph Acampora puts it, "The contemporary zoo has become a scientific park and aesthetic site. Its meaning is redemptive; it stands as an emblem of conservation policy, projecting a religious image of man-the-messiah—the new Noah: savior of species, the beasts' benign despot" (2008, 501). Zoo-goers are encouraged to make donations to conservation efforts by seeing the animals exhibited in the zoo and, therefore, developing an emotional connection not just to the captive animals but to their wild conspecifics (Braverman 2013, 8). In the process, zoo-goers get to feel that, by supporting the zoo, they have also done their part to help conservation efforts and make restitution to wild animals harmed in pursuit of human interests. Dale Jamieson points to this phenomenon when he says,

> In my opinion we should have the honesty to recognize that zoos are for us rather than for the animals. Perhaps they do something to alleviate our sense of guilt for what we are doing to the planet, but they do little to help the animals we are driving to extinction. Our feeble attempts at preservation are a matter of our own interests, values, and preoccupations rather than acts of generosity towards those animals whom we destroy and then try to save. In so far as zoos distract us from the truth about ourselves and what we are doing to nature, they are part of the problem rather than part of the solution. (2002b, 187–188)

Though zoos take themselves to be participating in the work of restitution, I will leave them aside and focus instead on sanctuaries serving wild animals, though some of what I say about wild animal sanctuaries may apply to sanctuaries working with other kinds of animals.[3] The ethical dimensions of sanctuaries are undertheorized and worth our careful attention given that the animals housed in them are captives.

Attention to the ethical dimensions of captivity for animals in sanctuaries may help explain the phenomenological experience of some sanctuary visitors. I cannot avoid returning continually to the mixed feelings I experienced when I visited the Cle Elum Seven or when I saw the tigers, cougars, and lions at Big Cat Rescue. The feeling of relief coupled with intense sadness haunts me and I struggle to make sense of how I can feel species pride that there are those among us humans who devote their lives to understanding these animals' group and individual needs and also overwhelming grief at the thought that holding them captive is really the best we humans can do for them. I am not alone in experiencing this mixture of relief, sadness, pride, and grief when visiting animals in a sanctuary. Better understanding the nature of the moral work sanctuaries undertake may help illuminate this complex emotional response.

There are also important theoretical and practical reasons to think carefully about how the necessity of captivity complicates the view that sanctuaries provide restitution for animals. Though my own views differ from Taylor's in many respects, I agree wholeheartedly with his view that thinking of ways to make restitution to animals is crucial to working through interanimal conflicts of interest where animals' interests are harmed in the service of humans' interests.[4] Taylor does not devote much space to considering how complicated interanimal restitution might be. He mostly takes it on faith that humans can "bring about an amount of good that is comparable (as far as can be reasonably estimated) to the amount of evil to be compensated for" (Taylor 1986, 305). But this is vastly important to get right. For if part of our justification for harming animals in the service of human ends is that we can make restitution, then we must be sure that restitution is possible. This matters in terms of how we assess Taylor's view, but more important for my purposes here, this matters for how we, as moral agents, think through our choices about how to resolve interanimal conflicts of interest. I worry that many people think of sanctuaries, if they think of them at all, as a good reason for species pride. The fact that animals (the lucky ones) can end their lives in sanctuary makes us feel better about having caused them harm in the first place. Trust in the healing capacity of sanctuaries enables us to cease dwelling on the choices we make to inflict harm on animals. This trust also enables us to set aside thinking about how we adjudicate these conflicts of interest because we believe that, through sanctuary, there is a way to make things right again for the animals who survive the harm we inflict. Note how similar this is to what Jamieson said about the mind-easing effect of zoos on zoo supporters. Just as zoos may serve to distract us from "the truth about ourselves," sanctuaries may unwittingly have the same effect. If, as I argue, sanctuaries are not in fact doing the work of restitution, then we must circle back to how we adjudicate interanimal conflicts of interest and reconsider giving primacy to humans' interests in cases where we think sanctuaries could be what mitigates the harm we decide to do.

CAPTIVITY AND RESTITUTION

It is a sad truth that the captivity animals face in sanctuaries poses problems for them that are similar to those they faced in their initial captive conditions. Of course, the conditions in well-run sanctuaries are far superior to those animals face as tools for human use in entertainment and research. Anyone who sees the research and transportation cage outside Chimpanzee Sanctuary

Northwest and then sees both their interior enclosure and their outside play area is struck by the improvement in the space they have access to. Still, animals in sanctuaries are permanent captives. As captives they face a life of confinement. Though we can give the animals more space than they had in exploitative captive environments, we can never give them a natural life that meets all their species-typical needs.

The confinement is not only morally relevant because it limits the animals' options, but because it reifies human control over these animals' lives. Writing about zoos, Marino, Bradshaw, and Malamud noted, "By definition, confinement subordinates its captives and gives the viewer complete power over them" (2009, 25). While animals in sanctuaries often have more control over this element of captivity than their counterparts in zoos and certainly over their counterparts in laboratories and other captive facilities, they remain subject to the humans who provide their care. The humans have far more control over the sanctuary situation than the animals living there. Unlike zoos, sanctuaries use confinement to protect and better serve the animals, rather than with the intention to control and display them. Still, Big Cat Rescue cannot have lions, tigers, and cougars roaming the streets of Tampa, or even the sanctuary grounds, at will. For their safety and ours, the animals living in sanctuary must be confined, thus curtailing their freedom.

In addition to confinement, animals in sanctuaries face the problem of boredom. Keeping captive wild animals stimulated, entertained, and happy is exceptionally difficult. Sanctuary staff work tirelessly to find sources of enrichment for their animals, but there is a limit to what can be done. Animals in sanctuaries are entirely dependent on humans and human artifacts for their amusement, and this limits the expression of their freedom in significant ways. As Diana Goodrich, director of outreach for Chimpanzee Sanctuary Northwest, said in a recent video, "We try to provide the best home that we can for them in captivity, but it's really a far cry from what they should be experiencing. They're very intelligent, they're very social, they travel really long distances every day and there's no way you can mimic the kind of rich life that they should be having with any kind of captive situation" (Chimpanzee Sanctuary Northwest 2013).

We must remember, too, that while there are basics of what each species of animal requires, the animals in sanctuaries are all individuals with their own personalities, interests, intellectual needs, and so forth (Goodall 2001, xxii–xxiv). There is no one list of enrichments that will speak to all captive animals of a given species. What they require will depend on their individual makeup but also on what past experiences they bring along with them to sanctuary life. It takes time, money, and enough human caregivers to have the resources to assess and provide what each individual animal needs to flourish. Some sanctuaries have more resources than others, and this will influence their ability to attend to individualized enrichment for their charges.

In addition to confinement and boredom, captive animals in sanctuaries are also prevented from exercising many of their natural activities. Good sanctuaries do not allow their animals to breed because doing so merely creates more captive animals. Sanctuaries ought not to be in the business of breeding more captive animals who will themselves experience lifelong captivity. At the same time, curtailing their reproductive freedom is certainly taking something important away from these animals; elephants and great apes, for example, remain with some of their family members for life in the wild. Jane Goodall summarizes the problems of captivity for chimpanzees as follows:

> Of course, chimpanzees belong in the wild, and if they are lucky enough to live in a protected area, or one remote from people, that is the best life. That life cannot be replicated in captive situations. In the forest, they have a great deal of freedom of choice. They can choose whether to travel on their own, in a small group, or to join large excitable gatherings. They can usually choose which individuals to associate with. Females can wander off, with their dependent young, and stay feeding peacefully and grooming together for hours, or even days. Close companions meet often, others may avoid each other. They know the excitement of participating in hunts or boundary patrols, and even aggressive, almost war-like encounters with individuals of neighboring groups. To survive they must spend time searching for and sometimes preparing their food—they are occupying their brains, using their skills. They are free. (2001, xx)[5]

It is interesting to note how the problems discussed here (confinement, boredom, limited expression of natural behaviors such as ranging, predation, and reproduction) are similar to those faced by animals living in the "very best" kinds of zoos. As I mentioned earlier, however, these parallels between captive animals in "good" zoos and captive animals in sanctuaries go entirely unnoticed in discussions of both. For example, Marino, Bradshaw, and Malamud note that "captivity (outside appropriate sanctuary conditions) imposes serious psychological stress" (2009, 27), yet they go on to say, "Even in zoos where an effort is made to provide nutritious food, some social contact, some kind of 'natural setting' and environmental enrichment, the animals suffer terrible deprivation because we can no more simulate the richness of a natural life for other animals than we could for humans in captivity." The second quote makes me wonder why the authors chose to make a parenthetical exclusion of sanctuaries in thinking about how captivity can contribute to psychological stress. Indeed, the next section of their paper is entitled "Sanctuary: The Remedy." Some captive environments are more stressful than others, but from what Goodall, Marino, and various sanctuary websites say, all captivity is a problem for animals just as all captivity is a problem for humans even if we observe that some forms of human captivity are more conducive to flourishing than others.

There are important differences between sanctuaries and zoos, of course. Marino and her coauthors are right to point out that, while zoos are designed to maximize for human entertainment and viewing opportunities, sanctuaries "are places created only to help animals who are hurt or displaced, where the culture of public viewing and entertainment do not compete with animal welfare" (2009, 27), though I suspect that sanctuaries' need to raise money does occasionally compete with animal welfare, a subject I take up shortly. Sanctuaries' missions are to make life better for animals and to put their interests above anyone else's. They do their best to manage a genuine moral dilemma that has no clear solution. Still, it is incumbent upon those of us who think about the problems of captivity to note that animals living in sanctuaries are, indeed, enduring the hardships of captivity. When we talk as though zoos, laboratories, and other captive facilities are the only places where captivity is a problem for animals, we miss an important opportunity to think about the long-term effects of humans' choices on animals' lives.

Another way in which the fact that captivity is a necessary component of sanctuary complicates the view that sanctuary provides restitution is more subtle than those I have been discussing thus far. Sometimes it is difficult to tell the difference between zoo rhetoric regarding educating and inspiring visitors to care about conservation efforts and the language used to describe sanctuary work. For example, in their essay "In Defense of Zoos and Aquariums" Michael Hutchins and his coauthors write the following about the zoo animals serving as ambassadors for their wild conspecifics: "Wild animals in zoos and aquariums are ambassadors for their species, helping to raise public awareness and funds to support education, research, on-the-ground conservation activities in range countries, and a host of other relevant activities" (2008, 513). Compare what they have said about zoos to Jane Goodall describing the educational mission of sanctuaries:

> The local people are amazed and fascinated when they see chimpanzees close up. We are trying to establish a wildlife reserve to protect the remaining forest.... When the fighting stops it may be possible to attract tourists and thus bring foreign exchange into the country. Although building and maintenance of chimpanzee sanctuaries is very expensive, we are not only caring for abandoned orphans but raising awareness through conservation education, and trying to protect the wild chimpanzees. (Goodall 2001, xix)

Most sanctuaries rely on private donations in order to do their work. It is a deeply saddening truth that those who breed, exploit, and abuse captive animals are not responsible for funding the very expensive care these animals require when they are released from their exploitative environments. This means that, despite Marino, Bradshaw, and Malamud's suggestion that sanctuaries are places where "public viewing" is not allowed to compete with animal welfare, this issue can be a factor for sanctuaries.

Some sanctuaries do not allow visitors, while others do. At those that do allow visitors, the animals are subject to the public gaze in ways that can replicate the experience of animals in zoos or other forms of entertainment. I have experienced this sensation myself. Big Cat Rescue does its best not to replicate the zoo experience. Whereas in zoos visitors are allowed to stroll unaccompanied by anyone who can provide education about the animals, my tour group at Big Cat Rescue was led by someone on the sanctuary staff who talked with us about each animal and about the terrible impacts of captive breeding and training for entertainment purposes. But even I, an animal rights activist since childhood and a graduate student working on animal ethics at the time, was distracted from hearing the message by the presence of these extraordinary animals, some of whom I had never seen up close. They were as subject to my gaze as are the animals in zoos. This troubles me. I am reminded of the analogy Ralph Acampora has drawn between the pornographic gaze and the objectifying gaze of humans upon animals in zoos (2008, 502). Though I intended for my gaze to be one of compassionate attentiveness, I cannot say for sure that I did not veer into the realm of the objectifying gaze when I was distracted from the sanctuary's message and caught up in the awe of seeing lions and tigers up close. Even though their work is motivated by meeting the best interests of the animals in their care, allowing people to walk through the sanctuary and view the animals complicates sanctuaries' missions. The Elephant Sanctuary in Hohenwald, Tennessee, puts this point nicely on their website where they explain why they are not open to visitors: "The Elephant Sanctuary is operated as a true sanctuary, and therefore is *not open to the general public*. Our elephants have lived their entire lives on exhibit, entertaining the public. Our goal is to create an environment where the elephants are not disturbed by human activity" (Elephant Sanctuary in Tennessee n.d.).

Not all sanctuaries are economically equipped to have a "no visitors" policy. I do not want to go so far as to follow the Elephant Sanctuary's view and say that sanctuaries that permit visitors are not "true" sanctuaries, but certainly allowing visitors complicates the work of restitution by subjecting the animals to extraneous human activity. The sanctuary animals are, to some extent, serving as ambassadors for their conspecifics still enduring the horrors of life in the research and entertainment worlds as well as for those threatened in the wild.

They can and do serve in this role because their lives are still those of captives being controlled largely by their human caregivers.

I have argued that captivity being a necessary component of sanctuary undermines the view that sanctuaries perform the work of restitution because animals living in sanctuaries live lives of confinement, curtailed activity, and boredom. Though sanctuaries do their best to mitigate these aspects of their animals' lives, it is unavoidably true that we are unable to alleviate all of the harms of captivity. In addition to these complications, I noted that sanctuary animals are still very much subject to human control. In the NEAVS's materials regarding the sanctuary part of their Project R&R, they note that, though the chimpanzees "can never be truly free, sanctuary can provide them with as much relative freedom as possible in captivity." They go on to say, "Even at the best sanctuaries, once removed from the wild or bred in captivity, no chimpanzee can ever be truly free again. We can never give them back what was taken from them: the right to be free and live autonomously" (NEAVS n.d. b). This is exactly right, which is why I find it puzzling that we continue to think of sanctuaries as sites of interanimal restitution.

Where making amends requires continued captivity for wild animals, compensatory restitution is rarely achieved. Those who work in sanctuaries often have a sense of the ways in which their work, though well intended, is morally problematic. In recognition of these moral problems, responsible sanctuary workers and volunteers see improving the lives of their captive charges as ongoing and vital work. They also seek to put themselves out of business by advocating to end the kinds of use and abuse that result in animals requiring sanctuary in the first place. This perspective is rather different from that of the general public and some policymakers who see sanctuaries as ways to right a wrong, as places where grief is held off for another day.

Writing about Superfund toxic cleanup sites, Sangamithra Iyer notes that some sites are not properly understood as "cleanup" projects because "radioactive materials aren't something you can clean" (Iyer 2010, 161). This is analogous to the trauma captive animals suffer at human hands. It can be assuaged, dealt with as compassionately and carefully as possible, but it cannot be cleaned up. We do what is best *given the circumstances*, but we do so knowing that the "best option" is so inadequate that we view the action in an overall negative light, something Stephen Gardiner would call a "marring evil" (2010, 301). Building, staffing, and maintaining sanctuaries for wild animals is often the only reasonable choice we have.[6]

Faced with the kinds of abuse, exploitation, and trauma the animals have endured, sanctuaries are likely our best chance to make amends. Yet, because the animals remain lifelong captives, we cannot think of the sanctuaries as washing away the harms we have done. Rather than thinking of sanctuaries as providing restitution, it is more appropriate to think of them as performing part of the work of moral repair.

TOWARD INTERANIMAL MORAL REPAIR

When we consider interanimal conflicts of interest and how we might go about making amends for the harms we cause animals, we should think in terms of moral repair rather than restitution. In the work of moral repair one does not see oneself as an individual providing restitution to another individual about whom one need not care, but rather we see ourselves as deeply connected to the suffering other and as engaged in her plight. Moral repair involves more than calculating a just compensation for harms done. It attends to the relationships between the parties; it involves noticing how the relationships are impacted by systems beyond the individuals and thus enables us to focus on features of those systems that need improvement. We recognize that the moral process of making amends is the work of responding to particular needs and that moral life, as Margaret Urban Walker puts it, will often involve "unfinished and ongoing business, compensations and reparations, postponements and returns" (Walker 1995, 145).

Whereas compensatory restitution is focused on trying to make the injured party whole again, moral repair "involves the restoration or reconstruction of confidence, trust, and hope in the reality of shared moral standards and of our reliability in meeting and enforcing them" (Walker 2001, 120). Moreover, unlike restitution, moral repair recognizes the incompleteness of the moral work undertaken. Moral repair is the sort of work that is "incomplete and imperfect; in which not all kinds of justice can be done; in which truths burn to be remembered but cannot always be fully told" (123–124). In moral repair we do not seek solely to compensate those harmed, but to "replenish the trust and hope on which moral relations depend" (124).

Walker's work on moral repair is focused on moral responses to interhuman tragedies. This is why she talks about restoring trust and hope in shared moral standards. In cases of genocide, for example, both victims and perpetrators must find a way to restore trust in one another that shared moral standards will be met. As a result, the concept of moral repair does not map perfectly to the interanimal realm, where it is not always clear that all the parties involved have a concept of normativity or shared moral standards. Some work needs to be done to provide a full account of what interanimal moral repair entails. Still, human/animal relationships are moral relationships requiring trust in one another and, for animals facing life in a sanctuary, some hope on their part that the new humans in their lives will share space with them with love, compassion, care, and empathy. I also see sanctuaries as doing important moral repair work with respect to humans. Sanctuaries help us restore moral trust in ourselves as a species. They remind us that humans can do something good in the midst of so much wrongdoing and give us hope that we can do better moving forward.

When we view sanctuaries as opportunities for the work of repair rather than restitution, we can more accurately see them as the best option available from an array of unsatisfying options. This should give us pause and spur us to further reflection. In particular, we have to go back and reflect on how we adjudicated the conflict in the first place, when it resulted in captivity as the best option for making amends. We must ask if the adjudication can still be seen as justifiable in light of the complexities of the work of moral repair. We must ask if we should reconsider how the interests should be prioritized the next time we face a similar decision. We cannot resolve interanimal conflicts in favor of human interests by promising ourselves that we will make things right again at the end in the form of prolonged captivity. This insight must influence future deliberations regarding interanimal conflicts.

For example, we should rethink our decisions to subject animals to biomedical research. In the mid-1980s, HIV researchers considered chimpanzees crucial to understanding HIV (Wolfe 2001, 151). Thus, breeding programs were set up and a chimpanzee population was maintained. In 2000, President Clinton signed the Chimpanzee Health Improvement, Maintenance, and Protection (CHIMP) Act, which created a federally mandated sanctuary system for retirement of the chimpanzees no longer required in research. Science moves along and notions about what animals are vital to understand which human problems shift. One can easily imagine another epidemic similar to HIV being used as justification to reinstate chimpanzee breeding programs where the moral qualms of doing so are mitigated by the fact that the chimpanzees will, later, be moved to sanctuaries. Given that we can never make things right again for the chimpanzees in biomedical research, we must not think of legislation like the CHIMP Act as a way to mitigate harms done to any future chimpanzees we decide to bring into "service" in the event of a human health crisis.

Finally, the insight that sanctuaries are doing the work of moral repair rather than restitution must enjoin us to take action to end the practices that bring about animal exploitation. In talking about what is responsible for our "pathetic response" to the current crisis of species extinction, Jamieson suggests that "What is to blame is the peculiar moral schizophrenia of a culture that drives a species to the edge of extinction and then romanticizes the remnants" (2002b, 178). Sometimes I wonder if something like this is happening with respect to people's attitudes toward sanctuary animals. Once an animal is in a sanctuary and people get to meet her, know her, hear her story

of exploitation and trauma, a caring response ensues. The animal is roman-
ticized, thought about, and held in awe in much the same way the animals
in zoos are. We feel relief at seeing an end to her suffering and have a sense
that things have gone well in the world. This is all good as far as it goes, but
in the meantime others like her continue to endure exploitation and trauma,
while very few among us feel called upon to take any personal steps to bring
the systems of exploitation to an end. We "adopt" and support the animals in
sanctuaries, but abdicate the responsibility for taking action to the sanctuaries themselves. Knowing that sanctuaries are imperfect solutions to horrific
problems must inspire us to take individual responsibility for our part in the
work of moral repair. Depending on our resources, talents, and particulars,
this work will look different for different people. Still, we cannot let the fact
that an animal has made her way to sanctuary do away with our sense of guilt
or grief. Sanctuaries are one step in the work of moral repair rather than the
final destination in a journey of compensation.

Contrary to Marino, Bradshaw, and Malamud's suggestion, sanctuaries are
not "the remedy" where remedy is understood as a cure. Sanctuaries are the
best we can do to make amends to animals humans have harmed. They are
sites of hope but also of pain, of triumph over trauma but also of continued
trauma, of new beginnings wrapped in an inescapable past and captive present.
Sanctuaries are places where we get a glimpse of humans doing the very best
kind of moral work. Yet where lifelong captivity is the best we can offer animals,
even the very best kind of moral work is tainted in some sense. As Sangamithra
Iyer puts it, "Recovery requires reconnaissance. We must all understand the
legacy of soiled human hands, and we must keep in mind that where we go
from here is also in our hands" (2010, 164).

ACKNOWLEDGMENTS

I am grateful to Ben Almassi, Sara Goering, Lori Gruen, and the members of
the Critical Animal Studies working group at the University of Washington,
in particular María Elena Garcia, Katie Gillespie, and Amy Reed-Sandoval for
comments on earlier drafts. My thanks to J. B. Mulcahy for talking with me
about sanctuary work as I wrote this chapter.

NOTES

1. Of course, it is a question whether an adjudication scheme based on assessing and
   ranking interests is the best way to approach conflicts of interest. I will set this issue
   aside for now. For a full analysis see Emmerman 2012.
2. Some animals tolerate life in captivity better than others. This is certainly true
   even among wild animals (as indicated in some of the chapters in Section 1 of this

volume). That said, I am setting aside discussion of farmed animal sanctuaries for the moment as it may be the case that there are important ethical differences in the problems faced by captive wild animals and captive farmed animals. Whether or not this is the case is a subject of some debate (see chapter 5 in this volume).

3. It is reasonable to ask at what point an animal bred in captivity who never knew freedom becomes a domesticated animal. I suspect that, as Braverman puts it, animals in zoos "exist in between the domesticated and the wild" (2013, 75; cf. 82 and 83 n. 66) and this will be as true of animals with a similar history living in sanctuaries. See also Jamieson 2002b, 184. Though this is an interesting question, I set it aside for the moment. When I refer to "wild animals" I mean animals who have not been "domesticated."

4. As I noted earlier, Taylor is a biocentric egalitarian. His theory is very much aligned with traditional, justice-based approaches to ethics. I identify as an ecofeminist animal theorist.

5. Goodall goes on to note that, given the dangers wild chimpanzees face, chimpanzees living in good zoos may be better off than their wild counterparts. I suspect this is more a commentary on the disastrous effects humans are having on wild chimpanzees and their habitats than on the living conditions of captive chimpanzees in zoos.

6. Some readers may note that there are alternative options to sanctuaries. One option would be to return the animals to the wild. Given their long-term captivity, conditions in the wild, and the special health concerns these animals face, rehabilitating and then releasing them into the wild is rarely an option (Goodall 2001; Jamieson 2002b). Another option would be euthanasia. Given what I have said about how captivity renders making restitution to animals very unlikely, it is reasonable to wonder if euthanasia is the most humane course of action. I suspect that there are animals in sanctuaries who, like some humans, would benefit from a permanent release from their trauma. Still, it was human hubris that got these animals into their present condition, and I am profoundly concerned about making similar sorts of mistakes with respect to what would be in their best interests regarding death.

REFERENCES

Acampora, Ralph. 2008. "Zoos and Eyes: Contesting Captivity and Seeking Successor Practices." In *The Animal Ethics Reader*, 2nd ed., Susan J. Armstrong and Richard G. Bolzer (eds.), 501–506. New York: Routledge.

Braverman, Irus. 2013. *Zooland: The Institution of Captivity*. Stanford, CA: Stanford University Press.

Chimpanzee Sanctuary Northwest. 2013. "Video Shown at Out of the Box Last Night." May 4. Accessed November 22, 2013. http://www.chimpsanctuarynw.org/blog/2013/05/video-shown-at-out-of-the-box-last-night.

Elephant Sanctuary in Tennessee, The. n.d. "Public Visits to the Sanctuary." Accessed November 22, 2013. http://www.elephants.com/visitPolicy.php

Emmerman, Karen S. 2012. "Beyond the Basic/Nonbasic Interests Distinction: A Feminist Approach to Inter-Species Moral Conflict and Moral Repair." PhD diss., University of Washington.

Goodall, Jane. 2001. "Problems Faced by Wild and Captive Chimpanzees: Finding Solutions." In *Great Apes and Humans: The Ethics of Coexistence*, Benjamin B. Beck, Tara S. Stoinski, Michael Hutchins, Terry L. Maple, Bryan Norton, Andrew Rowan, Elizabeth F. Stevens, and Arnold Arluke (eds.), xiii–xxiv. Washington, DC: Smithsonian Institution Press.

Hutchins, Michael, Brandie Smith, and Ruth Allard. 2008. "In Defense of Zoos and Aquariums: The Ethical Basis for Keeping Wild Animals in Captivity." In *The Animal Ethics Reader*, 2nd ed., Susan J. Armstrong and Richard G. Bolzer (eds.), 513–521. New York: Routledge.

Iyer, Sangamithra. 2010. "Soiled Hands." In *Primate People: Saving Nonhuman Primates through Education, Advocacy, and Sanctuary*, Lisa Kemmerer (ed.), 158–164. Salt Lake City: University of Utah Press.

Jamieson, Dale. 2002a. "Against Zoos." In *Morality's Progress: Essays on Humans, Other Animals, and the Rest of Nature*, Dale Jamieson (ed.), 166–175. Oxford: Oxford University Press.

Jamieson, Dale. 2002b. "Zoos Revisited." In *Morality's Progress: Essays on Humans, Other Animals, and the Rest of Nature*, Dale Jamieson (ed.), 177–189. Oxford: Oxford University Press.

Marino, Lori, Scott O. Lilienfeld, Randy Malamud, Nathan Nobis, and Ron Broglio. 2010. "Do Zoos and Aquariums Promote Attitude Change in Visitors? A Critical Evaluation of the American Zoo and Aquarium Study." *Society and Animals* (18): 126–138.

Marino, Lori, Gay Bradshaw, and Randy Malamud. 2009. "The Captivity Industry: The Reality of Zoos and Aquariums." *Best Friends Animal Society Magazine* (March–April): 25–27.

New England Anti-Vivisection Society (NEAVS). n.d. a. "About Project R&R." Accessed November 22, 2013. www.releasechimps.org/about/overview.

New England Anti-Vivisection Society (NEAVS). n.d. b. "Sanctuaries/Facilities." Accessed November 22, 2013. www.releasechimps.org/chimpanzees/sanctuary-facilities.

Taylor, Paul W. 1986. *Respect for Nature*. Princeton: Princeton University Press.

Walker, Margaret Urban. 1995. "Moral Understandings: Alternative 'Epistemology' for a Feminist Ethics." In *Justice and Care: Essential Readings in Feminist Ethics*, Virginia Held (ed.), 139–152. Boulder, CO: Westview Press.

Walker, Margaret Urban. 2001. "Moral Repair and Its Limits." In *Mapping the Ethical Turn: A Reader in Ethics, Culture, and Literary Theory*, Todd F. Davis and Kenneth Womack (eds.), 110–127. Charlottesville: University Press of Virginia.

Wolfle, Thomas L. 2001. "The Retirement of Research Apes." In *Great Apes and Humans: The Ethics of Coexistence*, Benjamin B. Beck, Tara S. Stoinski, Michael Hutchins, Terry L. Maple, Bryan Norton, Andrew Rowan, Elizabeth F. Stevens, and Arnold Arluke (eds.), 150–159. Washington, DC: Smithsonian Institution Press.

14

Dignity, Captivity, and an Ethics of Sight

LORI GRUEN ■

One of the chimpanzees I know living in sanctuary is now over forty years old. Every time humans come around he makes a ridiculous facial expression—he pops both of his lips out and folds them back so the inside of his lips show, making him look clown-like, with a big pink mouth. This chimpanzee was used in the entertainment business and presumably making himself look absurd garnered laughs and attention. He was undoubtedly taught to do this when he was young either by rewarding him when he did or, more likely, punishing him when he didn't. The aversive methods used by animal trainers in the entertainment industry have long been criticized for causing pain. The unnecessary suffering that animals endure to get them to perform bizarre behaviors is surely enough to raise strong objections to both the behavior and the suffering the animals experience to produce the behavior. And I think there is even more to object to when we observe the spectacles animals are forced to make of themselves for human purposes.

In *Ethics and Animals* (Gruen 2011) I recount Suzanne Cataldi's discussion of her visit to the Moscow Circus observing bears in bright-colored clown collars holding balloons and prancing around on tiptoes pushing baby strollers like clumsy "overweight ballerinas" (Cataldi 2002, 106). What is wrong with making bears appear as ballerinas or chimpanzees appear as clowns is that in getting animals to do these things, the animal's dignity is being undermined. That is what I will argue in this chapter. Generally the concept of dignity is reserved for humans; indeed, it is often thought to be what makes humans distinct. Yet the literature on human dignity is vague, and everyone writing on the topic seems to have her own conceptions about what dignity is. Despite the fact that it is already difficult enough to make sense of human dignity, I will take on the challenge of arguing for animal dignity and further argue that captivity is one of the conditions that poses a threat to dignity. Before I make that case, I will start by examining differing accounts of human dignity and then suggest how we might understand dignity for other animals. I will analyze dignity as a relational property. I will then explore the ways that captive conditions, particularly zoos and prisons, can undermine dignity through both visual and physical control.

WHAT IS DIGNITY?

In a wide-ranging article, Remy Debes unpacks the vagaries associated with the notion of dignity—historically, etymologically, in religious and philosophical discussions, and in law and policy (Debes 2009). He quite rightly notes that in the literature about dignity,

> Almost every author begins by leveraging her historical-etymological notes into the observation that dignity has been conceptualized in a multifaceted way. It is, she will say, dominated by the Kantian and Judeo-Christian traditions that make dignity a function of, respectively, rational autonomy or spiritual identity with God (imago Dei). But, she will hasten to add, despite those traditions, dignity has also been pervasively conceived as honor, rank, station, inherent worth, inalienable worth, equal worth, supreme worth, uniqueness, beauty, poise, gravitas, personality, integrity, bodily integrity, self-respect, self-esteem, a sacred place in the order of things, simply brute and unquestionable "specialness," and even, if she is being exhaustive, the apex of astrological influence. In short, pick any work on human dignity and you're apt to find the claim that "dignity" is beset by ambiguity in use. (Debes 2009, 45–46)

With dignity's ambiguity duly acknowledged, I want to argue that while the common-sense notion of dignity, one that links it to autonomy, can be helpful rhetorically, dignity is better understood as a relational concept.

The common sense version of dignity is meant to capture the inherent worth of human individuals. Dignity is usually thought to inhere in all humans as "some kind of inner transcendental kernel," as Michael Rosen has suggested (2012, 55). It is an intrinsic property that all humans share. This property is tied to our autonomous nature, and protecting or promoting dignity requires ensuring that people have the freedom to live life as they desire. People, as choosers of ends they find valuable, should be free to make those choices, and respecting their dignity is a way to recognize the value of their autonomous choosing.

When people are denied their autonomy, their freedom to chose the lives that make the most sense for them to live by their own lights, then it might be said that their dignity is also being violated. If dignity is, as many have suggested, tightly linked to autonomy, then in our current era of mass incarceration, it seems that millions of people are being denied dignity by virtue of being incarcerated. Incarcerated individuals do not have the opportunity to decide what to eat, when to sleep, where to go, who to spend time with (or not spend time with). Vocational, educational, and recreational opportunities are extremely limited, if they exist at all. Relationships with loved ones are curtailed. In some cases prisoners are shipped to federal facilities far from their families, often separating parents from their children for years. Choices are denied and their activities are almost completely controlled (see chapters 7 and 8 in this volume). For many prisoners, in the absence of rehabilitation, they have become so dependent on the carceral system that once paroled they cannot survive on their own. Not only are they prohibited from exercising autonomy as captives, the very capacity to do so can be deformed through incarceration and their dignity thereby undermined.

But denying incarcerated people both autonomy and dignity seems to be a heavy toll. And if all people are thought to have "the kernel" of dignity, an intrinsic property that humans have universally, then how can it be taken away when their freedom is denied? Perhaps what is happening here is that incarcerated people haven't lost their dignity, but rather their dignity, because of the loss of autonomy, is not being respected. Dignity is not reducible to autonomy.

While denying autonomy does not always equate to undermining dignity, it is also the case that having both the capacity and the opportunity to act autonomously does not guarantee that one's dignity should be respected. Some autonomous choices are not necessarily dignified or worthy of respect. Rosen describes a case that vividly pits autonomy against dignity in the person of M. Manuel Wackenheim. Wackenheim, who is a dwarf, apparently makes a living being tossed around by burly men in bars. In the commune of Morsang-sur-Orge, the mayor banned a dwarf-tossing competition and Wackenheim challenged the ban in court. After winning his first appeal, the ban was upheld by a higher court that argued "throwing a dwarf by members of the public leads to using a person affected by a physical handicap and presented as such as a projectile. An attraction of this sort was regarded as infringing the dignity of the human person in its very objective" (Rosen 2012, 67). Whatever one believes about the state's role in allowing or prohibiting Wackenheim from doing something undignified, the dwarf-tossing case illustrates a second sense of dignity, the sense in which what is at stake is not an individual's autonomous, perhaps even authentic, rational choice, but rather how that individual might be perceived in his community and whether his behavior is worthy of respect.

This relational conception of dignity drives social or civic demands for recognition and respect. This sense of dignity harkens back to its historical connotation that saw dignity as connected to one's station or status in society. As it has been deployed in contemporary global political contexts, dignity of this sort is, as stated in the Preamble to the Universal Declaration of Human Rights, "the foundation of freedom, justice and peace in the world." Conceptualized in this way, dignity is not some inalienable, intrinsic property possessed by all humans, but rather a relational property that, when recognized under the right circumstances, is conducive to social harmony and human fulfillment. Rather than focusing on the worth of individual rational agents making autonomous choices, a relational conception of dignity brings into focus both the being who is dignified and the individual or community who value the dignified in the right ways. This relational conception of dignity explains why concerns about dignity are often expressed in the contexts in which it has been or might be denied. It is rarely the case that we recognize or admire the dignity of people being respectful of one another in the ordinary course of things. But when a police officer singles out a black youth to stop and frisk or when a bus driver doesn't stop for a Hispanic woman carrying her groceries or when macho guys harangue lesbians walking out of a theater, we are concerned not just with the indignities experience by the youth and women, but we are struck by the lack of respect on the part of the offenders. They have failed to properly value the individuals with whom they are interacting and in that lose some of their own worth as a moral agent. In respecting someone's dignity, a valuer recognizes the equal worth of that individual, a worth they share, and value it accordingly.

In saying that dignity is a relational concept I'm not saying that it is subject to the whims of the perceiver or that dignity is merely a subjective or social projection about the worth of another. Rather, I'm trying to capture both the contextual nature of the notion and the broader normative implications of the recognition of dignity or the failure to recognize dignity on the valuer, the community of valuers, as well as the individual whose dignity should be respected. The relational concept of dignity is not necessarily incompatible with the view that there may be some essence or kernel of dignity that inheres in an individual (I will not take up these arguments here), but the focus of the relational conception is on apt perception and valuation rather than property identification.

Consider what the relational conception of dignity reveals in the case of Mr. Wackenheim. In choosing to be tossed, Wackenheim is not representing himself as dignified and the tossers are failing to value Wackenheim appropriately. It isn't tossing per se that is objectionable. It is hard to describe why that activity in itself would be morally objectionable. Rather, it is in the larger context in which the individual being tossed is a dwarf, and in most societies there is a social prejudice toward small people (in this case) or other individuals that do not conform to social norms. Willfully, autonomously choosing to engage in behavior that in the context of prejudicial social relations reinforces negative attitudes towards members of marginalized groups is problematic and not worthy of respect. If this is right, then it appears that dignity is not primarily tied to autonomy but rather to equality and the complex social meanings associated with it. If we think that certain people are the appropriate targets of ridicule or spectacle, that some people can be subject to harassment, humiliation, or simply ignored, just because they are different from the norm, even if some member of their group appears to autonomously choose to be targeted in dignity distorting ways, the values implicit in our commitments to equality are being compromised as are our very capacities as valuers.

ANIMAL DIGNITY

Traditionally it is thought that only humans have dignity, that it wouldn't make sense to apply the term to other animals. As Simon Blackburn notes, "I might treat your dog with friendly respect, although doggy behaviour can be fearfully undignified. Equally, if I am annoyed at someone littering a wilderness, I might say that they ought to respect it, but I would not know how to work in terms of its dignity. Magnificence, grandeur, sublimity perhaps, but dignity sounds to be a step too far" (Blackburn 2012). Alternatively, Aurel Kolnai suggests that while terms that capture dignity are chiefly applicable to human beings, they aren't exclusively so:

> much dignity…seems to me proper to the Cat, and not a little, which however different connotations, to the Bull or the Elephant. What about the monumentality of some trees and the silent life that animates plants in general?…And though man-made, cannot works of art (especially of the "classic," though not exactly "classicist," type) have a dignity of their own? (Kolnai 1976, 254)

Even though they disagree, what is interesting about what both Blackburn and Kolnai are highlighting is the complex relation between respect (and similar pro-attitudes) and dignity.

As I noted at the outset, when animals are forced to be something other than what they are, when they are made to be ridiculous, presented as laughable spectacles, this is disrespectful and their "animal dignity" is being denied. Martha Nussbaum has argued that animal dignity is based on the form of life that members of species have, those species-specific properties that are part of what it means to be a bear, a chimpanzee, an elephant, or a dog (2006b). She argues that the properties that are typical of proper species functioning, that allow an individual animal to live a characteristic life as a member of its species, should be respected. When an individual is denied the opportunity to behave in ways that befit his species, his dignity is being undermined. Nussbaum writes,

> Each form of life is worthy of respect, and it is a problem of justice when a creature does not have the opportunity to unfold its (valuable) power, to flourish in its own way, and to lead a life with dignity. The fact that so many animals never get to move around, enjoy the air, exchange affection with other members of their kind—all that is a waste and a tragedy, and it is not a life in keeping with the dignity of such creatures. (Nussbaum 2006a)

Similarly, when individuals are forced to perform functions involuntarily that aren't part of their behavioral repertoires, like making clown lips or walking on two legs and pushing a baby carriage, there is something wrong beyond the suffering they might experience. Their dignity is being violated.

One response to the idea that animals have dignity is to point out that beyond their suffering, the animals themselves don't care that they are being laughed at and ridiculed. Most other animals either don't have the capacity or the desire to think about what humans think of them.[1] People who spray paint their dogs and enter them into contests to see which dog looks the most like a ninja turtle, battleship, dinosaur, or panda, actually claim the dogs like it. And many animals appear to enjoy performing "stupid pet tricks." Some animals do seem embarrassed or guilty under certain circumstances, although as Alexandra Horowitz has shown, this is most likely a product of their "owner's" expectations (Horowitz 2009). Seeing other animals as embarrassed, ashamed, or indignant, or alternatively suggesting they enjoy being made to look absurd, always runs the danger of being a matter of human projection. Attributing dignity or noticing events that violate the dignity of other animals, critics may suggest, is simply another expression of our human inability to perceive anything outside of our anthropocentric perspective.

I agree that even if we oppose strong anthropocentrism—the view that maintains that human perspectives are superior perspectives—we cannot avoid the inevitability of our perspective always being a human one. One of the advantages of understanding dignity relationally is that it accommodates this inevitability. We do not have to discover an intrinsic property or species-typical function on which dignity supervenes, rather we recognize our human valuations as a central part of what dignity is. When discussing what I termed "wild dignity" I suggested that individuals with dignity-evoking capacities exist in relation to others with what we might call dignity-appreciating capacities and within specific contexts, often when something that matters is in jeopardy, we can opt to promote dignity (Gruen 2011). Dignity is akin to fragility; we don't worry about the fragility of a delicate glass until someone who tends to be careless starts to drink out of it, and it looks like it will break. Similarly, nonhuman dignity may only come into question when animals are part of a human social world in which questions of dignity arise. Whether or not an animal herself cares about her dignity is not the point.

While recognizing and promoting the dignity of other animals most likely leads to an enhancement of their well-being, the valuer who appreciates the dignity or recognizes and protests an indignity, has something significant at stake in aptly responding in the right contexts as well. When accurately perceiving the dignity evoked (or indignities experienced) the valuer is exercising her moral agency. This is not the context for a careful consideration of mature moral perception more generally,[2] nonetheless I would like to illustrate the importance of apt perceptions of dignity, not just to the animal, but to the perceiver, by briefly considering two photography projects.

The first is a project by Isa Leshko entitled "Elderly Animals," which began after she spent a year caring for her mother, who had Alzheimer's disease. She includes photographs of aging companion animals, but most of the photographs are of animals in sanctuaries who have been rescued from factory farms. Part of Leshko's motivation is to look aging and mortality straight on, to address her own fear of aging, but also to reveal something rather unusual—an aging farm animal. Farm animals are killed long before the end of what would be their natural life spans, so seeing them as elderly individuals challenges conceptions of who they are. As she notes, "By depicting the beauty and dignity of these creatures in their later years, I want to encourage people to question and challenge the way farm animals are currently treated." Through images of Handsome One, a thirty-three-year-old retired thoroughbred, Ash, an eight-year-old turkey, Bobby, an eleven-year-old duck, Phyllis, a thirteen-year-old sheep, and Abe, a twenty-one-year-old goat (pictured above) it is hard not to imagine them in the context of their full, but now dwindling, lives. Some look frail, all look tired, and it would be an error of perception to look at these individuals as "spent" resources and fail to recognize their dignity.

The other project, by Frank Noelker, became the book *Captive Beauty* (Noelker 2004). It is the result of almost ten years visiting over three hundred zoos all over the world and photographically capturing the beauty, the dignity, the loneliness, and the absurdity of the animals' captive lives. Two images of the fifty have haunted me since I first saw them; both were taken in 1997 in Washington, DC. One is an indoor photograph of a single giraffe in a small enclosure in which the walls are painted to give a faint impression of a distant

Abe, courtesy of Isa Leshko

savannah. At the front of the display there are mosaic panels of animals that are clearly not meant to look realistic. Nothing about the photograph looks realistic; in fact, in some ways it is comical, but of course the giraffe is real and that small space is where she will spend the rest of her life. To see this image as comical and not notice the giraffe's diminished dignity would again be a failure of perception.

The other photograph is of a hippopotamus indoors, walking down a set of cement steps into a very small, very shallow pool area. There are steps ascending opposite those the hippo is descending that are so close that it seems obvious the animal will not actually be able to get her entire body into the water. Behind the pool, on the wall is a painting of a vast body of water, and the cruel irony should not be lost on the viewer, for whom the painting was made. The photograph is framed by metal fencing.

Giraffe, Washington, DC, 1997, courtesy of Frank Noelker

The lives of the giraffe and hippopotamus captive in these small enclosures are undoubtedly bleak. Imagining how they are suffering is certainly part of what Noelker's photographs call us to do. But if one were to imagine the same animals in the same small indoor enclosures without the paintings in the background, there would be a different sense to the images and the scenes they capture. The enclosures' ornamental paintings, obviously meant for the gaze of the zoo-goer, are reminders of just how distorted this captive context is and reveal the indignities so poignantly displayed in Noelker's work.

More familiar photographs also elicit judgments about compromised dignity, beyond the suffering that may also be displayed. The shocking photos from Abu Ghraib are one obvious example; so are the images taken of the young women circulated on social media after she had been sexually assaulted; there are any number of culturally insensitive photographs taken by journalists or other outsiders that have appeared in popular magazines that raise questions about the role that representations can have in denying dignity. One of the things that I find interesting about reflecting on certain photographic representations is that the viewer's response to the indignity is part of what generates the recognition or judgment that dignity was violated, not necessarily the objections of the one who is photographed. In the case of other animals, a human recognition that dignity has been violated—that the animal is being made ridiculous, is not being allowed to live as she otherwise might, is being prevented from doing the things she would normally do, is not unlike the recognition of indignities we notice when confronted with certain images of humans we may not know and who will never know that we are looking at these images.

Dignity, understood relationally, can be compromised or undermined even when the individual whose dignity is at stake does not object or complain. And dignity can be promoted or respected even if the individuals whose dignity is being preserved are unaware that efforts are being made to do so. Of course in the case of dignity promotion, the individuals are likely to suffer less, and that is something that directly impacts their well-being. I would hope that by focusing not just on minimizing suffering but also on preventing indignities, the likelihood of inadvertently causing pain or distress will be minimized and well-being may be promoted. That other animals are not necessarily concerned about such things as dignity does not tell against their having it, and recognizing their dignity can actually benefit them. As I suggested, it also exercises our moral agency: being perceptive about dignity-enhancing or dignity-diminishing activities or conditions is a central part of our ethical capacity to treat others as they should be treated.

CAPTIVITY, DIGNITY, AND PERCEPTION

Perception is an important moral skill, and while apt perception is central in the promotion of dignity, being subject to the unwelcome gaze of others can be a threat to dignity. Seeing well is central to doing right, but looking too hard or too long can become problematic.[3] Here I want to explore the ways that the constant surveillance experienced by animals in zoos and incarcerated individuals in prisons negatively impacts the captives' dignity, over and above the impact it has on their well-being. There are similarities and differences in these cases that are important to be attentive to: in both cases annoyance, the lack of privacy, and inability to escape the gaze. In addition, lack of control can affect both the dignity and the well-being of the captives. In the case of human prisoners, humiliation can further erode dignity, and in the case of nonhumans, being the "objects" of the gaze is a dignity violation indicative of faulty human relationships with other animals.

Let's first consider zoos. Originally, zoos were designed to amuse, amaze, and entertain visitors. Enclosures were built to make the animals always accessible to the gaze of the zoo visitor, and animals were often presented as anomalous spectacles, sometimes fantastical, sometimes frightening. As public awareness of the plight of endangered species and their diminishing habitats grew, zoos developed more natural-looking enclosures and increasingly saw their roles as educational. While the motivation for the changes was primarily to educate the zoo-goers, in many cases there were also benefits for the captives. Living in more enriched and interesting environments can eliminate some of the boredom that captivity causes, and for social animals, living with others is centrally important to their well-being. But even with the advent of more naturalistic enclosures, captive animals are still on display, always under the visual control of humans.

Recently the Dallas Zoo underwent massive renovations and spent $30 million dollars to construct "Giants of the Savanna"—a multiacre enclosure in which giraffes, elephants, ostriches, zebras, and other animals mix in a naturalistic landscape that simulates their native habitat. One might expect that this highly touted innovation would contribute to the stated conservation education mission of the zoo and that the animals would be allowed to engage in more or less natural behaviors off in a distance as zoo visitors observe from afar. This would have provided animals an opportunity to find some place away from onlookers. Instead the zoo encourages visitors to actively engage with the captive animals as entertainment. The animals are trained to perform "naturalistic" behaviors during peak visiting times. "Animal activities will be strategically scheduled throughout the day, keeping the animals active and drawing people through the habitat." People will be able to buy biscuits to feed, but are cautioned not to pet, the giraffes, for example. Zoo director Gregg Edwards claims, "It's not a passive, 'let them out and loaf' kind of exhibit. It's a kind of habitat theater" (Fluck 2010).

Dale Jamieson has long been critical of the misguided messages that zoos express about human relations to other animals.

> Zoos teach us a false sense of our place in the natural order. The means of confinement mark a difference between humans and animals. They are there at our pleasure, to be used for our purposes. Morality and perhaps our very survival require that we learn to live as one species among many rather than as one species over many. To do this, we must forget what we learn at zoos. Because what zoos teach us is false and dangerous. (Jamieson 2002, 175)

One of the lessons learned from zoos is that we humans are better than the captives collected there. Ralph Acampora recounts research which shows that

> zoo-goers are much less knowledgeable about animals than backpackers, hunters, fishermen, and others who claim an interest in animals, and only slightly more knowledgeable than those who claim no interest in animals

at all (Kellert, 1979). Nearly 20 years later, [the] verdict still is dismal: "The typical visitor appears only marginally more appreciative, better informed, or engaged in the natural world following the experience... many visitors leave the zoo more convinced than ever of human superiority over the natural world." (Acampora 2005, 73)

The way animals are presented further distorts our relationships with them. Part of the problem is that zoos are not places in which animals can be seen as dignified. The painted indoor enclosures I mentioned in the last section and the more naturalistic enclosures seen more commonly in larger zoos are designed to create a relationship between the human observer and the object of the observation that obscures the individuality and dignity of the animals. The enclosures are designed to satisfy human interests and desires, even though they largely fail at this. At worst the experience creates a relationship in which the observer, even a child, has a feeling of dominant distance over those being observed. Minimally, as Acampora suggests, "The very structure of the human-animal encounter is disrupted, and the interaction that is sought—encountering the animals—becomes an impossibility as the 'real' animals disappear and the conditions for seeing are undermined" (2005, 71).

Thinking of animals as things to be looked at and believing that doing so makes for an enjoyable weekend outing, precludes seeing animals as having dignity. "There is no sense of awe, no veneration of nature, in watching an apathetic caged beast. This becomes debased amusement... teaching disrespect at worst, pity at best. It is little different from watching human prison inmates in the exercise yard" (Preece and Chamberlain 1993, 205). The relationship of watched and watcher under conditions of captivity, whether or not the watcher is the one who confines and controls the watched, is not one of respect.

In addition to undermining the possibility of regarding animals as having dignity, zoos usually do not allow animals to escape the human gaze. Without privacy, humans see animal behaviors that can be interpreted as debased or undignified. Part of the value of privacy is that, outside of the sight and judgment of others, we can experiment in living. I don't want to suggest that other animals are engaged in the same sort of projects of self-construction that we privately (and sometimes publicly) engage in, but never being able to escape the view of others undermines the "wild dignity" of animal captives. In the relative freedom of their native habitats, other animals can be seen or not and can watch humans, either seen or unseen by us. We may not like what we see when wild animals are aggressive, throw or eat excrement, masturbate, or hump each other. Often, in captivity, animals are forced to stop doing the things that make them indecent according to human norms and made to do things that they don't ordinarily do because humans want them to. This form of control is another feature of captivity that threatens dignity, both for nonhumans and for humans.

In prisons, incarcerated individuals are under constant scrutiny (see chapter 7 in this volume for a discussion). Though prisons are not quite designed the way that Jeremy Bentham envisioned panopticons, with rings of cells around a central observation tower, carceral environments succeed in making prisoners feel they are always being watched. In Bentham's time, surveillance was limited to what the guard's eyes could directly witness. Today, with cameras and other monitoring and recording technologies, prisoners can be fairly certain that they are in fact being watched every minute of every day. This denial of privacy has deleterious effects on psychological well-being—feelings of paranoia, anger, and resentment are not uncommon in the context of being under constant scrutiny. Being subject to a persistent gaze also impacts the dignity of those who are incarcerated. Like the animals in zoos, prisoners are watched as they engage in bodily functions, and there is usually no way to escape the invasive gaze. Unlike zoo animals, humans have adopted norms of keeping excretory functions private and thus experience the vulnerability of being on display as they defecate or urinate as an affront to their dignity. For incarcerated women being watched by leering guards while going to the bathroom or showering is particularly humiliating.

For prisoners, the gaze of the guards is often felt as one of contemptuous superiority. At best, prisoners may experience the looks of some correctional officers as pity. Over time, incarcerated individuals can become very attuned to small changes in the ways those in control look at them. In addition to constant surveillance and the lack of privacy that goes with it, being looked at as inferior or pathetic has an obvious impact on their dignity. This contemptuous or arrogant gaze, combined with very real power to control and dominate captives, and the limited conditions of choice and privacy, makes it impossible to preserve one's dignity as a captive.

Prisons and zoos are paradigm institutions of domination. Philip Pettit defines domination as occurring when an agent (or corporate agent) has dominating power over another "to the extent that 1. they have the capacity to interfere 2. on an arbitrary basis 3. in certain choices that the other is in a position to make" (Pettit 1997, 52). Captives in both prisons and zoos are under almost complete control. Though they are in a position to make very few choices, being so confined, even those choices are subject to interference on an arbitrary basis. In prisons, adult men and women are infantilized and denied basic options that most of us take for granted. Prisoners who are trying to turn their lives around while incarcerated are met with all manner of arbitrarily imposed obstacles. In zoos, even the most basic choices about mating and reproduction are controlled. Individuals are often taken away from the social group they have lived with and shipped to another facility to mate with individuals chosen for them.

For both humans and nonhumans captive domination and constant surveillance challenge the maintenance of dignity. And there is a difference between the experiences of those on the outside of the two institutions that also deserves mention. In the case of human captivity, the attitudes of those not incarcerated tend to be contempt or unease. Observing human captives can create a feeling of superiority, as was noted above in the case of observing captive nonhumans, but more often there is a discomfort experienced when humans view captive humans. For the most part prisons are kept out of sight, and there are limited "viewing opportunities" unless one is part of the prison industry. When outsiders do view those on the inside (actually, not as part of a fictional television series or dramatized documentary) the nature of the gaze and the attitude behind it is often quite different than the dominating gaze directed toward captive animals. In that case, other animals are readily available for viewing, and in addition to feelings of superiority, the attitudes behind the gaze are more relaxed, playful, and humorous. I would suggest that part of the difference is that despite attempts to normalize and rationalize human captivity by appeals to safety, security, or justice, there is a recognition of the wrongness of captivity—human beings who are captive are being denied their freedom and having their dignity threatened. It may be "justified"; indeed, that is part of the point of punishment, but the loss of freedom and dignity is nonetheless recognizable. The same wrong is not yet widely recognized in the case of other animals, and this is one more failure of perception.

CAPTIVE DIGNITY

Though there are many captive contexts that should not exist because they cause great harm and their only point is to satisfy human greed and/or amusement, there are some institutions of captivity that are not going away any time soon and that, arguably, serve important purposes for society and for the captives themselves. But as I have been arguing, captivity for humans and nonhumans poses significant challenges to the dignity of the captive. Is there a way to recognize the dignity of individuals while they are captives? There are some captive contexts, such as true sanctuaries, where the goal is not just to promote the well-being of the individuals who live there but to also recognize their dignity and treat the residents with respect (see chapters 5, 6, and 13 in this volume).[4] What might it look like to create captive conditions that allow those who exist within them to maintain dignity?

This is a large question to which I can only gesture towards an answer in closing. In addition to providing the basic needs for well-being, including a healthy diet, clean air and water, and enough space (and for some species that is not possible—see chapters 2 and 3), if I am right that dignity is relational, then focusing on improvements in what is possible for the three relata (the captive, the captor, and the context/conditions) would promote dignity. The dignity of a captive is enhanced when that individual is provided with opportunities for choice about who to spend time with, including captors and observers, but crucially, captives must be provided with the ability to escape the gaze of others. In the prison context that would mean providing more privacy. In the case of zoos, animals should be provided with places to hide that are recognizable to them as hiding places given their species-specific behaviors. In captivity, we can respect the wild dignity of animals by allowing them to be seen only when they wish to be seen and recognize that their lives are theirs to live without our judgments or interference. Certain features of current captive practices are fundamentally dignity denying. For example, sending prisoners far away from their families or breaking up social groups in zoo settings denies the most basic choices in addition to disrupting social bonds. Such moves can only be justified if they are clearly in the best interests of the captive, not to serve institutional ends. The relationship between captors and captives must also change. One change would be to develop an ethics of sight that works to achieve visual equality. Captives should be able to look at the captors and have their gaze respectfully returned. Being able to walk with one's head up and to look at others and be seen as an equal is a hallmark of dignity in humans. Seeing animals for who they are, as worthy of respect, and consenting to being what Phoebe Greene Linden calls "mutually viewed" is one way of promoting animal dignity.[5] Recognizing the limits of our own ways of seeing the world and being open to learning how others see it not only helps to promote their dignity but also has the potential to expand our perception; and perceiving well is an ethical skill in need of development.

ACKNOWLEDGMENTS

The title of this chapter was inspired by Timothy Pachirat's discussion of "the politics of sight" in his incredible book *Every 12 Seconds*. Thanks to Robert Jones, Joel MacClellan, and Matthew Barrett for helpful discussions of some of the ideas discussed. Thanks also to Isa Leshko and Frank Noelker for their photographic projects that address animal dignity and for permission to use their photographs here.

Notes

1. Those animals that live with us undoubtedly pick up on our judgments of them, and I am not denying that our judgments affect their behavior and often their well-being. My point simply is that I am doubtful that they see ridicule as dignity denying.

2. There are important debates in moral epistemology about moral perception—what is perceived, whether an account of moral perception is best understood to parallel color perception, whether intuition or principle supports judgments about accuracy and aptness of particular perceptions that I will not explore here. See Audi and Dancy 2010, Audi 2013, and Blum 1994 for discussion of some of these issues.

3. Perception does not necessarily require vision and is not exclusively visual. I am mindful of the ableist focus on sight in this chapter but I believe fully that nonseeing people often "see" more than those whose vision is not impaired and hope the language of "sight" is not inappropriate here. As Helen Keller once noted: "Now and then I have tested my seeing friends to discover what they see. Recently, I was visited by a very good friend who had just returned from a long walk in the woods, and I asked her what she had observed. 'Nothing in particular,' she replied. I might have been incredulous had I not been accustomed to such responses, for long ago I became convinced that the seeing see little" (quoted in Bradshaw et al. 2010, 152). For more discussion of what I'm calling "ethics of sight" see Ralph Acampora (2005), Marilyn Frye (1983), and Karen Warren (1990).

4. I say "true" sanctuary because there are some places that call themselves sanctuaries in which the animals are not being well cared for and are being used in a variety of ways to satisfy human ideological, economic, or psychological ends.

5. For more about this idea and other ideas about how to reimagine captivity for animals see Acampora 2010.

References

Acampora, Ralph. 2005. "Zoos and Eyes: Contesting Captivity and Seeking Successor Practices." *Society and Animals* 13(1): 69–88.

Acampora, Ralph, ed. 2010. *Metamorphoses of the Zoo: Animal Encounter after Noah.* Lanham, MD: Lexington Books.

Audi, Robert. 2013. *Moral Perception.* Princeton, NJ: Princeton University Press.

Audi, Robert, and Jonathan Dancy. 2010. "Moral Perception and Moral Knowledge." *Aristotelian Society Supplementary Volume*, Robert Audi (ed.), 84 (1): 79–97.

Blackburn, Simon. 2012. Review of *Dignity: Its History and Meaning. Times Higher Education.* March 29. http://www.timeshighereducation.co.uk/books/dignity-its-history-and-meaning/419440.article.

Blum, Lawrence. 1994. *Moral Perception and Particularity.* Cambridge: Cambridge University Press.

Bradshaw, G. A., Barbara Smuts, and Debra Durham. 2010. "Open Door Policy: Humanity's Relinquishment of 'Right to Sight' and the Emergence of

Feral Culture." In *Metamorphoses of the Zoo: Animal Encounter after Noah*, Ralph Acampora (ed.), 151–170. Lanham, MD: Lexington Books.

Cataldi, Susan. 2002. "Animals and the Concept of Dignity: Critical Reflections on a Circus Performance." *Ethics & the Environment* 7(2): 104–126.

Debes, Remy. 2009. "Dignity's Gauntlet." *Philosophical Perspectives* 23(1): 45–78.

Fluck, David. 2010. "Giants of Savanna the Latest Evolution at Dallas Zoo." *Dallas Morning News*, May 23.

Frye, Marilyn. 1983. *Politics of Reality: Essays in Feminist Theory*. Trumansburg, NY: Crossing Press.

Gruen, Lori. 2011. *Ethics and Animals: An Introduction*. Cambridge: Cambridge University Press.

Horowitz, Alexandra. 2009. "Disambiguating the 'Guilty Look': Salient Prompts to a Familiar Dog Behaviour." *Behavioural Processes* 81(3): 447–452.

Jamieson, Dale. 2002. "Against Zoos." In *Morality's Progress: Essays on Humans, Other Animals, and the Rest of Nature*, Dale Jamieson (ed.), 166–175. New York: Oxford University Press.

Kellert, S. 1979. "Zoological Parks in American Society." Address given at the meeting of American Association of Zoological Parks and Aquaria, St. Louis, MO.

Kellert, S. 1997. *Kinship to Mastery: Biophilia in Human Evolution and Development*. Washington, DC: Island Press.

Kolnai, A. 1976. "Dignity." *Philosophy* 51(197): 251–271.

Noelker, Frank. 2004. *Captive Beauty*. Urbana: University of Illinois Press.

Nussbaum, Martha. 2006a. "The Moral Status of Animals." *Chronicle of Higher Education* 52(22): B6.

Nussbaum, Martha. 2006b. *Frontiers of Justice: Disability, Nationality, Species Membership*. Cambridge: Belknap Press of Harvard University Press.

Pettit, Philip. 1997. *Republicanism*. Oxford: Oxford University Press.

Preece, Rod, and Lorna Chamberlain. 1993. *Animal Welfare and Human Values*. Waterloo, Ontario: Wilfrid Laurier University Press.

Rosen, Michael. 2012. *Dignity: Its History and Meaning*. Cambridge: Harvard University Press.

Warren, Karen. 1990. "The Power and the Promise of Ecological Feminism." *Environmental Ethics* 12(3): 125–146.

15

Coercion and Captivity

LISA RIVERA ▪

All these can be considered captives: a POW, a prisoner suffering the punishment of a ten-year sentence, a slave in the prebellum South, a victim of sex trafficking, a member of an extreme cult, a whale at Sea World, an elephant owned by Ringling Brothers, and a kidnapped child sold to a rug manufacturer to provide cheap labor. What can such different creatures have in common when materially their conditions are so dissimilar? Captivity is not a "You know it when you see it" phenomenon. Although the paradigm case of captivity is a free person who is held against her will by another, the existence of captive children and animals makes it clear that the denial of autonomy as it is usually understood is not a condition for captivity. Questions also arise about whether a captive must be held against her will. Further, the experience of captivity can dramatically alter a person's psychology and the choices she will make. If their capacities for free choice are sufficiently undermined, some captives may accept captivity or seek to remain captive. Captivity, it seems, takes multiple forms and has varying consequences.

The origin of the term "captivity" is in the word "captus," to take hold or seize a person or animal. A creature is captured when a captor holds her in a manner that prevents the captive from taking any action that is unwanted by the captor. Many types of animals can be captured, but the types of animals that are held in captivity are those that are capable of intentional self-directed movement. Captive animals generally will not be under a captor's control without some method preventing them from going elsewhere of their own accord. However, captivity is achieved through a variety of methods. For humans, especially, many of these methods are psychological.

Even if not the whole story, the imagery of a creature that is caught by someone does illuminate a central feature of captivity: the relation between captor and captive. Captivity is not simply a condition of confinement or unfreedom: it is a relationship between a being capable of intentional self-direction and someone who is substantially in control of that being's actions and movements. While we may loosely say a person has been held captive in his home by a landslide, such a person is not in captivity. A captive is always held by another person or set of persons who chooses to hold them.

A second significant feature of captivity is that it benefits the captor, and, in almost all cases, harms the captive. Captors benefit socially, economically, politically, and/or psychologically (e.g., from the pleasure of their power) by holding another captive. A captive creature's body, effort, labor, psychological response, or physical presence is used by a captor for his benefit. For this reason, we would be unlikely to call a woman with dementia whose freedom of movement is constrained for her safety or a toddler kept under his parents' constant control "captives" even if they would both strongly prefer not to be confined and are deprived of alternative options for action. The benefit of captivity for the captor alone is true even for the form of captivity that is the best candidate for justified captivity: imprisonment as punishment for crime. Benefiting the convicted is not the primary purpose of imprisonment. Although they have specific captors such as wardens and guards, convicts are captives of the state, and members of society believe that they benefit from the security captivity as a punishment is thought to facilitate.

This fact about the extreme lack of reciprocity of benefit in captivity also reveals why it makes more sense to see farm, zoo, and show animals as captives, but makes less sense to regard pets this way. I control my dog's options for action nearly as much as a free-range dairy farmer controls the options of his cows. However, the relationship I have with my dog is intended to be one of mutual benefit even if I am unable to confirm that my dog would choose it over other options (see the discussion in chapter 1 in this volume).

Thus, we can preliminarily say that the captivity occurs when there is a self-directed creature capable of independent intentional movement, and her movements, choices, and actions are subject to the control of another who benefits from this control. Captivity is a condition of powerlessness over one's options. Although captives need not be autonomous or have the complex deliberative capacities we ascribe to agents, the captor does need deliberative capacities since he must determine at the very least how best to maintain control over the captive's options.

My main focus here is human captivity. To understand the effects of captivity on people, I will look at three modes of captivity and the methods by which these are secured. The first type is physical captivity, which is primarily achieved by sequestration of the body and limitations on physical movement, as we see in prisoner-of-war camps, detention centers, and prisons. The second type is psychological captivity, as paradigmatically seen in totalistic cults, extremely abusive and controlling relationships, and the conditions of some members of completely totalitarian states such as North Korea. The third type is social and legal captivity, as in the case of legal slavery and certain forms of bonded labor.

These modes of captivity overlap with one another. Even when captivity is a physical condition of constrained movement, it is a psychological condition of constrained choice. All types of captivity cause enormous suffering for captives but may be experienced quite differently. I will first consider how each mode of captivity affects freedom and identity in different ways.

The examination of the effect of the methods of captivity on freedom brings me to consider these further questions: What is the relationship between captivity and coercion? Are the processes that create captivity always coercive? To answer, I will consider two different accounts of coercion. On the first account, argued for by Nozick and others, coercion is primarily a matter of conditional threats. This account purports to capture coercion of the will, but I will argue it overlooks the way in which situations such as imprisonment or legal enslavement unavoidably shape nearly all of a captive's choices in a way that clearly coerces her will. Given this, I argue an alternative, the enforcement account, better explains a central type of coercion at the heart of physical and legal/social captivity: the creation of barriers to disable a captive's options. However, we will find that psychological captivity straddles both accounts in an unusual way in that the captor harnesses and uses the captive's beliefs and emotions against her to eliminate her own power over her choices.

Before discussing modes of captivity, a few preliminaries about autonomy are in order. It goes without saying that captivity is the most extreme interference with human liberty and that it inhibits a person's autonomy. I will show below that there are various ways that captivity erodes or destroys some of the capacities necessary for autonomy, such as the capacity to think independently about one's choices or the capacity to execute choices that arise out of this reflection. In thinking about the effects of captivity on the person, however, it is more revealing to focus primarily on questions about basic capacities needed for free and independent action of any sort, rather than consider precisely how captivity constitutes interference with autonomy. Autonomously chosen desires may have a special dignity, and autonomy may be the true standard for full personhood. But given that autonomy is a standard some meet imperfectly or not at all, a focus on the interference with autonomy might be taken to imply that nonautonomous desires and preferences, especially when had by less autonomous people, are of less concern when we consider the wrongfulness of captivity. Although I cannot argue this at length, it does not seem plausible that there are degrees of wrongfulness for captivity that depend on how close the person comes to meeting standards of autonomy or how much her choices meet these standards. Rather, unjustified captivity violates something extremely basic that underlies the very possibility of autonomy: someone's ability to be a free agent in any respect, understood as the ability to make her own choices and act on those choices without the interference, control or domination of anyone else.

Different modes of captivity depend on different methods of interference, control, and domination of a person's choices and actions. The distinction between *autonomy of judgment* and *autonomy of action* is helpful in thinking about these methods (see Dworkin 1978, 163). A person has autonomy of judgment if she is able to think in a clearheaded way without internal or external interference about what she desires, cares about, and ultimately wants to do. Autonomy of action is her ability to act as she has decided she should, based on those judgments. Captivity is usually thought to impede autonomy of action. Physical captivity most certainly does; it sometimes leaves room for independent reflection and choice, but it may also undermine these as well. Psychological captivity directly impedes autonomy of judgment. Psychological captivity is secured by various means, among them information control, shame, guilt, harassment, and trauma. These techniques impede a person's ability to think clearly enough to independently form desires and choices. Social/legal captivity contains elements that impede both judgment and action. I have argued elsewhere that the ability to think clearly about what one wants can depend on the ability to act on what one has chosen (Rivera 2011). We will see in the case of captivity, how this occurs depends on the method of control.

PHYSICAL CAPTIVITY

We can understand physical captivity as a situation in which a person's movements and actions are controlled primarily by physical means rather than by psychological compliance or legal and social enforcement. Anyone whose captivity depends on the control of her body rather than of her mind can be regarded as a physical captive, even though a certain amount of compliance for a physical captive comes about through psychological methods such as threat and intimidation (see, for example, chapters 7 and 8 in this volume). Much physical captivity is outside the realm of law and it is uncontroversial that it is unjustified, for example, sex trafficking and forced labor. Here I will focus primarily on those who are serving prison sentences as a result of being convicted of crimes. Whether or not imprisonment for punishment is justified is not a question I take up. However, the lasting psychic effects of imprisonment should be relevant to anyone who cares about that question.

Unlike psychological captivity, it is not assumed or expected that a physical captive will willingly comply with the mechanisms to control his actions and the norms being pressed upon him in the absence of continual physical monitoring and force. In light of Bentham's panopticon, which causes prisoners to believe they may be watched at all times, some might argue that an important element of physical control depends on psychological domination. The prisoner's belief that he is being watched is significant in securing his submission. Since the prisoner modifies his behavior as the result of this belief, isn't physical captivity also a substantially psychological process? As we will see, physical captivity does have psychological elements as well as lasting psychological effects on a person's free agency. However, the important thing to note about the panopticon is that the prisoner is not thought to comply because of internalized acceptance of the norms of the prison, or from fear of guilt or shame at his behavior, but because he knows the norms he is violating will be enforced in a way that is physically or psychologically painful to him.

What causes a person to become a physical captive? First, physical captivity is generally initiated with some capture of the body, and it is secured over time by physical control over the prisoner's body and movement. A prisoner is arrested, handcuffed, shackled, held, and so on. His physical captivity over time always involves barriers such as walls, gates, and fences. Such barriers do have a psychological element, particularly given the fact that the prisoner becomes very dependent on those holding him prisoner for all his physical needs. Generally, a prisoner is only allowed to meet his physical needs such as eating, sleeping, elimination, cleaning, and exercise at the behest of those imprisoning him. (Prisoners in some poorer countries depend on their families to provide food, but they still depend on the prison to allow them to keep and eat the food brought by their families.) The physical space of the prison becomes the prisoner's only available space, and he may be confined to an even smaller space, as when confined to his cell or put into solitary. The prisoner's personal liberty is also curtailed within that space (e.g., what he reads, says, eats, etc. and what times he does all these things).

Second, the control that constitutes physical captivity is also secured by means of various direct penalties for disobedience. One type of penalty is to revoke privileges allowed in the prison such as the permission to read, write, watch television, make phone calls, receive visitors, or eat a variety of foods. A second type of penalty is to inflict physical or psychological pain for infractions of prison rules or policies. Some prisons employ direct physical harms such as whipping or being placed in a hot box. Some, including American prisons, utilize solitary confinement, in spite of the fact that it risks causing lasting mental illness (Grassian 2006). Although these penalties do inflict punishment after the transgression, their point is to deter: they are intended as a method to secure compliance and obedience on the part of all prisoners. Finally, the threat of death or of more extreme or lengthy punishment is often used to try to prevent prisoners from escaping their physical captivity.

Imprisonment is our paradigm for the loss of liberty. It absolutely eliminates the possibility of meaningful autonomy of action, and, during the period the person experiences captivity, it will also constrict autonomy of judgment, since her options are so severely limited. Yet one way that physical captivity in the case of prison differs from psychological captivity is that prisoners may have some small opening to choose their deepest identity constituting values. Prisoners are not forced to internalize the values and beliefs of their captors in the way that a victim of an ultra-totalitarian state, an abusive relationship, or an extreme cult is. Prisoners are not expected to have loyalty or fidelity to or even accept the norms of the prison. In his famous study of a maximum security prison, Gresham Sykes argues, "In the prison, power must be based on something other than internalized morality and the custodians find themselves confronting men who must be forced, bribed or cajoled into compliance" (2007, 47). Although prison undermines identity and agency, Sykes argues that some prisoners make it a goal to maintain these, for example by being a "real man," someone who tries to "[pull] his time" by refusing to let the custodians "strip him of his ability to control himself" (2007, 102).

Thus, compliance in physical captivity is primarily about behavior rather than internalized attitudes. And although it may leave room for some elements of identity and agency to be retained, maintaining these requires exceptional effort. A prisoner's success may depend on features of character or life experiences that he could not be responsible for. Thus, it would be unfair to expect physical captives to evade the agency and identity-destroying elements of their experience.

Physical captivity has significant psychological effects that may also affect a person's free agency for the period of time following captivity. Some of these effects may be permanent. The list of these is quite vast. Even if we confine ourselves to the supposedly more humane imprisonment by the state rather than illegal forms of imprisonment such as forced labor, it is impossible to detail all the ways physical captivity will alter people's future choices and choice-making abilities when they are free of the physical control they suffered: people's tolerance for imprisonment differs significantly, and some of the effects of prison are caused by traumas experienced in prison, such as rape and other forms of violence. If post-traumatic stress disorder or other mental illness is caused by imprisonment, this will affect a person's future free agency by damaging her capacities for deliberation and her ability and willingness to have certain kinds of experiences. It would be somewhat absurd to say that these effects are not from physical captivity itself. When you render someone powerless or near powerless in a social context as imprisonment does, you make the person

vulnerable to violence (see Haney, Banks, and Zimbardo 1973). Unless prisoners' rights are respected and continually enforced (which is very rare), it is
inevitable that some people may be psychically damaged or destroyed by the
physical insecurity and violence of imprisonment. Even so, certain effects of
the many kinds of mistreatment in physical captivity are not wholly intrinsic
to imprisonment itself. Physical captivity always contains an element of actual
or implicit violence in the form of bodily domination, but it is the irregu-
larity, fear, and insecurity of violence in prison that appears to do the most
psychological harm.

A thoroughly studied effect of prison life that *is* inherent to imprisonment is
institutionalization. Institutionalization directly impacts what we might refer to
as the internal capacities of free agency such as deliberation and choice. Almost
all of a prisoner's choices and actions are severely circumscribed by prison routine and by the dictates of prison personnel. Over time, the inability to exercise
deliberative and choice-making capacities over even the very basic aspects of his
daily life can erode a person's ability to act independently. A person shows signs
of institutionalization when he becomes dependent on other decision-makers
for basic choices, and disoriented or confused when forced to make choices on
his own. There are at least two different manifestations of the effect of institutionalization on freedom. First and more commonly, after a long period with
very few options, many ex-convicts experience discomfort with the wide variety
of options for action outside of prison. In rare cases, some prisoners become
altogether unable to make and act on their own decisions. There have been
instances where ex-convicts seek to re-enter prison because of their distress and
confusion in the absence of external control and regimentation. Such a person
can be regarded as a willing captive but only because captivity has so destroyed
his capacity for autonomy of judgment that prison becomes his only option.
Thus, although captivity generally involves some resistance on the part of captives, captivity can also destroy free agency to the extent that at least a few are
not held against their will. The possibility of willing captivity in this very narrow
sense exists for all physical, psychological, and legal/social captivity.

A second effect of institutionalization is the inability to self-regulate one's
behavior when outside the prison environment. Since the prison environment
immediately enforces conformity with rules, some prisoners become dependent on the swift and definite punishment within the prison structure to control their own behavior. Thus, the person (if imprisoned from a very young age)
fails to develop, or loses, that aspect of autonomy which makes it possible for
him to act on desires he wants to act on, since he is not in control of the desires
he acts on (see Frankfurt 1988). Prison may make some people more likely to
commit crimes because they are more prone to act on impulse when there is
no one but themselves monitoring their day-to-day actions (Haney 2003, 40).

Although institutionalization may seem pathological, it is better understood as an adaptation to the near total control in the prison environment. Those prisoners who refuse to submit to prison requirements will be met with harsh treatment. Physical survival in prison requires submission to prison rules and routine, and basic actions such as eating, bathing, and exercise all require compliance with the schedule and sometimes the explicit permission of guards. However, to submit in this way likely requires an initial act of will. Automatic obedience is psychologically difficult. Yet regular failure to obey commands in physical captivity incurs painful penalties. Thus, habitual compliance would likely have to be learned in part by suppressing the tendency to act on one's own accord over various domains. Further, the continual desire for more personal liberty over one's day-to-day life will only make prison more distressing. The more routine and habitual one can make one's compliance, the more secure one's well-being is (to the extent one can secure one's well-being in physical captivity). Thus, there is a form of internalized compliance in physical captivity but, unlike in forms of psychological captivity, it takes the form of habitual behavior rather than internalized belief that prison rules are intrinsically valuable or that the guards' power over oneself stems from legitimate moral authority.

Another relevant effect of imprisonment on free agency is the loss of self-worth that results from it:

> However painful the frustration or deprivation may be in the immediate terms of thwarted goals, discomfort, boredom and loneliness, they carry a more profound hurt as a set of threats or attacks which are directed against the very foundation of the prisoner's being. The individual's picture of himself as a person of value—as a morally acceptable, adult male who can present some claim to merit in his material achievement and his inner strength—begins to waver and grow dim. (Sykes 2007, 79. See also Haney 2003, 45)

Following Rawls, we can say that a prolonged period where one's agency is not shown respect by others and where one is unable to act on one's purposes or carry out a plan of life in any meaningful way is likely to damage or destroy "his secure conviction that his conception of his good, his plan of life, is worth carrying out" (Rawls 1971, 440). A person's confidence in her agency depends on the idea that what she intends to do is worth doing, and a confidence that the results she can bring about are valuable. Physical captivity leaves some room for this, but only in an extremely limited way. When permitted to, some prisoners do participate within their limited social sphere, try to benefit other prisoners, take up educational or artistic projects, and so on. However, to achieve the robust sense of self that can undergird these activities requires enormous effort on the part of the captive. And over time, the continual thwarting of one's opportunities and efforts to act independently may undermine a captive's motivation and sense of his own agency.

PSYCHOLOGICAL CAPTIVITY

We tend to think of physical captivity as the ultimate loss of freedom. However, because psychological captivity amounts to adopting a captor's intentions, it may involve a more extensive loss. What is given up is not only free agency but identity. Like the physical captive, the psychological captive's movements, actions, and body are under the control of a person or persons who benefit from this control. The psychological captive has very limited or no freedom to make choices that the captor disapproves of. Orwell's *Nineteen Eighty-Four* describes a society almost entirely made up of psychological captives.

There is a certain artificiality involved in talking of psychological captivity in the abstract. Paradigmatic cases of psychological captivity such as submission to an ultra-totalitarian state, extreme cults, or abusive relationships frequently occur in the presence of physical controls, threats, or harms. In real-life cases, each mode of captivity may involve elements of the other modes. What is distinctive about psychological captivity is that the near total control over someone's action that physical captivity achieves through physical barriers and force can be accomplished in the right context without those barriers and without force. Another significant feature of psychological captivity is that it often includes the expectation that the captor's preferences for the captive's choices will be internalized and acted upon by the captive as if these preferences are valuable. Thus, loyalty rather than mere behavior can be demanded by captors. Psychological captivity is effective only in some cases without violence or the threat of violence but the psychological captive is, in a physical sense, sometimes free to escape.

The apparent possibility of escape means that the psychological captive's innocence of complicity in her own captivity may be doubted. Such skepticism was seen in the Patty Hearst case, for example. [1] Thus, a conceptual problem with the idea of psychological captivity is that we often think of those who are under the near total psychological control of another person without any apparent physical control as being willing participants. Some may desire to hold them fully responsible for their actions. Whether they are fully responsible depends on whether people are always responsible to maintain autonomy and identity in circumstances of extreme pressure, duress, or coercion. Although this is beyond the scope of this paper, acceptance of a set of values, a religious or political doctrine, or a captor's rightful place as one's controller after a period of violence, coercion, or psychological manipulation does not meet the standards we ordinarily set for voluntary action.

Different methods are utilized to effect the psychological compliance necessary for psychological captivity, but what they tend to have in common is that they disorient the person and undermine her prior certainty about her beliefs and values in a gradual process of alienating them from their identity-constituting values and replacing these with those the captor regards as desirable. Robert J. Lifton describes a process of "thought reform" based on his study of former subjects of Chinese Communist schools of reeducation. Some of these were European and American prisoners of the Chinese Communist government. Some were Chinese intellectuals. Lifton argues that the process of thought reform in reeducation schools to initiate people into accepting "ideological totalism" is similar to that used in religious cults and on political prisoners. While it will always be controversial to claim that some instances of political and religious ideology are forced upon people, rather than genuinely held, Lifton's claim that this is the case depends on the fact that, when individuals describe the experience of belief formation after the fact, they describe not only acquiring a new set of beliefs and values but relinquishing many of their most cherished prior attachments such as love of their parents. They also claim to have believed things that they later regard as obviously false. This transformation of basic beliefs and primary identity-constituting values occurs in a manner that bypasses rational consent and endorsement. Nor is their transformation a matter of mere behavior. Lifton's subjects would later state that their confessions renouncing their former beliefs, values, and personal emotional attachments were sincerely felt (Lifton 1956, 1989).

According to Lifton, the process of thought reform can be successful without actual violence even if a fear of violence lies in the background. Thought reform primarily manipulates its subjects' social contact, beliefs, desires, and emotions so they eventually relinquish any doubts they have about the set of ideologies and beliefs the regime, group, or person desires them to have. He describes three main stages of thought reform when it was undergone voluntarily by Chinese students (even if the student was unaware of what his or her transformation would be). The first stage is group identification. For students who voluntarily underwent thought reform, the student was welcomed enthusiastically into the group, and "thought reform is presented to the student as a morally uplifting, harmonizing and therapeutic experience" (Lifton 1956, 77). The second stage is one where the milieu "closes in" on the student and the student was encouraged to regard himself as the object of study and consider his own deficiencies. Gradually, moral criticisms of the student (by instructors or other students) that were founded on the totalist ideology became more intense. The student was expected to make a full public confession of his deficiencies. Students began to experience acute anxiety. There was some latent background fear of violence because they were aware that the punishment for being found a reactionary could be grim. Instructors ascribed their physical symptoms of acute fear, loss of appetite, and inability to sleep to guilt that could only be relieved if they confessed to all their failings. Students who seemed resistant to the process of transformation or who appeared emotionally detached from the process were subjected to the highest level of pressure and public criticism. Finally, there was a period of "submission and rebirth" that required students to write scathing criticisms of themselves and their family. With this act of self-betrayal, they transferred their fealty to the group or regime (Lifton 1956, 77–82). Rather than excessive fear of bodily harm, most of what took place in this process utilized the power of students' natural sociality and their need to confirm their beliefs with others. Everyone socially available to the person undergoing thought reform showed utter conviction in the truth of the beliefs and value commitments being inculcated and in the extreme failings of any student who was suspected of clinging to his prior beliefs and commitments.

Lifton breaks this process down further into various elements that he argues also apply to other ideologically totalist indoctrinations such as cults and totalitarian states. Among these are

1. Milieu control: All information and ideas come from the tightly controlled milieu of students and instructors. Everyone surrounding the student agrees on the correctness of the ideology being presented and students monitor one another's statements and attitudes. Lifton compares this experience of information control and constant monitoring to the two-way telescreen in Orwell's *Nineteen Eighty-Four*. There, any lack of attention to the screen or any activity disapproved of by the screen would be reprimanded (Lifton 1956, 82).

2. Mystical manipulation: The student is enjoined to have faith in a higher purpose that justifies actions he might ordinarily reject. He is encouraged to believe in particular individuals, who have been chosen for this higher purpose and who should not be resisted (Lifton 1989, 400–401).

3. The demand for purity and guilt, shame and confession: The former life, identity, beliefs commitments, and values are regarded as impure. The person begins to feel guilty and ashamed. She is encouraged to confess her failings and begins to have a compulsion to do so. "Private ownership of the mind and its products—of imagination or of memory—becomes highly immoral . . . the milieu has attained such a perfect state of enlightenment that any individual retention of ideas or emotions can become anachronistic" (Lifton 1989, 404).

4. Belief transformation: Lifton discusses three elements that are fundamentally about providing a totally self-contained ideological framework to supplant

the person's prior frame of reference. First, the ideology is presented as an absolute body of truth that is absurd to question either from a factual or moral standpoint. Second, the language is loaded with "ultimate terms" and jargon such that the person's thought is constrained within that jargon. (This is also described in *Nineteen Eighty-Four* as the process of "newspeak," where words are removed from the language that express complex or nuanced ideas, and new words are promulgated that are ineffective in criticizing the totalitarian regime.) Third, Lifton states that the person is to prefer "doctrine over person." One's own beliefs are required to harmonize with the doctrine, and the doctrine is expected to supersede one's own beliefs, memories, and experiences. If contradictions occur, then new explanations and doctrines are expected to be accepted (Lifton 1989, 405–410).

5. The dispensing of existence: Those whose thoughts are being reformed are required to accept black-and-white thinking about groups. Members of some groups are good (e.g., the people), and members of others do not deserve to live (e.g., reactionaries and political criminals). This element of thought reform may not be relevant in every case of psychological captivity. However, it does explain how individuals in totalist situations such as cults commit senseless murders or mass suicides. Lifton also argues that this perspective creates fear of annihilation on the part of thought reform participants that makes them more willing to undergo the transformation of their belief system.

It is reasonable to question how perfectly and completely thought reform exercises control over individuals. Lifton points out that thought reform and submission to totalist belief systems often fail to be permanent or complete (Lifton 1989, 411). In the majority of cases, the belief system tends to fall apart when the milieu is no longer controlled. Thus, some escapees to South Korea from North Korea describe their deep love for the Kim family and continuing loyalty to the state even while experiencing starvation and imprisonment at the hands of the state (see Harden 2012 and Demick 2010). These feelings dissipate for most people once they become part of open societies. What is compelling about Lifton's account is that we do know of many cases where people come under the extreme control of others without initially desiring or endorsing this control. Thus, those who voluntarily enter extreme cults do not consent to their later submission to the cult leader's control. They are deceived about the cult's purpose and practices. It is not plausible to suppose the extent of power and control cult leaders have over their members occurs by the process of rational persuasion, and processes like thought reform do explain the blind obedience of these members. The fact that people come to sincerely believe and feel in the ways desired by these powerful others as well as act at their behest also needs to be explained when there is no overt threat of pain and punishment.

LEGAL/SOCIAL CAPTIVITY

Legal chattel slavery was a form of social and legal captivity. Its existence depended both on law and on widespread acceptance and social enforcement. I focus primarily on the form of slavery that existed within the United States prior to the Civil War. However, it is important to note that forced labor is not a historic phenomenon. An International Labour Organization report estimates about 12.5 million people are victims of forced labor (ILO 2005, 9). Some slaves are the victims of human trafficking for sex or manual labor, some are bonded agricultural laborers. Currently, this slavery is socially but not legally enforced as ownership of one person over another. Forced laborers are often physical captives who are held at their work sites, are physically threatened, or have their passports held. Debt bondage is sometimes both a legal and economic method of captivity. There are also cases of descent into forced labor where children are born into debt bondage (ILO 2005, 9). Although forced laborers are not legally property, it is difficult to draw a sharp line between forced labor and slavery. Victims of sex trafficking are often referred to as slaves because they are purchased and then regarded as owned by their captors. This is also true of child laborers who are kidnapped and held. Social and ethnic groups have also been enslaved as a result of war, and had their slavery legally institutionalized, as in the case of Nazi slave camps. Labor can also be forced by the state, as formerly in some Communist bloc countries and currently in Myanmar (ILO 2005, 25). Much forced labor depends on physical captivity and some, such as with victims of sex trafficking, may come about through psychological captivity.

Both physical and psychological captivity as described above were not primary in ensuring the captivity of chattel slaves. Although slaves were often physically free of barriers to movement and may have recognized the injustice of their captivity, they were unable to live independently of their master's control. Society gave them no such option. Slavery wherein the slave is the legal property of the master is a complex social phenomenon, however, and it is impossible to engage with all the social aspects of slavery here. The primary aspect of slavery relevant to this discussion is the total domination by the master over the slave. The slave has no place in society and therefore no recourse but to accept this complete control of himself. Orlando Patterson defines slavery as "the permanent, violent domination of natally alienated and generally dishonored persons" (Patterson 1982, 13). Its fundamental characteristic is social death. Patterson describes the slave's powerlessness as due to the fact he has no social role and no social power outside his role as the property of his master:

> The power relation has three facets. The first is social and involves the use of violence or threat of violence in the control of one person by another.

The second is the psychological facet of influence, the capacity to persuade another person to change the way he perceives his interests and his circumstances. And third is the cultural facet of authority, "the means of transforming force into right and obedience into duty...." (Patterson 1982, 1–2)

There are many physical and psychological aspects of a slave's captivity, but the primary method of making a person a captive through the practice of slavery depends on the social community's enforcement of captivity, which gave the slaves no options but enslavement. Masters had extreme power over slaves, but this power was legally defined. Slaves always faced the most brutal physical punishments for disobedience, yet even allowable punishment for slaves could be defined legally. Nor were all the restrictions on a slave's freedom up to the master. Laws directed at masters sometimes forbade what they were permitted to do with slaves. For example, in pre-Revolutionary South Carolina, teaching a slave to write or using him as a scribe carried one of the highest fines in the colonies. It was also illegal to employ slaves in jobs where they could learn about poisons or to teach them anything about poisons. Anyone employing them in an apothecary was subject to fine (Higginbotham 1978, 198).

Slaves, according to Patterson, did not lose all options:

He might, in relative terms, be powerless; but he always had some choice. He might react psychologically, play the slave, act dumb, exasperate. He might lie or steal. He might run away. He might injure or kill others, including his own master. Or he might engage in armed revolt. Barring all these, he might destroy his master's property by destroying himself. To be sure... most chose simply to behave with self-respect and do the best they could under the circumstances. Nevertheless I know of no slaveholding societies in which some slaves at some times did not rebel in some manner. (Patterson 1982, 13)

Nevertheless, after rebellion or disobedience the options narrow. All these possible actions either risk extremely harsh punishments or death, and so we cannot say a slave truly has a wide set of *genuine* choices. The frequency of slave rebellion indicates that, like a physical captive, a slave might maintain autonomy of judgment if the circumstances were right. However, a person born in slavery also had his entire social existence shaped by the system of enslavement and whatever self-concept or plan of life was constrained by that. The slave system is designed to disable whatever capacities the slave may develop for free agency. The slave is given no social resources, no education beyond the

minimum required to serve, and is subject to a continual fear of violent repri-
sals for actions disapproved by his master. These social barriers to developing
capacities required for free agency may also be true for some of those born into
extreme poverty and debt bondage, when debt bondage is a traditional social
practice and society only enforces the rights of those holding the debt over the
laborer.

COERCION

What is the relationship between captivity and coercion? It may seem intuitively obvious that the control a captor has over a captive depends on his power
to coerce the captive to behave, and sometimes to believe and feel as he desires.
There is no term or concept other than coercion that works so well to describe
the process that ensures a person becomes and remains a captive. However,
standard philosophical accounts of coercion do not correlate well with the
main processes that create captivity. So are these processes not coercive? Or
does captivity reveal that something is missing from standard accounts? I will
first discuss Nozick's account—which most contemporary views of coercion
follow—that coercion is a matter of controlling a person through conditional
threats. On this view, it looks as if the physical methods of making someone
unfree, such as chains or walls, are not coercive. (Behavioral controls through
threats common to prisons are coercive on the Nozickian account.) Slavery,
understood as the elimination of options for action by social and legal enforcement, is also not well conceptualized as coercion through conditional threats.
I will argue that failure to regard these processes as coercive is an oversight of
Nozickian-type accounts. This gives us a reason to regard coercion as having
various faces and, for some aspects of captivity, to favor an enforcement account
of coercion that focusses on the coercer's access and use of power to ensure the
captive behaves as he desires. But difficulties remain for both accounts if psychological captivity is regarded as coercive.

On Nozick's view, if a would-be coercer (P) wants to prevent a would-be
coerced person (Q) from performing some action A, Q is coerced when

1. P has communicated a (not necessarily verbal) threat to Q if Q does A.
2. Caused Q to believe that P will carry out his threat.
3. If P carries out his threat, doing A is a much worse alternative for Q
   than not doing A.
4. So Q doesn't do A.
5. Q's reason for not doing A is to avoid the situation in which P carries
   out his threat. (Nozick 1969, 440–446)

On this view, coercion is always successful. A person is only coerced if she alters her actions in order to avoid the bad consequence.

This type of coercion is biconditional: Do / do not do A or else I will do / not do B. However, offers are similarly structured this way and many offers, for example, to only sell someone a car if he pays a particular price, are clearly not coercive. On the conditional threat view, the main difference between a threat and an offer is that a threat if carried out would worsen the coerced person's condition (cf. Frankfurt 1988; Wertheimer 1987).

Yet things are not so simple since threats can come in the form of an offer. Nozick describes two very similar cases. In the first, Q's usual supplier of drugs (P) says he is not going to sell them to Q for a reasonable price, but instead Q can have the drugs "if and only if Q beats up a certain person" (Nozick 1969, 447). Nozick contrasts this with another case, where a stranger, who knows that P has been arrested, takes advantage of Q's desire for drugs and says he will give him drugs only if he beats up a certain person. The reason Nozick regards the first case as a threat but the second as an offer is that the expected baseline is different in the second: P usually comes through for Q and provides him with drugs. However, the option the stranger raises is an unexpected event.

The notion of a baseline can also depend on moral expectations rather than expectation about what is a usual occurrence. Nozick considers the case of a slave who is beaten daily but offered a respite from his daily beating if he performs some task well. If the baseline is what the slave expects to happen, this is an offer. But if the baseline lies in what we morally expect to happen, it is a threat. The appropriate baseline between a threat and an offer, Nozick says, depends on what the person prefers. The addict prefers the normally expected course of events as a baseline, and the slave prefers the morally expected course of events as a baseline.

The usually expected baseline won't resolve all questions; sometimes a person claims she will bring about a consequence that worsens another that she is regarded as having a right to bring about, for example, a landlord may threaten to evict a tenant if he does not give up his smoking habit as disallowed on the lease. This is not coercion. Thus, Alan Wertheimer (1987) argues, partly based on a view of what counts as coercion in the law, that coercion only occurs when the person is made worse than he has a right to be made. Coercion is therefore a moralized notion: Coercion is always wrong because the coercer has to threaten the coerced with a consequence he has no right to bring about. If imprisonment is justified captivity, on this view, it must not involve coercion.

Physical captivity does sometimes involve threats to enforce behavior, and these would seem to count as coercion if we set aside the issue of whether imprisonment is justified for the time being. There are various ways these situations could count as coercive in the Nozickian sense. There is an omnipresent

background threat of further punishment such as solitary confinement upon
failure to comply with prison rules. Escape is punishable by much more imprisonment. However, the physical barriers that create the condition of imprisonment are not coercive. Nozick claims that it is not coercive to force someone
into a space where they cannot leave:

> If I lure you into an escape-proof room in New York and leave you imprisoned there, I do not coerce you into not going to Chicago though I make
> you unfree to do so. (Nozick 1969, 440)

Although we might think a more pertinent question is whether you are coerced
to *stay in the room* by the fact you are trapped there, on Nozick's view, you do
not coerce someone if you remove all her options by force or constraint such
that she must choose to do as you wish. Rather, coercing someone appears to
involve getting the person herself to choose as you wish because she wants to
avoid the threat you have presented.

A similar question can be raised about slavery. Slaves comply with the specific wishes of their masters because of violence and threats of punishment. But
in the United States they did this because, until the abolitionist movement made
escape a viable option, slaves had no choice but to be slaves. They could not own
property, work, or subsist as free persons. They had no social identity separate
from their master's identity. Background violence and barriers to all alternative
survivable actions are not regarded as coercive on the Nozickian view. Only a
direct threat of harm (which many slaves did experience) is coercive.

It may help to consider the conceptual work that coercion is supposed to do
in explaining how one person controls another. Frankfurt raises a distinction
between physical coercion and coercion of the will. An instance of physical
coercion would be to put pressure on another's hand to make him drop the
knife. In such a case

> the victim is not made to act; what happens is that his fingers are made to
> open by the pressure applied to his wrist. It may in certain situations be
> difficult, or even impossible, to know whether or not an action has been
> performed. Perhaps it will be unclear whether the man dropped the knife
> because his fingers were forced open or because he wished to avoid a continuation of the pressure on his wrist. (1988, 26)

Likewise, McCloskey claims that a person whose choice is shaped by force or
physical barriers "does not act at all; rather [he] is acted upon... [However], the
coerced person acts... he chooses to do it". (McCloskey 1980, 340)

So do prison walls or social barriers to action simply amount to coercion
of the body but not coercion of the will? This seems to rely on the idea that

the prisoner who is in prison is not making a choice to remain in the prison; the walls and electrified fences give her no choice. We should reject physical barriers as coercive to the will, someone may argue, because coercion involves choosing (i.e., "using" one's will) and therefore there must be a set of alternatives to choose from even if the coerced choice is still unfree. (On the conditional threat model, the alternative can be very nasty as in cases like "Your money or your life," and so perhaps is not viable.) However, barriers do affect choices just as threats do. The effectiveness of the physical barriers in keeping the prisoner captive is precisely what shapes *all* the prisoner's subsequent choices. The prisoner obeys guards, eats, sleeps, exercises, and bathes because the physical barriers make her utterly dependent on the prison structure for her survival and she isn't able to go elsewhere. Without that context, these threats would not be meaningful. In acting on her only relevant options, the prisoner uses her will just as much as the person who is threatened, and just as unfreely. Thus one oversight in the Nozickian model is that it takes coercion to be a matter of discrete threats and overlooks the fact that even coercion via threats depends on a particular context, that is, the person's relative powerlessness against the threat.

On the Nozickian model, it also appears that coercion cannot be a prolonged over time since coercion must be a matter of discrete, actual threats. But it is particularly odd to characterize that the condition of being a slave as noncoercive except in cases where the slave faces a direct conditional threat. We might characterize prison walls as barriers or force, but it is clear that all slaves are not held in slavery by constant force. The power of the master over the slave and the master's ability to get the slave to do his bidding doesn't depend on the threat of force or violence alone (although it did depend on that at times), but on the social and legal power the master has over the slave. Without this legal and social control, and the social death of the slave, a threat of violence would not necessarily be effective over the slave since the slave would have some recourse or capacity to defend himself.

A view of coercion that better explains these cases is found in "the enforcement view" (Anderson 2010). This view of coercion depends on the fact that the coercer already is in a position of power over the coerced person that he uses to force or disable her actions. Thus, barriers to action, both physical and social, that render agents powerless and require them to submit to another's will, should count as coercive:

> On this account, the principle mode of coercion is *prevention*; inducement to perform specific acts typically follows on the ability to prevent many or even all other acts. When an agent acquires the power to inhibit another's action broadly, the powerful agent has the ability to alter radically what is practically necessary for the weaker agent, thus explaining the sense of

necessity invoked when coerces claim, e.g., that "I had no choice" or "he made me do it." (Anderson 2010, 9)

Anderson argues that this type of coercion should not be moralized: Imprisonment is coercive, whether it is justified or not.

This view sheds important light on the power of the captor over the captive. Captivity depends on power, but it is power of a special sort: The power to enforce the choice and action that the captor desires. Psychological captivity is perhaps the most effective means of control one person can have over another. However, an interesting question remains about whether psychological captivity is coercive on either of these views. On the one hand, psychological captivity can involve threats. If we consider the method of thought control, three types of threats were salient. First, there was the background threat of actual penalties (e.g., political imprisonment) for refusing to embrace the beliefs and values or have the feelings desired by the eventual captor. Does it matter if the threat is unstated? The fact that it exists should still make it coercive on the Nozickian account. Second, there is the (again, implied) threat of social ostracization because the social milieu demands of the proposed captive an agreement with the views others are expressing. Third, there is the threat of continual distress caused by the shame and guilt that prompts the confession. Interestingly, this emotional threat seems to finalize the result the captor seeks, wherein the captive fully embraces the beliefs, desires, and values the captor desires her to have. On the other hand, the enforcement model also could shed some light on psychological captivity because it seems to be most effective when the psychological captive loses her sense of identity and independent power. The would-be psychological captor's goal is to create a feeling of helplessness.[2]

However, neither view of coercion explains whether or not psychological captivity is coercive. Although threats are involved, there is no clear-cut Nozickian biconditional trade-off wherein the captive clearly gives the captor something concrete to avoid his carrying out the threat. Rather, what the captor wants as a result of his control is the psychological submission of the captive. The captive's submission is obviously not a choice of the type made when someone is told "Your money or your life," since the captive now accepts the captor's views. With respect to the enforcement view, the would-be captor has power, but it seems to arise from the would-be captive's helplessness. The captor's power is gradual and purely psychological in that he maneuvers the would-be captive into an ever-increasing state of guilt and shame. However, for psychological captivity without the threat of force, the barriers the captor creates are internal to the captive. The would-be captive comes to regard assent to the captor's control as practically necessary in order to avoid the psychological distress of the emotions she now feels when she resists.

It may be that this is the result because psychological captivity is imperfectly understood as coercive. Even so, the role of emotional reactions to pressure in causing someone to act as another desires suggests another thing missing from the Nozickian account of coercion: the fact that coercion depends on harnessing a person's motivations against her. If coercion is always a matter of biconditional threats, there are many threat situations where we cannot say the coerced person has no choice. Many things may count as a worsening that would leave the would-be coerced person unmoved. A suicidal person may not be motivated by someone's threat to kill her, for example. It seems that the actual result of coercing someone depends on whether the threat is enough to motivate him (see Frankfurt 1988).

A final question about psychological captivity (and the institutionalization that follows physical captivity) concerns the willing captive. If the captive no longer seeks to escape, does she continue to be coerced? In the case of psychological captivity, the captive now comes to embrace the captor's control over her. In the case of institutionalization, the prisoner willingly accepts imprisonment because he no longer has the capacities needed for free agency and fears a life that is independent of someone else's control. This suggests that one eventual result of coercion may be that continued coercion becomes unnecessary. Thus, one disturbing possible effect of coercion within captivity is the destruction of someone's free agency to the extent that she is wholly subject to a captor's will.

CONCLUSION

Captivity brings a multitude of harms to those who suffer it. It is no exaggeration to say that it is one of the most extreme assaults one person can make upon the self of another person. In rare cases, such as physical captivity that contains little traumatizing violence, the captive may retain his identity-constituting beliefs and values and there will be some room for the captive to retain autonomy of judgment and create a life plan, however constrained. Still, physical captivity frequently brings damage in its wake. Even if we assume imprisonment of the guilty is justified, we must acknowledge that current practices of imprisonment put the captive at risk for the erosion of capacities he needs for free agency, such as the inability to independently determine what he wishes to do or the belief that his own aims have value. Psychological captivity, on the other hand, potentially destroys identity and agency by its very nature. The psychological captor seeks the captive's submission to his desires, and this process involves replacing the captive's cares and values with his own. Social and legal captivity similarly destroy identity and agency, but for different reasons: a slave is stripped of an independent social identity and given an identity as an extension of his master. Thus, his choices are entirely constrained. The options that he might freely exercise, according to Patterson, all contain the threat of punishment or death. Thus, any exercise of freedom from control a slave might engage involves overcoming an omnipresent coercive structure.

When considering the role coercion plays in captivity it is reasonable to conclude that coercion involves more than using conditional threats as leverage against someone's will. Even the conditional threats that keep prisoners and slaves subject to their captors' desires depend on barriers to action that eliminate any options but submission. Thus, conditional threats do constitute coercion but do not constitute the whole of coercion. The full story of how physical and social/legal captives are coerced must also engage with the power of captors to utilize barriers to action that render captives helpless. Psychological captivity raises more difficult questions about coercion since the psychological captive is subject to a certain kind of nonexplicit, nonverbal threat and submits partly as a result of that threat. However, many of the processes that cause psychological captivity depend upon affecting the captive's own emotional states to create an internal pressure to comply. This process of harnessing a person's motives against her by making her feel powerless fits neither view of coercion perfectly, but, if it can be called coercion, it must be understood by drawing on aspects of both the conditional threat and the enforcement view.

NOTES

1. Patty Hearst was kidnapped on February 4, 1974, at the age of nineteen by members of Symbionese Liberation Army (SLA), a very small domestic militant group. On April 3, 1974, a tape was released with Hearst's voice claiming that she had joined the SLA, become a revolutionary, and taken the name "Tanya." On April 15, she was seen on videotape robbing a bank. In her trial she claimed to have been beaten, raped, and kept without food and water in a closet for many days prior to "joining" the SLA. However, she was convicted of bank robbery and sentenced to seven years in prison.

2. The destruction of independent motives to resist the captor's control that occurs in psychological captives, parallels the concept of "learned helplessness" developed by Martin Seligman at the University of Pennsylvania. Seligman discovered that dogs who received a series of inescapable shocks would eventually fail to jump out of their enclosures even when the shocks became escapable. Dogs who received shocks that were always escapable did not develop this persistent helpless response. Seligman later applied this concept to human behavior and argued that learned helplessness is a factor in depression (cf. Overmier and Seligman 1967 and Seligman 1975).

REFERENCES

Anderson, Scott A. 2010. "The Enforcement Approach to Coercion." *Journal of Ethics and Social Philosophy* 5(1): 1–31.

Demick, Barbara. 2010. *Nothing to Envy: Ordinary Lives in North Korea*. New York: Spiegel & Grau.

Dworkin, Gerald. 1978. "Moral Autonomy." In *Morals, Science and Sociality*, T. Engelhardt and D. Callahan (eds.), 156–171. Hastings-on-Hudson, NY: Hastings Center.

Frankfurt, Harry G. 1988. *The Importance of What We Care About*. Cambridge: Cambridge University Press.

Grassian, Stuart. 2006. "Psychiatric Effects of Solitary Confinement." *Washington University Journal of Law and Policy* 22: 325–383.

Haney, C. 2003. "The Psychological Impact of Incarceration: Implications for Postprison Adjustment." In *Prisoners Once Removed: The Impact of Incarceration and Reentry on Children, Families and Communities*, J. Travis and M. Waul (eds.), 33–66. Washington, DC: Urban Institute Press.

Haney, C., W. C. Banks, and P. G. Zimbardo. 1973. "A Study of Prisoners and Guards in a Simulated Prison." *Naval Research Review* 30: 4–17.

Harden, Blaine. 2012. *Escape from Camp 14: One Man's Remarkable Odyssey from North Korea to Freedom in the West*. New York: Penguin.

Higginbotham, A. Leon. 1978. *In the Matter of Color: Race and the American Legal Process*. New York: Oxford University Press.

International Labour Organization (ILO). 2005. *A Global Alliance Against Forced Labour*. Global Report Under the Follow-up to the ILO Declaration on Fundamental Principles and Rights at Work. May. Accessed May 5, 2013. http://www.ilo.org/public/english/standards/relm/ilc/ilc93/pdf/rep-i-b.pdf.

Lifton, Robert J. 1956. "Thought Reform of Chinese Intellectuals: A Psychiatric Evaluation." *Journal of Asian Studies* 16(1): 75–88.

Lifton, Robert J. 1989. *Thought Reform and the Psychology of Totalism*. Rev. ed. Chapel Hill: University of North Carolina Press.

McCloskey, H. J. 1980. "Coercion: Its Nature and Significance." *Southern Journal of Philosophy* 18: 335–352.

Nozick, Robert. 1969. "Coercion." In *Philosophy, Science, and Method*, Sidney Morgenbesser, Patrick Suppes, and Morton White (eds.), 440–472. New York: St. Martin's Press.

Overmier, J. Bruce, and M. E. Seligman. 1967. "Effects of Inescapable Shock upon Subsequent Escape and Avoidance Responding." *Journal of Comparative and Physiological Psychology* 63(1): 28–33.

Patterson, Orlando. 1982. *Slavery and Social Death*. Cambridge: Harvard University Press.

Rawls, John. 1971. *A Theory of Justice*. Cambridge: Harvard University Press.

Rivera, Lisa. 2011. "Harmful Beneficence." *Journal of Moral Philosophy* 8(2): 197–222.

Seligman, M. E. P. 1975. *Helplessness: On Depression, Development, and Death*. San Francisco: W.H. Freeman.

Sykes, Gresham M. 2007. *The Society of Captives: A Study of a Maximum Security Prison*. Rev. ed. Princeton, NJ: Princeton University Press.

Wertheimer, Alan. 1987. *Coercion*. Princeton, NJ: Princeton University Press